GOULD AND LINCOLN,

59 WASHINGTON STREET, BOSTON,

Would call particular attention to the following valuable works described in their Catalogue of Publications, viz.:

Hugh Miller's Works.
Bayne's Works. Walker's Works. Miall's Works. Bungener's Work.
Annual of Scientific Discovery. Knight's Knowledge is Power.
Krummacher's Suffering Saviour,
Banvard's American Histories. The Aimwell Stories.
Newcomb's Works. Tweedie's Works. Chambers's Works. Harris' Works.
Kitto's Cyclopædia of Biblical Literature.
Mrs. Knight's Life of Montgomery. Kitto's History of Palestin
Wheewell's Work. Wayland's Works. Agassiz's Works.

William's Works. Guyot's Works.
Thompson's Better Land. Kimball's Heaven. Valuable Works on Missions.
Haven's Mental Philosophy. Buchanan's Modern Atheism.
Cruden's Condensed Concordance. Eadie's Analytical Concordance.
The Psalmist: a Collection of Hymns.
Valuable School Books. Works for Sabbath Schools.
Memoir of Amos Lawrence.
Poetical Works of Milton, Cowper, Scott. Elegant Miniature Volumes.
Arvine's Cyclopædia of Anecdotes.
Ripley's Notes on Gospels, Acts, and Romans.
Sprague's European Celebrities. Marsh's Camel and the Hallig.
Roget's Thesaurus of English Words.
Hackett's Notes on Acts. M'Whorter's Yahveh Christ.
Siebold and Stannius's Comparative Anatomy. Marco's Geological Map, U. S.
Religious and Miscellaneous Works.
Works in the various Departments of Literature, Science and Art.

VALUABLE WORKS.

Diary and Correspondence OF THE LATE AMOS LAWRENCE. Edited by his son, WM. R. LAWRENCE, M. D. Octavo, cloth, $1.25; also, royal 12mo. ed., cl., $1.00.

Kitto's Popular Cyclopædia OF BIBLICAL LITERATURE. 500 illustrations. One vol., octavo. 812 pages. Cloth, $3.

Intended for ministers, theological students, parents, Sabbath-school teachers, and the great body of the religious public.

Analytical Concordance of the Holy SCRIPTURES; or, The Bible presented under Classified Heads or Topics. By JOHN EADIE, D. D. Octavo, 836 pp. $3.

Dr. Williams' Works.

Lectures on the Lord's Prayer — Religious Progress — Miscellanies.

☞ Dr. Williams is a profound scholar and a brilliant writer. — *New York Evangelist.*

Modern Atheism. Considered under its forms of Pantheism, Materialism, Secularism, Development and Natural Laws. By JAMES BUCHANAN, D. D., LL. D. 12mo. Cloth, $1.25.

The Hallig: or the Sheepfold in the Waters. A Tale of Humble Life on the Coast of Schleswig. From the German, by Mrs. GEORGE P. MARSH. 12mo. Cl., $1.

The Suffering Saviour. By Dr. KRUMMACHER. 12mo. Cloth, $1.25.

Heaven. By JAMES WM. KIMBALL. 12mo.

Christian's Daily Treasury. Religious Exercise for every Day in the Year. By Rev. E. TEMPLE. 12mo. Cloth, $1.

Wayland's Sermons. Delivered in the Chapel of Brown Univ. 12mo. Cl., $1.00.

Entertaining and Instructive Works FOR THE YOUNG. Elegantly illustrated. 16mo. Cloth, gilt backs.

The American Statesman. Life and Character of Daniel Webster. — *Young Americans Abroad;* or Vacation in Europe. — *The Island Home;* or the Young Cast-aways. — *Pleasant Pages for Young People.* — *The Guiding Star.* — *The Poor Boy and Merchant Prince.*

THE AIMWELL STORIES. Resembling and quite equal to the "Rollo Stories." — *Christian Register.* By WALTER AIMWELL. *Oscar;* or the Boy who had his own way. — *Clinton;* or Boy-Life in the Country. — *Ella;* or Turning over a New Leaf. — *Whistler;* or The Manly Boy. — *Marcus;* or the Boy Tamer.

WORKS BY Rev. HARVEY NEWCOMB. *How to be a Lady.* — *How to be a Man.* — *Anecdotes for Boys.* — *Anecdotes for Girls.*

BANVARD'S SERIES OF AMERICAN HISTORIES. *Plymouth and the Pilgrims.* — *Romance of American History.* — *Novelties of the New World, and Tragic Scenes in the History of Maryland and the old French War.*

God Revealed in Nature and in CHRIST. By Rev. JAMES B. WALKER, Author of "The Philosophy of the Plan of Salvation." 12mo. Cloth, $1.

Philosophy of the Plan of Salvation. New enlarged edition. 12mo. Cloth, 75 c.

Christian Life; SOCIAL AND INDIVIDUAL. By PETER BAYNE. 12mo. Cloth, $1.25.

All agree in pronouncing it one of the most admirable works of the age.

Yahveh Christ; or the Memorial Name. By ALEX. MACWHORTER. With an Introductory Letter, by NATH'L W. TAYLOR, D. D., in Yale Theol. Sem. 16mo. Cloth, 60 c.

The Signet Ring, AND ITS HEAVENLY MOTTO. From the German. 16mo. Cl., 31 c.

The Marriage Ring; or How to Make Home Happy. 18mo. Cloth, gilt, 75 c.

Mothers of the Wise and Good. By JABEZ BURNS, D. D. 16mo, Cloth, 75 c.

☞ A sketch of the mothers of many of the most eminent men of the world.

My Mother; or Recollections of Maternal Influence. 12mo. Cloth, 75c.

The Excellent Woman, with an Introduction, by Rev. W. B. SPRAGUE, D. D. Splendid Illustrations. 12mo. Cloth, $1.

The Progress of Baptist Principles IN THE LAST HUNDRED YEARS. By T. F. CURTIS, Prof. of Theology in the Lewisburg University. 12mo. Cloth, $1.25.

Dr. Harris' Works.

The Great Teacher. — The Great Commission. — The Pre-Adamite Earth. — Man Primeval. — Patriarchy. — Posthumous Works, 4 volumes.

The Better Land; OR THE BELIEVER'S JOURNEY AND FUTURE HOME. By Rev. A. C. THOMPSON. 12mo. Cloth, 85 c.

Kitto's History of Palestine, from the Patriarchal Age to the Present Time. With 200 Illustrations. 12mo. Cloth, $1.25.

An admirable work for the Family, the Sabbath and week-day School Library.

The Priest and the Huguenot; or, PERSECUTION IN THE AGE OF LOUIS XV. From the French of L. F. BUNGENER. Two vols., 12mo. Cloth, $2.25.

This is not only a work of thrilling interest, but is a masterly Protestant production.

The Psalmist. A Collection of Hymns for the Use of Baptist Churches. By BARON STOW and S. F. SMITH. With a SUPPLEMENT, containing an Additional Selection of Hymns, by RICHARD FULLER, D. D., and J. B. JETER, D. D. Published in various sizes, and styles of binding.

This is unquestionably the best collection of Hymns in the English language.

☞ In addition to works published by themselves, they keep an extensive assortment of works in all departments of trade, which they supply at publishers' prices. ☞ They particularly invite the attention of Booksellers, Travelling Agents, Teachers, School Committees, Librarians, Clergymen, and professional men generally (to whom a liberal discount is uniformly made), to their extensive stock. ☞ To persons wishing copies of Text-books, for examination, they will be forwarded, per mail or otherwise, on the reception of *one half* the price of the work desired. ☞ Orders from any part of the country attended to with faithfulness and dispatch.

SALVATION BY CHRIST.

A SERIES OF

DISCOURSES

ON SOME OF THE MOST

IMPORTANT DOCTRINES OF THE GOSPEL.

BY

FRANCIS WAYLAND.

BOSTON:
GOULD AND LINCOLN,
59 WASHINGTON STREET.
NEW YORK: SHELDON, BLAKEMAN & CO.
CINCINNATI: GEORGE S. BLANCHARD.
1859.

STEREOTYPED AT THE
BOSTON TYPE AND STEREOTYPE FOUNDRY.

PRINTED BY
GEORGE C. RAND & AVERY.

PREFACE.

SHORTLY after the appearance of the "University Sermons," the publishers desired that the title should be changed, inasmuch as the work was addressed no more to students in college than to inquirers after religious truth in general. I then declined to make any alteration. Of late, however, they proposed that I should modify the volume, in order the better to adapt it to the present state of religious feeling in many parts of our country. I saw that by the course which they suggested, the volume might be rendered more unique, and perhaps more useful. I have, therefore, omitted two discourses on the "Revolutions in Europe," and added six never before published, on subjects of greater practical importance.

The volume thus revised and greatly enlarged, appears under a title which the publishers consider appropriate. In this form it is now presented to all who feel the need of salvation by Christ, no less than to those whom it has been my pleasure, in former years, to instruct.

F. W.

PROVIDENCE, *December* 16, 1858.

CONTENTS.

a *

SERMON VII.

JUSTIFICATION BY WORKS IMPOSSIBLE.

SERMON VIII.

PREPARATION FOR THE ADVENT OF THE MESSIAH.

PART I.

SERMON IX.

PREPARATION FOR THE ADVENT OF THE MESSIAH.

PART II.

SERMON X.

THE WORK OF THE MESSIAH.

PART I.

SERMON XI.

THE WORK OF THE MESSIAH.

PART II.

SERMON XII.

JUSTIFICATION BY FAITH.

SERMON XIII.

CONVERSION.

SERMON XIV.

IMITATORS OF GOD.

SERMON XV.

GRIEVING THE SPIRIT.

SERMON XVI.

A DAY IN THE LIFE OF JESUS OF NAZARETH.

SERMON XVII.

THE BENEVOLENCE OF THE GOSPEL.

SERMON XVIII.

THE FALL OF PETER.

SERMON XIX.

CHARACTER OF BALAAM.

SERMON XX.

VERACITY.

SERMON XXI.

THE CHURCH OF CHRIST.

SERMON XXII.

THE UNITY OF THE CHURCH.

SERMON XXIII.

THE DUTY OF OBEDIENCE TO THE CIVIL MAGISTRATE.

PART I.

SERMON XXIV.

THE DUTY OF OBEDIENCE TO THE CIVIL MAGISTRATE.

PART II.

SERMON XXV.

THE DUTY OF OBEDIENCE TO THE CIVIL MAGISTRATE.

PART III.

SALVATION BY CHRIST.

THEORETICAL ATHEISM.

"The fool hath said in his heart, There is no God."
Psalm liii. 1.

It is scarcely possible for us to converse, even for a few moments, with another human being, without instinctively forming an opinion respecting his intellectual capacity. Although we may be unable definitely to express the reason for our judgments, yet every one has formed for himself a standard by which he estimates the ability of others. We readily and often rashly assign to the men whom we meet, a place among the ordinary, the distinguished, or the highly gifted; or among the inferior, the weak, or the very weak in intellect. These differences, however, may all exist within the normal conditions of the human understanding. We sometimes, however, meet with a man whose mind does not obey those laws which govern the operations of ordinary intelligence. We find ourselves in the presence of one with whom we can hold but partial and imperfect communion. We perceive that the being before us does not form his judgments in the same manner as the rest of mankind. He will believe, for instance, with unquestioning confidence, an assertion which to other men seems absurd. He will, on the other hand, refuse his assent to the plainest statement of fact, and hold out unconvinced against an accumulation of evidence of which a tithe would satisfy a man of sober understanding. A person of this character, I think, we always designate as a fool.

But this is not the only form in which folly exhibits itself.

We sometimes observe men who are convinced of the existence of a physical or a moral law, and yet act as if that which they believe to be true they certainly knew to be false. An idiot, though he may have been burned by the fire, will immediately expose himself to the danger of being burned again. He will learn wisdom neither from observation nor experience. Thus also we see men, for the sake of a momentary gratification, deliberately do an act which must work the wreck of character and the loss of reputation, and subject them through life to the gnawings of unavailing remorse. Thus the inebriate surrenders himself to a habit which he knows to be destructive of all peace of mind, and which must render him inevitably both loathsome and contemptible. Thus also we sometimes observe a young man, endowed with promising abilities, for whom parents and friends are making innumerable sacrifices, before whom the path to honorable distinction is plainly set open, basely squandering his time, associating with the frivolous, the reckless, and the profligate, and choosing for his portion poverty, remorse, and contempt, instead of affluence, conscious rectitude, and elevated standing. When we see men thus acting in deliberate defiance of the dictates of their own understanding, and in direct opposition to their clearly apprehended interests, I believe we always refer them to the class of fools. Though endowed with the power of forethought, they act as though they were deprived of it; and hence we number them with those on whom the power of forethought has never been bestowed. The former of these classes may be denominated theoretical, and the latter practical, fools.

It is, however, to be remarked, that the element of folly does not, by necessity, pervade the whole intellectual character. There seem to exist, in this respect, what may, perhaps, not inappropriately be denominated mental idiosyncracies. The man not unfrequently, on some subjects, reasons and judges like other men, while, upon other subjects, he is liable to the charge of incorrigible folly. In some cases, he may respect the precepts of practical wisdom, while in others he seems surrendered up to the dominion of hopeless fatuity.

Whatever may be the manner in which folly is displayed, the feelings with which we contemplate it are marked with sufficient distinctness. Where a man is a hopeless idiot, we pity him. The finger of God has touched him, and we are bound, by every tie of brotherhood, to treat him with thoughtful commiseration. When, however, we behold folly of a mixed character, — when a man is endowed with intelligence, and acts as if he were an idiot, — I think we are conscious of a very different emotion. The man can see some things clearly enough, while other things, equally evident, he utterly refuses to see. He will believe what he chooses, though it be ever so destitute of proof, while he refuses to believe that which displeases him, though established on the most irrefragable evidence. We cannot but believe that his state of mind is owing to some hidden and by no means commendable bias, and we can contemplate him neither with respect for his intellect nor confidence in his integrity.

The same sentiments, in most respects, are awakened by the exhibition of practical folly. If an idiot, who has never been able to appreciate the relation of cause and effect, throws himself a second time into the fire, from which, at imminent peril to ourselves, we have rescued him, we pity his sad calamity. But when a man possessed of a reasonable soul acts again and again in opposition to his acknowledged and most vital interests; when he sacrifices all that renders life a blessing for a contemptible gratification; when, in defiance of the plainest dictates of his understanding, he repeatedly calls down upon himself the direct penalties of inexorable law, — we may, it is true, pity him, but our pity is mingled with feelings nearly allied to contempt.

Indeed, I do not remember any emotions more universal than those with which we contemplate the intellectual character of our fellow-men. We admire, nay, we almost venerate, a powerful understanding united to vast reach of thought, and clear sighted, steadfast continuity of purpose. The very fact that we hold intellectual fellowship with a mind thus endowed creates within us, at times, an emotion akin to that of sublimity. On the contrary, as universal and deep-seated is the disgust awakened within us by striking exhibitions either of theoretical or practical folly. I do not know but we feel an emotion of self-esteem arising even from the contempt with which we never fail to regard it. Nay, " 'tis not in folly not to scorn a fool." The theoretical fool laughs at the practical fool. The practical fool despises the theoretical fool. Thus human nature, whether wise or unwise, bears testimony to the estimation in which this attribute is held throughout the universe of God.

Such, then, is the nature of the epithet by which the pen of inspiration designates the intellectual character of him who denies the existence of a God. It declares him to be a fool. Observe also the force of the expression. It does not make this affirmation solely of him who unblushingly avows his atheism, but even of him who cherishes it in the solitude of his own bosom — "The fool hath said *in his heart*, There is no God." Let us, then, during the remainder of this discourse, attempt to illustrate the truth of this sentiment of inspiration.

From what I have already said, it will at once appear that the denial of the existence of God may be either theoretical or practical. It is theoretical when we affirm that no such being as God exists. It is practical when, professing to believe that he exists, we act in all respects as though we believe that he did not exist. In the present discourse, we shall treat of the first of these errors.

I have already intimated that theoretical folly may manifest itself in two forms, either in that of absurd credulity, or of absurd incredulity. I think that in the denial of the existence of God both of those elements of folly may be discovered.

1. It is surely an evidence of absurd credulity to believe an assertion, respecting any subject whatever, when no evidence

is brought forward to sustain it; and especially when, from the necessity of the case, the evidence, if it did exist, is beyond the reach of the human understanding. There have frequently appeared impostors, who have affirmed that they should never die. Men have been found, who, without any evidence, have believed their assertions. Has not the whole world united in declaring them to be absurdly credulous? Have they not always been believed to be, so far as this subject was concerned, fools, on whose judgment, in future, no reliance could safely be reposed? Men have frequently predicted that, on a particular day, the world would be burned up, and they have found persons who believed that such would be the fact, simply on the ground of these predictions. Mankind have laughed at them as credulous simpletons, merely because, in a matter of importance, they believed an assertion unsupported by the shadow of evidence. Suppose that, on the ground of your affirmation, you could make a man believe that molten lava would not consume him, and that, relying on your declaration, he resolved to throw himself into the crater of a volcano; in what estimation would you hold his understanding? Or suppose that it were asserted that every star in the firmament is a glorified spirit, placed there to gaze forever on the events transpiring on this little earth. Were a man to believe this assertion, sustained by no evidence — nay, where, if the assertion were true, the evidence is infinitely beyond the reach of the human faculties, — could we believe him to be in possession of a sound understanding? We see, then, in general, that with the exception of intuitive propositions, the human mind, in the proper exercise of its faculties, can never believe, unless through the medium of evidence, and that, if it believe any assertion without evidence, we always consider it to be absurdly credulous.

Now, the atheist declares to us that there is no God. What is the proof of his assertion? By what syllogism does he demonstrate it? What is his major, and what is his minor premise? He tells us that he has never seen, nor felt, nor heard God; and, therefore, that God does not exist. But does nothing exist on earth which has never manifested itself either to his senses or to his consciousness? How does he know but, among the truths which have thus far escaped his notice, one may be the existence of God? Has he lived forever, and been present from eternity, throughout the immensity of space? Where was he when the morning stars sang together, and all the sons of God shouted for joy? How does he know but that God may have existed where and when he was not? On this subject, I take pleasure in introducing to your notice a remarkable passage from Foster's Essays — a volume of such inestimable value, that no young man should consider his education truly commenced, unless he has given it an attentive and thorough perusal.

"The wonder then turns on the immense intelligence by which a man could know that there is no God. What ages and what lights are requisite for this attainment! This intelligence involves the very attributes of divinity, while a God is denied. For, unless this man is omnipresent, unless he is at this moment in every place in the universe, he cannot know but there may be in some place, manifestations of a Deity, by which even he would be overpowered. If he does not know absolutely every agent in the universe, the one that he does not know may be God. If he is not himself the chief agent in the universe, and does not know what is so, that which is so may be God. If he is not in absolute possession of all the propositions that constitute universal truth, the one which he wants may be, that there is a God. If he cannot with certainty assign the cause of all that he perceives to exist, that cause may be a God. If he does not know every thing that may have been done in the immeasurable ages that are past, some things may have been done by a God. Thus, unless he knows all things, — that is, precludes the idea of another Deity by being one himself, — he cannot know that the being whose existence he rejects does not exist. But he must *know* that he does not exist, else he deserves equal contempt and compassion, for the temerity with which he avows his rejection and acts accordingly."

Such, then, my brethren, is the absurdity of the assertion that there is no God. It is an assertion not only unsustained by evidence, but one, the truth of which could not be certainly known, unless the assertor were himself endowed with the attributes of the Deity. In a word, I think that any one who reflects for a moment upon the fewness and feebleness of the faculties of man, and then upon the boundlessness of the universe, must be convinced, that the assertion that God does not exist, involves within itself all the elements of the most revolting absurdity.

I have, thus far, endeavored to show that atheism is absurd in its credulity. I shall next attempt to show that it is equally absurd in its unbelief. Not only does it believe without the shadow of evidence, nay, where evidence is by necessity impossible, but it disbelieves a proposition of which the evidence is interwoven with the very structure of the human understanding.

Before entering upon this part of our subject, allow me to suggest a single explanation. I am not about to prove to you the existence of God, as though it were to you a matter of doubt. You need no such proof. You all believe this all-important truth, and no illustration of mine could render it more evident. The belief in a First Cause, a superintending Providence, is one of the ideas common to our race, as soon as the mind is quickened into even incipient activity. So necessarily is this belief generated among the first forms of human knowledge, that it presses through the thick covering of ignorance which commonly overspreads our faculties when man is unenlightened by revelation. The mind of the creature needs the idea of a Creator, and it will associate this idea with the sun, the moon, or the planets, nay, with four-footed beasts and creeping things, rather than live destitute of a belief which is demanded by the necessities of our intellectual nature. It is not, then, my design to prove to you the existence of a God, but to illustrate to you the process by which the belief in his existence has become universal. In doing this, I hope also in another respect to exhibit to you the absurdity of atheism.

1. In the first place, the idea of power, of cause and effect, is the universal and spontaneous suggestion of the human intelligence. It springs up unbidden and irrepressible from the first perception of a change. We cannot conceive of a change without being conscious immediately of the notion of a cause by which it was effected. This law of the human mind is universal, and its operation may be as readily perceived in the case of a child as of a philosopher. You may easily make the experiment for yourselves. Remove a child's toy from one room to another, and he will instantly ask you who did it. This change of its place immediately suggests to him the idea of a cause. Tell him that no one did it, that it took place without the exertion of any sufficient power, and see if you can make him believe you. Let him burn his hand in the fire, and see if you can induce him to repeat the experiment. His own infantile intelligence has attained the conviction that like causes produce like effects, and no argument can possibly eradicate it. But suppose it were otherwise; suppose that you observed a child to be entirely destitute of this suggestion, that the notion of cause and effect never seemed to govern its conduct, but that it would place its hand in a flame as often as an opportunity occurred, without being able to arrive at the notion that the fire was the cause of its pain. You would decide at once that the child was an idiot; and you would not be mistaken. You see that a human mind cannot be deprived of this suggestion, without losing an essential element of its original intelligence.

The truth which I wish to illustrate was forcibly taught by Dr. Beattie, when he wished to impress upon his son the fact of the existence of God. Tracing the letters of the child's name in the fresh mould of the garden, he sowed in the lines some ordinary seeds. Very soon the son discovered his own name distinctly growing out of the ground, and demanded of his father the cause of it. Dr. Beattie at first told him it was produced by chance ; but the child would not believe it, nor could he be persuaded by all his father's ingenuity that it was not the work of some intelligent agent. From this incident, he was taught the idea of a universal cause. I think that every one who reflects upon this occurrence will declare that this child, in insisting upon the necessity of a cause, spoke the language of human nature.

Now, we are encompassed on every side by changes springing up around us in infinite variety. Every season of the year, every month, every day, and every night, nay, every hour, is crowded with them in numbers without beginning and without end, and every one, when we reflect upon it, by the constitution of our minds, suggests to us the idea of a cause. The necessity of this idea is, therefore, pressed upon us, by the very constitution of our minds, as soon as we begin to observe the changes continually occurring in the universe around us.

2. Secondly, when we examine this notion of cause and effect, we perceive that at first it is satisfied with observing the relation of antecedent and consequent combined with the idea of power. It is not long, however, before the mind proceeds farther, and asks not only for a cause, but for a sufficient cause. The child of Dr. Beattie could not be made to believe that the wind and the rain had by accident deposited the seeds in the order in which he perceived them. He knew that this must have been done by a cause that knew his name, and could spell it, and form the letters of which it was composed. Until such a cause could be suggested, his mind could not rest satisfied. So, when we are asked what causes the growth of vegetation, we reply, heat and moisture, the rain and the sunshine. At first, this explanation may seem satisfactory; but soon the elements of our intelligence require us to proceed a step farther. We observe the innumerable forms of beauty and utility springing up every where around us; we examine the wonderful laws by which every process of vege-

tation is governed; we trace the relations existing between the vegetable and animal kingdoms; we pursue our inquiries into the higher ranks of being, and learn the habitudes, the instincts, the uses of brutes, and the faculties, the intelligence, and the development of man. We at once conclude that our first conception of cause is wholly inadequate to account for the changes which we perceive. The drop of water and the beam of sunlight could never in strictness be the cause of the matchless beauty with which the earth is overspread. We cannot ascribe to senseless matter a power infinitely transcending that of the highest human intelligence. The most profound philosopher would be pronounced insane were he to attempt the formation of a blade of grass; and can we ascribe to brute matter the power to subject the elements of nature to complicated and mysterious law, or to create the blushing loveliness of spring or the rich abundance of autumn? We at once determine that, hidden behind these visible antecedents, there must exist an adequate cause, an intelligent power, competent to the production of all these changes, and to which all that we see is, from necessity, subordinate. We are thus led to conceive of an underived and absolute cause. When the mind arrives at this idea, it rests satisfied. It demands nothing more ultimate. The mind of the creature reposes upon the conception of a self-existent, all-powerful, and all-wise Creator, and it is henceforth at rest.

3. But, supposing that we have arrived at the notion of underived causation, the question may still be asked, May not several independent causes originate the changes which are taking place around us? This question is readily answered by examining the facts in the case. Every thing that we behold is manifestly a part of one universal whole. Every law is found to be in perfect harmony with every other law. Were the various forces which regulate the motions of our system in the smallest degree modified, universal ruin would ensue. Every thing teaches us that the universe, with all its changes, is nothing more than the realization of one single conception.

This fact excludes the idea of a multiplicity of causes, and teaches us, that the cause of causes, the absolute causation, is every where one and the same. We thus arrive at the idea of a universal cause, a sufficient reason why all things are, and why they are such as they are; that is, of a Creator infinite in power and unsearchable in wisdom.

4. When we reflect upon human conduct, we find that we always connect the outward act with the spiritual disposition, or intention, from which it proceeds. Observing them in this light, we perceive in every action the quality of right or virtue, or of its opposite wrong or vice. We know that the constitution of the moral beings around us is similar to our own. We refer their outward manifestations to their appropriate spiritual dispositions, and hence, from their actions, we judge men to be either virtuous or vicious. Virtue we cannot but esteem and venerate; vice we cannot but despise and abhor. These, I think, must be universally considered as the proper judgments of all moral intelligences. Let us now refer these obvious principles to our judgments respecting the first and universal cause. We observe by our own experience that our virtuous actions are always followed by happiness and that self-approbation which is, in itself, an exceeding great reward. We, on the contrary, observe that vicious actions are followed by pain and remorse, and a fearful looking-for of judgment. We observe that the same consequences follow the correspondent actions of others. We trace the vicissitudes of nations, and observe that they are regulated by the same law. We see that, irrespective of all human power and human foresight, nay, in despite of all the wisdom of man, virtue is indissolubly connected with happiness, and vice with misery. Here, then, is an order of sequence established, and it must have been established by the universal, the all-pervading cause. Here, then, we behold the perpetual acting of the Almighty; and from it we learn the moral attributes which compose his character. We thus are taught that he loves virtue and abhors vice, and we conclude that his moral, like his

natural, attributes are infinite. We thus arrive at the conception of an Almighty Cause who is infinitely holy. Thus our intellectual and moral natures unite in ascribing to the Creator every perfection of which we can conceive in an infinite degree. Such, it seems to me, is the result to which the unbiased faculties of the human mind would naturally arrive.

That mankind have generally arrived at this result is by no means asserted. The apostle Paul declares that men did not like to retain God in their knowledge, and, therefore, they exchanged him for false gods, and worshipped and served the creature rather than the Creator. What I intend to affirm is, that this is the result to which the faculties of the human mind arrive, whenever they are employed in the earnest and honest inquiry after God. Nay, more, this is the result to which they actually have in some cases arrived, even when deprived of the light of revelation. Thus saith the apostle to the Romans: " The invisible things of God, even his eternal power and Godhead, are clearly seen, being understood by the things that are made." Thus also saith the Psalmist: " The heavens declare the glory of God, and the firmament showeth forth his handy work." Accordingly, many of the heathen philosophers, but, above all, Socrates, from an observation of the works of creation and of the providential dealings of God, arrived at a conception of the character of the First Cause very similar to that which I have described. They attained to this knowledge without the assistance of revelation; and hence we learn that this attainment is within the reach of the unassisted human faculties. If, then, men have not commonly discovered these truths, or if, having discovered, they have not retained them in their knowledge, the reason is to be found, not in the inadequateness of their intellectual faculties, but in some cause of an entirely different character.

Now, the atheist, in defiance of this universal suggestion of the human intelligence, affirms that there is no God. He thus excludes from the human mind the idea of cause and effect, without which the essential nature of mind would be changed. Abolish this suggestion, and I do not say that we should be destitute of mind, but it would not be the mind of a man. Again, admit the idea of cause and effect, and suppose that absolute causation resides in mere physical antecedents, and we utter an assertion from which the mind even of childhood revolts. Again, admit the idea of absolute causation, that is, of almighty power and omniscient wisdom, and deprive it of all its moral attributes, — let such a being be neither holy, nor good, nor merciful, nor just, — and you have created a conception from which the nature of man recoils in unutterable dismay. Thus, atheism, in any form in which it can be presented, leads us at once to intellectual or moral absurdity. Thus, he who denies the being of God not only refuses to believe what is proven on incontrovertible evidence, but he denies the existence of the elementary principles of human intelligence. Were he thus to deny a fact in history, or a doctrine of philosophy, he surely could not escape the imputation of egregious folly.

In thus stating the necessity of the idea of a Deity to the human mind, as soon as its faculties are at all developed, I think I do not overstate the fact. A remarkable illustration of the truth of what I have said has been presented in modern history. You know that, during the French revolution, the national assembly decreed that there was no God, and that death was an eternal sleep. There speedily followed a dissolution of the elements of society, an anarchy baptized in blood. The authors of these blasphemies were soon alarmed at the results of their own labors, and quailed before the tempest which they had themselves excited. Robespierre himself was anxious to restore the worship of the Supreme Being, profoundly remarking, "Were there no God, it would be necessary for us to form one." The nation rejoiced to welcome back a belief demanded by the principles of our nature, and without which civil society could not long exist.

But, lastly, the belief of the atheist is wholly inoperative for the purpose for which it is intended. His object is, by denying the existence of God, to banish the idea of immortality and of a state of future moral retribution. Thus, in the case to which I have just alluded, the assertion that death is an eternal sleep immediately followed the denial of the existence of God. But, even were atheism true, it furnishes no argument whatever against either of these all-important truths. It is very obvious that we exist now, and the atheist asserts that we exist while there is no God. Why, then, though there be no God, may we not continue to exist forever? It is manifest that, in the present life, individuals and nations are the subjects of moral government, misery follows the gratification of lawless desire, and happiness attends upon self-denying virtue. The atheist asserts that all this occurs on earth, while there is no God; why, then, even were there no God, might not the same system of moral government be carried on through eternity? To these questions no answer can be returned; and hence, were atheism true, it would present no reason whatever why we should not exist forever, and forever reap the due reward of our moral actions.

We see, then, the absurdity of atheism. It asserts that which cannot be known to be true by any finite intelligence. It denies what cannot be disbelieved without denying the essential laws of human thought. It does this for a reason which would remain unaffected whether the assertion were true or false.

In conclusion, young gentlemen, let me urge you to place this truth at the foundation of all your knowledge, and to make it the ever-present idea by which all your moral character is formed. Eschew every system of ethics or philosophy that does not adopt as its elementary truth the existence and attributes of God, and our moral accountability to him. From this truth learn to draw succor in the hour of adversity, deliverance from the assaults of temptation, counsel in the day of prosperity, and sustaining grace in the article of death. Thus, by the teachings of the Spirit, shall you grow up into the stature of perfect men in Christ Jesus. And remember always to shun, as you would your most dreaded enemy, the man who either by precept or practice would diminish the power of this truth over your conduct. Remember that it is the fool who hath said in his heart there is no God, and observe that inspiration has assigned the reason of his unbelief — "Corrupt are they; they have done abominable works." Thus was it three thousand years ago, thus is it now, and thus will it be forever.

PRACTICAL ATHEISM.

"THE FOOL HATH SAID IN HIS HEART, THERE IS NO GOD."
Psalm liii. 1.

IN the preceding discourse, I attempted to illustrate the folly of theoretical atheism. I there intimated that this folly existed in another form — that, whilst we believe in the existence of God, we may yet act as though there were no God. This I termed *practical atheism.* To the consideration of this exhibition of folly let me now request your attention.

We are all, I trust, satisfied of the absurdity of theoretical atheism. Our reason imperatively demands a First Cause; our moral and intellectual nature imposes upon us the belief in his infinite perfections. But in your case this is not all. This belief has been instilled into your minds from your earliest infancy. As soon as you opened your eyes upon creation, you were taught that "the heavens declare the glory of God, and the firmament showeth forth his handy work." The first lesson that you learned was the prayer that your mother taught you. Night and morning, as you knelt by her side, you have lisped out your infantile petition to "Our Father who art in heaven." I trust that the influence of these blessed instructions has been obliterated neither by the turbulent sports of boyhood, nor the graver temptations of youth. I feel conscious, then, that I address a company of believers in the existence of God. Whatever may be your errors, theoretical atheism is not to be numbered among them. No argument could shake your belief in this great elementary fact which lies at the foundation of all true knowledge.

But while all this is so, may you not be justly liable to the charge of practical atheism? You believe that there is one God. You do well. But do your works correspond with your belief? If they do not, and just in so far as they do not, you are guilty of practical atheism. In order to examine this question more accurately, let us proceed to unfold the conception which you have formed of the existence and attributes of God.

1. We all, I presume, involve in our conception of God the idea of personality. One of the first lessons of science teaches us that qualities cannot exist without a subject, nor energies without an agent. Black, white, hot, cold, cannot exist of themselves, but only as there is something in which they inhere. So we can form no conception of the actual existence of power, wisdom, goodness, or justice, unless there be some being to whom these attributes belong; that is, some agent who is powerful, and wise, and good, and just. To speak of the First Cause, the real and sufficient reason of all things, as a collection of attributes without any actual essence to which they belong, is absurd. Equally absurd is it to speak of the First Cause as an abstract notion. An abstract notion, a generalized idea, has no existence whatever, but in our own thoughts. The abstract idea of power or goodness, as of whiteness or blackness, is a mere conception, a state of our own minds. To speak, then, of the all-sufficient cause as an abstraction, without personality, without positive existence, is, as it seems to me, to ascribe creative power and wisdom to the changing states of our own intellect. I do not know that any thing can possibly be more absurd than such a notion — for *belief* it can scarcely be called. In opposition to all such teachings we conceive of the Deity as an actual existence, an infinite being, whom, by the analogy of language, we term *person*, to whom all the attributes of Divinity by necessity belong.

2. To this Infinite Being we involuntarily ascribe self-existence. He is the cause of causes, the ultimate reason why every thing exists. If he be the all-sufficient cause for all

other existence, he must be the ultimate cause, or else there must be a succession of causes without beginning or end. which is absurd. As soon as we reflect upon such a supposition, we are conscious that it is, if I may be allowed the expression, an unthinkable conception. When, on the contrary, we attain to the idea of an underived and self-existent cause, the craving of our intellect is satisfied. It is as such a being that the Scriptures always speak of God. "Thus saith the Lord, I am the first and I am the last, and besides me there is no God. I am the Alpha and the Omega, the beginning and the ending, saith the Lord, which is, and which was, and which is to come, the Almighty."

This one truth admitted, we immediately perceive that there must exist an infinite difference between the Creator and the creature. Creation is derived, contingent, accidental. The Creator is underived and necessary. Creation might or might not have existed. The self-existent must always have been. Every thing else is from its nature changeable. He is essentially unchangeable. Were creation multiplied a hundred fold, he would be still the same. Were it all annihilated, he would still remain the unalterable, independent I AM.

3. Intimately associated with the attribute of self-existence is that of eternity, which reason, as well as revelation, teach us to ascribe to the Deity. The idea of eternity arises spontaneously in our minds, as soon as we begin to think upon duration. We know that we have existed but for a very few years, and that duration existed before we were created. When did it commence? We go backward to the origin of our race, we ascend to the dawn of the creation of our system, — still our idea of duration is unexhausted. We begin with the star that was last created; we think back to the moment of the creation of that which next preceded it; we go back to the era when one and another was not, until we arrive at the period when all was darkness, ere yet God had said, "Let there be light," — and we have not yet even diminished our conception of duration. We have exhausted our powers of measurement,

but duration still stretches backward to infinity. We have traced creation to its origin; but when did the Creator begin to exist? What limits can we assign to his duration? We feel at once that to affirm beginning to the uncreated one is absurd. We bow down in humble adoration, and exclaim with the Hebrew lawgiver, "Before the mountains were brought forth, or ever thou hadst formed the earth or the world, even from everlasting to everlasting, thou art God."

This is, however, only our notion of the eternity of the past. We turn and look forward towards an eternity that is to come. We go onward, in imagination, until we arrive at the period when our system, having finished its appointed course, shall be dissolved. Star after star, in the long lapse of millions of ages, goes out in darkness. The last light in the firmament flickers and is extinguished. The heavens have passed away as a scroll, and the material universe has ceased to be. Our power to measure the eternity to come is exhausted, but what shall measure the being of Him at whose word it was created, and at whose word it became nothing? When can underived existence end? We cannot even conceive of his liability to change or variableness, for this would involve the idea either of original imperfection or of force impressed from without. Either of these suppositions is absurd. "A thousand years" (the period of all created things) "in his sight are but as yesterday when it is past, and as a watch in the night." "Of old hast thou laid the foundations of the earth, and the heavens are the works of thy hands. They shall perish, but thou shalt endure; yea, all of them shall wax old as doth a garment; as a vesture shalt thou change them, and they shall be changed; but thou art the same, and thy years have no end."

4. To the Deity we cannot but ascribe infinite and absolute power.

Our conceptions of created power are by necessity limited. The beings with which we are conversant are endowed with it in different degrees. We readily observe the difference between feebleness and strength, but we soon arrive at a limit beyond which both sink to the level of equality. The insect that floats in the sunbeam, and " behemoth, chief of the ways of God," are alike powerless to heave the mountain from its foundations, or to uphold the earth in its orbit. Created power is limited in kind as well as degree. Leviathan, " when he raiseth himself up, may cause the mighty to be afraid ; " but he is a brute, for God hath denied to him understanding. The loftiest intellect that the world has seen, can neither protect the body which it inhabits from the poisonous miasma of the marsh, nor avert the death which is instilled into our veins by the venom of the gliding reptile. But no such limits restrict our conceptions when we reflect upon the omnipotence of the Creator. His power extends equally throughout infinite space, and every where it is measureless.

Nor does the power of the Creator resemble that of his creatures more in kind than in degree. Our power is ever relative. We can no more create the atom that floats in the sunbeam, than the planet that moves in the firmament. The changes which we seem to effect in the world around us, are nothing but the exhibitions of God's wonder-working power. The husbandman prepares the earth and scatters abroad the seed, but it is " God who giveth it a body as it hath pleased him, and to every seed his own body." But let man attempt by his own will to originate a single change in the creation, and he finds himself as powerless as the clods of the valley. To the Creator, on the contrary, we ascribe absolute and essential efficiency. By his simple will all things were created. " God said, Let there be light, and light was. By the word of the Lord were the heavens made, and all the hosts of them by the breath of his mouth. For he spake and it was, he commanded and it stood fast." And the God that in the beginning created, sustains and governs all ; upholding all things by the word of his power, and doing his will in the armies of heaven and among the inhabitants of the earth.

5. Again: To God we ascribe omniscient wisdom. Traces of this attribute are recognized in man. Having an end in

view, we can, with various degrees of skill, so adjust our means as to accomplish our purposes. But the profoundest wisdom of man reveals nothing so clearly as its own inherent feebleness. By what strange infatuation are its ends selected, and how sadly inadequate are the means by which it hopes to attain them! How puerile have been most of the objects of research of the wisest of men! How small is the amount of truth which can now be sifted out from the labors of the human intellect through the long range of by-gone ages! The plans of statesmen and conquerors have resulted in almost universal failure. The military and administrative talents of Napoleon were perhaps greater than those ever bestowed upon any other man. The means at his disposal were such as human intellect never before wielded. Yet, before his death, the lines which he had traced on the map of Europe were already effaced, and the political edifice which he had erected had crumbled into ruins. Thus must it be always with a creature of yesterday, blind to the future, and ignorant of the purposes of Him who doeth all things according to the counsel of his own will.

Infinitely dissimilar from our knowledge is that possessed by the Deity. Our knowledge is limited to time; his pervades eternity. We know nothing more than the relation which objects sustain to us; he knows all things absolutely. We know nothing but the outward act, the visible seeming; he, the motive hidden in the deepest recesses of consciousness. We know not beyond the present; to him the most distant future is open as the day. Our plans are continually thwarted by the interference of others; he, while allowing every created moral agent the unrestrained exercise of his free will, without variableness or the shadow of a turning, accomplishes those designs which were formed from the outgoings of Eternity. In conformity with these views are the teachings of the Scripture on this subject. "There is no darkness nor shadow of death where the workers of iniquity may hide themselves." "Neither is there any creature that is not manifest in his sight; but all things are naked and open to the eyes of him with whom we have to do." "He disappointeth the desires of the crafty, so that their hands cannot perform their enterprise. He taketh the wise in their own craftiness, and the counsel of the froward is carried headlong." "Surely the wrath of man shall praise thee, and the remainder of wrath shalt thou restrain."

6. To the Deity we ascribe every moral attribute in infinite perfection. He is the Holy One. By this we mean that his nature is spotlessly pure, not by accident, but by the necessity of his being; not only that he never did wrong, but that he could no more do wrong than cease to exist. Nor is this all. The holiness of God is not a mere negative quality, rendering it impossible for him to do wrong, but a positive attribute, rendering it equally necessary for him to do right. And, besides, with this perfection we always associate a moral affection, a love of goodness, and a hatred to sin, intense and ever operative. Virtue, throughout his moral universe, always meets his approving smile, while vice is every where confronted by his withering and all-consuming frown.

The immaculate purity of the divine nature is every where revealed, as we reflect upon the relations which he sustains to his creatures. The existence of moral agents, endowed with the power of affecting for good or for evil the destinies of each other, presupposes the necessity of government. There must exist a Judge of the earth, who will control the injurious and punish the wicked, as well as protect the innocent and reward the righteous. It is when we look up to God in this relation, that we adore him as a being of spotless justice. Never has an emotion been indulged, a word spoken, or an action performed, in the slightest degree tinged with virtue or vice, but he has, with perfect exactness, estimated its moral quality. He has thoroughly known either the palliations or aggravations by which it was attended. He has observed the degree of light which we have followed, or from which we have turned away; and the strength of the temptation which we have successfully resisted, or by which we have been overcome. He thus is perfectly acquainted with the desert of every action, and to every moral agent he metes out the retribution justly due to obedience or transgression. Nothing is too high to be reached by his award, nothing is so humble as to be neglected in his adjudication. From eternity to eternity, among the numberless ranges of existence that people the universe, this attribute has ever been exerted without the variableness or the shadow of a turning. "He is a rock, his way is perfect; for all his ways are judgment;—a God of truth and without iniquity, just and right is he." "The Lord reigneth; let the earth rejoice; let the multitude of the isles be glad thereof. Clouds and darkness are round about him, justice and judgment are the habitation of his throne."

7. But again: God is revealed to us not only as the Judge, but as the Father of the creatures whom he has made. Viewed in this relation, we behold him clothed in every attribute of parental goodness, desiring, with infinite love, the happiness of us his children. Every thing within us and around us bears witness to the existence of this perfection of the Godhead. Our senses and the objects which quicken them into enjoyment, the laws which govern the universe around us, the wonderful fabric of the intellect within us, our moral nature, its capacity for endless happiness, and its near relation to him whose image it bears, the provision which has been made for its ceaseless progress in virtue as it is changed from glory to glory, all teach us that God is love. But this is only a distant view of his beneficence. A more affecting conception of this attribute is derived from considering the relation which our Father who is in heaven sustains to every one of his individual children. By him the very hairs of our head are all numbered. He hears the cry of the raven, and scatters crumbs in the pathway of the sparrow. He invites you, and me, and every creature capable of knowing him, to approach him in all the confidence of filial affection, to unbosom to him all our sorrows, to spread before him all our wants, and, by intimate communion with him, to be transformed more and more into

his moral likeness. He is the Father of the fatherless, the Judge of the widow, the Helper of the helpless, and the Comforter of those that be cast down. "How excellent is thy loving kindness, O God! Therefore the children of men put their trust in the shadow of thy wings."

The most astonishing manifestation of the goodness of God is, however, made to us in the remedial dispensation. We are taught in the Holy Scriptures that our whole race is in rebellion against this holy and most merciful God, and that, had justice awarded to us the demerit of our sins, we must have been consigned to eternal banishment from his presence. The thoughts of our hearts were evil continually. We did not like to retain God in our knowledge, but said unto him, Depart from us, for we desire not a knowledge of thy ways. He had but to leave us to our own choices, and our everlasting dwelling must have been with the angels that kept not their first estate, to whom is reserved the blackness of darkness forever. But even here the tender mercy of our Father did not abandon us. When all the conditions of our first probation had been violated, he provided for us a second probation, established upon better promises. He accepted a propitiation for our offences, and offered again to receive us to his favor. "God so loved the world, that he gave his only-begotten Son, that whosoever believeth on him should not perish, but have everlasting life." Jesus Christ, having obtained eternal redemption for us, is now exalted a Prince and a Savior to grant repentance unto Israel and remission of sins. And now the God and Father of all is beseeching us, by every sentiment of duty and gratitude, to be reconciled to him. In every form of language, and by every affecting similitude, he assures us that he is not willing that any should perish, but that all should come to the knowledge of the truth. Though we have wandered far off into a strange land, the eye of our Father in heaven is still bent upon us in compassion. From time to time, his invitations to return fall upon our ear through the ministrations of his Spirit; and if he discover within us the feeblest emotion of penitence, he cultivates and strengthens it; and, as soon as we form the resolution, I will arise and go to my Father, —while we are yet a great way off, he hastens to receive us with the joyful welcome — "This my son was dead, and is alive again; he was lost, and is found."

Such are some of the conceptions which right reason, as well as revealed religion, present to us of the character of God. Every man must, I think, at once perceive that his moral nature could worship no other being without doing violence to itself. And yet more: as soon as we become acquainted with the existence and attributes of such a God, we become immediately conscious that it is our highest duty to love, to obey, and adore him. The capacity for such communion with God allies us to his moral nature. Destitute of it, we should be but in a small degree distinguished from the brutes.

But, if such be the character of God, and if we be his accountable creatures, that *he exists* must be infinitely the most important fact that can come within the range of our knowledge. If he is the universal, all-sufficient, and independent cause, upon him by necessity depend all that we now enjoy, and all that in the future we can hope for. If he is every where present, beholding the evil and the good, and has known our thought afar off, our whole history, as it essentially is, is perfectly spread out before his omniscient eye. If he be not only the omniscient but the impartial Judge, in whose sight the wicked cannot stand, we must at his hand receive the due reward of all our deeds, meted out by unspotted holiness. If he is all goodness, we are bound to render to him a tribute of gratitude as ceaseless as the stream of his beneficence; and the failure to do this is sin. If we must soon come into the unveiled presence of the Lord God Almighty, we can never behold him in peace unless our moral natures are in harmony with his. If he have so loved us as to give his well-beloved Son for our offences, and we have refused his offer of eternal life, there remaineth no other sacrifice for sin, and we must meet our Father in heaven guilty of having treated with contempt the message of redeeming love.

From these considerations it is, I think, evident that the existence of God, and specially of such a God as the Scriptures reveal, is by far the most *practical* truth of which we can possibly conceive. It is most intimately related to every action which we perform, every emotion in which we indulge, and every motive by which we are governed throughout our whole existence. We cannot conceive of a situation in which it is possible for us to exist where this truth ought not to exert an unlimited control over our conduct. It is the foundation of all that we hope for and of all that we dread. Were all other truth abolished, let this only remain, and the foundations of the moral universe would continue unmoved. Were every other being annihilated, let God and our individual selves only exist, and no essential source of our happiness would be dried up. Were the existence of God to cease, all other things, were it possible, remaining, this universe would become a hell. Hence you see that religion is not only a reasonable, but that it is infinitely the most reasonable, exercise of the powers of an immortal soul. All other obligations are finite; they bind us to duties of time, and place, and circumstances; this duty binds us always and every where, and the results that issue from it transcend all finite conception.

What, then, must be the condition of the man who believes in the existence of such a God, and yet suffers not this belief to exert any practical influence upon his conduct? He believes that he is dependent, and God all-powerful, and he acts as though God were powerless, and himself omnipotent. He believes himself to be ignorant, and God omniscient; he acts as though he were all-wise, and God incapable of knowledge. He believes that God beholds the inmost recesses of every spirit; and yet he acts as though he could conceal even the deeds of noonday from his all-seeing observation. He believes that God is a being of all-consuming holiness; and he acts as though the Eternal might be made his coadjutor in wickedness. He believes that every secret thing will be brought into judgment, and that the consequences of every sin are solemn beyond the reach of finite conception; and yet he labors assiduously to treasure up wrath against the day of wrath and revelation of the righteous judgment of God. He believes himself under infinite obligations to reverence and love his Father who is in heaven; and yet he says to the Most High, Depart from me; I desire not a knowledge of thy ways. He knows that the pleasures of sin are unsatisfactory and degrading, polluted and polluting; and yet, for the most insignificant of them all, he barters away the precious hope of glory, honor, and immortality. I ask, then, What folly can be compared with the folly of him who believes that all this is true, and then acts as though all of it were false? Language has no epithet which can adequately designate the madness of him who affirms the existence of the Deity, and yet lives without God in the world.

But now, turning from this general view of the subject, allow me to bring it at once to a personal application. Are there not among us this afternoon many young men whose lives have presented a practical illustration of this very folly? You all believe in the existence of God precisely as I have endeavored to set it before you. It is a belief from which you cannot escape, for it is interwoven with your intellectual and moral nature. In the moment of sinful excitement, tormented by the struggle between your passions and your conscience, you may wish there were no God; but it is not in your power to believe it. You know that, if God exists, his attributes are such as I have attempted to indicate; and yet I fear that many of you are living the life of the practical atheist.

While, however, I say this, I do not think harshly of you. Far be it from me to accuse you either wrongfully or unkindly. That we may bring this subject to a definite issue, let me suggest a few inquiries which every one may answer for himself in the solitude of his own bosom. Every one may thus decide the question whether the sin of practical atheism does not lie upon his conscience.

It will be remembered that I address you as believers in the existence and attributes of God, and the solemn consequences which result from this infinitely important truth. I would then inquire, Is there not in this assembly one, at least, who frequently passes days, and weeks, and months, without ever devoutly thinking of his God and his Redeemer; nay, by whose lips the name of God is never pronounced, unless it be to point a jest or give emphasis to an assertion? This young man surely is a practical atheist. Is there not another, who, at the transient solicitation of passion, or even from the dread of being considered precise, will do, and who is forming the habit of doing, that which he knows the eternal God to have forbidden? This young man is a practical atheist. Is there not one who left the home of his parents rich in all the instructions which piety could impart, and resolved that, in the new circumstances in which he was to be placed, he would seek first of all the favor of God, who is already living in the daily neglect of his soul's salvation, and on whom every religious truth is rapidly losing its wonted effect? This young man is a practical atheist. Is there not another, who professes himself a disciple of Christ, who has felt the powers of the world to come, and been, as he supposed, a partaker of the Holy Ghost, who has long since forgotten to bow the knee in prayer, who seeks neither the blessing of God upon his labors nor the pardon of God for his transgressions, who is fast forgetting his religious impressions and becoming recreant to his most solemn vows? This young man is a practical atheist. In a word, whoever there may be among us, who is living without respect to his obligations to his Creator and Redeemer, who is not, by patient continuance in well-doing, seeking for glory, honor, and immortality, whatever be his profession, he is a practical atheist.

Whence has arisen this atheism in the intelligent, responsible, and highly-favored creatures of God? How is it that thinking beings should deny the existence of their Maker, and that immortal and accountable spirits, convinced of the reality of his existence and attributes, should act as though these truths were a fiction of the imagination? To this question I think but one answer can be given, and it is found in the words of the apostle Paul — Because they did not like to retain God in their knowledge, God gave them over. It is because we do not love the moral attributes of God that we first refuse submission to his authority, and then either deny his existence or say unto him, Depart from us, for we desire not a knowledge of thy ways. Thus, as in other cases, we yield obedience to our passions rather than to our reason and our conscience, and testify to the truth of the assertion of holy writ — The carnal mind is enmity against God. Is not this true of every one of us who is living without God in the world? Would you not think of God if you loved him? Would you not obey him if you loved him? Retire within your own bosoms, and let each one decide for himself whether these things be so.

And, if this be so, whither, I pray you, doth it tend, and what must be the end thereof? When you put aside this tabernacle of flesh, how will you stand before God, with the temper of fixed enmity to his character unchangeably interwoven with your spiritual nature? What means do you possess for carrying on this warfare? Can you contend with omnipotence? Can you deceive omniscience? Can you sustain yourself under the frown of all-consuming holiness? Do you not perceive that enmity with God involves within itself the essential elements of unutterable woe?

What, then, remains for us but eternal death, unless our spiritual nature be transformed from enmity to love? Ye must be born again, is the dictate of reason as well as revelation. We are thus shut up unto the faith. We are, however, still in a state of probation. God, in the gospel of his Son, is offering to us reconciliation. I will, saith he, take from you the heart of stone, and give you a heart of flesh. To him, then, let us all approach in the temper of humble penitence and filial affection. Great as are our offences, our Father who is in heaven does not desire our destruction. He is not willing that one of us should perish. He has exalted his well-beloved Son as a Prince and a Savior to grant to every one of us repentance and remission of sins. Pardon and eternal life are freely offered to us in the gospel. Look unto me, saith the Lord, and be ye saved, all ye ends of the earth, for I am God, and there is none else. Let us, then, hearken to his merciful invitation, and let us do it now. Why should we continue to grieve him by our rebellion? Why should we harden our hearts against all the entreaties of redeeming love? Let us. then, now give to him our hearts, for now is the accepted time, now is the day of salvation.

THE MORAL CHARACTER OF MAN.
LOVE TO GOD.

"For all have sinned, and come short of the glory of God"
Romans iii. 23.

"I know you, that ye have not the love of God in you."
John v. 42.

In a preceding discourse, I had occasion to allude to the moral attributes of God. I then stated that reason and revelation unite in ascribing to the Deity almighty power, omniscient wisdom, spotless holiness, and infinite love. We cannot escape from the conviction that such a Being presides over the destinies of the universe, and that he is and ever must be intimately present to every one of us.

When we speak of the attributes of God, we always conceive of them as ever-acting energies, as the principles by which all his acts are, from necessity, governed. When we speak of his almighty power, we mean that he is ever acting, and when we speak of his omniscient wisdom, we mean that he is always directing. And, more than this, when we conceive of his moral perfections, we always suppose that his power and wisdom are governed by justice, and holiness, and love; that he is every where throughout the universe, rewarding virtue and punishing vice, and that he must, from the necessity of his nature, continue to do so forever. Thus the very conception of the character of the Deity involves the conception of an all-wise, all-powerful, and all-holy government, to which every moral creature is, from the conditions of his being, responsible.

If we be the moral creatures of God, it is then a matter of great consequence to us to ascertain the relation in which we stand to such a government. Are our desires in harmony with the laws by which we are encompassed? Is our character such, that, in conformity with the essential elements of his nature, God can make us happy? We are moral, voluntary agents; we can never take pleasure in any obedience, unless we obey from love. Do we then love the objects which God loves? do we hate the things that he hates? and, above all, do we love our Father in heaven, from whom comes to us every good and perfect gift? In a word, it is most reasonable to inquire whether or not our moral nature is in harmony with that of the Deity, for, if it be not, we must at last be miserable.

And these questions derive additional interest from the fact, that the present is with us a state of probation, and that it is the only probation which will ever be allotted to us. Every action is connected with consequences which attach to us forever. Every action is forming in us the habit of love or of enmity to our Creator. And besides, this being a state of probation, it is also a state of change. We may here prepare ourselves for either happiness or misery, by the formation of a moral character, and we may here reform our character, if we find that by any means whatever it has lapsed into sin. From all these considerations, it will, I think, be manifest, that the question, What is the moral character of the human race? is one of the greatest practical importance. Each one of us is an individual of that race, and is distinctly marked with the essential moral lineaments by which it is distinguished. Let us, then, candidly, and yet solemnly, inquire, what is the truth on this subject.

In considering the moral character of man, it is important to remark, in the first place, that there are two classes of beings to whom we stand in moral relations. These are our fellow-men and our Creator. It cannot for a moment be doubted that, in respect to both of these, we are under obligations to some courses of conduct in preference to others. Every one knows the difference between justice and injustice, truth and falsehood, gratitude and ingratitude in our dealings with our fellow-men; and that we are morally obliged to cherish the one class of affections and to eradicate the other. It is yet more evident that we must be under obligations greater than we can conceive, to exercise suitable affections towards our Father in heaven. If this be so, it will follow by necessity, that our moral character is to be determined by the manner in which these obligations are fulfilled. He who fulfils them is deserving of praise. He who fails to fulfil them is deserving of blame: how much more, he who cherishes moral dispositions to which they are directly opposed!

In order, then, to ascertain the moral character of man, it is essential to ascertain what are the moral dispositions which are required of him by his Creator. This is readily learned from the volume of inspiration. The moral law, under which we ars created, is expressed in these words: Thou shalt love the Lord thy God with all thy heart, and thy neighbor as thyself. To this rule, as soon as it is conceived, our conscience responds. Our whole moral nature bears testimony to its rectitude. No one can either pretend that it is unjust, or offer any other as a substitute for it, without involving himself in absurdity. This rule, then, being once admitted, we are provided with a criterion by which the moral character of man may be estimated. If it be found that men do love God with all their hearts, and their neighbor as themselves, then is their moral character perfect, and they may justly claim the reward of innocence. If, on the contrary, it be found that these affections are either imperfect or absolutely wanting, then must we abandon all pretensions to innocence, and we are exposed to the desert of wrong-doing.

It would be easy, in examining this subject, to spread before you the opinions of men, in all ages, who have reflected upon the moral character of our race. I might multiply quotations without number, from poets, satirists, and philosophers, to whose decisions, in all that concerns human nature, we are accustomed to yield the profoundest deference. These all unite in affirming that man is, in a great degree, ignorant of his duty, both to God and man; and that, when his duty is perceived, he is by no means inclined to perform it. I might also refer to the universal consciousness of guilt which pervades our race, and its natural consequence, the dread of futurity, and the fear of retribution, as evidences that our own consciences testify to the fact of our guiltiness. I might review the history of our race from the beginning, and point you to the instances of cruelty, oppression, treachery, and impiety, with which every page is filled, as illustrations of the moral bias of our nature. I might examine the systems of law which have been enacted in all nations, and of which the sole object is to defend the weak against the unhallowed aggressions of the mighty. But all these must be passed by for the present. They may seem too general and indefinite for the purposes of conviction, and moreover they all fail to teach us the origin from which all these evils emanate. Let us, then, turn from these human authorities, and inquire for the teachings of the Scriptures upon this subject. If God himself has revealed to us the moral character of man, we have the means of arriving at the truth with absolute certainty.

In appealing to the Scriptures in order to ascertain the moral character of man, you will, I trust, believe me, when I say, that I have no desire to teach you the doctrine of any particular sect. We desire to teach not what the sects have inculcated, but what the Bible reveals. Nor shall I attempt to illustrate or confirm the views of any class of theologians; this they are abundantly able to do for themselves. The Scriptures of the Old and New Testaments are our ultimate and only authority in all questions touching our moral relations to God. If we can ascertain what they teach us, we shall arrive at pure truth. If we present to you the dogmas of men, we shall at best set before you the truth, commingled with the results of human infirmity and error.

Nor have I the least design to defend the terms used by many writers on this subject. We desire to deal not with names, but with things; not with words, but with matters of fact. It has, sometimes, for instance, been the custom to designate the moral corruption of man by the term "total depravity." Definitions, I know, may be given of this phrase which would render it not inconsistent with what I suppose to be the revealed truth; still I think that this truth might be expressed by more fitly chosen words. When we modify an adjective by the epithet "total," we mean, I think, to declare that the quality pervades the subject without admixture or alleviation. That thing is not *totally* black which presents any intermingling of colors. If *depraved* mean sinful, *totally depraved* would seem to mean sinful in such a sense as to exclude the existence of virtue. Now, I do not perceive that such a character is ascribed to man in the Scriptures. If, on the other hand, this expression indicates that though there may be virtue in human action irrespective of divine grace, yet that in no case it fulfils the conditions of the laws of God, this may be true, but the truth might, as I think, be expressed by more appropriate terms.

Ruined and helpless as the moral condition of man is represented to be in the Scriptures, they do not assert that there is in his nature none of the elements of goodness. So far as we can discover, they nowhere assert that filial or parental affection, patriotism, generosity, or benevolence, are either vicious, or to be classed with the instinctive and therefore morally neutral impulses of brutes. The principles of ethics would teach us that such a view was erroneous. The intentional fulfilment of a moral obligation must, as it seems to me, be virtuous. It may not be as virtuous as it ought to be. It may be wanting in some of the elements necessary to a perfect moral action, and, therefore, it may *come short of* the praise of God. So far, however, as it is the intentional fulfilment of a moral obligation, it is virtuous, and I think that all men correctly honor it as such. There are surely gradations in moral character irrespective of the transforming influences of the grace of God. When the young ruler came to inquire of Christ, there was much that was wanting to render him acceptable to God; yet the Savior looked upon him and loved him. Our Lord clearly beheld in him a character very different from that of the scribes and Pharisees who surrounded him.

Let us, then, while we attempt to examine this subject, endeavor to cast aside our prejudices, and inquire for the simple truth. Let us deal with facts, instead of words. On the one hand, let not our natural indisposition to find ourselves in the wrong render us blind to our real condition; and, on the other hand, let not our adherence to preconceived opinions lead us to deny what is obvious to our own observation. It becomes us to allow to human nature all that it can reasonably claim, and, at the same time, to state the facts concerning it precisely as they exist. No benefit can ever arise from adherence to error, under what guise soever it may be concealed.

I have already remarked that the standard by which the moral character of man is to be judged is the law, Thou shalt love the Lord thy God with all thy heart, and thy neighbor as thyself. He who obeys this rule is innocent; his moral character is perfect; he will receive praise from God. He who fails to obey it is imperfect, sinful, and is shut out from all claim to justification on the ground of the law. We shall proceed, on this occasion, to examine the declarations of revelation respecting the character of man, in view of the first part of the precept, Thou shalt love the Lord thy God with all thy heart.

From the multitude of passages that might be offered to illustrate this subject, I have chosen the two which form the text of this discourse, as among the most definite and explicit. The apostle declares that all men, the whole human race, have sinned; and, if we examine the context, we shall see that he means also to affirm they are sinners. He adds, as a consequence of this, they have *come short* of the glory of God. "Glory," in this place, means "praise," the praise of well-doing. "To come short of" is to fail of obtaining. The text, then, asserts that all men, by sinning, have failed to obtain the divine favor. The truth therefore, revealed, is this: God has given us a perfect rule of conduct; we have not obeyed it, and hence we have lost all claim to his approbation. That this is his meaning is evident from the conclusion which he draws from these premises; "therefore, by the deeds of the law can no flesh be justified."

The words of our Savior also affirm distinctly what is our moral character in respect to our obligations to God. "I know you," said he, "that ye have not the love of God in you." That this assertion was not intended to refer exclusively to his immediate hearers, but that it is universally true, is evident from his declaration on another occasion. "This is the condemnation," said he, "that light is come into the world, and men loved darkness rather than light, because their deeds are evil."

In attempting to illustrate this doctrine, I remark, first, that the Scriptures always proceed upon the admission that the great moral relation of man — that which involves and infinitely transcends every other — is his relation to his Creator. In comparison with this, every other dwindles into insignificance. All others, in comparison with it, are as finite to infinite, as time to eternity. The love of God throughout the moral universe is the alpha and omega, the beginning and the end, of all essential and permanent goodness. The presence or the absence of this attribute constitutes the difference in this world between the saint and the sinner, and in the unseen world that between an angel and a demon. All other relations change, and the obligations and duties thence arising change with them; this relation alone is changeless and immutable as the throne of the eternal. God cannot be otherwise than he is, and hence the duty to love him supremely must be unalterable. From this affection all essential goodness, throughout the universe, emanates, and by this alone is it sustained and invigorated. This alone would create universal love; withdraw it, and every passion would tend to universal hatred. Without it, the creature is fallen, shut out from the companionship of the holy, delivered over to the blindness of his own ignorance and the turbulence of his unrestrained desires. Like the principle of gravitation in the material world, while it exists in its native energy, the mightiest planet in its remotest orbit performs with unerring rectitude its appointed revolution, whilst the veriest mote that floats in the sunbeam finds unbidden its appropriate place. Abolish it, and suns, and stars, and planets, would rush in wild confusion through the abyss; and though here and there a crystal or a gem might for a while retain its fair proportions, yet all things would be rapidly crumbling into void and formless chaos.

Now, the Bible charges it upon man, with the most emphatic precision, that of this element — the supreme love to God — he is utterly and entirely destitute. The messages of the prophets to the Jews repeated in every form this appalling announcement. "They say unto God," saith Job, "Depart from us, for we desire not the knowledge of thy ways." "A son honoreth his father, and a servant his master; if, then, I be a father, where is my honor? and if I be a master, where is my fear? saith the Lord of hosts." Lest, however, it should be said that these expressions are the figurative language of poetry, our Lord, in the words of the text, in terms that cannot be misunderstood, declares, with an emphasis that cannot be mistaken, "I know you, that ye have not the love of God in you."

Here, however, a distinction may be taken. It is not charged upon man, that he may not love his own conceptions of the Deity. It is not said that a Greek or Roman might not have loved the fabulous creations of his own mythology, if their attributes were in harmony with the tendencies of his own corrupted nature. The text simply affirms of both Jew and Gentile, that they had no love for the holy God whom the Messiah came more perfectly to reveal. Nor would the Scriptures deny that we, at the present day, might love the natural attributes of the true God. We may admire a poetical conception of the Creator, as the Author of all that is sublime and beautiful, the God of sunshine and of storms, of spring-time and of autumn, "who bringeth forth Mazzaroth in his seasons, and guideth Arcturus and his sons," while we have no one proper affection towards the God and Father of our Lord Jesus Christ. Our Lord addresses us not as tasteful but as moral creatures; not as admirers of the beautiful, but as responsible agents, every one of whom must give account of himself unto God. It is with reference to the moral attributes of the Most High, his spotless holiness, his unchanging truth, his boundless love, and his paternal goodness, that our Savior speaks, when he declares, "I know you, that ye have not the love of God in you."

2. But the Scriptures go further than this. It is evident that, under the present constitution, it is the will of our Creator that we should derive happiness from a great variety of external objects. Things sensual, social, and moral, things of time and of eternity, are designed to furnish for us sources of pleasure as well as impulses to action. So long as these were enjoyed within proper limits, and in due subordination to the will of the Creator, the happiness of man was perfect and his virtue untarnished. The love of God was the all-controlling principle of his action, and to this affection every other rendered homage. But when the love of God was banished from his bosom, the love of some created object immediately occupied its place. The restraining powers of his moral affection being removed, his affections were surrendered to the things that perish. Hence we became sensual, carnal, having not the spirit. We obey the desires of the flesh, without regard to the will of God. We seek the present, regardless of the future. We ask, "Who will show us any good?" instead of asking what is right and well-pleasing to our Father who is in heaven. Thus was it in the garden of Eden. God had said of the tree of knowledge, "Thou shalt not eat of it nor touch it." But when the woman saw that the tree was good for food, and that it was pleasant to the eyes, and a tree to be desired to make one wise, she took of the fruit thereof and did eat." "Thus saith the Lord by the prophet Jeremiah, Be aston-

ished, O ye heavens, at this, and be horribly afraid; be very desolate, saith the Lord. For my people have committed two great evils; they have forsaken me, the fountain of living waters, and have hewn them out cisterns, broken cisterns, which can hold no water."

Hence, as man obeys his appetites in the place of God, the Bible charges upon us universal sinfulness. We are told not only that the love of God is not in us, but that we practically disobey him. "When God looked down upon the children of men to see if there were any that did good, they had all gone out of the way, they had all together become sinful." The apostle Paul, in treating upon this subject, declares concerning Jew and Gentile, — that is, the whole human race, — "There is none righteous, no not one, there is none that understandeth, there is none that seeketh after God, there is none that doeth good, no, not one." After stating in detail the various forms of this sinfulness, he concludes as follows: "Now we know that whatsoever the law saith, it saith to those that are under the law, that every mouth may be stopped, and all the world become guilty before God." The love of God being withdrawn, no action can proceed from this motive, but all must proceed from motives sensual and earthly. Or, if we act from higher and more worthy, as, for instance, from social motives, or the dictates of moral obligation to man, the love of God being absent, we are shut out from communion with the Holy One, and come short of the praise of God.

3. Let us proceed to another consideration. While this change has taken place in man, the law of God has remained unaltered. The command, holy, and just, and good, continues as at the beginning: "Thou shalt love the Lord thy God with all thy heart." Man has fixed his affections on the creature, instead of the Creator, and finds his only happiness in enjoyments which God has forbidden. The creature is thus placed in direct opposition to the Creator, and hence there arises in his bosom a dislike to God and the government of God. Man does not love the divine omniscience, because it looks into the

secret recesses of his heart. He does not love the divine holiness, because it is opposed to the courses which he chooses to pursue. He does not love the divine justice, because it will assuredly recompense to every man the due reward of all his deeds. He does not love the divine goodness, because it will make only the holy, obedient, and penitent happy. We can easily conceive what must be the result of so universal an opposition — an opposition that encompasses us every where and at all times, and which must reveal itself without a covering in the world of truth, to which we are tending.

This result must be hostility. We cannot but dislike a power which is every where thwarting our plans and uttering its solemn rebuke at the moment when we are revelling in our choicest gratifications. Hence the Scriptures charge upon us not only dislike, but even enmity to God. Our first parents fled from the presence of God, to hide themselves among the trees of the garden. The apostle Paul declares that men do not like to retain God in their knowledge, and that so intense is this dislike, that they shut out the idea of the true God, by substituting in his place the most degrading objects of idolatry. "Professing themselves to be wise, they became fools, and changed the glorious and incorruptible God into an image made like to corruptible man, and to birds, and four-footed beasts, and creeping things." Thus also saith he in another place, "The carnal mind is enmity against God, for it is not subject to the law of God, neither indeed can be;" that is, so long as a man is carnal, determined to derive his happiness from sources forbidden by his Creator, he must from necessity be at enmity with God. Nor is this all. The Scriptures teach us that this enmity is capable of resisting the strongest conviction of the understanding. Thus saith the Savior: "Light has come into the world, and men have loved darkness rather than light, because their deeds are evil." Nay, more, this enmity is unaffected by the longest experience of the goodness of God. "Despisest thou the riches of his goodness, and forbearance, and long-suffering; not knowing that the goodness of God leadeth thee to repentance?" But, above all, the inflexible nature of this hostility has been illustrated in the reception which has been given to the message of mercy by Jesus Christ. In the gospel, God draws near, beseeching us to be reconciled to him; but his offer is universally rejected. Men, with one consent, begin to make excuse. They deliberately choose to remain at enmity with him, rather than to confess their sins, renounce their idols, and be received as his children, through faith in his well-beloved Son.

Here, however, let it be observed, I do not assert that this enmity against God is a sentiment of which either you or other men are of necessity conscious. You may, on the contrary, be shocked when you hear that the Scriptures charge such a degree of wickedness upon us. You will then naturally ask, "How can this enmity exist without manifesting itself to our consciousness?" The answer, I think, is obvious. We cherish affections directly opposed to the law, and at variance with the character of God; but we have learned so habitually to banish the thought of God from our minds, that the hostility which really exists does not become a matter of reflection. We shut out the light, and choose to abide in darkness, and are at ease; but this by no means proves that we shall remain at ease when the light of day shall burst upon our sin-distempered vision. The Scriptures, when treating on this subject, always speak of our moral condition as it actually is, and as it must of necessity manifest itself, whenever the proper opportunity shall arrive. We cherish feelings directly at variance with the holy government of God; but he reveals himself to us at present, not as a God doing justice, but as a God desiring to be reconciled. He is long suffering, and not willing that any should perish. He is striving by his goodness to lead us to repentance. But this cannot continue always. He must render to every man according to his deeds. When the veil of flesh shall be removed, the full blaze of all his perfections must burst upon us, and then must the opposition of our character to his, reveal itself in all its intensity.

Once more, and I have done. The Scriptures teach us that, by steadfast continuance in sin, we are forming for ourselves a fixed and unalterable character. It is the law of habit, that, whether we will or will not, the frequent repetition of an act produces upon us a permanent effect, creates a stronger and stronger tendency to this act, and renders a change of character more and more difficult, and, at last, practically impossible. Such is the effect of the indulgence in sin. That it should be so is according to all the analogies of our probationary state. That this effect has been produced upon us, every one may learn from his own experience.

I might easily refer to various passages of Scripture in which this truth is clearly set forth. Thus saith the prophet, "Can the Ethiopian change his skin, or the leopard his spots? Then may ye also do good that are accustomed to do evil." This whole subject is, however, set forth by the apostle Paul in the seventh chapter of the Epistle to the Romans, with a graphic power, which leaves no room for misconception. He had before shown that we are all sinners, and hence under condemnation for our past offences. He here teaches that, by sin, our moral nature is so disordered, that we are moreover helpless in our iniquity. In illustrating this truth, he uses the first person, for the purpose of designating the universal condition of man. "We know," saith he, "that the law is spiritual; but I am carnal, sold under sin. For that which I do I allow not, for what I would, that I do not, but what I hate, that I do. I find, then, a law that when I would do good, evil is present with me. I delight in the law of God after the inward man; but I find another law in my members, warring against the law of my mind, and bringing me into captivity to the law of sin in my members. O wretched man that I am! who shall deliver me from the body of this death?" In such language as this does he describe the internal warfare between the conscience and the passions, and the constant failure of man to live in obedience to the law which he acknowledges to be right. Such, then, is the condition in which we find ourselves after the habit of sin has been formed. We are not only guilty, but helplessly guilty. Hence, by the deeds of the law can no man be justified.

We learn from this discussion what is briefly the charge which the Scriptures bring against man, so far as his moral relations to God are concerned. They declare that he is destitute of love to God; that his affections are given to things which God has forbidden, or in degrees that he has forbidden; hence, that there has arisen in the bosom of man a sentiment of hostility to his Maker; and lastly, that, by a course of ceaseless transgression, this hostility has become the fixed habit of his soul. If such be the facts, we must perceive that every act of man must come short of the praise of God. God demands and deserves our supreme affection. Every one of our actions is destitute of this element; nay, more, it acknowledges the supremacy of the passions to the conscience, and of the creature to the Creator. Thus saith the text, "All have sinned and come short of the praise of God."

If this be so, we must be aware that we can present no claim of innocence, on the ground that there yet may be discovered some traces of virtue in man when his relations to his fellows alone are concerned. That such virtues do exist in different degrees among us, is not denied. The Scriptures do not deny it. But this admission in no way invalidates the truth of the doctrine in question. The charge in the text has respect to our relations to God. But it would be easy to show that as our duty to God is involved in every action of our lives, the action, how right soever in other respects, yet wanting in this essential element, is eminently faulty. No one of us can therefore conclude that his life is right in the sight of God on account of the existence in his character of much that is lovely, and excellent, and of good report, in his relations to his fellow-men.

Again: No one of us is warranted in the belief that he loves God because he is not conscious of the sentiment of hostility towards him. Our Father in heaven is not satisfied with this negative moral condition, were such a condition possible, in his children here on earth. His command, the obedience to which is essential to our happiness both here and hereafter, is, "Thou shalt love the Lord thy God with all thy heart;" and this command cannot surely be obeyed by merely refraining from hating him. But can we be convinced that we are entitled to the praise of even this negative virtue? Is it not the fact that we have no consciousness of hostility to God because we really think nothing about him? "The wicked," saith the Psalmist, "through the pride of his countenance, will not seek after God; God is not in all his thoughts." We cannot indulge in hostility to a nonentity; and what is not in all our thoughts is truly a nonentity to us. But if we could conceive of the character of God as it really exists, and behold him scrutinizing every thought, registering every word, and observing every action, bringing every secret thing into judgment, and justly offended at every thing unholy, is it at all certain that we would not instantly feel that God and ourselves were at irreconcilable variance?

But we shall all very soon behold God as he actually is. When we lay aside this earthly tabernacle, our spirits will be at once in the presence of the omnipresent Spirit. Then we ourselves, as well as all things around us, will appear as they are. What then must be our condition, if we find ourselves destitute of love to God, hostile to all his perfections, and by our own act fixed in this condition forever? God is immutable. We have hardened ourselves in unchangeable opposition to his character and law. What result can possibly ensue but eternal banishment from his presence? And who could be so appropriate associates for us as those whose moral feelings harmonize with our own? Our own consciences must approve of the sentence by which we are consigned to the dwelling-place of those who kept not their first estate. What can we say when he shall punish us?

If these things be so, I am sure that every one of us must be convinced of the necessity of a radical moral change in the character of man before he can meet God and be at peace. Reason reëchoes the saying of the Messiah — "Unless a man be born again, he cannot see the kingdom of God." Whatever, then, may be our hopes, unless we have been renewed in the spirit of our mind, we are still enemies to God by wicked works. Are we willing to cherish this enmity, and reap its results forever? No one would dare to choose for himself such a doom. Let us, then, escape it by penitence and faith now, while change is possible. Penitence, even were it possible beyond the grave, would there avail us nothing. "Let, then, the wicked forsake his way, and the unrighteous man his thoughts, and turn unto the Lord, for he will have mercy upon him, and unto our God, for he will abundantly pardon."

THE MORAL CHARACTER OF MAN. LOVE TO GOD.

"EVEN AS THEY DID NOT LIKE TO RETAIN GOD IN THEIR KNOWLEDGE, GOD GAVE THEM OVER TO A REPROBATE MIND."

Romans i. 28.

IN the preceding discourse, I attempted to exhibit the teaching of the Scriptures in respect to the moral character of man. I suppose that the Bible charges us with being destitute of love to God, alienated in our affections from him, and enemies to him by wicked works; it also declares that we are steadily pursuing a course which must render these moral dispositions fixed and unalterable so long as we exist. I propose, on the present occasion, to pursue this subject somewhat further, and to show that these declarations of the word of God are perfectly in accordance with the facts that have been disclosed in the history of our race.

That man at first was created in his present moral condition has not generally been deemed probable. It seems scarcely credible that a holy and most merciful God would have made originally a creature, and specially a probationary creature, with such a proneness to evil as man has every where displayed. Hence the opinion that there has come over our race some great moral change, has been almost universal. The classical mythology represented the progenitors of our race as guileless, virtuous, and pious, the inhabitants of a world where the curse came not, but where all things ministered to their happiness. Man, however, soon degenerated.

The golden age gave place to the age of brass, and this in turn to the age of iron; thorns and thistles mocked the labors of man, who had become a sinner; diseases cut short his days; the box of Pandora was opened, and mourning, lamentation, and woe became the inheritance of our apostate race.

This idea, thus dimly shadowed forth in heathen mythology, is clearly and definitely presented in the Holy Scriptures. They teach us that God created man upright, with moral powers holding such a relation to his sensual appetites that he was fully prepared to enter upon his probation with every prospect of success. "God created man in his own image, in the image of God created he him." "And God saw every thing that he had made, and behold it was very good." Under these circumstances there was nothing to restrict the intercourse between the Creator and man, any more than between the Creator and any other holy being whom he had made. Hence the communion of heaven with earth was free and unrestrained. God revealed himself personally to man, made known to him his will, and taught him the consequences which must result both from obedience and disobedience. Thus we learn that, at the beginning, man was well instructed in the knowledge of the character and law of his Creator.

But man, having been created a moral agent, in addition to reason and conscience, and appetites and passions, was endowed with the awful power of will. The motives for his conduct having been presented, he was left in absolute freedom to choose between them.* But man, being in honor,

---

* "——— I made him just and right,
Sufficient to have stood, though free to fall.
Such I created all the ethereal powers
And spirits, both them who stood and them who failed:
Freely they stood who stood, and fell who fell.
Not free, what proof could they have given sincere
Of true allegiance, constant faith, or love,
Where only, what they needs must do, appeared,
Not what they would? What praise could they receive?

abode not. He chose to disobey God, led astray by the allurements of sense, and fell from the high dignity in which he had been created. Renouncing his allegiance to God, he became of necessity the slave of his passions. The supreme affection of man having been withdrawn from God, it was bestowed upon the creature. Conscience was dethroned, and her sceptre was surrendered to appetite. Yet, though the just subordination of his powers among themselves was thus overthrown, the powers themselves remained. Neither conscience, nor passion, nor reason, nor taste, nor memory, nor will, had been annihilated. Sin neither abolished our knowledge of God, nor our capacity for recognizing his attributes as they are displayed in the things that are made. Hence, notwithstanding his fall, man was still capable of a true conception of the character of God, and a clear conviction of the obligations by which we are bound to obey him.

Under these conditions, the results of this early trial of our race were abundantly disastrous. The wickedness of man became so intolerable, that, with the exception of a single family, God swept away from the face of the earth its entire population. "God saw that the wickedness of man was great upon the earth, and that every imagination of the thoughts of his heart was only evil continually. And it repented the Lord that he had made man on the earth, and it grieved him at the heart. And the Lord said, I will destroy man whom I have created from the face of the earth." Such was the character and such the destiny of the antediluvian fathers of mankind.

After the race had been thus destroyed by the flood, a second parentage was, if I may use the expression, granted to mankind, and granted under the most favorable circumstances.

What pleasure I from such obedience paid,
When will and reason, (reason also is choice,)
Useless and vain, of freedom both despoiled,
Made passive both, had served necessity,
Not me?"

Paradise Lost, Book III. 98—110.

Noah was a just man and perfect in his generations. And Noah walked with God. "Thee have I seen righteous before me in this generation." It seems as though God had selected the most virtuous man on earth to be the second father of our race, in order that our probation might proceed with every prospect of success. After the catastrophe, in which the millions of his contemporaries were swept away, God revealed himself to Noah, and made to him most gracious promises of favor and protection. There is reason to believe that, for a long period after this event, mankind enjoyed a clear and extensive knowledge of the character and law of God; a knowledge rendered the more impressive by the recent vindication of his justice. We find that the patriarchs, in their extensive migrations, met among different nations the devout worshippers of the true God. Abraham, the father of the Hebrew commonwealth, paid tithes to Melchizedek, as to a person more pious than himself; and was afterwards rebuked by the righteous king of Gerar for base equivocation. A similar event occurred in the history of the patriarch Isaac. Very distinct traces of a knowledge of the true God may be discovered among the Gentile nations at as late a period as that of the entrance of the Jews into the land of Canaan. None of the inspired prophets have spoken of the character of the Most High in sublimer language, or have been more fearfully impressed with the vision of his holiness, than Balaam, the mysterious seer of Moab. And even at the present day, as the enterprise of our missionary pioneers is discovering new tribes of the human family, we occasionally perceive clear indications of traditionary knowledge, which could have descended from none other than an inspired source. That such is the fact in respect to the Karens, a people scattered throughout the jungles of Burmah, I fully believe. These ignorant barbarians, destitute of a priesthood, and without a written language, had retained among themselves a collection of moral precepts, which for purity and beauty surpass every thing that has come down to us from the most refined nations of antiquity; and which are intimately allied to the teachings of revelation itself. Whether, therefore, we take the Holy Scriptures or profane tradition for our authority, we are, I think, justified in believing that the race of man commenced the second period of its probation with a competent knowledge of the existence, attributes and moral requirements of the Creator.

But, although this knowledge of God remained in the possession of man, his moral nature continued unchanged. His passions were still at war with his conscience, and in every contest they came off victorious. The ever-present idea of a holy God gave energy to the moral sense, and rendered its rebukes more intensely painful. The man would sin in spite of his knowledge, and he suffered at every transgression the pangs of remorse. Thus the knowledge of God became a source of incessant moral anguish, and it was natural that he should endeavor to escape from it. He did not like to retain God in his knowledge. God, justly indignant at the wickedness of the creature, gave him over to a reprobate mind; that is, he left him to his own choices, and suffered him to work out the inevitable results of his deliberate transgression.

The manner in which these results were accomplished may, I think, be observed by a reference to the moral history of man.

We have seen that, as long as man yielded himself up to the dominion of passion, the knowledge of God must have been painful. But his intellectual nature demanded the acknowledgment of a first cause, while his moral nature required some object of veneration. As the idea of the true God had become painful, he naturally sought to satisfy these primary wants of his spiritual constitution by providing for himself some object of veneration, which might be worshipped without giving additional power to the stings of conscience. To accomplish this has been the object of mankind from the earliest ages to the present moment.

The first, and perhaps the most natural, step in the path of moral degradation, was to deify the distinguished dead. While living they had conferred benefits on man, and received the tribute of his grateful homage. The feelings of the human heart could not consign them to forgetfulness. If the dead existed in another state, they might there exert some power in behalf of the living. If to this we add the susceptibility of the heart under sorrow, and the disposition to praise when applause can awaken no envy, it is not unreasonable to suppose that the custom of deifying deceased men would become extensively prevalent.

Such, I think, seems to have been the origin of the mythology, both of classic and barbarian antiquity. The original deities of heathen idolatry were manifestly, I think, distinguished monarchs or remarkable benefactors. Jupiter, the father of the gods, was, as we are told, born in the Island of Crete, and the names of his parents are even indicated. Ceres was the first instructor of the human race in the arts of agriculture. Vulcan was the discoverer of the uses of iron. The same idea may be traced throughout the Egyptian and Hindoo mythology. Such were the *dii majores*, the original deities which men first received to a participation in the worship due only to Jehovah.

The same fact is further illustrated by the multiplication of demigods which succeeded this first deification. Hercules, Castor and Pollux, the Muses, Esculapius, Achilles, and a thousand others, were the *dii minores*, the lesser gods, the offspring of a deity and a human being. This parentage indicates, I think, the origin of the gods themselves, since deified men would naturally be connected by the ordinary ties of passion with those from whom they sprang. Hence arose the universal disposition to claim consanguinity with the gods, until, at last, the relationship became so universal as to confer no title to honor. At the time of Alexander the Great, these notions had passed into desuetude, and his claims of descent from Jupiter were laughed at by his contemporaries.

Here, however, I think it important to remark, that these deities were not originally introduced as substitutes for the true

God. They were merely intercessors, mediators, who might influence the supreme Divinity to be favorable to us. Something approaching nearer to the frailty of humanity seemed a more desirable object of worship than the holy God himself. Soon, however, this preference gradually excluded God from the conception of man, and the deified hero, at first only an intercessor, was at length worshipped in the place of the supreme Divinity. Still the original conception was not completely blotted out, and hence we observe that Jupiter and all the gods were governed by an invisible and overruling fate, to which they were obliged to yield unquestioning obedience. This tendency may, I think, be distinctly observed in all the phases of idolatry.

This was the first step in human degradation; it was, however, a descent from heaven to the abyss. It was exchanging the Creator for the creature. It was taking from the object of worship all that was peculiar to the Deity, and all that gave to our conception of him legitimate authority over the conscience. It was removing the incorruptible God from the throne of the universe, and substituting in his place a fiction of our own imagination, a being like to ourselves, debased by sensual appetites, delighting in polluted gratifications, liable to sorrow and disappointment, and grieving over misfortune like any one of us.

While, however, I suppose that such was the more common manner in which the creature, as an object of worship, was substituted for the Creator, I would by no means assert that it was universal. I have said that men were deified on account of the benefits which they had conferred. The same principle would lead to the deification of things as well as persons. In this manner every external object that is capable of doing us good may become a deity. Such would be the case in sparsely settled communities, where the passions of men are less powerfully excited, and among an agricultural people, where success in labor depends upon agents which we cannot control The Persian object of adoration was the sun or fire, which they believed to be the source of life, both animal and vegetable. The Egyptians worshipped the Nile as the cause of fertility, and, on the same principle, the ichneumon that destroyed the crocodile, the ox that tilled the land, and at last the leek and the onion, which were their favorite articles of food. Our aborigines worshipped several animals of the chase. And, in general, among idolatrous nations we find that animals frequently are held sacred, either on account of the benefits which they confer or the injuries which they inflict. It is for this latter reason that many of the inhabitants of the islands of the Pacific hold the shark in religious veneration.

Let us here pause for a moment, and observe what must be the effect produced upon the moral condition of man by this substitution of the creature for the Creator. I think it evident that the conscience of man can never maintain its supremacy over the passions, unless its decisions are enforced by a belief in the existence of such a Deity as the Scriptures reveal; an omnipotent Being, of almighty power, boundless goodness, immaculate purity, and inflexible justice. Nothing less than this will hold in check the violence of human passion, and repress the all-grasping tendency of human selfishness. But by this change in the object of worship all this restraint is removed, and conscience is left single-handed to struggle against the united strength of sensual and selfish impulses. I say single-handed, but this does not adequately express the truth. The unseen powers to which conscience looked for aid have more commonly become treacherous friends, who were themselves in league against her. The deities above were the patrons of crime and the exemplars of impurity. They, in the hour of trial, took part with her adversaries, and hence the triumph of the passions was complete.

But other results flowed from the increased intensity thus given to human passion, which rendered the moral degradation of man yet more hopeless. When the passions are vehemently excited, desire for gratification absorbs every other idea. At such a moment man specially feels his own impotence, and perceives that the future is wholly beyond his control. After having done his utmost to command success, he naturally looks upward to some higher power to render the means which he has chosen effectual. The warrior, on the eve of a battle, knows that the victory which shall lead to dominion cannot be rendered certain either by the penetration of his own sagacity or the prowess of his own arm. After his last order has been issued, he is conscious that the result is in the hands of some power higher than himself. His mind naturally turns to some being whose aid he may invoke in directing, for his advantage, the unseen events of the morrow. His soul, agitated by contending emotions, turns to some one of the conceptions with which his imagination is filled, and to it he commends himself and his fortunes. Should he prove victorious, the object of his worship will henceforth be to him and to his army the god of war. In the same manner the glutton and the drunkard would wish for a deity who might mitigate the paroxysm of fever or avert the stroke of apoplexy. The miser, devising schemes of unrighteous gain, would need a deity to grant him success, and the robber would sacrifice to a god before he proceeded on his errand of burglary.

You see thus that man, having assumed to himself the power of creating gods, would naturally multiply them almost without number. No passion can be conceived of, so base that it did not desire a deity whose aid it might invoke; and its desire was rarely for a long time unsatisfied. Profligacy, ambition, and sensuality in every form, readily created deities, who were their especial patrons. Hence vice appeared on earth armed with the authority of the Divinity. Yet even here the voice of conscience was not altogether silent. There would yet remain some to whom these excesses would appear morally odious. Even licentious men, when the storm of passion had subsided, might doubt whether a life of violence and sensuality must not meet its appropriate reward. It was necessary to advance a step farther, and silence the monitions of the moral sense, by bringing them into harmony with the will of the deities. When this was done, the reign of passion must be absolute.

This step was easily taken. If the gods above presided over the human passions, and taught men the means by which they could be gratified, the acts which passion dictated would of course be their most acceptable worship. As there was a god devoted to every passion, it only remained to ordain for each such rites as were in accordance with his attributes. Thus the veneration for the gods, which conscience itself teaches, would be the very means of sanctioning the most shocking immoralities. Conscience and passion would henceforth teach the same lesson, and no obstacle would exist to the universal indulgence in unblushing licentiousness. To aid in working out this result, temples were erected without number to every conceivable divinity, and to preside over the rites of each, a numerous and well-fed priesthood was appointed. The most exquisite artistical skill was lavishly employed to surround the worship of sensuality with the most attractive charms. Shrines, the admiration of all succeeding ages, crowned every hill-top and adorned every grove. Statuary of exquisite beauty realized in marble the most revolting conceptions. Every grotto and fountain acknowledged its tutelary divinity, and sent forth its priests to summon the people to its idolatrous rites. The slavery of man to the senses and the passions was fast rivetted upon him, as it seemed, forever. The secret chamber and the solemn temple, the distant grove and the thickly-peopled city, resounded with nothing but the struggle for mastery and the revel of licentiousness. Men did not like to retain God in their knowledge, and God gave them over to a reprobate mind.

These remarks, as you perceive, have been made with special reference to the nations of classic antiquity. But the same principles have wrought out the same results, wherever the progress of civilization has cherished their natural development. This fact is illustrated, for instance, in the history of the Hindoo mythology. The early divinities of the religion of Brama were, as I have suggested, deified men. These, in the process of time, were greatly multiplied. Next were added gods to preside over the human passions. Worship was made to conform to the character of the deity to whom it was offered, until, at the present time, there is not a crime so nefarious that you may not commit it as an act of devotion to some one of their millions of deities. Hence the moral character of the people is, in many respects, intimately allied to that of Greece and Rome at the period of their deepest degradation. The modern traveller cannot describe to us the scenes depicted on the walls of Herculaneum and Pompeii; and the missionary returning from Bengal refuses to utter the abominations that are witnessed by assembled thousands as the most acceptable sacrifice to the gods, on the days of their solemn devotion.

Now, if man had possessed no other knowledge of God than that derived from tradition, this downward tendency in our race would surely have seemed remarkable. We might have expected that intelligent and moral creatures would have cherished a knowledge of their Creator as a most invaluable treasure, and transmitted it unimpaired from generation to generation. But, during all this period, " God did not leave himself without a witness, in that he did good, and gave us rain from heaven, and fruitful seasons, filling our hearts with food and gladness." That knowledge of God which might be obtained by the study of his works is in all ages open to mankind. " The heavens ever declare the glory of God, and the firmament showeth forth his handy work. Day is uttering speech unto day, and night unto night is showing knowledge; and there is no speech nor language where their voice is not heard." The writings of Socrates indicate to us the extent to which the knowledge derived from this source may be attained, and the facts from which he reasoned were spread before all men. Notwithstanding this, there was none that was seeking after God. No one was asking, Where is God my Maker? unless as a question of metaphysical speculation. They remained, even in the days of the intellectual glory of Greece, the slaves of a debasing and abominable idolatry. I do not know that any clearer illustration can be presented of the truth of the assertion in the text than that which these facts exhibit. If men had liked to retain God in their knowledge, such a tendency, working out such results, could not have existed. The moral history of man bears witness to the truth of the divine declaration, that all men have sinned and come short of the glory of God; and that, as they changed the true God into a lie, and worshipped and served the creature more than the Creator, who is blessed forever, — for this cause God gave them over to vile affections. If there be a God, and we have thus forsaken him, surely no other result than this could reasonably be expected.

Thus far I have attempted to exhibit the moral tendency of man when he has been destitute of a written revelation. The subject, however, is capable of yet further illustration.

It was when the whole world was lying in the wickedness of which I have spoken, that the Messiah appeared to take away sin by the sacrifice of himself. By the light of nature we might have discovered the justice and goodness of God, and our own deep and inherent sinfulness; but we could never discover a way in which he could be just, and justify the guilty. But Jesus Christ came to reveal to us God in the character of a Father, willing to be reconciled, offering to us, as a free gift, pardon, reconciliation, and eternal life. "As Moses lifted up the serpent in the wilderness, so was the Son of man lifted up, that whosoever believed on him might not perish, but have everlasting life." The thick cloud which veiled the mercy-seat was dispersed, and every man might in humble confidence approach our Father in heaven, through the mediation of his well-beloved Son. The gospel of Jesus Christ is a message from God, beseeching men to repent of their sins, and yield to him that affection which is his most righteous due.

It is not needful that I here refer to the manner in which this offer of pardon was received, or the enmity which its promulgation excited in the breasts both of Jew and Gentile. It is, however, difficult to account for the fact, that an offer of restoration to piety and holiness should excite men to wrath, unless they were intensely sinful. But passing by this consideration, I proceed to remark, that this declaration of the willingness of God to receive us again to his favor, was made in a language at that time universally accessible, and thus it was rapidly disseminated throughout the civilized world. The written revelation was accompanied by the living preacher, and the good news of salvation was proclaimed in every city and village of the Roman empire. The truth thus promulgated, after centuries of persecution, aroused the slumbering conscience of man, and revealed the absurdity of the rites of heathenism. It banished the classical mythology from the earth, and among all the nations of the then known world, established its claim as a revelation from the Most High. Multitudes of men, in every place, were the examples and the witnesses of its transforming power. Now, it might well be asked, Could such a revelation, committed to writing, universally disseminated, and enforced by the precepts of the disciples of Christ, be again hidden from the eyes of men? Could the worship of God, which it taught, be exchanged for a sensual idolatry, and the pure doctrines of Jesus be made the ministers of sin? If all this were done, it would surely present a still stronger illustration of the truth of the text, — they did not like to retain God in their knowledge.

What have been the facts in this case? We are obliged to answer, that the downward moral tendency of our race, even under these circumstances, was, in a remarkable manner, analogous to that which we have already described among the heathen.

The church of Christ had scarcely escaped from the persecution of centuries, before the priesthood began to lay claim to the authority of mediating between God and man. This claim, strange as it may seem, was admitted, and an order of men, united under an infallible head, was acknowledged to be the only medium through whom any spiritual blessing could be conveyed to mankind. Their teachings were alone held to be obligatory upon the conscience, and in their hands were deposited the keys of heaven and hell. Where such an institution existed, the Scriptures, of course, could be of no practical importance; for of what value can be a written law, in the presence of the infallible lawgiver? The word of the living God was thus exchanged for the doctrines and commandments of men, and salvation was to be looked for, not from the Redeemer himself, but from him whom he had appointed to be his vicegerent on earth.

This was the first step in the progress of Christianized idolatry. It did not, however, remove man far enough from God to silence the voice of conscience, or render him the sufficiently passive slave of an ambitious hierarchy. Heavenly intercessors were proposed, who might present our prayers to the all-seeing God, and through whose influence we might be rendered acceptable to our Father in heaven. The Virgin Mary, as the mother of God, was first proposed for the adoration of the faithful. Peter and the rest of the apostles soon shared in this modified homage. To them very soon were added beatified martyrs, confessors, bishops, and saints, good and bad, without number, until the calendar was crowded with the names of those whom Christian men were commanded to worship. These were at first introduced merely as intercessors; but, as they were recognized as the immediate authors of our blessings, prayer was soon addressed to them, instead of to God himself. As in ancient paganism, so here, again, the cloud of inferior deities rendered the divinity invisible to man. The beatified saint took the place of the deified hero, or the half-mortal demigod; the true God was again exchanged for a false one, and the professed disciples of Christ worshipped and served the creature rather than the Creator. Nor did this infatuation stop here. Images, pictures, relics, became objects ot worship, and thus the works of men's hands, or the mouldering relics of his earthly tabernacle, were adored in the place of the ever-blessed God.

In this case, as in the other, the passions formed an alliance with the natural tendency of man to seek for aid from some supernatural power. As the ancient pagan selected his demigod, so the paganized Christian selected his saint, who should aid him in the accomplishment of his purposes, or avert from him the retribution which he had deserved. Even at the present day, the Greek pirate invokes his patron saint as he leaps on board the vessel which he has devoted to destruction; he mutters his prayers as he does the deed of murder, and, returning home, offers a portion of his spoils to the Virgin, in thankfulness for her aid in his nefarious enterprise. The Italian assassin repeats his pater noster as he whets his stiletto, and devoutly crosses himself as he withdraws it, reeking from the bosom of his rival. Nor was this all. If God have established a vicegerency on earth, and man has power to forgive sins, he may well be supposed to have power also to dictate the terms on which forgiveness may be obtained. Nay, more; it is going but a single step farther to assert that the authority which could absolve from guilt after the commission of crime, might also remit the penalty in anticipation. Now all this was, at one time, actually believed throughout Christendom. It is easy to perceive that a licentious age would gladly avail itself of such a doctrine to silence the voice of conscience, and that an ambitious priesthood would eagerly inculcate it as a means for the attainment of universal power. Such were the results that actually followed. At the time of the reformation, Christianity was supposed merely to consist in the performance of rites, and in obedience to the priesthood, without holding the most remote connection with purity of manners or holiness of life. It was conceded that a man might be spotless in piety, and yet live in the practice of the most revolting immorality. Thus, not only was the idea of God excluded from human thought, but the moral power of the world to come was nothing better than a scourge in the hands of the hierarchy. There was nothing left to arrest the downward and sensual tendencies of our nature. The corruption that reigned triumphant in city and country, in church and state, among ecclesiastics and laymen, was almost without a parallel, except in the grossest periods of pagan idolatry. Thus, again, was the truth illustrated, that men did not like to retain God in their knowledge, and God again gave them over to a reprobate mind.

He who will duly consider these facts, will, I think, scarcely fail to arrive at the conclusion that there is in the heart of man a moral temper averse to the character of God; that he naturally strives to substitute a fiction of his own, as an object of worship, in the place of the true God; that, this having been done, all safeguards of virtue are removed, man is given over to a reprobate mind, and becomes the willing slave of passion and sensuality.

But has this tendency in human nature been even yet eradicated? I wish that there was sufficient reason for answering this question in the affirmative. At the reformation, the Scriptures were again given to the people, and the pure light from heaven shone once more among the nations. Yet, even in Protestant Christendom, if I mistake not, undeniable traces of the same idolatrous bias have from time to time discovered themselves. The priesthood, in some instances, has again asserted its claim to the right of mediating between God and man; of being the exclusive interpreters of the holy oracles, and the only medium through which the grace of Christ can be conferred upon his disciples. Nay, more; we have been told that our acceptance with God does not depend absolutely on faith in Christ and holiness of heart, but also on the reception of ordinances from the hands of men whom God has intrusted with the monopoly of salvation. I cannot but regard these arrogant assumptions, and the passive acquiescence with which they are so frequently received, as another illustration of the tendency to which I have alluded. Nor would I confine the application of these remarks to any period or to any sect. Wherever the ministry assumes to be lords over God's heritage, instead of being ensamples to the flock; wherever rites and ceremonies of any sort whatever are exalted above holiness of heart and a humble walk with God; wherever the Christian pastor claims for himself exemption from that law which Christ has imposed upon all, or assumes the right of modifying that law for his own convenience; and whenever these doctrines are believed and these claims allowed by the people, — then and there the seeds of idolatry have been sown, and they will bear the fruit of apostasy from the faith. While, however, I affirm all this, I would by no means speak lightly of the honesty or the piety of many who believe to be true what I believe to be most lamentably false. God alone can determine the point beyond which error becomes incompatible with piety. That which is false can never be made true by the piety of him who affirms it; it only derives greater power to deceive from his blameless life and devout conversation.

I have thus far spoken of this tendency of man, as it has been exhibited in the history of nations and communities. But the subject admits of a more personal application. If such be the character of man, it is the character of every individual, and every one of us may discover its lineaments engraven upon his own moral nature. Let, then, every one of us answer for himself the question, Is the love of God within me? In order to do this, we must appeal to our own consciousness. Are we conscious of any love to the God revealed to us in the Scriptures? Nay, I will go further. Can none of us recollect the time when we would have rejoiced beyond measure, could we have satisfactorily demonstrated that an all-seeing and all-holy Lord God Almighty never existed? When the claims of God upon our universal love and obedience have been pressed upon us, do none of us remember how our whole nature has revolted against them? Have we never been conscious of a settled dislike to such an all-pervading government, and wished that there was some other universe, over which God did not reign, that we might flee to it, and escape the notice of his all-seeing eye? Our own consciousness, therefore, bears witness to the truth of the text, and confesses that, by nature, we did not like to retain God in our knowledge.

If such, then, be the facts disclosed by the history of man, they abundantly confirm the truth of the assertion in the text. Man by nature does not like to retain God in his knowledge, and he resorts to idolatry in every form, in order to escape from the presence of his Maker. Shutting out God from his thoughts, he of necessity surrenders himself to the dominion of the passions and the senses, and is thus given up of his Creator to a reprobate mind. If such be the facts, let every one of us ask himself what must be the end thereof.

THE MORAL CHARACTER OF MAN.
LOVE TO MAN.

"And the second is like unto it, namely, Thou shalt love thy neighbor as thyself."

Matthew xxii. 36.

I have, in previous discourses, attempted to illustrate the first commandment of the law, and to prove that, judged by it, every man must stand guilty before God. I suppose it to have been shown that we do not like to retain God in our knowledge; that this dislike is so intense as to lead us, by the most absurd idolatry, to violate the dictates of our understanding, in order to escape from the idea of an all-seeing and most holy God.

Taking these facts for granted, we proceed to consider the second commandment of the law, and to inquire whether man can plead innocence on the ground of obedience to its requirements.

Before, however, proceeding to consider this part of the subject, a preliminary truth deserves a passing reflection. It is obvious to every one who bears in mind our relations to God, that our obligation to obey him extends to every action of our lives. We ourselves, our possessions, our faculties, our fellow-men with whom we are conversant, are not our own. God is the universal Proprietor of all, for in him we live, and move, and have our being. He is the Father of all, and he justly requires us to treat our brethren, who, equally with us, are his children, as he shall command. And yet more, he is entitled

6*

not merely to obedience in the outward art, but to filial obedience; that is, the obedience which springs from love. Hence, in all our transactions with our fellow-men, we are required to recognize the existence of both these commandments — "Thou shalt love thy neighbor as thyself," and, "Thou shalt love the Lord thy God with all thy heart." This latter principle, filial obedience to God, must enter as a motive into every action before it can either lay claim to innocence, or deserve the praise of the Creator. It is this sentiment alone that can sustain virtue when assaulted by temptation, or unite us by any tie of moral sympathy with our Father who is in heaven.

You perceive, then, that every moral act, in order to merit the praise of God, must be pervaded by the element of love to him. If this element be wanting, I do not say that the action is destitute of virtue, but I say that it is destitute of piety, and that it would have been performed in just the same manner if there were no God. Such an action could never be pleasing to God; nay, more, by the amount of all this deficiency it would be displeasing to him. Suppose, then, a man to obey perfectly the second commandment of the law, while he was wholly indifferent to the most blessed God, nay, while he was deliberately cultivating in himself the habit of settled opposition to his law — must not the displeasure of the Most High rest most justly upon him? But we have already shown that this latter is actually the moral condition of man; that the love of God is not in him, and that he does not like to retain God in his knowledge. Hence it is, I think, evident that, were the second precept of the law faithfully obeyed, yet so long as man was at enmity with God, he would still remain a sinner by reason of the absence from all his actions, of the element of piety.

We always judge in this manner respecting any other case. The keeping of one precept is no excuse for the violation of another. If a man obey the precept, "Thou shalt not kill," this can in no manner justify him in the violation of the precept, "Thou shalt not steal." Much less is the keeping of a minor and subsidiary precept a justification of the violation of a universal and all-controlling precept. If a man be guilty of treason against his country, can he lay claim to perfect innocence because he has always paid his debts? The chief magistrate of a nation is under paramount obligations to conform his whole conduct, both public and private, to the dictates of justice, veracity, and patriotism. But suppose his whole administration is disgraced by acts of oppression, violence, and treachery, — can he be held innocent because he is proved to be a kind husband and an affectionate parent? When, in years long gone by, it was urged against a monarch of Great Britain, that he had repeatedly, and on deliberation, violated his coronation oath, and conspired to overthow the constitution of the realm, it was never held to be a justification of his conduct, to assert that he had taken his little children on his knee, and kissed them.

I think, then, it may easily be granted, that while the love of God is excluded from the heart of man, even though he should love his neighbor as himself, he would still fall under the condemnation of the law to which he was rendered amenable by his Creator.

And here we may pause for a moment to observe that this general truth affords an easy explanation of the passage in the Epistle of James — "Whosoever shall keep the whole law, and yet offend in one point, he is guilty of all." By this he means simply to assert that a single deliberate violation of any particular precept of the law of God sets at nought the authority of the Lawgiver, and demonstrates that the creature has usurped the place in our affections due only to the Creator. The love of God is not in him, for, if it truly exist at all, it must be supreme, and hence, all his actions, being destitute of this element, are in the sight of God sinful, and, of course, deserving of his displeasure.

Leaving this preliminary consideration, we proceed to inquire what is the character of man when subjected to the test of obedience to the second precept of the law, "Thou shalt love thy neighbor as thyself."

Our Lord himself has explained the meaning of the term *neighbor* in this passage. It means man, every man, every child of Adam, the being to whom we are connected by no other tie than this, that he is a brother of the human family.

We are commanded to love such a one as ourselves; that is, not as we do love ourselves, but as we may rightfully love ourselves. To enter upon a complete analysis of this precept, and illustrate the various classes of actions which it renders obligatory, would transcend the limits of this discourse. It will be sufficient to observe that self-love incites us to love our own happiness upon the whole, and to desire the uninterrupted enjoyment of those means which God has given us, in order to secure it. It causes us to feel injured and aggrieved if the full enjoyment of these means is in any manner curtailed by our fellow-men. All this is innocent and proper. Now, in this manner we are commanded to love our fellow-men. We must as intensely desire that our neighbor may, without interruption, enjoy the means of happiness which God has bestowed upon him, as we desire to enjoy them ourselves; and we must feel the same sense of wrong when he is injured as we feel when we ourselves are injured. We can claim for this precept no less comprehensive signification than this; and I think that every man's conscience will bear witness that, thus interpreted, it really expresses the obligation existing between man and his fellow-men.

With respect to the natural disposition in man to obey this second precept, the Scriptures do not speak as definitely as in respect to the first and great commandment of the law. They have nowhere declared that the love of man is not in us, or that we do not like to retain man in our knowledge. While they speak of our obedience to it as universally deficient, they do not definitely find the limit of that deficiency. This would be impossible, since, in respect, to this precept, our obedience falls short of the praise of God in very dissimilar degrees. The Bible presents us with instances of men who have made various attainments in virtue, all, however, by acknowledgment, imperfect; and also of men who have been in various degrees guilty of crime, but of none as so bad that they could not wax worse. It clearly teaches us that the tendency of man is to vice rather than to virtue; that there is not a just man on earth that sinneth not; that the attainment which individuals and nations have made in virtue has been owing to gracious influences bestowed on us from on high; and that the moral degradation to which society universally tends is the natural consequence of the bias towards evil which has existed in us since the fall. To define, however, the extent of our sinfulness, it has not attempted; it only asserts that all men have sinned, and come short of the glory of God.

Nor, indeed, is a definite statement on this subject in any manner necessary. Our fellow-men are every where around us. In almost every action of our lives, we have the opportunity of testing both their dispositions and our own, in respect to this precept. We have to deal with this matter practically. Every man can judge for himself whether or not his fellow men are inclined to obey the law of reciprocity when they can make gain by disobeying it. Every one arrived at years of discretion knows whether the ordinary and applauded maxims of business do or do not proceed upon the principle, that men actually love their neighbor as themselves. Every parent knows whether children, at a very early age, do or do not manifest this tendency. Nay, we can all determine this question, each one for himself, by referring to the testimony of his own consciousness. We can easily tell whether selfishness or disinterestedness is the natural bias of a human soul, and whether it does or does not require an effort to do justice to our neighbor when we can only do so by the sacrifice of our own interests. We all know whether pure and impartial justice, in the dealings between man and man, is the rule or the exception; and whether he who should describe a perfectly good man as an actual existence, would not be looked upon as a retailer of fiction. Nay, were such a man to appear on earth, we could be by no means sure that he would escape the fate of Aristides, who was banished from Athens for the reason that his fellow-citizens could not bear to hear him always denominated *the just.*

Such is, I believe, the universal testimony of man. The Scriptures every where confirm it, though they never deny that some portion of justice exists among men; nor do they designate the particular degree in which man has, in this respect, gone astray from original righteousness. I shall, in the remainder of this discourse, attempt to present some considerations which may tend to illustrate these declarations of the word of God.

In treating this subject, I shall not set before you particular instances of wickedness exhibited in the conduct either of individuals or of nations. These, it might be said, are extreme cases, owing to particular circumstances, and not therefore justly to be laid to the charge of men universally. We shall, therefore, draw our argument, not from particular cases, but from facts of the most general character, which meet the eye wherever it is turned thoughtfully upon actions of mankind.

I think, then, it is evident, that the moral disposition of man, in this respect, must, by necessity, determine the form of social organization wherever individuals unite in a community. In establishing the principles by which a society of moral and intelligent creatures should be governed, you would proceed in one way if every one of them loved his neighbor as himself, and in a very different way if every one of them loved himself better than his neighbor. Safeguards, limitations, punishments, would be necessary in one case that would be unnecessary in the other. Thus, also, by observing the framework of any society, it would not be difficult to discover what was the kind of beings for whose benefit it was constructed. In examining a machine, there is little difficulty in determining whether it is designed to float in the air like a balloon, or tear up the greensward like a plough. So, by examining the principles on which human society is formed, it will not be difficult to ascertain whether it was intended for beings who were by nature disposed to obey, or for those by nature disposed to disobey, the commandment in the text.

I. I remark, then, in the first place, that our first conception of social organization proceeds upon the supposition that men are naturally inclined to violate this law.

Every man is endowed by the Creator with the perfect right to the enjoyment of life, liberty, and the pursuit of happiness; that is, with a perfect right to use as he will the means which God has placed in his hands for the attainment of his own happiness, provided he do not interfere with the same perfect and equal right which every other man enjoys in common with himself. To act in obedience to this elementary principle, is to obey the law of reciprocity; that is, to love our neighbor as ourselves, in the sense which I have already explained. Were men naturally inclined to obey this precept, they would need no organization to prevent them from violating it. It is absurd to take pains to prevent men from doing that which they have no disposition to do. We make no provision for obliging men to eat when they are hungry, or to rest when they are weary. When there exists a natural disposition to any particular course of conduct, we leave it, if it be innocent, to itself, never attempting to do what nature can do so much better without us.

But, if we will attentively consider, we shall perceive that the first, and by far most important object for which human society is established, is to prevent the violation of the law of reciprocity. It proceeds upon the principle that every man will, if he can, employ for his own happiness not only the means which God has given him, but also those which God has given to his neighbor. But it is evident, that, were this principle admitted, it would lead to universal and interminable war, until the race was exterminated. And, besides, although every man is disposed to infringe the rights of his neighbor himself, he is by no means disposed to concede this power to another. The moral sense acts correctly when it is not biased by selfishness. Hence men instinctively combine together for the purpose of obliging each other to obey the law of reciprocity. If any one attempt to infringe the rights of his neighbor, the rest of the community, with one voice, command him to forbear. They find that human society cannot exist without employing the power of the whole in favor of right, and thus obliging every individual, by the authority of the whole, to respect the rights of his fellows. It is from this function of society that all law emanates. Society confers no rights; it only guaranties to every man the enjoyment of those rights which have been conferred upon him by his Creator.

We see, then, that the first conception of human society is that of an instinctive arrangement for the purpose of preventing the violation of the rule in the text. Civilization advances, and the happiness of man, both individual and social, is promoted, just in the proportion that this purpose of society is more and more perfectly accomplished. So soon as this purpose of society is abandoned, right is universally violated with impunity, and a nation becomes a prey to universal wickedness. The power of society to repress crime being withdrawn, anarchy ensues — a word which instantly suggests to us all the misery which man can suffer from violence and injustice. It is the rule of might uncontrolled by right. It is a condition in which every man is at liberty to seek his own gratification, however small, in violation of the rights of his neighbor, however sacred. A partial illustration of this condition of humanity was presented by the city of Paris in some periods of the first French revolution. An illustration yet more striking was several times exhibited during the Peninsular war, when cities taken by assault were delivered up to the will of the soldiery by the orders both of the French and British commanders. An innocent and unarmed population — men, women, and children — were in these instances left, without law, entirely to the mercy of their fellow-men. The victors might do with the vanquished precisely as they chose. The atrocities of such a scene, as I have been informed by eye-witnesses, are too horrible for recital. Men, under such circumstances, are transformed from human beings into demons, and a city surrendered up to their lusts, presents a more vivid picture of hell than can be found elsewhere on earth. If, then, the elementary conception of a social organization assumes as a fact the selfishness of man; if the great object of this organization is to protect the individual from the infringement of his rights; if the most horrible condition of humanity of which we can conceive is that of men left without control to do exactly as they choose, and seek their own gratification without regard to the happiness of their neighbors, — it would seem that there can be no question respecting the natural disposition of man. Such things could never exist among beings who were by nature disposed to love their neighbor as themselves.

In the second place, —

II. The history of the various forms of human government illustrates the truth that man does not love his neighbor as himself.

Suppose a society to be organized for the purpose I have specified above, — it is necessary that its power be confided to the hands of comparatively few individuals. The whole of the society cannot act in every case that requires its interference. The authority of the whole must be delegated to a part, who thus become what we call the government or magistracy. The object, therefore, for which a magistracy is appointed, is so to administer the power of the whole, that every individual shall be confirmed in the enjoyment of every right bestowed upon him by his Creator; that is, that every individual shall be obliged to obey the law of reciprocity.

Now, I need scarcely remind you that the best talent of the human race has from the beginning been employed in the attempt to devise a form of government which shall accomplish this object, and that thus far (unless our republic shall prove an exception) the attempt has signally failed. It has been found practically impossible so to balance the various powers of the state that the individual shall be free to do right, while he is at the same time restrained from doing wrong. It has taken ages of reasoning and reflection, and it has cost torrents of blood, to ascertain, with any thing like precision, even what are the limits within which society has any right to interfere with the actions of the individual. And after this limit has been discovered, how shall we construct a government which will not transgress it? If we bestow too much or too irresponsible power upon rulers, they become tyrants, and the government is overthrown by reason of its oppression. If we bestow upon them too little power, violence will neither be prevented nor injury redressed, and the individual, despairing of redress or of protection from society, seeks it for himself; and thus ensues universal anarchy.

Hence it has happened, I think, that the most stable governments on earth have been civil or spiritual despotisms. When the rulers form an intelligent and vigilant caste, and can withhold from the people a knowledge of their rights; or when a priesthood can persuade them that their eternal salvation depends upon unquestioning obedience to the mandates of a hierarchy; and specially when these two forms of despotism can be united, — that is, when you can deprive men of the exercise of reason and conscience, until, in some of the most important respects, they cease to be men, — then they may be governed in quietness. If you can turn men into brutes, you may govern them like brutes. But restore them to their rank, as the intelligent and responsible creatures of God, and their passions, stimulated by liberty, defy restraint, and render a permanent government almost impossible. Hence it has been so often remarked, that the civil institutions of man have, in all ages, trodden, with greater or less rapidity, the same invariable circle from anarchy to despotism, and from despotism again to anarchy. The forms of government which have endured the longest, have been those which have vibrated, from time to time, between these opposite extremes. When this invariable circle has been trodden slowly, the changes have been less violent, and mankind have, at intervals of peace, been permitted to enjoy the blessings bestowed upon them by their Creator. Where, on the other hand, this circle has been rapidly passed over, and civil institutions, by the turbulence of passion, have been frequently overturned, the race of man, worn out with the struggle, has ceased from the earth; and thus it has happened, that whole regions, once the abode of wealth and civilization, are now a wilderness; and the remains of once populous cities have become the lair of the lion and the hiding-place of the jackal.

Or, if we pass by the interior history of civil societies, the same truth is illustrated in the principles which have generally governed the intercourse of nations with each other. Where is the nation to be found that ever treated other nations, specially if they were weaker, on the principles of reciprocity? Do men ever even expect it? Nay, do they not frequently applaud the successful violation of right? Who has ever reaped so abundant a harvest of human applause as the military conqueror? What, besides his incomparable talent for war, has crowned with imperishable renown the name of the late emperor Napoleon? When a battle has been fought, which has covered the earth with slain, and carried mourning, and widowhood, and orphanage, to every village throughout the land, the only question that we ask is, Which of the armies has been victorious? Alexander, Cæsar, and Napoleon, are celebrated as the heroes of our race; but we never think of the millions who were slaughtered to glut their lust of power. Now, I ask, if we loved the rights of our neighbors as our own, could such things be done? or, if they were done, could they fail to awaken a universal sentiment of intense moral indignation? Can we conceive of a more atrocious crime than that of butchering our fellow-men for the sake of increasing our fame or advancing our personal interests, or the interests of a political party? And yet, we not only do such things, but have pleasure in those that do them.

It may be asked, Is not our country an exception to these remarks? In the formation of our civil constitution, I suppose that the law of reciprocity has been more thoughtfully considered than in the formation of any other that history has recorded. The principle of the universal equality of human rights, with one lamentable exception, has here been fully recognized. But does any one believe that our constitution can endure, if it rely for support on nothing but the natural love of justice in the human bosom? Thus far, owing to the religious principles in which we have been educated, it has stood. This, however, is a superinduced influence; it is the result of the teaching of revelation accompanied by power from on high. But, I ask, was there ever before a people among whom such a government as ours could have been maintained even for a single year? Nay, abstract from this people the influences diffused abroad by the religion of Christ, abolish the Bible, the Sabbath, the instructions of the sanctuary, abandon us all to the natural workings of the human heart, and let any one ask himself how long such a government as ours could possibly exist.

III. I do not know but any additional proof on this subject may seem superfluous. I am, however, unwilling to close the argument without suggesting another consideration, nearly allied to this last, to which I have alluded.

Were men universally, or even generally, inclined to obey the precept in the text, it is manifest that the making of laws, and the carrying them into execution, would be the easiest labor imaginable. Infringement of right, if it existed at all, would result simply from imperfection of the understanding, and never from pravity of the heart. The legislator need not, in any case, do more than merely to indicate to his fellow-citizens the rule of right, so that those less well informed than himself might not fall into error. Every man would receive with gratitude any instructions which would enable him to avoid doing wrong to his neighbor. And, if any one, through inadvertence, had infringed the rights of his fellow, of all the men in the community, he would be the most anxious to acknowledge his error, and make all the reparation in his power. We should, in such a state of society, stand in no need of penal enactments, since every one would, of his own choice, do all that justice could prescribe. Law would be nothing else than instruction in our duty, unaccompanied by the threat of punishment for disobedience. Sheriffs and constables, prisons, penitentiaries, and executions, would have been unheard of among men. The just and disinterested disposition which ruled in the heart, would render all these sad mementoes of our depravity utterly without use and without object.

But what do we observe to be actually the fact? No one is so childish as not to know that a law without a penalty would be deemed the greatest of practical absurdities. The legislator who should propose the enactment of such a code, would, by universal consent, be esteemed insane. And then reflect upon the number of laws necessary for the government of the human race. In all civilized countries, a large portion of men, reputed to be preëminent for intelligence, is constantly employed in the labor of legislation; that is, in framing enactments whose object it is to prevent man from doing injury to his neighbor. It is, moreover, found that the greatest practical skill is required in order to construct a law so that it shall not be rendered inoperative by evasion. Even such skill can but imperfectly, and for a short period, resist the pressure of human selfishness. The most perfect rule that man could devise for to-day, would, in a few years, need addition, alteration, or amendment, in order to protect the innocent from modes of injury which, at the beginning, would never have been dreamed of. Hence, in every country which has made any considerable progress in civilization, laws and commentaries upon them, form, of themselves, libraries of appalling magnitude. The laws, for instance, of Great Britain constitute, of themselves, the study of a lifetime. And yet, even these are insufficient to prevent an extent of crime which we cannot look upon without dismay. These laws are enforced by the severest punishments; and yet prisons and penitentiaries are crowded, transport ships are loaded, the gallows groans under its sad burden; yet crime increases, though not one out of ten who deserve it, ever comes within the reach of the officer of justice.

In addition to this, consider the talent that is daily employed in the administration of the law. Judges, jurors, counsellors, and executive officers, are laboring incessantly throughout the length and breadth of the land. They toil on without intermission; but the burden, like the stone of Sisyphus, returns upon them, year after year, with redoubled weight. The philanthropist and the Christian aid the efforts of the legislator by all the eloquence of love. Education is scattered broadcast among the people. The pulpit and the Sabbath school unite their energies in the attempt to prevent crime and reform the criminal; but the work of violence and dishonesty still goes forward. We seem surrounded by a pestilential moral atmosphere, which cannot be excluded, unless life itself be extinguished. At last, every one but the disciple of Christ, gives up, in despair, the effort to reform the race; and it is acknowledged that unless the moral nature of man can be changed by power from on high, the all-grasping selfishness of the human heart can never be reduced to obedience, to reason, and to conscience.

Such being the acknowledged facts, I think there can no longer remain any doubt on this subject. The conclusion is pressed upon us on every side, that mankind is guilty of the violation of the second precept of the law as truly as of violation of the first. Such are the truths revealed by our moral history. They belong to that class of general facts which need not be established by argument, but which meet us at once as soon as we open our eyes upon the condition of the world around us.

It would seem, then, from a review of the facts which we have endeavored to establish, that, in the words of the apostle, all men have sinned, and come short of the glory of God. Instead of loving God with all his heart, the love of God is not in man; and, more than this, he is cherishing those moral habits which must issue in direct, and intense, and endless enmity to his Maker. Instead of loving his neighbor as himself, his love to his neighbor easily yields to the demands of selfishness or passion; and the result has been, that, from the beginning, notwithstanding all the monitions of conscience, and all the restraints of society, the earth has been filled with violence. Mankind must, therefore, plead guilty to the charge of disobedience to both of the great commandments of reason and revelation.

Suppose all this to be so, and men to enter the unseen world with this very moral character unchangeably rivetted upon them for eternity. They would find themselves at enmity forever with infinite holiness and goodness, sustained by almighty power and guided by omniscient wisdom. This in itself would create despair, rendered more agonizing by the reproaches of conscience — that worm that dieth not, that fire that cannot be quenched. Nor is this all. They have deliberately refused to submit to the law of God, and God withdraws and leaves them to a state in which there is no law. They preferred the government of their passions, and God surrenders them to the rule which they have preferred. Suppose then, that, intelligent creatures, knowing no law but passion, and each one seeking his own gratification, at the expense of the happiness of all the rest, to be separated from the other moral creatures of God, and left to the indulgence of uncontrolled desire. The result must be enmity growing more and more intense and terrific, and this must be forever.

Such is our condition by nature, and such the destiny for which, if divine grace prevent not, we are preparing. The wages of sin, that which it deserves, and to which it by necessity tends, is death. The gift of God, that which proceeds from his boundless and unmerited love, is eternal life, through Jesus Christ our Lord.

THE FALL OF MAN.

"BY ONE MAN'S DISOBEDIENCE MANY WERE MADE SINNERS."
Romans v. 19.

I HAVE, in previous discourses, attempted to place before you the scriptural account of the moral character of man. The question here naturally arises, How could a race of sinners have been created by a holy and most merciful God? The answer to this question is contained, in part, in the words of the text. By one man's disobedience many, or "the many," became sinners. That is, the Scriptures teach us that the race of man was created upright, that our first parents sinned, and that, in consequence of that sin, their descendants are found to be universally depraved. My object, in the present discourse, is simply to present the statement of the Scriptures on this subject, and to consider some of the objections that have been urged against it.

1. The Bible asserts that God created our first parents perfect. "God created man in his own image; in the image of God created he him. And God saw every thing that he had made, and behold it was very good." By this I understand that God created man with a perfect moral nature, such that every impulse and affection was in harmony with the relations in which he was placed. But man was endowed with the gift of free agency. He had the same power to disobey the law of God as to obey it. Without such power he could have been neither virtuous nor vicious. The consequences of obedi-

ence and disobedience were placed before him, and thus his destiny was left in his own hands.

2. It pleased God, at an early period in the history of man, to place before him a trial of his obedience. "And the Lord God commanded man, saying, Of every tree of the garden thou mayest freely eat; but of the tree of knowledge of good and evil thou shalt not eat of it, for in the day that thou eatest thereof thou shalt surely die." Whether this narrative be understood literally or figuratively, its lesson is precisely the same. It teaches the all-important truth, that there is a moral limit affixed to the gratification of human desires; that under our present constitution, we have the power to enjoy objects which God has forbidden, and to pursue the gratifications which he has allowed, beyond the limit which he has assigned; and that the perfect subjection of all our desires to the holy will of God is made the test of our moral character, and the universal means of our improvement in virtue. This is my interpretation of this history. I look simply at the moral lesson which it teaches. The drapery with which it is clothed is a matter of inferior consequence.

3. The Scriptures proceed to inform us, that our first parents were tempted by Satan to disobey the plain commands of God. "The woman said unto the serpent, We may eat of the fruit of the trees of the garden, but of the fruit of the tree which is in the midst of the garden, God hath said, Ye shall not eat of it, neither shall ye touch it, lest ye die. And the serpent said unto the woman, Ye shall not surely die; for God doth know, that in the day ye eat thereof, then your eyes shall be opened, and ye shall be as gods, knowing both good and evil. And when the woman saw that the tree was good for food, and that it was pleasant to the eyes, and a tree to be desired to make one wise, she took of the fruit thereof, and did eat, and gave also to her husband, and he did eat."

How other men may look upon this narrative, I know not. To me it presents a perfect analysis of every act of sin against God. In the first place, there is a conviction, more or less distinct, that the act is a violation of the known will of God. Then there is a dallying with temptation, and a contemplation of the pleasure which we may enjoy by sin. This is succeeded by obtuseness of conscience and the hope that the desire may be indulged, and yet the consequences which God has threatened be averted. Then follows an intenser desire for pleasure, the power of passion waxes stronger, and the power of conscience waxes weaker. At length, the balance between these opposing forces is destroyed, the will consents, the act is done, the sin is committed. I do not know that the literature of our race presents a more accurate account of the process of wilful transgression than is here recorded in the first pages of our history. They speak a language that finds a response in every human bosom.

4. This one act changes at once the moral condition of the creature. It is not merely a sin, — it is a fall, a fall into a fathomless abyss. It is a victory of the passions over the conscience, a defeat that can never be retrieved. It is a declaration of rebellion against God, a deliberate preference of the pleasures of sense to the favor of our Father who is in heaven. With the change of the object of his supreme affection, the man himself is radically changed. God, who is unchangeably opposed to this new choice of the creature, ceases to be lovely and adorable in his eyes. Henceforth, he becomes an object of suspicion and dread. Adam and his wife hid themselves from the presence of the Lord among the trees of the garden, just as their children ever since have endeavored to hide themselves from the gaze of omniscience. Instead of confessing their sin, they strove to impute their guilt to each other. Henceforth all their character becomes tinged with moral corruption.

5. After this, the Scriptures always speak of the race of man as corrupt and sinful. The first-born of our common parents was the murderer of his brother. Soon "God saw that the wickedness of man was great upon the earth, and that every imagination of the thought of his heart was wholly evil

continually." Throughout the volume of inspiration man is every where spoken of as morally depraved, a sinner against God, and, in consequence of this sin, under the condemnation of his most holy law.

But the Scriptures go farther. Unless I wholly mistake their meaning, they assert that there is a definite connection between this sin and the consequent sinful character of our first parents, and the sinful character of their posterity. By one man's disobedience, the many were made sinners. "By one man, sin entered into the world, and death by sin, and so death passed upon all men, in that all have sinned." The Bible, however, does not assert that we committed Adam's sin, or that we are guilty of Adam's sin, or that we shall be punished for it, or that we had any part or participation in it. It, on the contrary, declares that every man shall be judged for what he has himself done. Every man shall give an account of himself to God. But the Bible does, nevertheless, inform us that such a connection exists between us and our first parents; that we become sinners in consequence of their transgression. Of the manner of this connection, it gives us but little information; yet some important light may possibly be discovered if we diligently reflect upon the truth which has been revealed to us.

Such is a brief statement of the doctrines of the Scriptures on this subject. Are they in any respect at variance with right reason? Is there in them a single assertion repugnant to the human intelligence and conscience? To these questions let us now direct our attention.

The substance of the Scripture statements may be, I think, expressed briefly as follows: —

I. Our first parents were created free agents, that is, moral intelligences.

II. They were placed under circumstances in which their virtue was subjected to trial.

III. By the constitution under which our race was created, the conditions of our probation were so interwoven with theirs, that, if they became sinful, we should become sinful also.

Let us briefly consider each of these statements, for the purpose of inquiring whether in either or all of them there is any thing revolting to an enlightened conscience, or at variance with the moral attributes of God.

I. Can any objection be urged against the truth that our first parents, and all the race of man, have been created free agents, that is, moral and accountable beings?

I might here observe, that the doctrine of man's free agency is not a doctrine of revealed religion, or, in fact, of religion at all. It is the simple dictate of the human consciousness. To object to it is just the same absurdity as to complain because God has given us hands or feet, a heart or a brain, or a reasoning soul; it is, in fact, to revile the great Giver on account of his gifts.

But, farther: a moral agent differs from a brute mainly in this — that he is capable of distinguishing right from wrong, and of choosing freely between them; that he is capable of deserving moral praise and blame, and is held responsible for his actions before the tribunal of a righteous and all-seeing Judge. Brutes are endowed with none of these powers, and are charged with none of this responsibleness.

Now, can any one impugn either the justice or the goodness of God, because we, and all the orders of higher intelligences, were not created brutes? Would it have been more consistent with the perfections of the Holy One to fill creation with beings unable either to admire or adore his goodness, who could neither love him or be loved by him, who were, by the necessity of their existence, incapable of virtue — sensual, irrational, brutish Or would it be good or wise for the Deity at this moment to withdraw from all created intelligences the gift of moral agency, and transform men and angels, cherubim and seraphim, into brutes that perish? Should we desire that ourselves or our friends should become oxen of the stall or swine of the sty? We cannot, then, make any objection to the goodness of God because he has created us and other of our fellow-creatures moral agents.

But, in this very idea of moral agency, there is involved, as we have already intimated, the power of choice, the absolute freedom of the will. When the good and evil are set before us, we must be left entirely free to choose and to refuse, or there could be no moral desert, and we could not justly be the subjects either of reward or of punishment. To the truth of this every man's consciousness bears witness. We do not feel deserving of either praise or blame for the pulsations of the heart or the heaving of the lungs, or for being either hungry or thirsty, but only for those acts which we know to be dependent on our own volitions. As soon as an act is placed beyond our own control, we disclaim all responsiblity both for it and its results.

Again: I think that our notion of moral agency involves the additional idea that there are certain limits established beyond which the Deity does not interfere with the actions of his creatures. If he have conferred upon him the power of free choice, he does not interfere with that power, nor retract the gift which he has bestowed. He places before men motives, and leaves them free to act, in view of them, as they will. Having created a man or an angel, he ever treats him as a man or an angel, and neither as a brute nor a stone. Hence, if God have created man free, and fixed the just limits beyond which he will not interfere with his actions, the Deity is not responsible for the result. An invaluable source of happiness is placed in the power of the creature, and he is at liberty to use or to abuse it. Let him do either, the character of the Most High is unsullied.*

Is it said that thus far the exercise of this power has been productive of misery, rather than happiness, inasmuch as our whole race has abused it? I answer, this world occupies an

* I do not here bring into view the doctrine of the agency of the Holy Spirit. This is a free gift, the result of the mediation of Christ, to which we could lay no claim, and which, under a system of law, has no place. Besides, even this agency is exerted in perfect harmony with the free agency of man.

almost infinitely small space in the whole universe of God It may be that this is the only spot, in the whole creation, in which this constitution has produced any thing but happiness. Incomparably the greatest portion of the creation we believe to be holy and happy; and wherever there are holiness and happiness, they are the result of this very gift of moral agency. It is this which has filled heaven with myriads of spirits, who have passed through their probation without sin, and are now rejoicing before the throne, clothed in a holiness that cannot be sullied. Let us, then, learn to look upon the ways of God with humility; and, least of all, let us speak lightly of that endowment by which we become specially allied to the divine nature.

II. If, then, it was just and merciful in God to create a race of moral intelligences, was there any thing at variance with his perfections in the circumstances in which our first parents were placed?

They were created innocent, in the image of God.

They were endowed with moral powers capable of appreciating their obligations to the Creator, and an intellect by which they became aware of the consequences of their actions. All the conditions which were necessary to influence their decision, were within the sphere of their vision, and they were endowed with the unrestrained liberty of choice.

The trial to which they were subjected was by no means unreasonable for beings thus endowed. The preponderance of motives was such as might naturally be expected to lead them to choose the path to virtue and happiness. The word of the tempter was set against the word of the Creator. A momentary sensual gratification was opposed to the displeasure of the eternal Father. The finite was put in comparison with the infinite. It was under such circumstances that man was required to hold fast his integrity during the brief period of his probation, with the promise, if he were found faithful, of immortal felicity. More favorable conditions of probation can scarcely be conceived. If there must be a moral trial, it could not take place under more favorable auspices.

Still, it is to be remembered that the result is left dependent upon man's free will. After all, he is, and from the necessity of his nature he must be, liable to sin. He may act in opposition to every noble and generous motive, and yield himself up to the seductions of sense. Unless there existed this liability, he would be as incapable of virtue as of vice.

Do you ask me how a being so constituted and so conditioned could ever sin? This question can be answered in no other manner than by an appeal to the observation and consciousness of every man. Why is it that we see such things done every day? And why is it that every thoughtful man feels himself liable continually to just such moral disasters? Why is it that men, by a single vicious indulgence, or the gratification of a single unholy desire, cover themselves with infamy? Why is it that men, perfectly convinced of the truth of the gospel, reject the offer of salvation, and prefer those very sensual pleasures which they confess are empty, vain, and absolutely despicable? Can any man tell us why such things should be? And yet, every one knows them to be matters of daily occurrence.

If, then, any one will calmly consider these facts, I think that he will be persuaded that the conditions of probation, under which our first parents were placed, were eminently favorable. In all this there seems nothing at variance with the perfections of God.

III. But an important question yet remains to be considered. The Scriptures teach us that the conditions of our probation were affected by the conduct of our first parents. "By one man's disobedience, many were made sinners." It is said that such a constitution is inconsistent with the justice of God.

Suffer me here to repeat what I have before asserted. The Scriptures never assert that we are guilty of the sin of Adam, or that we are punished for it. They every where declare that every man is guilty simply of his own voluntary transgressions of the law, and that the guilt of every man is to be estimated by the degree of moral light which he has voluntarily resisted. Every man is thus held responsible for just so much moral illumination as he has enjoyed, and no more. Nothing, surely, can be more equitable than this.

What, then, is it that the Scriptures assert respecting the connection between us and our first parents? To me it seems to be simply this: If they had kept the law of God perfectly, their children would have passed through their probation under more favorable circumstances than themselves; and thus, through successive generations, the conditions of man's probation would have become more and more favorable. If they disobeyed God, the conditions of the probation of their children would be less favorable than their own; and it would, through successive generations, become less and less favorable. In the one case, there would be created a tendency to holiness, and in the other, a tendency to sin, each growing stronger as long as the succession continued. In both cases, however, it is to be remembered that the moral character of each individual is subject to the power of his own free will.*

Now, I think it obvious that there is no practical injustice in such a constitution as this. It is manifestly the fact that our subsequent condition depends upon our present acts. He who does a conspicuously good or evil act, feels its consequences ever afterwards. If, then, our good or evil condition is made to depend upon the act of another, and if the circumstances, in which the trial was made, were decidedly in his favor, as well as ours, there seems no practical injustice in making the trial in his person instead of our own. We

* I wish it to be remembered, that I here speak of this tendency as a fact, without discussing the manner in which it is produced. On this subject, various opinions have been held by theologians, some believing in a physical change; others, in a spiritual bias; others, again, in the power of external circumstances. Into this controversy it did not suit my purpose, in this place, to enter.

should have realized the benefit if he had acted worthily, as we suffer the injury from his acting unworthily.

But the question still returns, Why was such a constitution established? Why were moral agents so connected in destiny with those who have gone before them? or, in other words, Why is our probation rendered either more or less favorable in consequence of actions in which we had no agency?

I answer, This is a universal principle of the divine government, and we never object to it except in this particular instance.

Who of us is ignorant of the fact, that the conditions of his probation have been influenced most materially by the character of his parents? Their virtue, their self-denial, their example, has given you a position which, under opposite circumstances, you never could have held. Had your parents been dishonest, intemperate, degraded, would not your condition have been far less favorable than it is? I do not say that in either case your destiny would have been taken out of your own hands; I only say that the circumstances which I have mentioned, would have rendered the conditions of your probation either more or less favorable. But what had you to do with their character or actions? Manifestly no more than you had with the character or actions of Adam.

Again: let any man cast his eyes over our beloved country. Let him survey its fields loaded with harvests, its villages resounding with the hum of industry, its harbors crowded with shipping, and its cities becoming the markets of the world, and every where the rights of person and property protected by equal laws, and still more by a moral sentiment which has become a part of our social nature. Let him enter the family, and observe how closely virtue clings to the domestic hearth, and how strongly filial and parental affection bind together the members of the same household. Let him enter our schools, academies, and colleges, and take notice that the door is thrown wide open to intellectual improvement, and that facilities in abundance are every where afforded for the cultivation of meritorious talent. Let him frequent the house of God, and observe in what manner, throughout our land, every man is engaged in the worship of his Creator according to the dictates of his own conscience; that the Bible is found in every house, and that the Sabbath school and the Bible class are instilling its blessed truth into minds of those of every age and of every condition. Having observed all this, let us ask why is it that our probation has been granted to us under circumstances so favorable to moral improvement, and from the millions of New England there will arise but one answer, — we owe it all to the piety, the intelligence, the earnest faith, and the self-denying energy, of our Puritan forefathers. But what had you or I to do with the charaeter or actions of the Puritans? Nothing. Yet it is owing to that character and those actions that our probation is passed under circumstances so eminently favorable.

The illustrations of this principle are innumerable, for its application is universal. Our probation has been materially affected by the printing press. But what had we to do with the invention of the printing press? The present age derives innumerable blessings from the invention of the mariner's compass. But who of us had any agency in the invention of the mariner's compass? We all enjoy the advantages resulting from the invention of the steam-engine. But what agency had any one living in the labors of the marquis of Worcester, of Watt, or of Fulton? In fact, the conditions of our probation, in instances that defy enumeration, are materially affected by the acts of those who have preceded us, while with these acts we have no more connection than with that act of our first parents by which we became sinners.

Such, then, is the law of our constitution. It is manifestly a merciful law. On it alone depends our capability of social progress. Abolish it, and every generation of men, without advancing a single step, would stand immovably fixed in the footprints of that which preceded it. Advancement in the arts and sciences, in wealth, power, and civilization, would be impossible. All our relations both with the past and the future would cease. History would become an unmeaning word. Society would be dissolved, and every human being become an isolated and solitary unit. Let it once be granted that no man's condition shall be affected by the actions of any other being, and the whole constitution under which we exist must be abolished; and in what manner a better one could be established the objector himself must inform us.

Such, at all events, is the law under which we are created. It seems to me a good and merciful law, absolutely necessary to our social and individual well-being. But you will observe that the conditions under which we were made sinners are only a particular instance under this general law. If, then, the law be wise, and good, and merciful, absolutely necessary to our well-being, why should we object to it in this particular instance?

Here, however, let me recur again to the distinction which I would ever bear in mind. We are not either virtuous or happy simply because those who went before us were so. We are not either ignorant, vicious, or miserable, simply in consequence of the character of our ancestors. The law of which I speak merely asserts that our condition for becoming either the one or the other is more or less favorable in consequence of the acts and character of those who have preceded us. Every individual is still free to resist or conform to the tendencies by which he is surrounded. Our free agency is in neither case either destroyed or even affected. The New Englander is just as free to choose as the Hottentot. The descendant of the Puritans may resist all the influences that would train him to virtue, and become preëminently vile, while an example of virtue that shall attract the admiration of the world, may be produced on the banks of the Amazon, in the deserts of South Africa, or among the islands of the Pacific. The conditions of our probation alone are affected by this law;

our own character remains by necessity dependent upon our own free will.

Such, then, as it seems to me, is the explanation which the Bible offers of the acknowledged fact of man's universal sinfulness. It teaches us that God created man innocent. He, however, created him a moral agent, and placed him on earth to form a character for eternity under circumstances as favorable as could be conceived for attaining to everlasting life by his own obedience; and he established a constitution by which the conditions of the probation of those who should succeed should be rendered either more or less favorable by the acts and character of those who preceded them. Under these circumstances our first parents sinned; and the conditions of our probation are rendered less favorable than theirs at the beginning; less favorable, indeed, to such a degree, that every one of us, as soon as he becomes capable of moral action, becomes a sinner.

It may, however, be asked, Why did not the Deity, by some merciful agency, so influence man that his fall might have been prevented? To this I know not that any answer can be returned. It is not to be expected that we shall be able to fathom the depths of the wisdom and goodness of the Eternal. It may be that this could not have been done without infringing upon the limits of the free agency with which he has endowed us. It evidently did not originate in any want of love to man. The same page that records the history of our fall and the sentence of our condemnation, reveals to us the wonderful fact that "God so loved the world that he gave his only-begotten Son, that whosoever believeth in him should not perish, but have everlasting life." "He that spared not his own Son, but delivered him up for us all, how shall he not with him freely give us all things?" Here, surely, a devout mind may rest satisfied.

What, then, in conclusion, are the practical reflections that this discussion should bring home to the bosom of every individual?

1. While I have been speaking of the probation of Adam, has it not occurred to every one of you that his condition and ours are similar in more respects than we had at first supposed? The law of God, the free agency of man, the nature of temptation, and the motives to holiness, are the same in the circumstances of both. One all-important fact alone distinguishes the character of his probation from ours. Under the dispensation of law, to which he was amenable, one sin was decisive of his destiny. To us, under the dispensation of the gospel, a way of salvation is revealed which extends the hope of eternal life throughout the whole period of our probation. No matter how much we have sinned,—we have a High Priest who is able to save even to the uttermost. "He that believeth on the Son hath everlasting life." It is under such merciful conditions that we are now passing our probation.

2. How infinitely momentous is the condition of an immortal being endowed with the gift of free will! The good and the evil are set before him. Eternal life and eternal death are both placed within his reach, and, as he puts forth his hand either to the one or to the other, he seals his destiny forever. Such is the condition of every child of Adam. When we urge you to seek the salvation of your souls, to turn from the love of the world to the love of God, to become new creatures in Christ Jesus, we know that the weight of this solemn responsibility rests upon each one of you. Let each one of us bring this thought home to his own heart, and cherish it there until it bring forth its legitimate results. A being thus situated has no right to trifle with himself. Procrastination under such circumstances, when our probation may close at any moment, is suicide far worse than madness. Be not, I pray you, guilty of such wickedness. Arouse yourselves to a true conception of your condition, your responsibility, and your infinite destiny. Say not, "Go thy way for this time; when I have a convenient season, I will call for thee." "Behold, now is the accepted time; behold, now is the day of salvation."

JUSTIFICATION BY WORKS IMPOSSIBLE.

"THEREFORE BY THE DEEDS OF THE LAW, THERE SHALL NO FLESH BE JUSTIFIED IN HIS SIGHT."

Romans iii. 20.

THESE words express the conclusion at which the apostle arrives after a full investigation into the character and condition of man.

In the previous portion of his Epistle, he had exposed the universal and intense sinfulness both of the Jews and Gentiles, and the utter inexcusableness of both, inasmuch as all had sinned against clear and adequate light. He sums up the argument in the words of the text—"Therefore by the deeds of the law, there shall no flesh be justified in his sight; for by the law is the knowledge of sin."

By the term "deeds of the law," we are to understand those deeds which the law commands. By "flesh" is meant human nature, the whole race of man. The word "justified" is susceptible of two meanings. It may indicate that he who is accused is declared innocent of crime, "*rectus in curia*," as by a judicial tribunal, when he has been proved guilty of no wrong. Secondly, it may mean, to be treated as though he were just, although he be not innocent; as, for instance, when a man is freely pardoned, all proceedings against him being quashed, and he is restored to the standing of a just man. It is in this sense that the word is used, when men, who by acknowledgment are guilty, are declared to be justified by faith. The text evidently uses the word in the former of these two significations. It speaks of justification through the deeds of the law, that is, through the doing of those deeds which the law requires. If a man does all that the law requires, he may manifestly plead the law in justification. He may demand that it declare him innocent on his own merits. It can have no further demand upon him, and he is as free of it as though it had never existed. The assertion of the text, then, is, that our whole race, and, of course, every individual of it, is incapable of ever being justified on the ground of having kept the requirements of the moral law of God.

This assertion of the apostle may be easily illustrated by a brief reference to some of those declarations of the Scriptures which we have previously considered.

1. The Bible declares that the moral law, under which we have been created, commands us to love the Lord our God with all our heart, and to love our neighbor as ourselves. This, as we have reason to suppose, is the law which is extended over the whole moral universe. Sin is the transgression of this law. The wages of sin — that is, what it deserves — is death. Indignation and wrath, tribulation and anguish, are upon every soul of man that doeth evil. This law is declared to be holy and just, and good; that is, in perfect harmony with the attributes of the most high God.

2. The Scriptures assert that man is destitute of that love which the law of God requires; and that, in the place of it, he cherishes a spirit of enmity to his Maker. "I know you," saith Christ, "that ye have not the love of God in you." We do not like to retain God in our knowledge. Nay, more: "the carnal mind is enmity against God, for it is not subject to the law of God, neither indeed can be." Instead of being filled with the love of man, we are declared to be filled with envy, deceit, malignity, and every evil passion." The constitution of civil society every where proceeds upon the assumption that men are selfish, faithless, violent, and cruel, and laws are every where made to counteract these hateful tendencies.

3. The Scriptures go farther, and reveal to us our moral condition with still greater precision. They teach us that the conditions of our probation were made contingent upon the obedience or disobedience of our first parents. They disobeyed God, and their character became sinful. The conditions of our probation became thus less favorable, so that we find man every where a sinner as soon as he begins to act under moral responsibility. Thus we see that sin is not an accident to which a part of mankind are exposed, but a universal fact in human nature. "By one man, sin entered into the world, and death by sin, and so death has passed upon all men, in that all have sinned."

Such are the declarations of Scripture, and to the truth of them our own consciousness bears undoubted testimony. As soon as any one of us begins to compare himself with the law under which he is created, or even with the imperfect moral standard held forth by his own conscience, he acknowledges himself a sinner, coming short of the praise of God. Nor does any one find himself alone in this condition. He is surrounded by just such beings, an inhabitant of a world lying in wickedness. Examples of sin abound on every side. Men find their passions too powerful for the control of conscience; they are led captive by sin, and are clearly destitute of those affections which are justly required of us by our Father who is in heaven. So deeply rooted is the conviction of our universal sinfulness, that if a man, in any age or country, should believe himself entirely free from sin, we should either look upon him as a superhuman being, or else, by universal consent, pronounce him insane.

And, if any man entertain any remaining doubt on this subject, we would suggest a single practical test, by which he may easily satisfy himself. Let him reflect upon the character of God, and our relations and obligations to him, as they are revealed in the Scriptures, or even indicated by natural religion. Let him form some conception of the love, the veneration, the obedience, which such a creature should exercise towards such a Creator, and then let him honestly make the attempt to exercise these affections. Let him retire from the business of the world, enter his closet, and hold with his Creator such communion as is meet for a child of the dust to hold with his Father in heaven; and let him maintain this temper through life. Let any man fairly make this experiment, and I think he will have but little reason to entertain a doubt respecting the moral character of his heart. With the apostle, he will exclaim in despair, "The law is holy, but I am carnal, sold under sin."

Now, such being the statements of the Scriptures respecting the law of God and the moral character of man, the conclusion in the text is irresistible. The law requires that he love God with all his heart. How can it declare him guiltless, when he has not the love of God in him, much less when his mind is at enmity with God? The law declares that the wages, the equitable desert of sin, is death. How can it, in the same breath, declare him, who is by acknowledgment a sinner, innocent, and therefore deserving of eternal life? You see that these two assertions are absolute contradictions. If the law justly require us to love God with all our heart, and we are at enmity with him, we must be under condemnation. In this direction, then, there is no possibility of escape. Every mouth must be stopped, and the whole world lie guilty before God.

So much as this, I think, has, with different degrees of distinctness, been very generally conceded. Men, both pagan and Christian, confess themselves sinners, if they admit a single moral principle. Hence the universality of the feeling of human guiltiness, and the dread of the judgments of God, as the desert of transgression. But here the question arises — Are there not some means in our power by which we may make reparation for our sins, so that, although we are guilty, we may yet, by our own doings, escape the condemnation to which we are exposed? Since we cannot be justified on the ground of innocence, may we not by our own merits, or sacrifices, present a claim to be treated as just, and thus inherit everlasting life?

This question, from the beginning, has deeply agitated the human soul. The confession of sinfulness is the unbidden utterance of every man's conscience. The agitated spirit was hence impelled to devise some means by which the consciousness of guilt might be removed and the fear of retribution allayed. The first expedient, which seems universally to have suggested itself, was the offering of expiatory victims. Hence, among the fathers of our race, sacrifices were numbered among the duties of almost daily observance. Thus Abel offered to God of the firstlings of his flocks. Job, when his children had been feasting, offered a sacrifice for each one of them. Abraham, wherever he pitched his tent in his pastoral migrations, builded an altar, and offered upon it a victim. Thus, when, by the command of God, the Jewish theocracy was established, almost all things were purified with blood, and without the shedding of blood there was no remission. Morning and evening the sacrifice smoked upon the altar for the daily offences of the people, while the trespass of every individual was acknowledged by an expiatory offering. The idea shadowed forth in all these observances was the same. The worshipper acknowledged that he was a sinner. He offered, as a victim, the most valuable thing that he possessed, in the place of himself, in the hope that the Deity would accept of the substitute, and that the wrath which he had incurred might be appeased by the immolation of a brute.

This idea, however, was by no means confined to the children of Abraham. It seems to have been as universal as our race itself. You all remember the hecatomb offered by the Greeks, when they desired to appease the wrath of Apollo whose priest, Agamemnon, their king, had insulted; and throughout the whole range of classical poetry, from the epic of Homer to the lyrics of Horace, nothing more frequently meets us than allusions to sacrifices intended to render placable the gods when offended by the past, or to propitiate their favor when their aid was deemed specially needful for the future. Jupiter, Apollo, Bacchus, Juno, Minerva, and Mars, had each his appropriate offerings and appointed priesthood, and each was worshipped with mingled feelings of doubt or confidence, and, it may possibly be, in some cases, with some imperfect sentiment of solemn adoration.

But this feeling of the human heart did not even thus exhaust itself. On occasions of more than usual solemnity, and in times of unwonted emergency, even human victims were sometimes offered up. Such was the case in seasons of wasting pestilence, always supposed to be an indication of the divine displeasure. Sometimes a captive, taken in battle, was deemed a sufficient atonement. At other times, the choicest specimen of humanity that the nation could select was doomed to bleed upon the altar. Thus the history of the early age of the Hebrew commonwealth records the sad narrative of the sacrifice of Jephtha's daughter; and Grecian tragedy has selected for one of its most affecting representations the intended offering up of Iphigenia, the daughter of Agamemnon.

But such an expedient as this inevitably loses its efficacy as soon as man listens to the voice of his own consciousness. He then feels that guilt is a personal thing, an affection of the spirit, and that he himself is a sinner. It is he, in his own person, that must answer at the bar of offended justice. Guilt cannot be transferred to a brute, nor can it at will be laid upon the conscience of another. The brute has no moral life; it can neither keep the law nor break it, and can never assume the responsibility which belongs solely to an immortal spirit. Hence the worshipper returned from the sacrifice unsatisfied and unblessed. The Jew, though performing the rites appointed by the Most High, confessed that it was not possible that the blood of bulls and of goats should take away sin. The pagan retired from the flowing libation and the smoking hecatomb bearing about within him a conscience still burdened with the guilt of unpardoned sin. The controversy between the spirit and its Creator was still unadjusted. The power of sin remained unbroken within him, and his soul was, as before, self-condemned and despairing.

And hence it came to pass that, long before the time of Christ, confidence in the whole system of sacrifices was rapidly passing away, before the progress of intellectual culture. I do not say that sacrifices were not offered. Unless this had been done, the nations had sunk into atheism. They had, however, lost all moral power over the minds of thinking men. The educated classes externally conformed to the popular belief for the sake of enforcing upon the common people the notion of a superintending Providence. The common people worshipped as their fathers had worshipped before them. At the era of the introduction of Christianity, the moral efficacy of such sufferings had ceased, and their inability to restore peace to a wounded spirit was universally felt.

This, however, belongs to a time that has passed away. A reference to it is, however, not without its utility, inasmuch as it reveals to us a universal human sentiment, and illustrates the course of action to which that sentiment so generally led.

Another view of this subject has been frequently taken by those who have been conscious of the guilt of sin. They have supposed that reparation to the violated law might be made by repentance and reformation. This idea would naturally suggest itself to a thoughtful mind, earnestly inquiring for reconciliation with God. It has at all times sought to ingraft itself upon Christianity, and thus render needless the atoning sacrifice of Christ. As the consequences, both theoretical and practical, which result from it, are important, I will examine it with as much care as the remaining time allotted to this discourse will allow.

The doctrine in question is, I suppose, essentially this: Although man be a sinner, as the word of God declares him to be, yet, by repentance and reformation, he may make such reparation as will entitle him to be treated as just or innocent; and thus he may become justified by the works of the law.

Repentance is the temper of mind which is appropriate to a moral agent who has done wrong. If a man have violated a good and righteous law, it becomes him to regret his action, to take the blame of it upon himself, to acknowledge the justice of the law, and submit himself, without reserve, to its enactments. He dislikes the act, not on account of the consequences which follow it, but on account of its own essential turpitude.

Repentance towards God is nothing other than the exercise of these tempers of mind in view of our relations to him. We have sinned against him, and violated his holy law. If we repent, we regret our fault sincerely, and without reserve; we take the blame of our conduct upon ourselves; we abhor ourselves for our wrong doing, and acknowledge the equity of the law which condemns us. "Against thee, thee only have I sinned and done evil in thy sight, that thou mightest be justified when thou speakest, and be clear when thou judgest." Now, if I understand the doctrine which we are considering, it declares that he who exercises this temper of mind is thereby justified, and, on this ground, may claim to be treated as though he had been innocent.

On this subject I would offer a few obvious considerations.

1. If this doctrine be true, it must proceed upon an entire change of the moral law. The law which the Scriptures have revealed is, that the wages of sin is death. This is its equitable desert. To declare, however, that if a man repents of his sin, he is entitled to justification, is to introduce another law, and to declare not that sin of itself is deserving of death, but only sin unrepented of. Now, I ask, where do we find the authority for announcing such a law? Revelation does not teach it. The laws of civil society do not present any analogies which would lead us to believe it true. No government on earth could be administered upon this principle. I know well that the Scriptures abundantly promise that he who repents of his sins shall find mercy; but to me they seem with the utmost precision to declare that repentance is not the

procuring cause of pardon, and that it can give the offender no claim to the remission of sins. "We are justified freely by *his grace* through the redemption that is in Christ Jesus." "In whom we have redemption through his blood, even the forgiveness of sins." "He hath made him to be sin (a sin-offering) for us, who himself knew no sin, that we might be made the righteousness of God" (righteous in the sight of God) "in him." Pardon for the race of man having thus been made possible by the work of the Messiah, it is freely offered to all who will repent and believe in the Lord Jesus Christ. Repentance itself has no power to justify us; it is only the condition on which the atonement of Christ is made available to the sinner.

2. This doctrine would, as it seems to me, lead to new views of divine justice. If a sinner can claim justification at the hands of God in virtue of repentance, then there would seem but little distinction to exist between innocence and guilt. He who had kept the whole law without fault, and he who had broken every commandment through life, and at last repented of his sins, would both stand in the same moral condition before God; both, on the ground of their own doings, being entitled to be treated as innocent. Now, if this be true, the desert of *sin* could not be death, but only of sin *unrepented of.* Sin repented of, and innocence, would both deserve the same treatment. I cannot persuade myself that the Scriptures present this view of our relations to God.

3. If this doctrine be true, we should, I think, believe that God himself entertained no moral displeasure against sin, but only against sin unrepented of. The announcement of his law would seem to be, that holiness and sin repented of were equally lovely in his sight, inasmuch as they were by his law entitled to the same reward. The Deity would thus seem to entertain less abhorrence to sin than the penitent himself. The penitent acknowledges that his whole life has been morally loathsome; that, on account of it, he deserves to suffer the penalty of the law; while, upon this supposition, God is repre-

sented as assuring him that there is nothing deserving of punishment in sin, but only in unrepented sin; and that now, since he has repented, he may make the same claim to justification as if he had ever been innocent. I by no means suppose that these sentiments are entertained by those who believe the doctrine in question. I merely assert that these are the consequences to which, as it seems to me, the doctrine by necessity leads.

And, lastly, were this the law of the divine dispensation, I think that it would defeat its own object; for, were this the law, repentance would be impossible.

Repentance can only arise from a conviction of the moral turpitude of sin; it is an abhorrence of the act purely on account of its moral wrong. But, upon the supposition in question, sin itself is not wrong, or odious in the sight of God, but only sin unrepented of. But, if the act itself be not morally detestable, of what is there for us to repent? We are to be penitent not for the act, but for our impenitence, while penitence itself is impossible, because the act is not in itself worthy of condemnation.

As soon as we abstract from an act its desert of the displeasure of God, there is no need of any change of mind towards it; and sorrow for it cannot possibly exist. It may be said that we may be sorry for the consequences; but then this is not repentance, nor is it at all a moral exercise. To expect that this would justify us, would be to declare that a man should be treated as innocent, as soon as he became afraid of the consequences of his crime.

To me, then, the Scriptures seem to assert that repentance can offer no atonement for sin. If the law be holy, and just, and good, it is holy, and just, and good, that it be enforced. If a man repent of his sins, this is right, and he shall have the advantage of it; but under a system of law, this can make no reparation for past transgression. The man confesses that the law is just; but this confession does not render it less just. He acknowledges that he deserves to perish:

but this does not alter his desert. He still deserves the just award of his past guilt. "Therefore, by the deeds of the law can no flesh be justified, for by the law is the knowledge of sin."

Such seems to me to be the result to which revelation leads us, considered as a system of law. Such was the dispensation under which we were originally created. But the conditions of this form of probation were violated originally by our first parents, and they have been violated by their descendants ever since. Hence, were there in the Scriptures no other announcement, the Bible would be to us nothing else than a sentence of universal condemnation. But, blessed be God! it contains something else than condemnation. It is an offer of universal pardon to the race of man, through the mediation of Him who "loved us, and gave himself for us." As the conditions of our first probation were rendered void, and the commandment, which was ordained unto life, was found to be unto death, God provided for us a second probation, established upon better promises. "God so loved the world that he gave his only-begotten Son, that whosoever believeth on him should not perish, but have everlasting life." This is the great message of eternal love to the lost and perishing race of man. It is in virtue of this atonement, made by the Messiah, that pardon and eternal life are now freely offered to every penitent believer.

To reveal this great and astonishing truth is the great design of revealed religion. Natural religion intimated to us our sin, and dimly foreshadowed the doom of our transgression. But from natural religion itself, — merely a system of law, — no news of reconciliation could proceed. It is the gospel of Jesus Christ alone that brings life and immortality to light. It is by Jesus Christ that we are justified from all things from which we could not be justified by the law of Moses. For the announcement of this great central truth, the whole previous history of our world was one magnificent preparation. For this end, empires arose, flourished, and fell.

To prepare the way for the Desire of all nations, seers foresaw, and prophets foretold; "for the testimony to Jesus is the spirit of prophecy." And when the second Adam, he who was thus, by his life and death, to change the terms of our probation, appeared, the blind saw, the lepers were cleansed, the dead were raised, the elements were stilled, and malignant spirits were obedient to his all-powerful word. All things, material and spiritual, did homage to him, "the brightness of the Father's glory," who had come by himself to purge away our sins.

Although, then, by the deeds of the law no flesh can be justified, though of ourselves we are helpless and undone, yet we may not despair, "for our help is laid upon one that is mighty," one who is able to save to the uttermost every one that believeth. "This is a faithful saying, and worthy of all acceptation, that Christ Jesus came into the world to save sinners." The way of life is just as open to us as the way of death. The blessed message to every one of us is, "Whosoever will, let him come and take of the fountain of the water of life freely." If, then, any of us should finally perish, it will not be because we are sinners, nor because we had ruined ourselves, but, in addition to all this, because we have rejected the gift of eternal life freely offered to us in the gospel.

PREPARATION FOR THE ADVENT OF THE MESSIAH.

PART I.

"WHEN THE FULNESS OF TIME WAS COME, GOD SENT FORTH HIS SON."
Galatians iv. 4.

"THE WORLD BY WISDOM KNEW NOT GOD."
1 *Corinthians* i. 21.

THE Scriptures, my brethren, distinctly teach us that our race was at the beginning placed under a system of probation; that the conditions of that probation were not only equitable, but merciful; that these conditions were violated by our first parents; and that, in consequence of that event, every one of their descendants has been voluntarily sinful; and hence, that, by the deeds of the law, — that is, on the ground of our obedience to its precepts, — no flesh can be justified; but that every one of us is, on account of his own transgressions, justly exposed to its righteous condemnation.

Viewed in this light alone, nothing can be more appalling than the condition of humanity. We are all sinners. We choose to be sinners. Not liking to retain God in our knowledge, we have surrendered ourselves to the dominion of our own passions. We do this in opposition to all the instructions and all the warnings both of nature and revelation. "We know our duty, but we do it not." The moral law, under which we were created, and which, in every act, we have violated, is holy, and just, and good; and therefore it is unchangeable. Its requirements cannot be abated, nor can its sanctions be abrogated. Supposing, then, that no other terms of probation could be offered to us, the law must take its course, and we must sink without remedy under its unmitigated curse.

Were this all, were we still "under the law," — to use the language of St. Paul, — sad would be the revelation presented to us in the Holy Scriptures. It could do nothing more than make manifest to us the wrath of God "revealed from heaven against all ungodliness and unrighteousness of men." Like the roll of the prophet Ezekiel, it would be "written within and without with mourning, and lamentation, and woe." It could do nothing more than lift that veil which hides from our view the dwellings of the lost, and bid us listen to the despairing blasphemies which ascend without ceasing from the bottomless abyss.

Such would be to our sinful race a revelation of simple law. But, thanks be unto God for his unspeakable gift, such is not our hopeless case. God has revealed himself to us, in the gospel of his Son, as a "God forgiving iniquity, transgression, and sin." In infinite mercy he has granted to us a new probation, and has provided for us a new covenant, established upon better promises. To a race by their sin shut out from all hope of eternal life, — "for by the deeds of the law shall no flesh be justified," — he has made the offer of free, full, universal pardon. To men steeped in sin he has made known a way of restoration to purity, holiness, and eternal life. I say *restoration*, but this word expresses but a part of the truth, for God has done infinitely more. He has promised to raise those of our race, who accept of the terms of reconciliation freely offered to all, to blessings vastly greater than those which have been lost by our apostasy. "God so loved the world that he gave his only-begotten Son, that whosoever believeth in him should not perish, but have everlasting life." The believer enters heaven, not in the image of the first, but of the second Adam. He pauses not at the outer court of the temple made without hands, but entereth within the veil, "whither the forerunner has for us entered, even Jesus, made a High Priest forever after the order of Melchisedek."

The great object of the New Testament is to teach us the means by which this change in the conditions of our probation was effected, and the manner in which we may avail ourselves of its advantages.

But the inquiry will readily suggest itself to every thoughtful mind, Why was not this way of salvation made known to man as soon as he had apostatized? Why was not the remedy administered as soon as the existence of the disease was discovered? I answer, The purpose to redeem our race was formed in the counsels of Eternity. A mysterious intimation was given in the garden of Eden, that though all was lost, yet, in the unfathomable wisdom and mercy of God, all was not irrecoverably lost. "Her seed shall bruise thy head," were the enigmatical words in which were wrapped up the promise of our final victory over all the powers of evil. To the parents of our race they must have been but imperfectly understood; yet they shed down a ray of hope upon the thick darkness which enveloped us. He who uttered them, alone comprehended the fulness of the blessing which he purposed to confer upon our race, and he then commenced, and he has ever since continued, that course of administration which has for its object the regeneration of our world, and the giving unto the Messiah "the heathen for his inheritance, and the uttermost parts of the earth for his possession."

Ages now rolled away. A world was drowned by a flood. A second parentage was selected for our race. Empires rose, flourished, declined, and were forgotten. Other empires, to whom even the record of the existence of their predecessors had never been handed down, arose upon their ruins. These again flourished, declined, and were forgotten. Age after age stumbled on in darkness, and, in quick succession, groped their way downward to the regions of despair. Four thousand years had each presented its myriads before the bar of God, and yet the destiny of our race, to all but an insignificant tribe, remained shrouded in impenetrable darkness. Sages and philosophers had looked on every side for light, but still they gazed upon nothing but starless midnight. At length "the morning star took his station over the stable of Bethlehem." The day dawned. The Sun of righteousness arose with healing in his beams, and discovered to an astonished world the gates of heaven thrown wide open to every one that believeth in Jesus.

But, even here, we naturally ask, Why was this delay? Why did not the Messiah appear at an earlier period, and at once put away sin by the sacrifice of himself? To this question various satisfactory answers might, I think, be returned. It might be said that this was a question to which our reason offered no means of solution; or it might be suggested that he who, in boundless mercy, provided for us such a way of salvation, would, also, in the exercise of the same mercy, select the most appropriate time for revealing it to us. Or, again, it might be said that perhaps God chose to exhibit to the moral universe the evils of sin, and hence he suffered it for ages in our world to work out its legitimate results. The text, however, suggests a reason at once definite and satisfactory; it teaches us that when the *fulness of time* was come, or, as perhaps we, using another illustration, should say, when every thing was ripe for this august event, God sent forth his Son. From these words we learn that before the Son of God could be sent, there must be a preparation made for his appearing. A connected series of intellectual, social, and moral changes must take place, before the coming of Christ could produce its intended results. Until these preliminary events had transpired, the Messiah could not, in accordance with the all-wise purposes of God, appear. When, however, this preparatory work had been accomplished; when, in the words of the text, the fulness of time had come; at the very moment selected by infinite wisdom, — "then God sent forth his Son, made of a woman, made under the law, to redeem them that were under the law, that we might receive the adoption of sons." *

If now we consider this subject somewhat more attentively, several views will readily present themselves.

In the first place, then, we observe that the word of God had proclaimed the universal sinfulness of man, and the moral corruption of our whole race, and had declared that by the deeds of the law no flesh could be justified. It seems to have formed a part of the plan of the Deity to subject mankind to the test of experiment; so that it might be evident to the whole universe that his assertion was true; and that thus a practical demonstration might be given of the necessity of the work of redemption in order to our salvation.

For this purpose man was left in general to the light which he had received from the beginning. To this was added, in the Gentile world, the teaching of natural religion; while to the Jews was superadded the teaching of a written revelation. For four thousand years our race was left to these moral influences, that it might be seen whether any would "feel after God, though he was not far from any one of them." The experiment showed conclusively that the word of God was true to the letter, that men "did not like to retain God in their knowledge;" and, yet more, that "the thoughts of the imaginations of their hearts were only evil continually."

During these four thousand years, there appeared, as I have

* When I here speak of the necessity of preparation in order to accomplish a purpose of the Almighty, I trust I am understood. There is nothing here said which is intended to signify any limitation to the absolute power of the Almighty. He might, if he had chosen, have abolished all the intellectual and social laws to which man was subjected, and have established new ones. This would, however, have been to create man anew. What is meant is simply this — that, the laws existing as they were at the beginning, such a preparation was necessary in order to the accomplishment of the purposes supposed. It is not, therefore, meant that God could not have done otherwise, but that he could not have done otherwise without abolishing the laws which he had established.

said, no tendency in man to grow better. There had been formed no true or even rational conception of the Godhead. The ignorance of the character of the Deity, and of our relations to him, which overspread our race, became, age after age, more profound. Moral corruption, at once the cause and the effect of this ignorance, became more and more intense, until, at the time of the advent of the Messiah, the world had attained to a preëminence in wickedness such as no period, either before or since, has ever witnessed.

I do not, however, affirm that this course of moral deterioration was in the line of straight and uniform descent. From the nature of the case, this could not be, since, then, the race would have perished from the unrestrained indulgence of every evil passion. The process was in fact something like the following. In infancy, poverty, and feebleness, nations are comparatively virtuous. They cannot be otherwise, since the struggle for existence leaves no leisure to listen to the seductions of vice, and consciousness of inferiority renders successful aggression hopeless. But, with progress of wealth and power, the means of vicious gratification stimulate the passions of the human mass. Sensuality, even to loathsomeness, corrupts the sentiments of the entire people, and gradually expels every generous impulse. Selfishness usurps the place of patriotism. The insane love of pleasure, utterly reckless of consequences, becomes the ruling passion of the soul. The body politic is enfeebled by moral corruption, and the nation becomes the prey of some barbarous but less vicious horde. These, again, erect the standard of empire, and flourish on the ruins of a slaughtered or enslaved people. But they breathe an atmosphere already tainted with moral infection. They draw their nourishment from a soil poisoned by intense sensuality. The conquerors are in turn subdued by the vices of the conquered, and, by a quicker transition, become the slaves of luxury and vice; until they themselves become the victims of another people, destined to pursue the same sad round of wickedness and retribution. Such was the history of the world for ages. Such would it be forever were not some moral force introduced from without to arrest its downward tendency.

But, besides this general fact, it deserves more particularly to be remarked, that this experiment upon the moral character of man was made under every possible variety of circumstances. In the first place, the legislators of antiquity were not unaware of this propensity in man to evil; and they strove, by all the means which they could devise, to correct it. For this end, they constructed every conceivable form of government. Monarchy, aristocracy, democracy, were all tried, under every modification that the wit of man could suggest. Power over man was lodged in the hands of the one, of the few, or of the many. All these expedients were found equally and totally ineffectual. There seemed but little difficulty in originating a form of government, which, under favorable external circumstances, might raise a poor and industrious people to power and wealth; but the attainment of this very object seemed to render their downfall inevitable. The moral tendency was towards deterioration. The mass gravitated to the earth, and by no change in its form could you either check its progress, or arrest the operation of that law by which it was evidently governed.

Legislation, then, during this long interval, seemed to have ended in nothing but failure. It could offer no successful resistance to this propensity to evil. Thus it became evident, that no system of laws, and no constitution of government, had power either to elevate the tone of private morals, or to foster such attainments in public virtue, as could save them from dissolution. Hence it was demonstrated that hope from the principles of our social nature was not to be expected; and that, unless help should arise from some other source, the condition of our race was desperate, and our moral reformation impossible.

But this was not the only trial to which the moral character of our race was subjected. During these ages of political change, the human mind, in many nations, had made astonishing acquirements in the power of philosophical research. From the time of Pythagoras to that of Socrates, especially among the Greeks, men had ceased not to inquire for the reason of the facts, physical, intellectual, and moral, which were transpiring around them. Questions were continually asked concerning the character of the Deity, and our relations and obligations to him. During this long interval, however, while an increasing multitude of educated men were directing their attention to subjects of spiritual philosophy, they continued, age after age, to wander farther and farther from the truth. This downward tendency reached its lowest level at the period of the intellectual reign of the sophists, — a name which has ever since been synonymous with treachery and falsehood. Setting aside, as worse than useless, all questions of practical duty, their only object was to cultivate the intellect to the highest refinement of subtlety, that so it might become more exquisitely skilful in the arts of deception and intrigue. They boasted of their ability to prove the same act to be either right or wrong, wise or unwise, true or false, as occasion might require. Hence they baptized the intellect itself in falsehood, and subverted, at their foundation, the very principles of virtue. Thus philosophy, which was designed to lead men to truth, to goodness, and to piety, became the unblushing pander to vice. It not only darkened counsel by words without knowledge, but it steeped the conscience itself in corruption, — a corruption the more incurable, because it seemed to flow from the sources which Nature herself had opened in the fountains of the human understanding.

It was at this eventful period that Socrates appeared, who, with a self-sacrificing earnestness which indicated a pure love of virtue, combatted the enormous errors of his age. From the things that are made, he proved the existence and attributes of their Maker. From the character of God, he taught men, in many respects, the relations which they sustain to him. Attacking the sophists of Athens, sometimes by argument and sometimes by ridicule, he was exposing them to the contempt which they merited, when his life was cut off by an act of judicial murder. The philosopher died, but his sentiments still lived. They inspired with new life the mind of Plato, a name destined to enduring immortality. The intellect of this remarkable person was perhaps more preëminently gifted than that of any man who has ever devoted his attention to spiritual inquiry. To an acuteness which nothing could elude, a taste which found its models in its own faultless conceptions, he added an imagination, which, in the opinion of the first critic of antiquity, has entitled him to the rank of the Homer of prose. His discourses are, at the present day, to be numbered among the choicest specimens of composition that the human mind has produced. But, if I do not mistake, he was wanting in the simple humility and virtuous earnestness of his master, and hence his splendid talents were too much directed to the purpose of displaying their own magnificence. Truth, virtue, duty, nay, the character of the Deity itself, became matters of refined, abstruse, though glorious, speculation. The guide-post which Socrates had erected, was entwined so thickly with roses, that it was difficult to discover the direction in which it pointed. The path which he had opened was planted so densely with shrubbery, it was adorned so profusely with statues and shrines, that the wayfarer was bewildered in a labyrinth of beauty; and, pausing so frequently to admire, forgot the object for which his journey had been commenced.

To Plato succeeded Aristotle, a name which ruled the human mind with undisputed sway, in many departments of science, from his own era to that of Bacon, and of which the influence is acknowledged even to the present day. Endowed with but little imagination, he was, perhaps, the most clear-sighted reasoner the world has ever seen; while in amplitude of learning, exactitude of inquiry, and power of philosophic generalization, succeeding ages have rarely furnished his equal. He so expounded the doctrines and perfected the sciences of logic and rhetoric, that, as they fell from his hand, so they have remained, almost without addition or alteration, through the lapse of more than two thousand years. The existing knowledge of physical science was moulded into shape by his plastic hand, while it received vast additions from his scrutinizing investigations. But while Science thus gratefully acknowledges her obligations to the philosopher of Stagira, religion owes him no homage. In no respect, that I am aware of, did he enlarge our knowledge of God, or of our relations and obligations to him. It is true he taught the world wisdom. He explained to us the laws in obedience to which the mind advances in the pursuit of truth or in the detection of error; and he unfolded those canons of criticism which enter even now into our course of collegiate study; but he taught us nothing concerning the way of deliverance from sin. He scattered light upon every path but that which leads us to God. If it had been in the power of the human intellect to regenerate the moral character of man, this regeneration would have been effected by Aristotle. No man was ever possessed of a surer or wider mental vision. No man had ever a greater power of moulding the mind of following ages into the form of his own conceptions; yet, in respect to religion, he left the race just where he found it. None of his precepts have ever, by their transforming energy, regenerated the souls of his disciples. No change from vice to virtue was ever known to follow the teaching of his doctrines. His works have been the chosen study of Pagan and Mohammedan, of Protestant and Catholic; and every where they have stimulated the intellect, but they have left the moral nature untouched. They satisfied every aspiration of the understanding; but when the sinner inquired, How shall man be just with God? they gave him no answer. They found man under the bondage of sin, the slave of passion, drunk with sensuality; and they left him having no hope and without God in the world.

I might easily pursue this subject farther, by presenting illustrations from other periods of civilization. But it is useless. The experiment, under what circumstances soever it has been tried, has led to the same result. Had it been possible to deliver man from the moral condition in which he is every where found, by any exertion of the human intellect, it would have been done by the men to whose labors I have just alluded. But it was not possible. The direction which the human intellect has always taken, confirms the truth of the declaration of St. Paul,—" The world by wisdom knew not God." Nay, we see, from the instances to which we have referred, that a true conception of the character of God, and of our relations and obligations to him, is distasteful to the human mind. Socrates taught more important truth on these subjects than all the other heathen writers combined. For doing this the common people persecuted him to death, and the philosophers whom he had taught, instead of pursuing his doctrines to their natural results, treated them merely as the starting-point for metaphysical speculations. Thus is also confirmed that other declaration of the apostle, " They did not like to retain God in their knowledge, but when they knew God, they glorified him not as God, neither were thankful, but became vain in their imaginations, and their foolish heart was darkened." It thus became manifest that man did not sin by reason either of ignorance or of mental imbecility, and that no attainment of intellectual power could change his propensity to evil. Here, then, from another point of view, was made evident the helplessness of our moral condition; and thus it was shown that, without some special effort of divine mercy, we must ever abide under the condemnation which we had incurred.

But one other hope remained. It has been said that the moral and æsthetic elements of the human character are nearly allied, if, indeed, they be not identical; that, at least, the beautiful and the good are twin sisters; and hence it has been conjectured that the cultivation of the taste must lead to reformation in the moral nature of man.

The period that elapsed previously to the advent of the Messiah, furnished an opportunity for the trial of this form of the moral experiment, of which we have been speaking. The age of Socrates, and Plato, and Aristotle, was the golden age of the arts of Greece. Neither before nor since this time, has the marble been ever chiselled into forms so instinct with majesty and loveliness. It is probable that painting had attained to similar perfection, though, unfortunately, none of its productions have come down to us. Architecture then had exhausted, in one direction at least, all the forms of beauty and grandeur of which the mind can conceive. Poetry had already furnished those faultless models of verse on which all succeeding generations have gazed with reverential despair. Eloquence then, with a power which has never since been equalled,

> "Wielded at will that fierce democracie,
> Shook the arsenal, and fulmined over Greece
> To Macedon and Artaxerxes' throne."

But had this wonderful development of the taste any power to reform the moral character of man? Far from it. Taste became itself the pander to vice. The very fountains of literature were defiled. Poetry became at last the stimulant to undisguised licentiousness. Painting and statuary lent their aid to render unblushing vice attractive, and to fascinate the taste with whatever could defile the conscience. The eye could scarcely be opened in any street of a Grecian or a Roman city, without resting upon some finished specimen of art, which filled the imagination with all that was morally revolting. Taste, revelling in licentiousness, presided over every department of the arts. Its dominion was not confined to places of public resort. It painted the walls of dressing-rooms and chambers; it sculptured the statuary of private gardens; nay, it fashioned personal ornaments of the young and old, of the daughter and the matron. And thus it became evident that taste, far from exerting any power of moral reformation, tainted with our own corruption, disseminates more widely, and renders yet more intensely fatal, the poison with which it is itself infected.

Scholars and artists have mourned for ages over the almost universal destruction of the works of ancient genius. I suppose that many a second-rate city, at the time of Christ, possessed a collection of works of surpassing beauty, which could not be equalled by all the specimens now existing that have yet been discovered. The Alexandrian library is believed to have contained a greater treasure of intellectual riches than has ever since been hoarded in a single city. These, we know, have all vanished from the earth. The Apollo Belvidere and the Venus de Medicis stand in almost solitary grandeur, to remind us of the perfection to which the plastic art of the ancients had attained. The Alexandrian library furnished fuel for years for the baths of illiterate Moslems. I used myself frequently to wonder why it had pleased God to blot out of existence these magnificent productions of ancient genius. It seemed to me strange that the pall of oblivion should thus be thrown over all to which man, in the flower of his age, had given birth. But the solution of this mystery is found, I think, in the remains of Herculaneum and Pompeii. We there discover that every work of man was so penetrated by corruption, every production of genius was so defiled with uncleanness, that God, in introducing a better dispensation, determined to cleanse the world from the pollution of preceding ages. As when all flesh had corrupted his way, he purified the world by the waters of a flood, so, when genius had covered the earth with images of sin, he overwhelmed the works of ancient civilization with a deluge of barbarism, and consigned the most splendid monuments of literature and art to almost universal oblivion. It was too bad to exist; and he swept it all away with the besom of destruction.

You see that for four thousand years this experiment was continued upon the moral character of man. The point to be determined was, as we have supposed, whether man, left to the conditions of his first probation, would ever recover himself from his apostasy from God. The experiment was tried under every form of government, under the most favorable conditions for intellectual culture, and during the period of the most perfect development of human taste. But under none of these influences was there exhibited the remotest tendency to moral reformation. Hence it was practically demonstrated that "the world by wisdom knew not God;" and that, without some merciful divine interposition, the condition of man was hopeless. It was at the close of this protracted experiment, when Rome, following the example of Greece, had sunk into gross licentiousness; when men had not only lost the knowledge of God, but had become universally corrupt beyond all previous example; when, as it would seem, nothing further remained but for God to destroy our race and blot out the memory of man forever, — it was then that the "fulness of time had come," that God sent forth his Son, made of a woman, made under the law, to announce that a new probation had been granted to us, and to utter that astonishing truth, "God so loved the world that he sent his only-begotten Son, that whosoever believeth in him should not perish, but have everlasting life."

It was my original intention to have illustrated, at some length, the results of the moral trial to which the Jews were subjected previously to the advent of the Messiah. I have, however, already occupied the time ordinarily allotted to a discourse, and I will therefore allude to this part of the subject in very few words.

The same experiment was made upon the Jews as upon the Gentiles, but it was made under vastly more favorable circumstances. They were selected and set apart from the idolatrous nations around them; they were rendered a peculiar people by a burdensome but imposing ritual; they were the sole depositaries of the law which God had given to our race; and their history, from the time of the call of Abraham, was replete with most astonishing illustrations of the attributes of God, whether exhibited in judgment or in mercy. It was, however, essentially a dispensation of law. It declared the precept and the penalty, the reward for obedience and the punishment for sin. Its language was, "Indignation and wrath, tribulation and anguish, upon every soul of man that doeth evil; but glory, and honor, and peace, to every man that worketh good." Having given these precepts, there it rested. I know that it also foreshadowed the blessings of the new dispensation; but its teaching, in this respect, was enigmatical, and could have taken no permanent hold upon the national mind. It did not reveal the manner in which "God could be just and the justifier of him that believeth in Jesus." Hence, like the dispensation of natural religion, it was a dispensation of law, yet of law plainly and evidently set forth. It left man with a clear knowledge of his duty, to act with no other impulse than that derived from the consequences of his action. The failure that ensued cannot, as in the case of the Gentiles, be learned from the volumes of contemporaneous literature, for in the case of the Hebrews such works do not exist. The apostle Paul, however, declares that, at his time, they had become even more corrupt than the heathen themselves. While they boasted of their knowledge of the law, "through breaking the law they dishonored God," insomuch that "through them, the name of God was blasphemed among the Gentiles." Thus it became evident that our whole race — Jew and Gentile — was under sin; that hope of reformation, from any power within ourselves, was groundless; and hence, in the words of the apostle, that "by the deeds of the law no flesh could be justified."

From this view of the subject, I think, then, that a reason may be discovered why the Messiah did not appear in the beginning to take away sin. The delay of his advent was for the purpose of rendering it practically evident that our moral condition, under a system of law, was helpless; that there existed in our nature no recuperative energy; that having broken loose from his obligations to God, the course of man was in the line of perpetual retrocession; and that, without the introduction of some new condition into the elements of his probation, there remained for him nothing but a fearful looking for of judgment. When this had been made evident, under every phase, both of civilization and barbarism, under every form of government, and under every degree, both of intellectual and æsthetic development, then "the fulness of time had come, and God sent forth his Son."

PREPARATION FOR THE ADVENT OF THE MESSIAH.

PART II.

"PREPARE YE THE WAY OF THE LORD, MAKE STRAIGHT IN THE DESERT A HIGHWAY FOR OUR GOD. EVERY VALLEY SHALL BE EXALTED, AND EVERY MOUNTAIN AND HILL SHALL BE MADE LOW; AND THE CROOKED SHALL BE MADE STRAIGHT AND THE ROUGH PLACES PLAIN, AND THE GLORY OF THE LORD SHALL BE REVEALED, AND ALL FLESH SHALL SEE IT TOGETHER, FOR THE MOUTH OF THE LORD HATH SPOKEN IT."
Isaiah xl. 3, 4.

IN the last discourse, I attempted to illustrate the doctrine that the advent of the Messiah could not have occurred immediately after the apostasy. Various events must have transpired before the fulness of time could come. Before God publicly interfered, if I may so say, with the conditions of the first probation, he chose to show by experiment that such interference was necessary. It thus became evident that neither in the social, intellectual, nor æsthetic departments of human nature, did there exist the elements adequate to restore us to virtue and piety. Under all forms of government, through every grade of intellectual progress, and in the midst of the most successful cultivation of taste, man's moral tendency was ever downward, until he had arrived at so universal depravity, that the Deity, in ushering in a new dispensation, consigned to oblivion by far the greater part of the intellectual labors of preceding generations.

In this manner was it practically demonstrated that a remedial dispensation was absolutely necessary. But these suggestions have by no means exhausted the subject. If we look at it from another point of view, we shall see that a positive preparation of the race itself was necessary, before the plan of redemption could be successfully revealed. This preparation was gradually going forward at the same time that our moral helplessness was so amply illustrated. It is to this series of events that the prophet alludes in the beautiful language which I have selected for the text. He represents the Messiah as a conquering prince appearing to take possession of his newly-acquired dominions. It was customary among Oriental nations to render such an occasion in the most signal manner impressive. Every road by which the conqueror was to proceed was put in perfect repair; obstructions were all removed; the valleys were exalted and the hills were levelled; the crooked were made straight and the rough places smooth, so that, when the triumphant procession appeared, its progress might be wholly uninterrupted. Under this figurative language the prophet conveys to us the idea that before the glory of the Lord shall be revealed, all things must be put under requisition for the purpose of rendering the event more illustrious and its results more universal. In other words, we are thus taught that the previous history of our world was overruled by infinite wisdom with special reference to this event; and that when the revolutions of four thousand years had completed this mighty preparation, the fulness of time arrived, and God sent forth his Son.

In order to obtain a correct view of this subject, it will be proper to observe the conditions which seem necessary * to the successful promulgation of the gospel, and the manner in which these conditions were fulfilled in the history of the world previously to the advent of the Messiah.

If we reflect upon the nature of the Christian revelation, I

* The meaning of necessity, as here used, is explained in a note to the preceding sermon, p. 110.

think we shall be convinced that its conceptions belong to an advanced period of civilization. It addresses itself, I may say, exclusively to the spiritual nature of man. But, in the earlier periods of our race, our conceptions are all from without; they have to do almost exclusively with sensible objects. This is evident from the history of all language. Conceptions from within belong to a later period, and only appear in the progress of civilization. Hence the ideas made known to us in the New Testament could scarcely have been comprehended, until man had passed from the region of objective and become familiar with the region of subjective thought. The gospel has to do with thought, feeling, sentiment, motive, and all their various attributês; and it could not be well understood until the mind of man had become somewhat at home in these conceptions.

Nor is this all. The Christian religion addresses itself to the moral nature, the conscience of man. It is to this faculty that its commands are specially addressed. The harmony of its precepts with the law, originally written there, is one of the universal proofs of its authenticity. It is for the purpose of providing a remedy to the moral disorders of the soul, that the gospel is revealed. The need of this remedy can only be made evident as the universality and intensity of this disease are discovered. Hence I think it will be seen that a remedial dispensation would naturally be delayed, until the moral character of man, both individual and social, had been fully displayed; and mankind had become in some degree capable of appreciating the facts thus presented to their notice.

But, besides this, the gospel is a revelation communicated to man by language, and its authenticity, as is meet, is attested by miracles. Now, I think that considerable progress must have been made in civilization before such testimony could be given as we would be willing to receive on a question of so vital importance. Until the laws of nature are to some extent known, we cannot determine whether the Creator has or has not in a particular case departed from them. Savages, in these respects, possess but the intellect of children. They seem almost to court deception, and we admit their testimony with doubt and hesitation. Hence we pay very little respect to the early history of the primitive nations. An ignorant age is governed by the imagination rather than by the reason, and we look upon its traditions rather as allegorical pictures than indubitable statements of matters of fact. The fact here to be substantiated is no other than this — the Messiah, God manifest in the flesh, appeared on our earth to teach us the way of life, and to offer himself up as a sacrifice for the sins of mankind. I ask, Could any one believe so stupendous a statement as this, upon the testimony of a barbarous age?

And this leads us to observe, again, that a revelation from God to man, informing him of this wonderful change in the conditions of his probation, — a revelation designed for all ages to the end of time, and destined to work a perfect transformation in the moral character of our race, — could not have been completed until language, that most mysterious of all the products of the human intellect, had arrived at a considerable degree of perfection. It was necessary that the doctrines and motives peculiar to the new dispensation should be promulgated with all possible explicitness, and yet guarded from all tendency either to incompleteness or excess. No medium of communication would be competent to the transmission of such all-important truth, but a language capable of expressing the most delicate modifications of human thought; and so perfect in its construction, that its meaning, in subsequent ages, might be determined by the most definite laws of exegetical inquiry.

To understand the necessity of which we speak, it is only requisite to remember the ordeal through which the Christian revelation has passed during the period that has elapsed since the days of the apostles. There is scarcely a doctrine which it contains that has not frequently been made the subject of earnest, I had almost said of bitter controversy. Its enemies have denied the truth of every one of its assertions, and its professed friends have, in countless instances, endeavored to interpret its doctrines in such manner as to gratify their lus. of civil or ecclesiastical power. Every atrocity, which has for ages been perpetrated by either lay or clerical despots throughout Christendom, has claimed the authority of some passage from the word of God. And, on the contrary, men have always been delivered from despotism by stripping off from the Scriptures the covering by which they had been veiled, and making them to speak out plainly the simple truth of the Most High. Now, unless the gospel had been revealed in a language capable of expressing the truth, the whole truth, and nothing but the truth, and of so expressing it that the meaning of every word could be verified, it would surely, at this distance of time, have been scarcely possible for even a candid man to discover what had been really revealed. Suppose that, eighteen hundred years since, the Gospels had been written in a language similar to that of our aboriginal Indians, — who, at this age, would pretend to be able to interpret it? Nay, I doubt if the doctrines of the New Testament could have been given to all subsequent ages, even in the ancient Hebrew. How could the subtle reasoning, and the wide generalizations of the apostle Paul, have been conveyed in a language which had attained its highest perfection in the time of Moses and of Job, and which was adapted only to an age of primitive manners and objective thought? Nay, had the revelation for all ages been delivered in Hebrew, I doubt whether, at this late period, its meaning could be verified. The Hebrew possessed no literature save that which existed in the sacred books themselves. Hence, when a difficulty in interpretation occurred, there would have been no contemporaneous authority to which we might appeal for illustration. I think that these considerations will be sufficient to convince us that this language was an inadequate medium for the transmission of a revelation that was destined to endure to the end of time, and, thus enduring, to regenerate a world.

If we reflect upon these plain conditions, I think it will be evident that at no era preceding that of the advent could the new dispensation have been with so much propriety ushered in. And still more, I think that, by a slight reference to previous events, we shall be led to believe that the hand of God may be distinctly traced in directing the course of civilization with respect to this great transaction.

Amidst all the agitations of society, throughout all the overturnings of empire, the human mind, during this long period, had been gradually attaining maturity. Each nation, during its brief existence, had either added something to the stock of human knowledge, or made some contribution to the materials for human thought. Every revolution had illustrated in some new phase the principles of conduct, and had bequeathed the lesson to succeeding generations. Prosperity and adversity, war and peace, despotism and freedom, anarchy and order, had tended to widen and deepen the course of philosophical speculation. The very wickedness of man, overturning empires and dissolving the cement by which the elements of society are held in cohesion, had obliged men to reflect more or less upon moral cause and effect. Patriotism, as well as natural virtue, nay, self-interest, as well as the love of right, had, to some extent, forced men to turn their eyes upon this changeless plague-spot of our common nature. The very love of power, so rife in all ages, had directed attention to those spiritual impulses by which all outward action is modified, and from which alone it frequently proceeds. From all these sources, the mind of man, at the time of our Savior, had become a subject of very general investigation; and its various processes had been examined with acumen and earnestness. It is also probable that this kind of inquiry was prosecuted with greater vigor on account of the existing state of religious opinion among the ancient nations. The system of mythology had long since lost its power over the public mind; and hence the priesthood dared not protect it from contempt by the exertion of physical force. Let a man believe what he chose, or advocate what he pleased, in matters of pure science or intellectual speculation, the mythology had little to do with it.

Hence the mind, left mainly to its own impulses, pursued thought wherever it led; and hence arose that prodigious mental activity, that far-reaching love of research, that fearless range of speculation, which distinguished the Augustan age of Rome, but more especially the age of Pericles in Greece. Nay, Greece and Italy, during the universal prevalence of pagan idolatry, enjoyed the blessing of soul-liberty in a much higher degree than they have done for ages under the dominion of the (so called) Christian hierarchy, by which these nations have so long been enslaved.

But while this progress was so rapidly made in the intellectual development of the ancient nations, specially of the Greeks, this latter people was, at the same time, cultivating, with unparalleled success a language which has been for ages the admiration of the human race. It is a language which scholars have ever since considered the most perfect vehicle of thought that human intelligence has yet invented. Combining the opposite extremes of strength and flexibility; capable alike of fixing with precision the most refined distinctions in metaphysics, and of giving utterance to the tenderest emotions of sentiment; bursting forth now in all the thunder of resistless eloquence, and now warbling in numbers softer than the breathings of maternal love; affording free scope to the giant spirit of Demosthenes, and yet yielding itself up to utter, as if in sport, the songs of Anacreon; in its youth pouring forth in matchless verse the epic of Homer, and in its manhood clothing the conceptions of Sophocles and Pindar with perennial beauty; unexhausted by the boundless imagination of Plato, and yet laying down with mathematical exactness the canons of Aristotle,—it seems to have been created for the purpose of transmitting to all coming time that spiritual truth by which a world should be created anew. And yet more: This language had naturally so attracted to itself whatever was valuable in science or delightful in literature, that many of its greatest works could not be lost. Hence, whatever has at any time been written in it can even at the present day be definitely interpreted. Hence, also, wherever in the old world the human mind has awaked from the slumber of ignorance, the knowledge of this language has been revived. And it deserves to be remarked, that those remains of it that have come down to us, are specially rich in the expression of spiritual conceptions — in terms which are most readily adapted to illustrate the truths of revelation. Hence, when the new and astonishing doctrines of the gospel were to be promulgated, hardly a term required to be modified in order to adapt this language to the purpose. St. Paul was esteemed by Longinus as one of the most distinguished of Grecian orators; and the discourses of many of the earlier Christian writers are numbered among the purest specimens of this remarkable tongue. Thus was the language prepared in which the gospel of our salvation was to be written, and by which it was to be transmitted to succeeding generations to the end of time.

And here, in passing, let us pause, for a moment, to inquire, by whom was this language enriched by every form of expression, and endowed with so remarkable a power of exactness and precision? It was by poets who sung of barbarian wars, of the contests of fabulous gods, and the loves of unholy sensualists; by historians who wrote for fame, and orators who contended for power; by philosophers who inquired not for truth, and sophists who taught falsehood for hire. Even these last, by their endless disputations, their subtile distinctions, and their crafty sophistry, gave a fixedness to language which it could by no other means have attained. Thus is it ever in the government of God. He makes the wrath of man to praise him, and the remainder of wrath he restrains. Thus, while men, utterly forgetful of him, were following each one the desires and devices of his own heart, they were accomplishing his purposes, and preparing the way for the coming of Him who was the desire of all nations. Thus, while God allows all his moral creatures to act as they will, by far-reaching wisdom, he overrules all things for his glory, and causes wicked, sensual, and atheistic men to subserve the purposes of virtue and righteousness and true godliness.

Such was the preparation necessary in order to prepare a language in which God should reveal to us the doctrines of the new dispensation, and usher in the hope of everlasting life. But this was not all. It was also necessary that this language should be diffused throughout the civilized world. This was also accomplished.

At the period in which the Greek language had attained to its highest perfection, Alexander, frequently called the Great, was born. This remarkable man, perhaps the most remarkable conqueror whose history has yet been written, immediately after his accession to the throne of Macedon, having subdued the states of Greece that had dared to resist his sway, commenced that series of victories which have rendered his name immortal. Having overrun that portion of Europe that lay to the eastward of Greece, he carried his conquests into Asia; and, in a few years, Asia Minor, Syria, Palestine, Egypt, Assyria, and Persia, were his tributary provinces. He even penetrated into India; and, but for the resistance of his own soldiers, would have planted his standards upon the banks of the Ganges. The theatre of these conquests comprehended by far the most populous and highly civilized portions of the then known world. Every where throughout these vast regions, he established the Grecian authority, and by consequence introduced the Greek language. Every where he brought the science and intelligence, the courage and freedom, the manners and arts of Greece into contact with the puerile thought, the servile timidity, and barbarian wealth of Oriental civilization. Power and wisdom, when they strike their roots into such a soil, are not easily eradicated. Greek, in all these regions, soon became the language of intelligence, rank, and station. From the higher classes it was gradually disseminated among the middle ranks of society; and hence, among these countless millions, it had soon established a universal sway. Of the extent to which it had prevailed we may learn from the fact, that as early as the year 285 before Christ, it had become necessary to translate the Old Testament Scriptures into Greek, for the use of the Jews residing in Alexandria. Greek had already become more familiar to them than the language of their ancestors, and, lest they should lose their knowledge of the word of God, it was rendered, for their benefit, into a tongue that had become to them vernacular. Flourishing schools of Grecian philosophy were established in several of the cities of Asia Minor. Among these, Tarsus, the birthplace of the apostle Paul, at an early period, obtained no inconsiderable preëminence. These, like so many centres of illumination, diffused on every side the light of western civilization, and rendered a knowledge of the Greek language a necessary attainment for every educated man. These remarks, however, as you will perceive, have respect principally to the countries to the eastward of Greece.

With the death of Alexander, the political preëminence of Greece was nearly at an end. She, however, still continued immeasurably in advance of the surrounding nations, in the arts, in science, and in civilization. As the Roman empire was rising in the west, her citizens felt the necessity of intellectual cultivation as well as of martial glory; and they began to resort to Athens, the seat of knowledge and the cherished abode of eloquence and philosophy. Thus the poets and orators of Rome first imbibed a taste for elegance of language and refinement of thought. At last Greece was subdued by the arms of Italy, and Achaia was added to the catalogue of Roman provinces. From this time, there was nothing to prevent the universal influx of Grecian literature into Rome. The statues, the paintings, the poetry, the eloquence, and the philosophy of Greece, were transferred from the banks of the Ilyssus to the banks of the Tiber. Roman authors aspired to little else than to copy into their own language those models which they ceased not to study with an almost idolatrous admiration. In fact, Roman literature became almost a mere reproduction of those works which were universally acknowledged to have attained the perfection of æsthetic excellence.

The result of all this is very easily conceived. The Latin language was itself modified by the literature which it imitated, and became the second in power of the languages of antiquity. But this was not all. Greek, throughout the Roman empire, became the language of educated men. Hence, when Paul addressed the Roman governor, Claudius Lysias, in this language at Jerusalem, it was at once perceived that he was a person of consideration, and not the lawless freebooter for whom he had been at first mistaken. Thus, also, Cæsar relates, that on one occasion, when he wished to communicate important private intelligence to one of his lieutenants, in a besieged city, he wrote a letter in Greek, and directed his messenger to attach it to an arrow, and shoot it over the walls. This language, he knew, would be unintelligible to the Gauls, but would be well understood by the officers of his own army.

In this manner, during the gradual progress of Rome to universal dominion, this language came into general use throughout the civilized world. It was spoken and read in all the countries bordering on the Mediterranean, in Europe, Asia, and Africa. In all these regions, it became the language of educated men. Whatever was written in Greek was accessible to millions, and these millions comprehended all the men who gave character to their age, or conferred distinction upon their nation.

We see, then, in the second place, that God not only prepared a language in which this revelation for all coming ages could be written, but he diffused that language over the civilized world. He created a suitable vehicle for the truth, and he made that vehicle, as far as was necessary, universal. And this work, let us observe, was accomplished by means of the ambition of Alexander, and the all-grasping love of dominion of the citizens of Rome. Men ignorant of the existence and character of the true God, bowing down to the senseless images which their own hands had fashioned, indulging without restraint their own corrupt passions, were thus advancing his purposes, and opening the way for the advent of his Son. Thus, again, was that saying verified, "He maketh the wrath of man to praise him, and the remainder of wrath he will restrain."

One other condition remains yet to be observed. You well know that the nations inhabiting the shores of the Mediterranean were originally distinct in government, dissimilar in origin, diverse in laws, habits, and usages, and almost perpetually at war. To pass from one to the other, without incurring the risk of injury, nay, even of being sold into slavery, was almost impossible. A stranger and an enemy were designated by the same word. Beginning with Spain, and passing through Gaul, Germany, Italy, Greece, Asia Minor, Syria, Palestine, Egypt, and Carthage, until you arrive again at the Pillars of Hercules, every state was most commonly the enemy of every other. It was necessary that these various peoples should all be moulded by the same pressure into one common form; that one system of laws should bind them all in harmony; and that, under one common protection, a citizen might be able to pass through all of them in security. This seems to have been needful, in order that the new religion might be rapidly and extensively promulgated.

In order to accomplish this purpose, as I suppose, was the Roman empire raised up, and intrusted with the sceptre of universal dominion. Commencing with a feeble colony on the banks of the Tiber, she gradually, by conquest and conciliation, incorporated with herself the many warlike tribes of ancient Italy. In her very youth, after a death-struggle of more than a century, she laid Carthage, the former mistress of the Mediterranean, lifeless at her feet. From this era she paused not a moment in her career of universal conquest. Nation after nation submitted to her sway. Army after army was scattered before her legions, like the dust of the summer threshing-floor. Her proconsuls sat enthroned in regal state in every city of the civilized world; and the barbarian mother, clasping her infant to her bosom, fled to the remotest fastnesses of the wilderness, when she saw, far off in the distance, the sunbeams glittering upon the eagles of the republic.

Far different, however, were the victories of Rome from those of Alexander. The Macedonian soldier thought mainly of battles and sieges, the clash of onset, the flight of satraps, and the subjugation of kings. He overran; the Romans always conquered. Every vanquished nation became, in turn, a part of the Roman empire. A large portion of every conquered people was admitted to the rights of citizenship. The laws of the republic threw over the conquered the shield of her protection. Rome may, it is true, have oppressed them; but then she delivered them from the capricious and more intolerable oppression of their native rulers. Hence her conquests really marked the progress of civilization, and extended in all directions the limits of universal brotherhood. The Roman citizen was free of the civilized world; every where he might appeal to her laws, and repose in security under the shadow of her universal power. Thus the declaration, "Ye have beaten us openly and uncondemned, being Romans," brought the magistrates of Philippi suppliants at the feet of the apostle Paul; his question, "Is it lawful for you to scourge a man that is a Roman and uncondemned?" palsied the hands of the lictors at Jerusalem; and the simple words, "I appeal unto Cæsar," removed his cause from the jurisdiction even of the proconsul at Cæsarea, and carried it at once into the presence of the emperor. You cannot but perceive, that this universal domination of a single civilized power must have presented great facilities for the promulgation of the gospel. In many respects, it resembled the dominion of Great Britain at the present day in Asia. Wherever her red cross floats, there the liberty of man is, to a great extent, protected by the constitution of the realm. Whatever be the complexion or the language of the nations that take refuge beneath its folds, they look up to it every where, and bid defiance to every other despotism.

You see, then, in conclusion, that an extensive work of preparation was needed before the glory of the Lord should be revealed, and that new dispensation ushered in, which should endure to the end of time, and transform the kingdoms of this world into the kingdoms of our Lord and of his Christ. It was requisite that the powers of the human mind should arrive at vigorous manhood, that a language should be created capable of enunciating the message from on high with a distinctness that should bear the scrutiny of all coming ages; that this language should come into universal use, and that the civilized world should be united under a uniform government. After four thousand years, all this was accomplished. The fulness of time had come, and God sent forth his Son.

If this be so, we perceive that the overturnings of forty centuries were required in order to prepare the world for the advent of the Messiah. The same omniscient wisdom has ever since been engaged in carrying forward the work which was then commenced. Not only the revolutions of empire, but the astonishing changes in civilization produced by the discovery of America, the invention of the printing press, the steam engine, the railroad, and the electrical telegraph, have all been ordained with reference to the same grand result. The wrath of man still praises God, and the remainder of wrath he restrains. Centuries may roll away before the universal reign of the Messiah shall commence; but, if so extended be the work of preparation, what limit can be imagined to the duration of that kingdom which Christ shall establish over a redeemed and emancipated world? Ages of peace and righteousness may be confidently anticipated, in comparison with which the preliminary ages of sin and misery will in the retrospect dwindle to an almost invisible point. The number of the lost will be to the number of the saved as the small dust of the balance; the victory over sin will be triumphant; and this earth will again become a glorious light in the moral firmament of God.

Do I read the past history of our world aright? Is this the

true unveiling of the mystery that has covered so large a portion of the history of the human race? How astonishing a conception, then, is here presented of the far-reaching wisdom of the Deity! The myriads of our race, in the untrammelled exercise of all their powers, each one carrying forward the purposes of his own heart, and working out the problem of his probation for eternity, have been, at the same time, accomplishing the will of Him "who is wonderful in counsel," "in whose sight a thousand years are as one day, and one day is as a thousand years." "The weakness of God is stronger than man, and the foolishness of God is wiser than man." "The Lord reigneth, let the earth rejoice; let the multitude of isles be glad thereof." This is the God against whom every sinner is in rebellion, and with whom every one of us "has to do." Can there be any hope in such a contest? Can we oppose ourselves to such a God, and hope to prosper? "Be wise, then, O ye kings; be instructed, ye judges of the earth. Serve the Lord with fear, and rejoice with trembling. Kiss the Son, lest he be angry, and ye perish from the way when his wrath is kindled but a little. Blessed are all they that put their trust in him."

THE WORK OF THE MESSIAH.

PART I.

"GOD SENT FORTH HIS SON, MADE OF A WOMAN, MADE UNDER THE LAW, TO REDEEM THEM THAT WERE UNDER THE LAW."

Galatians iv. 4, 5.

THE apostle Paul, in the chapter preceding that from which the text is taken, illustrates the superiority of the gospel revealed to us by Christ over the law delivered to the Israelites by Moses. In accomplishing this purpose, he teaches us that the law, being merely preparatory, was, of course, an inferior dispensation, which ceased as soon as that to which it was introductory commenced. It accomplished, however, an important purpose, during the long interval that elapsed between the calling of Abraham and the appearance of the Messiah. "The law was our schoolmaster to bring us unto Christ." When, at last, every preparation had been fully made, — when the time, the set time, to favor Zion had come, — then "God sent forth his Son, made of a woman, made under the law, to redeem them that were under the law, that we might receive the adoption of sons."

These words, my brethren, seem to me to unfold to us some of those remarkable conditions under which the Messiah visited our world to do away sin by the sacrifice of himself. In the attempt to direct your meditations at this time, I propose simply to illustrate and develop the sentiment which they contain.

12 *

1. The text asserts that "God sent forth *his Son*." Who is intended to be designated by the term *Son*, I need scarcely pause to inform you. It is that divine Being who is elsewhere called "the Word," "who was in the beginning with God, who was God," "by whom all things were made, and without whom not any thing was made that was made."

2. God sent forth his Son, "*made of a woman.*" The term "made of a woman" intends, as I suppose, to assert that the Son appeared on earth a human being; that he took upon himself a human, in opposition to an angelic or any other nature. If this be true, then the Messiah possessed a perfect human constitution, endowed with all the powers and faculties belonging to such a constitution, just like any one of us. He possessed an understanding, a taste, a conscience, a will, appetites, passions, senses, just like our own, save only that they were not defiled with the stain of sin. "Wherefore he is not ashamed to call us brethren."

The same idea is frequently expressed in other passages of the Scriptures. Thus we are told, John i. 14, "The word *became flesh and dwelt* among us, full of grace and truth." Thus, also, 1 Tim. iii. 15, 16: "The pillar and ground of the truth, and without controversy, great is the mystery of godliness; God was manifest in the flesh." So, also, Romans ix. 5: "Whose are the fathers, and of whom, as concerning the flesh, Christ came, who is over all, God blessed forever." Thus, also, Philippians ii. 5—7: "Christ Jesus, who, being in the form of God, made himself of no reputation, and *took upon himself* the form of a servant, and was made in the likeness of men, and, being found in fashion as a man, he humbled himself, and became obedient to death, even the death of the cross." And lastly, for I need not multiply quotations, Hebrews ii. 14: "For as much then as the children are partakers of flesh and blood, (that is, of a human nature,) he also himself likewise took part of the same, that through death he might destroy him that had the power of death, that is, the devil." The meaning of these and similar passages, I suppose to be the following: The divine Being designated by the term *Word*, or Son of God, was united with a perfect human nature, in the person of Jesus of Nazareth; and this mysterious being was Christ, the Messiah, the anointed One, God manifest in the flesh, by whose obedience, sufferings, and intercession alone, the race of Adam can hope for eternal life.

3. God sent forth his Son, made of a woman, *made under the law*. What is the meaning of this last phrase — "made under the law"?

The law spoken of here must be either the ceremonial or the moral law.

The word *law* is used twice in the sentence which forms the text. In both cases it must have the same signification. It is said, in the latter clause, Christ came to redeem those who were under the law. The word here cannot mean the ceremonial law, since this exposition would restrict the blessings flowing from the atonement of Christ to the Jews, who were the only people under this law; and would also make the salvation of the gospel nothing more than a deliverance from ceremonial observances. It would thus teach us that the whole purpose for which Christ came upon earth was to emancipate the Jewish nation from the thraldom of the Mosaic ritual. Besides, in the clause succeeding the text, the meaning of the words "redeem those who were under the law" is explained by adding, "that we might receive the adoption of sons." Now, our receiving the adoption of sons could not be consequent upon the subjection of Christ to the ceremonial law; nor could it mean emancipation from that law, since, of those who received this adoption, the greater part never were under its dominion. I think it clear, then, that, in this case, the word *law* means, not the ceremonial, but the moral law. If such be its meaning in the one case, it is also its meaning in the other. When we say, therefore, that Christ was made under the law, we mean the moral law, that under which the human race was created, which they are bound to obey, and by which they will all be judged in the day of final account.

What, then, does the apostle mean, when he declares that Christ was *under* the moral law? You observe that Christ was made under the law "to redeem those that are *under* the law." It is evident that the expression in these two places has the same signification. We cannot, then, escape the conclusion that Christ was made under the law in the same sense that we are under the law.

When we say that we are under the law, we, I think, mean that we are under a constitution such that we suffer or enjoy in consequence of our disobedience or obedience to a law that has been made known to us. The assertion may be explained in a few words, thus: We were endowed, at our creation, with all the requisite powers, and surrounded with all proper inducements for keeping the law of God. We were gifted with an intellect to know, a conscience to admonish, and a will to determine; and sufficient motives were set before us to incline us to act virtuously. The law of God which we were required to obey was briefly this: "Thou shalt love the Lord thy God with all thy heart, and thy neighbor as thyself." Under these circumstances we were placed in a state of probation, and our eternal destiny was suspended upon our obedience or disobedience. If we had kept the law, eternal life would have been bestowed upon us through the merciful ordinance of God. If we failed even for once, our claim to salvation on the ground of law was forever annulled, and we became exposed to the righteous penalties of the precept which we had violated. But this is not all. It is manifestly an element of the constitution under which we are placed, that those who come after us must suffer or enjoy in consequence of our acts — acts with which they could have had no personal connection. Such is the constitution under which we all find ourselves to have been created, and to which Adam was in a particular manner subjected. Had Adam passed through his probation without sin, no one can tell in how far the moral peril of the probation of his posterity would have been diminished. He sinned, and involved all who came after him in the catastrophe of his transgression.*

Now, when we say that the Messiah was made under the moral law, it seems to me the same as to assert that he appeared upon earth, and lived, and died, under these same conditions. He placed himself under the same moral constitution as that under which the race of man was placed; or, in other words, the same as that under which Adam was originally placed in the garden of Eden.

When, however, I assert this, it is proper to remark that the Messiah voluntarily placed himself under this constitution. He was, in his divine nature, infinitely removed from the moral law proper for human nature. "He was before all things, and by him do all things consist." "The Word was in the beginning with God, and the Word was God." "Being in the form of God, he thought it not robbery to be equal with God, but *made himself* of no reputation, and *took upon him* the form of a servant." The Creator cannot, from his nature, be subject to the law of the creature. He, of his own incomprehensible benevolence, placed himself under the law which he had appointed for the creature in order to work out our redemption.

After, however, the Son of God had placed himself under the law of human nature, he became subject to it, in the same manner as that nature; that is, specially as Adam was subject to it, when he commenced his probation.† He was exposed to all the consequences of disobedience, and entitled to all the rewards of obedience, just as we suppose our first parent to have been before his fall. This, however, includes several particulars, which may properly be stated somewhat more explicitly.

On this part of our subject I would remark, first, he took upon himself a nature liable to sin. Were it otherwise, it would not have been a human nature; and he would neither have

* See Sermon p. 80. where this subject is more fully illustrated.

† This is manifestly the appropriate condition of human nature. The *sinful* condition of our race is an accident, and is evidently no part of the constitution under which our race was originally created.

been under the law, nor would he have been of the seed of Abraham. Had he not been liable to sin, I do not see in what would have consisted his virtue, either in resisting temptation or in triumphing over evil. What may be the forms of virtue in other states I know not, but, under the conditions of human nature, I think we never attribute virtue to an action unless the two courses, right and wrong, are both open before a man, and with entire freedom of will he chooses the one in preference to the other. The way of sin is therefore as fully open before a human being as the way of holiness; and from the conditions of his being, he is as liable to the one as to the other.*

Secondly. It follows, I think, from what I have said, that, if the Messiah had sinned, the consequences to himself would have been the same as to any one of us. The words of the law are, "Indignation and wrath, tribulation and anguish, upon every soul of man that doeth evil," and "glory, and honor, and peace to every man that doeth good." And "we know that what things soever the law saith, it saith to *them that are under the law.*" This was the law under which the Son of God was made.

* It may be proper here to remark, that in every case of human action there may be both a physical and a moral possibility or impossibility. Thus a man of tried virtue and goodness has it physically as much in his power to commit murder or theft as any other man. He has by nature passions and appetites which may be gratified by these or any other sins. His hunger, for instance, may be appeased by forbidden food. There is nothing to restrain him but his virtue. But that virtue may be so superior to this temptation, that, were it presented before him forever, he would never be overcome. We say, in such a case, that it is morally impossible for him to commit this sin. We recognize this distinction every day in our ordinary conversation. If a man is, from sickness, unable to move, he is incapable of crime in the one sense. If he be so virtuous that temptation is unable to seduce him, we say that he is incapable of crime in the other sense. Thus we frequently say of a good man, that he is incapable of lying; of a kind man, that he is incapable of cruelty. We suppose, then, that the Messiah was physically capable of sin, and liable to temptation, and that the only reason why he did not sin was his transcendent virtue.

By keeping it, he would, in his inferior nature, have been entitled to all its rewards; by disobeying it, he would have been exposed to the punishments which it threatened. If, however, it be here asked, How could punishment be inflicted on this mysterious Being, in whose person were united the divine and human nature? I willingly confess that I cannot explain it. There seems, however, to have been recorded various facts in his life which show that even this was not impossible. When on earth, without sin, his soul was exceedingly sorrowful even unto death. His nature, then, even here, was capable, as also we see in the garden of Gethsemane, of the direst extremity of pain. When on the cross, his Father's face was hidden from him. If his nature were capable of such a condition as this for an hour or a moment, it was capable of it for any period whatever.

Thirdly. But far other consequences than those that came upon himself were to result from the probationary existence of the Messiah. I have alluded to the element of the constitution under which our race was created by which we suffer or enjoy in consequence of acts in which we have had no participation. In virtue of this law, our first parents became, from the necessity of the case, in some sort representatives of their race. They fell. "By one man sin entered into the world." Their posterity have ever since been sinners. "By one man's disobedience, the many were made sinners." In what manner these consequences become entailed upon us, it is not necessary here to inquire. It is sufficient for us to observe the fact that results directly from what is here asserted, namely, that, in consequence of the sin of our first parents, the door of eternal life became practically closed to the whole of that race which came after them.

Now, it seems that this very element of the constitution under which we were created, and by which our race was ruined, is precisely that by which we are redeemed. By the sin of Adam, his posterity became sinners, the law of God was dishonored, the paternal authority of God set at defiance, and thus the way of life to man became closed. It was necessary, in order to our salvation, that this law should be perfectly obeyed by one in human nature; and obeyed in such a manner, and by one of such a character, as would reflect more honor on the purity of the law, and illustrate more gloriously to the universe the holiness of God, than we could have done by our obedience, or even by suffering forever the penalty which we had incurred. This was the great purpose for which Christ was manifest in the flesh. "He took not hold of the nature of angels, but he took hold of the seed of Abraham; wherefore *in all things* it behoved him to be made like unto his brethren."

The Messiah then came as the second Adam, to obey the law, which, in consequence of the disobedience of the first Adam, the whole race of man had broken. The possibility of the salvation of the whole race was conditioned upon his obedience. If he kept the law spotless and without blemish, if he magnified the law and made it honorable, God the Father would be well pleased for his righteousness' sake. If he passed triumphant in virtue through all the moral trials to which our nature could be exposed, a way of escape from eternal wrath was provided; the gate of heaven, before closed by our sins, was thrown wide open to every child of Adam; justice and mercy would meet together; God could be just, and yet the justifier of him that believeth in Jesus; the throne of God would be encircled with a more venerable and yet more lovely effulgence; and a manifestation of the attributes of the Eternal, more august than cherubim and seraphim had yet beheld, would burst forth upon principalities and powers in heavenly places. But if, on the other hand, the Messiah had sinned,—if the wickedness of man, or the temptations of Satan, had seduced him by word, or thought, or deed, from the line of perfect obedience to the holy law of God,—all this would have been reversed. The Messiah himself must have borne, with ourselves, the curse of that law under which he, in common with the race of man, had placed himself. The gate of heaven, closed a second time to our race, would have been sealed without the possibility of hope;

and our whole apostate family, not one exempt, would have peopled the regions of despair. Nay, more: the plan of redemption, on which the wisdom of Omniscience had been exhausted, would have proved abortive. That effort of infinite compassion, by which it was intended to save a race of perishing sinners, would have only rendered their perdition more hopeless by the very sacrifice of his well-beloved Son. The counsel of Heaven would have been covered with confusion. Infinite mercy would have wrought nothing but misery.*

On this conflict, then, we may well suppose that the destinies of the universe were suspended. By the obedience of the Messiah was it to be determined whether sin or holiness should be henceforth in the ascendant. Well may we suppose that our earth, at that moment, presented a spectacle on which all intelligent creatures were gazing with all-absorbing interest. Well might the Holy Spirit descend in a visible form on the head of Him who was first girding himself for this mighty contest. Well might the Eternal Father cheer him with his presence, and declare to the universe, "This is my beloved Son, in whom I am well-pleased." Well might Moses and Elias seize an opportunity on the mount of transfiguration to speak with him respecting the decease which he should accomplish at Jerusalem. Well might angels be seen ministering to him, when his nature, exhausted by fasting, or pressed

* It may be objected to the view here taken, that I have not duly considered the class of passages which lay a peculiar stress on the blood of Christ as a sacrifice for sin, the death of Christ as procuring our redemption, the offering up of Christ, &c. To this I would reply, that I by no means have forgotten these passages, nor am I disposed, in the least degree, to attenuate their meaning. No view of any subject of revelation can be correct if it do not allow the full and obvious meaning of every class of passages which treat upon that subject. It may, therefore, be proper to remark that, in treating of the work of Christ, the Scriptures seem to me to develop two ideas — the one, the obedience of Christ to the law; the other, the offering up of himself as a sacrifice for sin. It is to the first of these alone that the attention of the reader is directed in the present discourse. The subject is further considered in the following sermon.

down by the weight of a world's redemption, was sinking beneath its burden. No wonder that the earth quaked, and the rocks rent, and the sun was shrouded in darkness, on that fearful hour in which was decided the fate of the whole moral universe. But, if all the powers of heaven were thus interested in the event of this conflict, we may well believe that the powers of hell beheld it with the intensest apprehension. By the result of the Messiah's mission was it to be decided whether they were to defeat the purposes of the Holy One, or be covered with tenfold confusion, and made the scorn and abhorrence of the universe of God. Hence all their hosts were summoned to the onset. A peculiar and unusual power over the race of man seems at this time to have been conceded to them. This was, no doubt, exerted to the uttermost. Nor this alone. The Messiah himself seems to have been exposed more directly than any of us to the temptations of the hosts of Satan. Every means that infernal cunning could suggest, or desperate malignity direct, was plied to the uttermost, in order, if possible, to seduce the Messiah into sin, and thus defeat the purposes of infinite goodness. Well was it for our race that our help was laid on one that was mighty. What created virtue could have passed through such a trial unscathed? None but God manifest in the flesh could have accomplished the work which was given to the Redeemer to do. And hence do we see how immeasurable a meaning is given to the words, "God *so* loved the world that he gave his only-begotten Son." Eternity itself will fail to explore the length, and breadth, and depth, and height, of the love of God, which passeth knowledge — that love which so put in jeopardy the whole interests of the universe, to save from perdition a race of creatures who had rebelled against a holy and most merciful law.*

---

* If the view here taken of the conditions of the Messiah's mission be correct, it will, I think, throw some light upon the question so frequently asked, *In what manner* did Christ's appearing upon earth have any effect upon our moral relations? To this various replies have been presented. It has been said that his unparalleled humil

II. Let us now survey this transaction from another point of view, and endeavor to form a conception of the life of Christ under the conditions which we have endeavored thus imperfectly to explain.

1. Every one of us may possibly know, from experience how oppressive is the weight of solemn and important responsibility. There are critical moments in the life of almost every man, when the whole color of his destiny has been determined by a single decision. He who remembers these eras in his history needs not to be reminded of the fear and trembling with which he approached them. The soul, in such circumstances, bowed down beneath the responsibility under which its decision must be pronounced, feels distinctly that it could not possibly exist, were this anxiety to be long continued. So intolerable is the pressure of this overwhelming care, that men generally hasten to almost any decision in order to be relieved from it, preferring any consequence whatever to the torture of insufferable doubt.

The case, however, becomes vastly more oppressive when

iation, or his lowly and painful life, his bitter death, were of the nature of a suffering of the penalty of the law. I, however, apprehend that this explanation has not always been satisfactory to those who have borne in mind the character of the law which we have violated, and the awful holiness of the Being against whom we have sinned. Besides, the sufferings of Christ, considered by themselves, were not severer, nor was his death, in itself, more excruciating than that of many martyrs, confessors, and missionaries. And yet, again, when the question is asked, how does such a life, if this be all, meet the demands of the law? how is it in so special a manner a moral victory? I think we generally feel that this transaction is a mystery of which we would like to see a clear solution. If, however, we go beyond this outward appearance, and consider that this life was really spent under a liability to all the consequences of sin, and that this virtue, thus exhibited, did really triumph over every attack that could be made upon it by all the hosts of hell, we seem, to me, to approach nearer to an answer to these questions; while, at the same time, the whole transaction assumes a moral grandeur, in comparison with which every other fact in the history of the world turns pale.

not only our own destinies, but those of others, are deeply affected by our decisions. I can conceive of no situation more intensely painful to a benevolent mind than that in which the happiness or misery of multitudes is suspended upon the deliberations of our own finite intelligence. A crisis of this kind, happily, does not frequently occur in the ordinary walks of life. There are, however, rare situations, in which men are called habitually to act under the pressure of such responsibility. Where this is the case, the heart, unless sustained by the highest attainments in virtue, becomes callous and indifferent to the result; or else the intellect itself gives way beneath a burden of anxiety too heavy to be borne by human nature. Politicians and statesmen, more directly than other men, are placed in the circumstances to which I have referred; and hence it is that their annals are so replete, on the one hand, with instances of remorseless and revolting selfishness, and, on the other, with those of derangement, suicide, and sudden death.

In the case of the Messiah, however, not temporal but eternal interests were suspended upon his decisions. It was not merely the result of his actions upon his own happiness or misery, but their result upon the happiness or misery of innumerable millions that pressed with overwhelming anxiety upon his holy soul. It was not merely the happiness or misery of created beings, be they ever so numerous, or how largely soever susceptible of pleasure or pain; it was the honor of that holy law which, in the presence of the universe, he had undertaken to magnify, which was perilled upon the condition of his sinless obedience. And yet more: these stupendous consequences were not suspended upon a single hour, or day, or year of the Messiah's life, but upon every action, every word, every thought, every motive, throughout his whole probationary existence. Every moral bias, during his continuance under the law, was put forth under the pressure of this infinite responsibility. Had he but once disobeyed God; had he acted from one guilty or even one imperfect motive had he, for a single moment, exercised any thing less than the full measure of that love which was due to his Father in heaven, and to his brethren of the human race,—all would have been lost; the scheme of man's redemption would have stood recorded in the annals of eternity a solemn failure, and the cunning and malice of hell would have triumphed over the wisdom and holiness of heaven.

To spend a life on earth, with a full knowledge of the consequences which were thus suspended upon every moment, must have been awful beyond any thing of which the human mind can adequately conceive. There were, however, circumstances in the life of the Messiah which must have aggravated, beyond description, the agony which he suffered.

It will assist us to form a conception of the life of Christ, if we, for a moment, in the first place, compare it, in this respect, with that of Adam. Adam is styled, in the Scriptures, the type or emblem of Him who was to come. The reason of this designation is obvious. Our first parent stood in a relation to the race similar to that held by the Messiah. Had our progenitor kept the law inviolate, and passed through his probation without sin, the course of human life would have commenced, and perhaps would have continued, sinless; just as, "by the transgression of one," on the other hand, "the many were made sinners." So the Messiah, the second Adam, standing in the same relation to our race, on his obedience or failure, the destiny of us all was a second time contingent. But how immeasurably different were the conditions of these our two representatives! The soul of Adam awoke to consciousness in a pure and holy world. Nothing was reflected back from every object around him but the unsullied image of the Creator. God himself was his instructor and his companion. There was no example of sin to corrupt him. There was no infliction of injustice to exasperate him. There was no act of ingratitude to grieve him. Every thing around him was very good; and every thing was created with the express intention of fostering the principle of holiness within him. And, moreover, he entered upon this state without ever having seen any thing more glorious. It was comparatively easy for him to pass through his probation unharmed, and thus to impress the seal of righteousness upon his whole posterity.

The Messiah, on the contrary, entered a world lying in wickedness; a world without God. Every face that he saw had been marked with the image of the prince of darkness. The very elements of its society had received their form and pressure from the enemy of all righteousness. What a contrast did it form with the world that he had left! He had exchanged the peace and harmony of heaven for the war and discords of earth; the anthems of seraphim for the blasphemies of men. The adoration of the hosts of heaven, who accompanied him to the confines of our world, had hardly ceased, when he was assailed by the scornful revilings of the worms upon his footstool.

Again: when men are placed in circumstances of peculiar trial, they are of necessity intimately associated together. The chief actor in a momentous enterprise unites with himself others who sympathize in his motives, comprehend his plans, carry forward his designs, and who would cheerfully sacrifice their lives in behalf of the cause in which all are equally engaged. How much this tends to alleviate anxiety, and soften the pressure of otherwise intolerable care, I surely need not remind you.

None of these ameliorating circumstances, however, relieved the anxieties of Jesus of Nazareth. Of all the beings who have dwelt upon our earth, none was ever so emphatically a lone man as the Messiah. In the prophetic language of Isaiah, "he trode the wine-press alone, and of the people there was none with him." At the commencement of his public ministry, all his family, his mother only excepted, discarded him as a madman. Though he selected his immediate companions from his most promising disciples, yet not one of them could comprehend his plans, or form even a remote conception of the nature of his mission. Even after his resurrection, their views of the result of his advent reached not beyond the establishment of a temporal sovereignty, and the conferring of universal dominion upon the descendants of Abraham. "Lord," said they unto him, "wilt thou at this time restore the kingdom to Israel?" Nay, on the very night in which he was betrayed, when, about to enter upon his bitter passion, he was attempting to prepare them for the coming events, they interrupted him by an altercation arising out of the question, who should be the greatest in the approaching revolution. Thus, without sympathy, wholly without a helper, he bore the weight of his own sorrows; while he was working out, unaided, the deliverance of a world from the condemnation of the law.

But while thus destitute of friends, who were capable of sympathizing with him, he suffered, as no other being on earth ever suffered, the unmitigated infliction of this world's enmity. If any thing could have moved him to wrath, he must have been so moved by the treatment which he received from those whom he came from heaven to seek and to save. He came to suffer the will and obey the law of God, to rescue us from eternal perdition; and how was he welcomed? In infancy his life was sought for by Herod. As he travelled on foot over the plains of Judea and the mountains of Galilee, the common hospitalities of life were denied him. "The foxes have holes, and the birds of the air have nests, but the Son of man hath not where to lay his head." If he did not work miracles, his authority was denied; if he wrought them on the Sabbath, he was accused of breaking his Father's commandment; if he wrought them on any other day, his power was ascribed to collusion with the prince of devils. If he taught plainly, he excited the malice of the scribes, and they conspired against his life; if he spoke in parables, they scoffed at him as a madman and a demoniac. Every truth that he revealed was uttered in the presence of avowed enemies, or of treacherous friends, who, with fiendish ingenuity, wrested his words and strove to distort his holy precepts into blasphemy. To have refrained from speaking would have displeased his Father, for he came from heaven to be a light unto the world. To speak was to arouse that ceaseless enmity which was only awaiting a fit occasion to raise the universal cry, "Crucify him! crucify him! away with such a fellow from the earth!" Every act, which fiendish ingenuity could invent, was plied to the uttermost to tempt him to sin; and had he but once sinned, his tempters, with their whole race, would have been consigned to remediless perdition.

But this is not all. I have already remarked that he was incessantly exposed to the most subtle temptations of all the powers of darkness. Of the manner of these temptations we have a recorded example in two of the evangelists. From this single instance, we may learn that every circumstance of his eventful life was employed with consummate address to lead the Messiah into sin. In the extremity of hunger and exhaustion, he was pressed to put forth his miraculous power in a manner not permitted by his Father, that so he might betray impatience to the allotments of Providence. In his loneliness and humiliation, when, his mission not having been confided to a single soul, he was a solitary being on earth, all the kingdoms of the world are offered him as the reward of a single act of transgression. And when, strong in holy confidence, he had repelled every temptation, even this confidence is employed to tempt him to a mode of reliance on God not warranted by his dealings with men.

This, however, is but a single incident in the Messiah's life from which the veil has been removed by the hand of inspiration. But if the acts of the tempter were thus plied in loneliness, in the wilderness, when the Savior had retired for the purposes of devotion, with what earnestness must they have been redoubled in the city, among the multitude, when the successive incidents of his life afforded incomparably better hope that they might be tried with advantage! What must have been the suggestions of the adversary, when the malignity of enemies and the ingratitude of friends tried his tender spirit to the uttermost? And let us not forget that thus tempted from without, and assaulted from within, every action of his life was performed under the fearful responsibility of a world's salvation. Who, but the Son of God, was equal to such a trial? Had not our help been laid on One that was mighty to save, where could have been the shadow of hope for any of our race?

Such was the life of Christ. But he had yet a baptism to be baptized with, in comparison with which all that he had yet undergone was tolerable. In view of this, he prayed his Father that, if it were possible, this cup might pass from him. He prayed thus three times. The anticipation of the trial through which he must pass, so overwhelmed his physical nature, that the blood gushed from every pore, forced out by agony too great for human endurance.

In order to estimate the intensity of the Messiah's suffering, consider, for a moment, the elements of agony that were concentrated in the crisis of his passion. The slight consolations that he had received from human sympathy were withdrawn, and he was delivered up into the hands of merciless ruffians. His disciples leave him alone, and one, the oldest and the most zealous, denies, with imprecations, that he had ever even known him. Human malice is unchained, that it may exert upon him its whole power without control. The Lamb of God is smitten with the fist, spit upon, and crowned with thorns. All this is but the prelude to death in its most agonizing form. The immaculate Son of God must endure the public death of an ignominious felon. What death is, no one of us can know from experience; much less can we know what is endured in a violent, lingering, and cruel death by murder. But every one, who has stood by the bedside of a departing friend, can form some, though it be an inadequate, conception of that hour when the powers of the mind are prostrated by disease, and the soul, environed on every side by the extremity of suffering, feels the power of self-government giving way under the pressure of intolerable anguish. If such be death to any one of us, what must it have been to pass through this hour as the Messiah did, with the destinies of the world suspended on his sinless obedience?

But this was not all. The infernal spirits had thus far tempted him utterly in vain. The warfare was nearly accomplished, and as yet they had achieved no victory; one conflict only remained. The last effort was now to be made, and with better prospect of success than they had before dared to hope for. They had succeeded in isolating the Savior from every human aid. The moment of nature's weakness was the time of their chosen opportunity. The Messiah must come specially within their power, as he was delivering the race of man from it forever. "It was their hour, and the power of darkness." Every earthly support had been withdrawn from him. The very power of self-control was trembling under the pressure of agony too great to be endured. The will could scarcely retain its authority amidst the struggles of expiring nature. Now, now, could the Messiah be tempted to sin; now, could he be made to yield even to an unholy thought, or put forth an impatient desire, their whole work would be accomplished. The whole power of hell was therefore concentrated to overwhelm him at this awful crisis. Under such conditions did the Savior pass through the hour of death.

But lastly: up to this hour, the Spirit had been poured out without measure upon him. Thus far he had been upheld by constant and reciprocal communion with his Father and our Father, with his God and our God. But at this moment, even this light, that had thus far cheered him, was withdrawn, and he passed through the valley of the shadow of death in utter darkness. All support, created and uncreated, was removed, and he was left to the unaided strength of his own personal virtue. What an hour was that in the annals of eternity! The endless destiny of countless myriads, the honor of the law of

God, the decision of that contest which must end in the triumph of heaven or the triumph of hell, the question whether Messiah should sink under the curse of the law to which he had subjected himself, or be raised in his assumed nature to the throne of the universe, — all were suspended upon the strength of the Savior's virtue under this awful trial. He cried, "My God, my God, why hast thou forsaken me?" There was darkness over all the land. There was silence in heaven. Seraphim and cherubim, awe-struck, looked down upon this unparalleled moral contest. On its issue there seems to have depended the happiness or misery of the moral universe of God.

The moments of agony slowly rolled away. The powers of hell had gained no advantage. The Messiah, strong in his own unaided virtue, had baffled every attack of earth and hell, and shone glorious in untarnished holiness. His last moment has arrived. Doth he yet maintain his integrity? Doth he, amidst these unfathomable trials of his benevolence, still love his neighbor as himself? Hearken to the prayer that quivers upon his parched and feverish lips: "Father, forgive them, for they know not what they do." Although forsaken of his Father and his God, doth he yet trust in him with filial confidence? Hearken again: "Father, into thy hands I commit my spirit." The warfare was accomplished. The victory was won. He said, "It is finished, and gave up the ghost."

The work was done. The victory was achieved. He had sustained his unparalleled trial, holy, harmless, and undefiled. The law of God was magnified and made honorable. An illustration of the holiness of God had been made, so glorious that the condemnation of the race of man would have been as nothing to it. The subtilty of the hosts of hell was turned to foolishness. The malignity of Satan was covered with eternal shame. The seed of the woman had crushed the head of the serpent. The race of Adam was delivered from the curse of the law, and a way, even into the holiest of holies, was opened to us, through the blood of the everlasting covenant. "Mercy and truth had met together, righteousness and peace had kissed each other." Every attribute of God shone forth upon the whole moral universe with a new and more resplendent effulgence. And all this was accomplished by means of the Messiah's holiness. "Wherefore, also, God hath highly exalted him, and given him a name which is above every name; that at the name of Jesus every knee should bow, whether of things in heaven, and things in earth, and things under the earth, and that every tongue should confess that Jesus Christ is Lord to the glory of God the Father." And hence, also, as he ascended to his native heaven in triumph over all the powers of darkness, a new song burst forth from the redeemed of every kindred, and tongue, and people, and nation, and from all the angels round about the throne, saying, with a loud voice, "Worthy is the Lamb, that was slain, to receive power, and riches, and wisdom, and strength, and honor, and glory, and blessing;" while this song was reëchoed from every creature in heaven, and on earth, and under the earth, saying, "Blessing, and honor, and glory, and power, to him that sitteth upon the throne, and to the Lamb, forever."

THE WORK OF THE MESSIAH.

PART II.

"THOU HAST ASCENDED ON HIGH, THOU HAST LED CAPTIVITY CAPTIVE, THOU HAST RECEIVED GIFTS FOR MEN, YEA, FOR THE REBELLIOUS ALSO, THAT THE LORD GOD MIGHT DWELL AMONG THEM."

Psalm lxviii. 18.

IN the last discourse, I endeavored to present a conception of the manner of life of the Messiah on earth. I then took occasion to show that he perfectly fulfilled that law under which he had voluntarily placed himself; he triumphed over all the powers of darkness, and, having accomplished his whole work on earth, he said, "It is finished," bowed his head, and yielded up his spirit. He, in human nature, obeyed the law which we had violated, in the words of the apostle, "condemned sin in the flesh," "and spoiled principalities and powers, making a show of them openly."

This, however, was only a part of his work as the Messiah. He took upon himself *human* nature. He was made of a woman, made *under the law*. It behoved him to pass through all the changes to which those born of women are subjected. Until all this was accomplished, his work, as our representative, was not completed. Let us see whether we are able, by the light of revelation, to trace out his work any further.

The Scriptures, I think, teach us that the human race must exist in three successive states. First, in the state of a spirit united to a mortal body — such are we at present; secondly, in the state of spirit disconnected with a body; and thirdly, that of spirit united with a glorified, or, as the apostle terms it, a spiritual body.

Our blessed Lord, during his residence on earth, had passed through the first of these conditions of human nature. "He was in all points like as we are, yet without sin."

At death, the Messiah entered upon the second state to which we are appointed. His body was laid in the tomb of Joseph, and it continued there from the evening of the sixth to the morning of the first day of the week. The body was actually dead, the executioners themselves being witnesses. And to make assurance yet more sure, a soldier, by a wound in the Savior's side, that must have severed organs essential to life, rendered all deception or error impossible. The spirit or soul of the Messiah was then separated from his mortal body. It dwelt in the place of departed spirits. All this is stated in the first sermon that was preached after the resurrection. Quoting from the sixteenth Psalm, the apostle Peter says, "I foresaw the Lord always before my face, for he is on my right hand, that I should not be moved; therefore did my heart rejoice, and my tongue was glad; moreover, also, my flesh" (my human body) "shall rest in hope, because thou wilt not *leave* my soul in hell, neither wilt thou suffer thy holy One to see corruption," (to suffer decay;) "thou hast made known to me the ways of life," (thou wilt bring me to life again,) "thou wilt make me full of joy with thy countenance," (thou wilt raise me to the fulness of joy at thy right hand.) The apostle shows that these words could never have been true of David, since he never rose again, but his flesh saw corruption and decay, like that of any other human being. They are, however, perfectly true of the Messiah. "David," said he, "being a prophet, and knowing that God had sworn with an oath, to him, that of the fruit of his loins, according to the flesh, he would raise up Christ to sit upon his throne, he, seeing this before, spake of the resurrection of *Christ*, that *his* soul was not left in hell, neither did *his flesh* see corruption."

The word translated *hell* here is "*hades*," a word signifying, originally, the *invisible*, and used, commonly, for the invisible world, the place of the departed. It differs generically from the word *gehenna*, which is used invariably to designate the place of future punishment reserved for the ungodly. You see, then, that the apostle does not teach us that the soul of the Messiah, at death, entered heaven; but merely hades, or the abode of separate spirits.

But what do we know of the residence of Messiah in this unseen world? I must confess our knowledge on this subject to be but limited. We know that this invisible world is a place either of pleasure or of pain. The apostle speaks of being absent from the body and present with the Lord. He says, that so far as his own choice was concerned, he would rather be thus transferred from the present state of trial to that of eternal rest. Our Savior promised to the thief on the cross, "This day shalt thou be *with me in paradise*." It was a promise to a dying penitent. It spoke to him of consolation, and of future happiness. It could have meant neither annihilation, nor unconsciousness, but exceeding joy. It was, then, to the bliss of this invisible state that the Messiah was himself drawing near. He was about to conduct this first-born of the redeemed to the mansions which he was going to prepare for all those that love him.

On the other hand, this same hades, the place of the departed, is spoken of as a place of hopeless misery. "The poor man died, and was carried of angels to Abraham's bosom." "The rich man also died, and was buried, and in *hell* he lifted up his eyes, being in torments, and seeth Abraham afar off, and Lazarus in his bosom." From such passages as these, we may, I think, learn that there is a state into which all men pass between the hour of death and the morning of the resurrection; a state in which the soul exists separate from the body; a state of joy unutterable to the pious, and of sorrow intolerable to the wicked; and that into this state the Messiah entered, and continued there until, by his own power, he rose again from the dead.

What was the object of the Messiah in entering this state? I must confess myself unable fully to answer this question. We shall all be satisfied on this subject when we ourselves have entered it. In our present state, there is much about it that is mysterious. One or two suggestions may, however, throw some light upon this interesting inquiry.

The Scriptures, as you must all have perceived, speak with great emphasis of the *death* of Christ, of his *offering up himself*, and being by his death specially the means of our redemption. It may be that there were some parts of this great transaction that could be perfected only at or after his death. It may be that in death he offered himself up as an expiatory sacrifice, ready and willing to bear all that the law of God might require as the price of our redemption. This may be the meaning of the apostle when he says, "If the blood of bulls and of goats sanctifieth to the purifying of the flesh, how much more shall the blood of Christ, who, through the eternal Spirit," (in his eternal spiritual nature,) "*offered up himself without spot* to God, purge your consciences from dead works to serve the living God?" Here the apostle seems to refer to the offering up of himself after he had shown himself to be without spot. This would lead us to believe that a part of this great work of the Messiah was to be performed after death. It seems to intimate that after his obedience on earth was complete, he surrendered himself up, to suffer in our behalf all that was necessary in order to render our pardon and redemption consistent with infinite holiness. His obedience, however, had been so transcendent in virtue, he had so triumphantly vanquished all our spiritual enemies, and put to shame all the powers of darkness, that I know not whether any thing more was demanded. "The Lord was well pleased for his righteousness' sake," (his obedience,) "for he had magnified the law and made it honorable." That this was the case would seem probable, because there is no reference in the Scriptures to his suffering after death. This offering up of himself, however, may have belonged to the invisible world. Earth had no theatre on which such a scene could have been enacted. It belonged to the spiritual world; it had respect to the whole creation of spiritual intelligences, and before them alone could it be appropriately displayed.

Again: the unseen world is the place in which the race of man spend by far the greater portion of their existence prior to the resurrection. Christ had established his dominion on earth by triumphing over all our enemies. It may be that it was necessary for him to establish his dominion in that other state, through which also we must pass. In what manner his residence and triumph, there, will affect our condition, I know not that I am able to affirm. I can, however, very well conceive that it would have been a very different state for the believer, if Christ had not entered it, and thus triumphed over all our enemies, as our forerunner, representative, and head. I know that where he went, there it will be safe and glorious for the believer to follow. I know that where he established his dominion, there it will be blissful for a holy soul to rest. I know that where he has prepared a place for us, there we shall be filled with joy unspeakable and full of glory.

Besides, we all know and feel that, in consequence of the mission of Christ to our world, the race of man, in its present state, is brought immeasurably nearer to God. God becomes our Father, and believers are his children. His spirit dwells on earth, and holds communion with the spirits of the contrite. We may thus hold direct and filial intercourse with God. Nothing but our worldliness and sin prevents him from manifesting himself to us here, perhaps as unreservedly as he did to our first parents before they transgressed. Heaven has thus been opened to us, and the angels of God are now ascending and descending upon the son of man. The meaning of this symbolical language is, I think, apparent; Messiah is the medium of intercourse between earth and heaven.

Now, it may be that the abode of the Messiah in the place of departed spirits, and the accomplishment of his work there, may have brought that state also into more intimate communion with Heaven, and rejoiced the spirits of the just with new displays of the character of the Most High. Who can tell how much more brightly the beams of eternal love shine upon that spiritual world, in consequence of the veil which he drew aside, when he burst the bars of death, and rose triumphant over the grave?

I know not but this may also explain to us the passages in which believers, at death, are said to be present with the Lord. It may be, that, in consequence of his triumph there, the communication between heaven and the believing soul is so fully and unreservedly established, that it is even as though he were there continually present. It may be, that, in consequence of his work there, he is able, through the long period of separate existence, to manifest himself to the spirits of the redeemed by such immeasurable outpouring of his Spirit as could not else have been possible. Thus his abode there once, would render it the same to the believer, as though he were always present. Again: we are informed of the triumph which attended his entrance upon his work of humiliation. Who can tell how glorious in holiness and love must his manifestation of himself have been there, when his work of sorrow was completed, and he had begun to taste the joys of his well-earned victory! How delightful would it be could we here on earth listen to the history of the Savior's life, from the lips of those who were eye-witnesses of his acts, and who, with their own ears, had received his instructions! But how much more glorious may we expect will be the narrative of his appearing from all the company of the redeemed, who consorted with him during the period of his residence in the spiritual state! The few words which have come down to us of his teaching on earth have furnished matter for profoundest contemplation to the most gifted and holy men who have lived since his advent. How wonderful may we suppose to have been the light which Christ in his spiritual state has shed upon all that has gone before in the lapse of ages, and all that shall follow in the cycles of eternity!

But I must turn from this subject to another. Before leaving it, however, I beg to say that I do not offer all these suggestions as a part of revealed truth. I offer them rather as probable suppositions. They may be all, or some, or none of them, true. But one thing, I am sure, is true; we shall find, when we enter the spiritual state, that the reasons for the Savior's existence there were both more numerous, and more glorious than we, in our present state, can possibly conceive.

Whatever may have been the reasons for the abode of the Messiah in the separate state, which we denominate *death*, it was not possible that he should be holden of it. When his work there was accomplished, it was appointed that he should enter upon the third state to which our nature is to be raised. Of his own power he returned to life, for he "had power to lay down his life, and he had power to take it again."

The reason given in the Scriptures for his appearing again in human nature is twofold. "He died for our sins," saith the apostle Paul, "and was raised again for our justification." The terms "for our justification," I do not suppose, mean, that we may be justified, but that the *evidence* might be given, that our justification had been effected. Jesus Christ had predicted to his friends and his enemies that he should rise again. "Destroy this temple," said he, speaking of the temple of his body, "and in three days I will raise it again." "After I am risen again, I will go before you into Galilee." If he had not risen as he had said, there would have been wanting proof, notwithstanding all his miracles, that he was *the Messiah*. We should have known that a divine personage had come upon earth to teach us, and that he had undertaken, by his mediatorial work, to accomplish our redemption; but whether his undertaking had been successful would have been ever doubtful. Who could tell whether his mediation had been accepted, and whether a way into the holiest of holies had yet been opened to every one that believeth? But, by his resurrection, all these questions were answered. It was now evident that he was all that he claimed to be, and that God was well pleased for his righteousness' sake. He had triumphed over death, the result of our transgressions; and hence it was evident that, as our nature had vanquished death, it had become to us a conquered enemy, and that sin, which was the cause of it, might now be pardoned, and sinners of the human race justified.

But this was not all. Thus far, there had been no clear revelation, either of the fact or the manner of man's immortality. The ancients generally had a belief of the existence of the human spirit after death. The Hebrews, as we have seen, called it *hades*, the place of the invisible. They also believed that it was a condition of rewards and punishments. A most magnificent poetical description of this state is found in the triumphal song of the Hebrews over the king of Assyria, in the fourteenth chapter of the prophecy of Isaiah. But how long this state would continue, whether it was to extend without change forever, or to be terminated at some remote period, by the return of the soul to this world, they knew not. It seems to have been necessary, by a visible illustration, to bring life and immortality to light; and thus to abolish death, by showing that the power of Death had been destroyed, and his sceptre broken forever.

Now, this was accomplished by the resurrection of the Messiah. He subjected himself to death. His mangled corpse was laid in the tomb of Joseph. A great stone was laid over the door of the sepulchre. The seal of the governor was placed upon it. A Roman guard was stationed around it, for the express purpose of preventing deception. "We remember that this deceiver said while he was yet alive, After three days, I will rise again: command, therefore, that the sepulchre be made sure until the third day." Every means that power or ingenuity could devise, was employed to retain the body of the Messiah in the grave, and thus baffle the hopes of his bewildered disciples.

On the morning of the third day, when his followers were covered with shame, because they had expected that this had been he who was to redeem Israel, while his few remaining friends were already preparing spices to embalm the corpse of the teacher whom they loved, that body underwent a most miraculous transformation. That change passed upon it which we have ever since called a resurrection. The spirit was again reunited to it. It became once more instinct with life. Remarkable prodigies attended the event. There was a great earthquake, "for the angel of the Lord descended from heaven, and came and rolled back the stone from the door, and sat upon it. His countenance was like lightning, and his raiment white as snow, and for fear of him the keepers did shake, and become as dead men." Henceforth the Messiah appeared as the first fruits of them that slept.

But what is the meaning of the words, "the *first fruits* of them that slept"? How was the Messiah the "*first fruits*"? Several cases had before occurred in which the dead had been restored to life, and the spirit recalled to inhabit again its tabernacle of clay. The young man whose dead body touched the bones of the prophet Elisha, arose again to life. The prophet himself restored from the dead the son of the Shunammite woman. Our Lord had raised to life the son of the widow of Nain. In a more solemn and public manner, in the presence of a multitude, he had recalled the spirit of Lazarus, who had lain four days in the grave. These were all cases in which the spirit had been reunited to the body after they had been for a greater or less time separated from each other. In what sense, then, was it true that the risen Messiah was the *first fruits* of them that slept?

I answer: the difference between the two cases is exceeding great. Those which I have spoken of were merely instances of revivification. The spirit was recalled to inhabit again a mortal body, still under the power of death, and, by the conditions of its being, again, by necessity, to die as it had died before, and crumble back to its original dust. In these cases, the power of death was only for a time arrested. It was demonstrated that there was a being who had authority, when he chose, and in particular instances, to loosen for a moment the bands of death. But in these cases, Death again resumed his dominion. Those who had been raised to life, were raised only to a mortal life, and were still subject to corruption. It was not by these instances shown that an immortal life was in reserve for us, and that we were at last to come off victorious over the grave.

But with the resurrection of the Messiah, the case was far otherwise. This was not a revivification; it was a resurrection. The mortal body was changed into a glorious, an immortal, an incorruptible body, no more liable to death; and with this body the spirit of Christ was again united. It was in this glorified body that he appeared after his resurrection. It was in this that he ascended. It is this that he wears on the right hand of God. It is in this that he is the head over all things to his church; and thus will he continue, until he shall have delivered up the kingdom to God, even the Father. It is in this respect that he is the first fruits. And as he, our representative and head, has been clothed with this body, so shall every one of us be clothed with a similar, an incorruptible body.

But what is this spiritual body? I confess I cannot tell. There is nothing like it among things material. Neither I nor any one on earth has ever seen it; nor, probably, could we cognize it by any of our senses. The apostle Paul, who, in the fifteenth chapter of the First of Corinthians, has treated on this subject more at large than it is elsewhere treated of, speaks of it as a mystery. He pretends not to describe it, but reasons analogically to show that our inability to cognize it is no proof that it does not exist. All the information which he gives is summed up in these words: "It is sown in corruption, it is raised in incorruption. It is sown in dishonor, it is raised in glory. It is sown in weakness, it is raised in power. It is sown a natural body, it is raised a spiritual body."

Now, with this description, — if indeed description it may be called, — the body borne by the Messiah, so far as we can see, corresponded. It seems to have changed all its relations to matter. The stone at the mouth of the sepulchre could not confine it. That stone was rolled away, not to allow the spiritual body of the Messiah to come forth, but to allow the weeping disciples, who had come to embalm him, to see the place where their Lord had lain. Bolts and bars could not exclude it, for when the doors were shut, where the disciples were assembled for fear of the Jews, came Jesus, and stood in the midst, and saith unto them, "Peace be unto you."

It seems to have been a body henceforth incapable of suffering from any form of material injury. It yet bore, unharmed, the print of the nails in its hands, and that ghastly wound in the side, made by the spear of the soldier. "Then saith he to Thomas, Reach hither thy finger, and behold my hands, and reach hither thy hand, and thrust it into my side, and be not faithless, but believing." But these wounds created neither pain nor suffering to this glorified body. Nay, are we not taught that the spiritual body of the Messiah yet bears those scars which it received in its last conflict with our spiritual enemies? "I beheld, and lo, in the midst of the throne, stood a Lamb, *as it had been slain.* And I heard the voice of many angels round about the throne, saying with a loud voice, Worthy is the Lamb *that was slain,* to receive power, and riches, and wisdom, and strength, and honor, and glory, and blessing."

This body of the Messiah seems to have been in all respects subject to the will of the spirit which inhabited it. It could, at pleasure, be present or absent, in the upper chamber at Jerusalem, or in the mountains of Galilee, or on the shore of the lake of Genesaret. Even its outward manifestations to others seemed to depend wholly upon the volition of the spirit with which it was united. Now, the Messiah seems to his disciples as an humble wayfaring man, on the road to Emmaus; on the instant, he appears to them in his proper person, and vanishes out of their sight. Sometimes he is not only visible, but tangible, so that they can have no doubt of his identity. All these manifestations are wholly inconsistent with the ordinary laws to which matter is subjected. They belong not to a natural, but to a spiritual body.

All this, I know, is profoundly mysterious. We know of nothing on earth like it. We must receive it as a matter of testimony, and we can go no farther. I do not suppose that in our present state, we possess the faculties for obtaining any more perfect knowledge on the subject. The apostle Paul does not pretend to explain it. He, however, teaches us, that this doctrine finds its analogy in the ordinary process of vegetation. We plant a seed; it decays in the ground. Soon it germinates, and appears in a form wholly unlike the grain which we had planted; "God having given it a body as it hath pleased him." So, now, in the autumn of the year, a dry and unsightly seed falls, and is buried in the earth. It lies for months beneath the snows of winter. At length, the sun, emblem of the Sun of righteousness, warms it with his beams, and it rises from its lowly bed in a new and beautiful form, resplendent in color, and refreshing in fragrance, to show forth the praises of Him who hath clothed it by an act of his omnipotent power. Thus the body of the Messiah was laid in the grave, mortal and corruptible; but soon it appeared clothed in the garments of immortality, prepared to ascend and take its appointed place at the right hand of the Majesty on high, where he ever liveth to intercede for us.

It was in this glorified body that I suppose our Savior to have dwelt for some weeks on earth, showing himself alive by many infallible proofs. In this body, as he was blessing his disciples on a mountain in Bethany, "he was parted from them, and carried up into heaven, and a cloud received him out of their sight." In this body he still lives to intercede for his people. In this body he will come to judge the world. For, said the angels at his ascension, "This same Jesus, who is taken up from you into heaven, shall so come in like manner as ye have seen him go into heaven." When this last act shall have been performed, the mystery of redemption will have been completed, the history of this world will be closed, and the Messiah will surrender up the mediatorial kingdom unto the Father, that God may be all in all.

We see, thus, the nature of the mediatorial work of the Messiah. He took upon him our nature; he subjected himself to the law appointed for humanity; he, by his obedience unto death, magnified the law which we had dishonored; he offered himself without spot in our stead; he entered that spiritual state which is appointed for us; there he established his dominion, and prepared a place for us; he left the abode of the dead, bearing with him a glorified body, like to that in which his disciples shall be clothed; he ascended to his Father and our Father, to his God and our God, as our forerunner and head, to take possession, in our behalf, of that glorified state, to which all his members shall, after the final judgment, be introduced.

If this be so, we can well perceive that the advent and work of the Messiah is the one great event in the history of our world. It is the visit to our globe of Him "before whose face the heavens and the earth shall flee away, and there shall be no more place left for them." It is the pivot on which the destiny of man was turned from everlasting despair to immeasurable and inconceivable hope. It is the act by which the condemnation of the second death is lifted off from our race, and the way is laid open for us to enter into the holiest of holies, through the blood of the everlasting covenant. If this be so, well may all the previous history of our world have been one series of preparations for the coming of the Son of man. Well may we anticipate that all its subsequent history will be so ordained as to unfold the results of this great transaction. "The heathen have been given to the Son for his inheritance, and the uttermost parts of the earth for his possession." He is now rapidly unfolding his purposes, and claiming the promise that was made to him of universal dominion. "Because he was made obedient unto death, the death of the cross, God hath highly exalted him, and given him a name that is above every name; that at the name of Jesus, every knee shall bow, and every tongue confess, that Jesus Christ is Lord, to the glory of God the Father."

A few reflections naturally arise from this subject, to which I would call your attention before I close this discourse.

I remarked just now that Jesus Christ is called the first fruits of them that slept; that is, he is the first of those born of woman who has passed through all the changes to which humanity is appointed. In all this, he is the representative of our race. Every one of us must therefore pass through all the changes to which I have alluded. We are now in the condition of earthly humanity. Soon we all shall lay aside these tenements of clay, and enter upon the state of the departed. There shall we reside until the morning of the resurrection, "when the Lord himself shall descend from heaven with a shout, with the voice of the archangel, and with the trump of God; and the dead in Christ shall rise first; then shall we which are alive be caught up together in the clouds to meet the Lord in the air, and so shall we ever be with the Lord." Every one of us will then be clothed with an incorruptible body. Death can no more have dominion over us. The seal of immortality will be impressed upon us, never to be erased forever. Such are the changes that await every one born of woman. Such is the life and immortality which Jesus Christ has brought to light. Irrespective of the truth which he has taught us, all beyond the grave is shadows, clouds, and darkness. The light which shines from the cross of Christ, under which the believer reposes, streams through the dark valley of the shadow of death, until it is reflected back from the throne of the King eternal, immortal, and invisible. But this is not all. While we are thus taught the nature of the changes through which humanity must pass, we are also taught that, at death, an eternal separation must take place between the righteous and the wicked. In the spiritual state, the rich man and Lazarus were separated from each other by an impassable gulf. At the final judgment, Jesus Christ will say to those on his right hand, "Come, ye blessed of my Father, inherit the kingdom prepared for you from the foundation of the world," and to those on the left hand, "Depart from me, ye cursed, into everlasting fire, prepared for the devil and his angels." "And these shall go away into everlasting punishment, but the righteous into life eternal."

It was because we were all exposed to the condemnation of the second death, that the Messiah came to our earth, assumed our nature, and undertook the work of our redemption. For this purpose, he left the glory which he had with the Father before the world was; was born of a woman; was made under the law; endured the contradiction of sinners; was made obedient unto death, even the death of the cross; under the hiding of his Father's face, he triumphed over our enemies, and said, "It is finished," and gave up the ghost; for us, he entered the place of the departed, and there prepared a place for us; for our justification, he rose again, in an immortal body, like unto that with which we shall be clothed; for us, he ascended and is "seated on the right hand of the Majesty on high, having obtained eternal redemption for us." This work was accomplished for the whole race of man. The conditions of our probation have thus been reversed. Irrespective of the work of the Messiah, the announcement from the throne of God was, "Cursed is he that continueth not in all things written in the book of the law to do them;" "but now God can be just and the justifier of every one that believeth in Jesus." "Whosoever believeth in him shall not perish, but have everlasting life."

The offer of eternal life, through the merits of a crucified Redeemer, is freely made to every child of Adam. "It is a faithful saying, and worthy of all acceptation, that Christ Jesus came into the world to save sinners." "The Spirit and the bride say, Come. And let him that heareth say, Come. And let him that is athirst come. And whosoever will, let him take the water of life freely." "Now, then, we are ambassadors for Christ; as though God did beseech you by us, we pray you, in Christ's stead, be ye reconciled to God." Such is the most merciful invitation of the gospel. The gate of heaven, through the mediation of Christ, is as wide open to us as the gate of hell. If, after all this, we choose the pleasures of sin, and refuse the mercy of God in Christ Jesus, our doom must be inevitable, for there remaineth no other sacrifice for sin. We ourselves must confess that we are without excuse, and unite with the whole moral universe in pronouncing the sentence of our own condemnation. "He that despised Moses' law, died without mercy under two or three witnesses; of how much more punishment shall he be thought worthy, who hath trodden under foot the Son of God, and hath counted the blood of the covenant, with which he was sanctified, an unholy thing, and hath done despite unto the Spirit of grace."

Can we endure an eternity under such a condemnation as this? Let us, then, now, while it is an acceptable time, seek to escape from it. Let us now turn to God by repentance, and surrender our whole souls unto him. Like the returning prodigal, let us arise and go to our Father, and say unto him, "Father, I have sinned against Heaven and in thy sight, and am no more worthy to be called thy son." While we are yet a great way off, our Father in heaven will see us, and meet us in love, and say, "Bring forth the best robe, and put it on him, for this my son was dead, and is alive again, he was lost, and is found."

JUSTIFICATION BY FAITH.

"A MAN IS JUSTIFIED BY FAITH, WITHOUT THE WORKS OF THE LAW."
Romans iii. 28.

To be justified, as I have elsewhere said, may have two meanings. It may signify that a man has committed no crime, and therefore the law has no demand upon him; or that, though he be guilty, yet he is treated as though he were innocent; the demand of the law against him having been, for some cause, set aside. That it is used in the context, in the second of these senses, is manifest. The apostle is here speaking of those whom he has shown to be sinners exceedingly, and of whom justification, on the ground of the works of the law, — that is, of obedience to the law, — could in no manner be predicated. It is while speaking of such men, who have "sinned and come short of the glory of God," that he uses the words of the text, — "therefore we conclude that a man is justified by faith, without the works of the law."

The meaning of the phrase, "without the works of the law," may be easily explained. It clearly does not mean that there is *no* connection between justification and keeping the law, or between salvation and obedience. Such a sentiment as this would be utterly at variance with every word uttered by Christ and his apostles; nay, with the whole tenure of the Scriptures. "He that keepeth my commandments," saith the Savior, "he it is that loveth me; and he that loveth me shall be loved of my Father, and I will love him, and will manifest myself unto him." "Whosoever heareth these sayings of mine, and doeth them, I will liken him to a wise man, which built his house upon a rock." "And every one that heareth these sayings of mine, and doeth them not, shall be likened to a foolish man, which built his house upon the sand." So, also, the apostle Paul: "What shall we say then? Shall we continue in sin that grace may abound? God forbid. How shall we, who are dead to sin, continue any longer therein?" "Know ye not that so many of us as were baptized into Jesus Christ were baptized into his death? Therefore we are buried with him by baptism into death, that, like as Christ was raised up from the dead by the glory of the Father, even so we also should walk in newness of life." "Knowing this, that our old man is crucified with him, that the body of sin might be destroyed, that henceforth we should not serve sin." In fact, the whole object of the apostle, in the sixth, seventh, and eighth chapters of the Epistle to the Romans, is to show that holy obedience is by necessity the result, and the result only, of faith in Christ.

When the text, then, asserts that we are justified without the deeds of the law, it cannot mean to teach us that the connection between justification and good works is severed by the gospel. The passages which I have quoted show, beyond question, that good works are essential both to justification and faith; that without good works faith is impossible, and the hope of justification a fallacy. Their meaning, then, must be, that good works, the works of the law, are not the ground of our justification in the sight of God, but that the ground of our justification is faith in Christ. It is by virtue of faith in Christ that we are pardoned and justified; and the result of this change in our moral condition is a new life, which, by necessity, manifests itself in works acceptable to God. The order of these acts is then the following: In consequence of faith in Christ we are justified, that is, pardoned, treated by God as just; by faith, also, a new life is commenced in the soul; and this life ever makes itself known by corresponding actions. Thus saith the apostle: "For what the law could not do, in that it was weak through the flesh, God, sending his own Son in the likeness of sinful flesh, and by" (a sacrifice for) "sin, condemned sin in the flesh, that the righteousness of the law might be fulfilled in us, who walk not after the flesh, but after the spirit."

If this be true, it follows that it is of the utmost importance for us to ascertain, as accurately as possible, the nature of faith. This is the subject which I propose to consider in the present discourse. It is my desire to present it before you with the greatest simplicity, so that every one of us may be the better able to determine for himself whether he be, or be not, a believer in Christ Jesus.

I think it must be evident, on inspection, that faith can be no one external act. It is spoken of in the Scriptures in connection with acts of the most dissimilar character. It is referred to, from the commencement to the close of the Bible, as that alone which is well pleasing to God under every variety of dispensation by which the Most High has made himself known. Thus, we are told of the faith by which we understand that the worlds were made; of the faith by which Abel offered a sacrifice, by which he obtained witness that he was righteous; of the faith by which Enoch had the testimony that he pleased God; of the faith by which Noah prepared an ark to the saving of his house; of the faith by which Abraham obeyed the call to go out into the place which he should after receive for an inheritance, and by which he sojourned in the land of promise as in a strange country; of the faith by which, when he was tried, he offered up Isaac; and of the faith by which "Moses refused to be called the son of Pharaoh's daughter, choosing rather to suffer affliction with the people of God than to enjoy the pleasures of sin for a season." We read also of the faith of Rahab, of Gideon, of Barak, of Samson, of Jephtha, of David, of Samuel, and the prophets. In the New Testament we read of the faith by which miracles were performed, as well as of that faith by which a sinner is justified, and made a new creature in Christ Jesus.

Now, from these examples, it is manifest that faith cannot

be any particular act; for the acts by which it is exemplified are as diverse as any of which we can possibly conceive. The faith of the Scriptures must then be some *temper of mind pervading all these acts*, which distinguishes them from other acts of the same external character; a temper of mind of a nature sufficiently comprehensive to embrace them all, how diverse soever they may appear outwardly; and which shall render them all, under all these various external circumstances, acceptable to God. It becomes us to inquire, What is this temper of mind? To this question, let us, in the next place then, direct our inquiries.

In order to illustrate this subject, allow me to call your attention to the fact, that all the social relations existing among men give occasion to the exercise of various and dissimilar affections. The relation of parent and child renders imperative, on the one part, the feeling of affectionate guardianship, and, on the other, of filial love and obedience. The relation of brethren of one family imposes upon every member the duty of mutual aid, forbearance, and sympathy, and the universal feeling from which such acts proceed. The magistrate is bound to protect the citizen in the exercise of his rights; the citizen to obey the magistrate in the performance of his duty. And, in general, the tempers of mind, emanating from these relations, spontaneously arise in our bosoms as a part of our common nature.

Take, for instance, the filial relation. Every one knows that the child is bound to love, reverence, and obey its parent. We cannot conceive of the character of a parent worthy of the name, without feeling that these affections are his rightful due. We, on the other hand, ascribe to a child who displays them in an eminent degree, a high attainment in virtue. Were filial obedience the controlling motive in the bosom of a child, we perceive that all his acts, of what kind soever, would be pleasing to his parent, considered simply as a parent. Whether they were important or unimportant, wise or unwise; whether they had reference to his own happiness, or the happiness of others; if they were done from simple, unaffected filial love, the parent could not but look upon them with respect, and, in some important sense, with approbation.

Now, God stands to us in the relation of a heavenly Parent, the Creator and Preserver of all, endowed with every moral excellence of which we can conceive. His parental character demands from us the temper of filial obedience, or the obedience of love; while every one of his attributes demands from us some especial form of moral affection. It is manifest that he being such as he is, and we being such as we are, it becomes us, from choice, to regulate our entire conduct by his most blessed will. And, besides this, the veracity of God demands that we repose the most implicit confidence in his promises. The goodness of God should awaken within us unceasing gratitude. The justice of God should create within us unwavering trust in the success of virtue. The holiness of God should fill us with profound veneration, and an earnest desire to be transformed into his image. All these, and various other moral affections, are manifestly incumbent upon us as the children of our Father who is in heaven, who has formed us in his likeness, and who designs that we should be made partakers of his moral nature. They may all be appropriately comprehended under the simple temper of filial love; for of this affection they are all the different manifestations. It is this affection, or temper of mind, which I suppose the Scriptures to designate under the term *faith.*

But it may be asked, How does this affection differ from that which exists among the glorified beings in heaven? They continually exercise these moral dispositions; and yet faith is never spoken of in the Scriptures as a grace of the heavenly rest. Faith is an affection of this present probationary state; and the field for its exercise is limited to the constitution which exists on this side the grave.

All this is true, and it serves still further to illustrate the subject. In the upper world, where we see as we are seen and know as we are known, there is no opportunity for the exercise of any other affection than perfect love, unmodified filial obedience. In the present state, however, this affection is modified by the circumstances under which it is called into exercise. Here every thing around us is continually tending to counteract the exercise of this holy affection. If a man will live godlily, he must suffer persecution. The world around us commands one thing, and God commands another. The punishments which the world will inflict, if we disobey it, are visible and present. The rewards of obedience to God are invisible and distant. God, in the present state, reveals his will and makes known his promises, and then retires, and leaves us to contend with the counteracting influences that surround us. Faith is the exercise of filial love, successfully resisting the pressure of things present, sensual, and unholy. It is acting as God would have us, not when all things incite us to obedience, but when all things around us incite us to sin. It is the temper of mind which thus gives to things unseen their appropriate mastery over things seen ; it is the overcoming of the world by the power of holy trust in God ; reliance upon his perfections, when every dictate of human wisdom would lead us to distrust him.

If we review the illustrations of the victories of faith presented in the eleventh of Hebrews, I think that we shall find them all to be pervaded by this element. Thus it was the commonly-received opinion, at the time of the apostle, that matter was eternal. In opposition to this, it is by faith, simple confidence in the testimony of God, that "we know that the worlds were framed by the word of God, so that things which are seen are not made of things that do appear." It was by virtue of this filial disposition, that Abel offered to God a more excellent sacrifice than Cain. It was by trust in the word of God, in defiance of the sneers of an unbelieving world, that Noah prepared an ark to the saving of his house. And thus Abraham left his father's house, and all the allurements of home, and went out, not knowing whither he went, sojourning in tabernacles in a land of which he was not permitted to occupy more than a cave for a burial-place. But I need not to multiply instances. In these, and all the other instances of triumphant faith, you will ever observe the same element. It is the temper of filial love, confidence, and obedience, triumphing over the counteracting influences arising from our present state of ignorance and sin, whether they proceed from the passions that agitate us within, or the trials that disturb us from without.

And still further: I think that, in the dispensations of his providence, God honors the principle of faith, under what circumstances soever it may be exhibited. Whenever a creature, even though he may not be in other respects obedient, yet on any particular occasion, acts from simple confidence in the perfections of the Most High, — in that particular case, God fulfils to him his promises, and grants to him the benefit of that single act of confidence. In this manner Rahab and Gideon, and Samson and Jephtha, obtained the rewards of faith. It is not necessary, in order to understand the declarations concerning them in the Epistle to the Hebrews, to suppose that they were persons of real piety; though they may have been really pious. All that we need to believe is, that they, under particular circumstances, reposed special confidence in the promises of God, and acted accordingly. This would insure to them, in a particular instance, the benefit of faith; and hence their success may be enumerated among the triumphs that belong to this moral attribute.

The view of faith which I have here taken is beautifully illustrated by an anecdote from Cecil's Remains. His little daughter was one day playing with some beads, which delighted her wonderfully. He told her to throw them into the fire. "The tears," said he, "started into her eyes. She looked earnestly at me, as though she ought to have a reason for such a cruel sacrifice. 'Well, my dear, do as you please; but you know I never told you to do any thing which I did not think would be good for you.' She looked at me a few moments longer, and then, summoning up all her fortitude, her breast heaving with the effort, she dashed them into the fire. 'Well,' said I, 'there let them lie; you shall hear more about them another time; but say no more about them now.' Some days after, I bought her a box full of larger beads and toys of the same kind. When I returned home, I opened the treasure, and set it before her. She burst into tears with ecstasy. 'Those, my child,' said I, 'are yours, because you believed me, when I told you it would be better for you to throw those two or three paltry beads into the fire. Now, that has brought you this treasure. But now, my dear, remember, as long as you live, what faith is.'" I know of nothing that could more clearly illustrate my idea of faith than this beautiful incident. Had the father brought the larger toys first, and told the child to exchange the smaller ones for them, she might have been obedient and grateful; but she would have manifested no faith. It was when the spirit of filial love overcame every other impulse, and enabled her to act in view of things unseen, that her faith revealed itself. To act towards God, in any case, as she acted towards her father, is faith.

God has taught us in the Scriptures that when a sinner cherishes this disposition towards him, he pardons his sins, and receives him into the number of his children. It must, however, be a feeling which pervades his whole nature, and overcomes every opposing impulse. It is the temper of universal filial obedience. Having broken the law of God; on the ground of having kept that law, justification is impossible. We are, therefore, said to be justified without the deeds of the law. God, in virtue of the work of the Messiah in our behalf, pardons us, and treats us as just, as soon as he perceives in us this filial disposition. And still more: this disposition can manifest itself in no other manner than by performing those acts which, by necessity, emanate from it; that is, by good works and holy affections. Thus the very disposition, on account of which we are justified, insures, by necessary consequence, that change of character without which we could never be acceptable to God.

Such, then, is the nature of faith. It is, as we immediately perceive, the essential element of piety. It at once places our moral nature in harmony with the moral character of God; and thus triumphs over the impulses to evil arising from our present probationary and sinful state. And yet more: as it is a temper which places us in harmony with every attribute of the divine nature that has been revealed to us, it may exist under every form of dispensation, and with every degree of spiritual illumination. The patriarch Abraham is held forth for our imitation as the model of a faithful man, although his knowledge of the way of salvation must have been obscure, and his knowledge of preceptive duty comparatively imperfect. As, in subsequent ages, God revealed his character and his will more clearly, the same disposition manifested itself in devout submission to all the requirements of the Mosaic ritual. It is the principle of correspondence in the creature with the moral nature of the Creator; and it is unfolded more and more perfectly with every new revelation which God makes of himself to us, the humble dwellers upon his footstool.

Hence we see at once in what manner the manifestation of faith must be affected by the wonderful truths of the new dispensation. It must transform the soul into practical conformity to the truth which God has revealed concerning his Son. Let us, then, observe the effects which the revelation of the gospel must have upon a believing soul.

1. Jesus Christ died to save sinners justly condemned, and, therefore, unable by their own works to justify themselves. "God commendeth his love to us, in that, while we were yet sinners, Christ died for us." "When we were without strength, Christ died for the ungodly." Faith teaches us to place ourselves in precisely the condition which the word of God assigns to us; to confess ourselves helplessly sinful and justly exposed to the righteous condemnation of the law of God. Thus saith the apostle, under the full impression of this truth, "O, wretched man that I am! who shall deliver me from the body of this death?"

2. To sinners in this condition God makes known the offer of salvation through Christ Jesus. "God so loved the world that he gave his only-begotten Son, that whosoever believeth in him should not perish, but have everlasting life." Faith would teach us, then, renouncing all hope of saving ourselves, to confide our souls to Christ as our only and all-sufficient Savior. "That I may," saith the apostle, "be found in him, not having mine own righteousness, which is by the law, but the righteousness which is of God by faith.

3. Christ is the revealer of the Father's will. "He is the brightness of his glory, the express image of his person." Faith teaches us to yield up ourselves without reserve, in holy obedience to the precepts which Christ has given us. To them we must conform our wills, our thoughts, our words, our actions, our whole being. "We are not our own; we are bought with a price, that we should glorify him in our bodies and spirits, which are his." Nor this alone. The revelation which he has made to us is replete with exceeding great and precious promises. Faith teaches us to give to them the power of a present and vivid reality. It is thus that it gives "substance to things hoped for, and evidence to things not seen."

4. The Father has given to us the Son as our example. "He took upon him the form of a servant, and was found in fashion as a man." "He was made under the law." Yet he was holy, harmless, undefiled, separate from sinners. In all the various trials of a most persecuted and tempted life, he was ever the same spotless Redeemer, victorious over every spiritual enemy. Thus was there exhibited to us an illustration of what the law of God requires of each of us; thus are we taught the manner in which we should live so as to please our Father who is in heaven. The temper of filial obedience would, then, lead us to strive with our whole spiritual might to copy the example which Christ has set before us, to love the world as he loved it; to be crucified to it as he was crucified to it; and, under all the circumstances of a human proba-

tion, to esteem it our meat and drink to do the will of our Father who is in heaven.

5. And yet more: while we are maintaining this conflict with all the powers of evil, and fighting the fight of faith, it is by the aid of Christ alone that we can come off conquerors He has promised, if we do his will, to dwell with us and to be in us. He is not only the way, and the truth, but the life, the source, and sustainer of life, to every true believer. Faith would, then, teach us, renouncing all dependence upon ourselves, to rely wholly for spiritual strength on the grace that is in Christ Jesus. Thus the apostle declared, "When I am weak, then am I strong; I can do all things through Jesus Christ, which strengtheneth me." And thus every believer knows that he has power to overcome his spiritual enemies only as, in deep self-distrust, he learns to confide in the aid bestowed upon him by the Captain of his salvation.

If it be demanded what are the counteracting influences which oppose themselves to prevent a sinner from thus believing in Christ, I answer, they arise sometimes from without, in the form of allurement or of menace; but always from within, in the resistance of a fallen and sensual nature to the holy and spiritual doctrines of the gospel. We do not like to acknowledge ourselves in the wrong; the gospel teaches us that without this acknowledgment we cannot come to Christ. We do not like to surrender ourselves without any claim of merit to the pure mercy of God in Christ; but, until we thus surrender ourselves, we are under the law. Nothing is more difficult than to renounce our own will, and submit ourselves to the will of another; but until we thus subject our whole nature to the will of Christ, we are not his disciples. And, finally, there is not a corrupt, proud, selfish disposition in our whole character, to which the example of Christ is not in direct opposition. All these must be crucified, if we would follow his example, and imitate his life. It is the spirit of filial obedience triumphing over every unholy passion, that constitutes a man a new creature in Christ Jesus, and makes him a partaker of the peace that passeth all understanding. Thus, in general, we find, I think, that all the scriptural instances of faith by which we must be saved, are pervaded by the same element; it is every where the spirit of heaven gaining victory over the opposing influences of earth, subduing every sensual passion and every selfish affection of a human soul.

1. If, now, the above explanation of the nature of faith be correct, it will teach us the inaccuracy of some of the notions which have commonly prevailed on this subject. It has, for instance, been frequently affirmed, that faith is the belief of the individual that Christ died for him in particular. If he can by any means persuade himself that he is included in the number of those for whom an atonement is made, then he is included in that number; he is an heir of everlasting life and a partaker of the glory that is to be revealed. But, if faith be what I have supposed it to be, such a belief as this has not the most distant resemblance to it. It has, in fact, no moral quality whatever; it places us in no new moral relations to God, and is not productive of any change in character. All that is necessary to produce it, is a determined resolution to believe a proposition, whether the evidence in support of it be or be not sufficient. And hence, when we would direct the anxious inquirer into the way of salvation, our effort should not tend to produce in him the belief that he is accepted, but to lead him to that state of true submission to God and love to his character, in which faith originates, and which is the essence of all real piety. To urge a man to the belief that he is saved without this temper of heart, is to practise upon him a gross deception. If his moral affection to God be right, peace of mind will be its necessary result; while peace of mind without it is a lamentable delusion.

2. If the preceding remarks be correct, we easily learn what is meant by the prayer of faith, and the efficacy that is ascribed to it. Faith is a moral disposition of the creature in harmony with the divine character. The prayer of faith is the prayer of a soul in whom this moral disposition predomi-

nates, and is such prayer just in so far as our desires are in harmony with the attributes of God. That prayer shall be answered in proportion to its conformity to the will of God, is a matter of necessity. That prayer, then, which God promises to answer, is the prayer which proceeds from ardent love to him, and unshaken reliance on the perfections of his character, no matter how dark and discouraging may seem the circumstances that surround us. It is at once obvious, that the promise of God to answer such prayer, is a very different thing from the promise to answer our prayers if we only persuade ourselves that he will certainly hear us.

3. The view which I have here taken will, I think, enable us to understand all the various passages in the Scriptures, in which faith is the subject of discourse. The faith of Abel, of Abraham, of Moses, of Samuel and the prophets, and of Paul and the apostles, as well as of the humblest Christian at the present time, all are comprehended under the same idea. In every case, it is the temper of filial love triumphing over the opposing influences of sin; and, under the new dispensation, it is this same disposition exalted and rendered more all-pervading, in consequence of the infinite love of God revealed to us in Jesus Christ our Redeemer. Thus the company of the faithful, on earth and in heaven, are all pervaded by one spirit; all are in fellowship with God and his Son Jesus Christ; all are members of one body, of which Christ is the head, and all heirs of God and joint heirs with Christ, to an "inheritance incorruptible, and undefiled, and that fadeth not away." Such are the members of the church of the first born whose names are written in heaven.

4. We learn from the nature of faith, the reasonableness of the terms on which salvation is offered to sinners. God requires of us, in order that we be saved, nothing more than would be our duty if no salvation were promised — nothing more than the exercise, on our part, of filial love towards our Father who is in heaven. This he deserves on account of the excellence of his own nature, no less than of his

exceeding compassion towards us. He surely could demand no less of his intelligent and moral creatures; and we surely could desire to exercise no other feelings towards the infinitely Good, the Giver of every good and perfect gift. And yet, through the abounding mercy of the gospel, he offers to all who exercise such an affection, and through it triumph over the allurements of sin, eternal life. I do not see how it is possible to conceive of more merciful terms of salvation than those which are offered to us in the gospel. Well saith the apostle, "As ambassadors of Christ, as though God did beseech you by us, we beseech you, in Christ's stead, be ye reconciled to God."

And if this be so, if God has made the most merciful offer of salvation of which we can conceive, this must be his final tender of reconciliation. No man can surely either desire or expect that Almighty God would do more than he has done to save the guilty from the condemnation which they have merited. After this, "there remaineth no more sacrifice for sin, but a certain fearful looking for of judgment and fiery indignation, that shall devour the adversary."

It is under these fearful conditions that our probation is now passing away. We have merited eternal banishment from God. He has given his Son for our offences, and now proclaims that "whosoever believeth in him shall not perish, but have everlasting life." We ourselves must confess that no more favorable conditions could be offered. The only requirement which he makes is, that we exercise towards him a filial, obedient disposition; that we love, with all our heart, Him who is infinitely worthy of our love; and obey, from affection, him who is infinitely deserving of all our service. If we refuse, and prefer to continue in causeless, unprovoked rebellion against our Father who is in heaven, we are condemned of our own consciences. When he shall enter into judgment with us, every mouth must be stopped. What wilt thou say when he shall punish thee?

CONVERSION.

"THEREFORE, BEING JUSTIFIED BY FAITH, WE HAVE PEACE WITH GOD, THROUGH OUR LORD JESUS CHRIST."
Romans v. 1.

THERE is, if I mistake not, a very perceptible difference to be observed between the examples of piety recorded in the Scriptures and those which we now meet with in the ordinary intercourse of life. With such men as the apostles, martyrs, and confessors of old, unshaken trust in Christ, full assurance of salvation, and an abiding consciousness of the indwelling of the Savior, formed the foundation on which their religious character was built. These very confident beliefs led them to sacrifice every thing for Christ, and gain such astonishing victories over the world. They *knew* in whom they believed ; they were confident that they were pardoned sinners ; they were assured that they were children of God, and heirs of eternal life, and that their light afflictions, which were for a moment, were actually working out for them a far more exceeding and an eternal weight of glory. The joy of the Lord was their strength. They were as confident of their coming salvation, as they were of the veracity of God, who had said, I give unto them eternal life, and they shall never perish, neither shall any man pluck them out of my hand. Nor was this steadfast expectation of future glory confined to the apostles and their immediate associates. They always spoke of it as something attainable, and generally attained, by their brethren to whom they wrote. *We know*, said the apostle, that if this earthly house of our tabernacle be dissolved, we have a building of God, a house not made with hands, eternal in the heavens. Ye took joyfully, said he to the Hebrews, the spoiling of your goods, knowing in yourselves that ye have in heaven a better and an enduring substance. The same apostle prays in behalf of the Ephesians, that they may be strengthened mightily by the Spirit, in the inner man, that so they might know the love of Christ which passeth knowledge, and be filled with all the fulness of God.

I doubt whether this individual confidence in our good estate could be affirmed of Christians in general at the present day. I rather fear that the full assurance of faith has come to be the exception rather than the rule. We have a hope, frequently a very feeble one, that our sins are pardoned, and that we are the children of God. We have occasional glimpses of the prospect before us, but too commonly clouds and darkness rest upon it. We strive to keep the law of God, we continually come short of our expectations; we do wrong, and our hope of final salvation is obscured. We plead for pardon and strength, and we are helped; but again our vigilance fails, and our faith falters. We hope and fear, trust and distrust; we seem to rely in part on Christ, and in part upon ourselves; hence our course is wavering and unsteady, and we make little moral progress. We seem, in fact, to be vibrating between the law and the gospel, and thus fail to receive the fulness of the blessing purchased for us by the sacrifice of Christ. The same remark quite commonly applies to the case of recent converts to Christianity. After the first flush of religious joy has subsided, and they begin to look for the evidences of piety in their own hearts, they discover so much that is imperfect, they come so far short of the mark to which they had hoped to attain, that they fall back in discouragement, and doubt whether they have ever been accepted of God.

It is evident that this is a state of mind not anticipated by the gospel of Jesus Christ. He came to deliver us not only from the curse of sin, but from the fear of the curse. It is the will of Christ that we should be strong in faith, giving glory to God. There is in the gospel every ground for firm confidence to those who have fled for refuge to lay hold on the hope set before them. Can we do nothing to encourage the faith of the weak believer? Will there not be something accomplished, if we can, in the plainest and most direct manner, set before him an intelligible outline of the way of salvation? In regeneration there is a personal dealing of the soul with God. There are acts of the soul with God, and there are acts of God with the soul. God has made unchangeable promises: when the soul believes, he fulfils them, and by the power of his Spirit creates the soul anew in Christ Jesus. If we can see these truths clearly, and apply them to our own individual case, it may help us to discover more distinctly the evidences of our adoption, and enable us to rely with more confident assurance on the promises of God. To attempt this is the object of the following discourse.

The whole doctrine of regeneration takes its rise from the fact that every man is a sinner against God, helplessly and hopelessly guilty. The law of the moral universe, under which we were created, is holy, and just, and good. It requires that we shall love the Lord our God with all our heart, and our neighbor as ourselves. It requires of us, as of necessity it must, perfect obedience. To such obedience God has granted the promise of eternal life. But the law makes no allowance for any wilful transgression. Cursed is he that continueth not in all things written in the book of the law to do them.

But our whole race has broken this law, and risen up in rebellion against God. In thought, and word, and deed we have violated every commandment. All have sinned and come short of the glory of God. There is no man that liveth and sinneth not. We love our sin, and deliberately prefer it to holiness. We are convicted by our own consciences as transgressors. Every right affection to God has vanished from the soul. We prefer our will to his. We deliberately obey the impulses of our passions and appetites, in direct violation of his commandments. Our whole moral nature is in opposition to the character of our Father in heaven. The carnal mind is enmity against God, for it is not subject to the law of God, neither, indeed, can be. Here, then, we behold a race of moral and intelligent beings in rebellion against God, enemies to him by wicked works, defying his authority, and exposed to the righteous curse of his violated law. This is the character of the race, and of every individual of it, so that every mouth is stopped, and the whole world is guilty before God.

Such being our condition, salvation through obedience to the law is manifestly impossible. The commandment, which was ordained unto life, has become death to us by our wilful violation of it. Under these circumstances our ruin seemed inevitable. A most favorable probation had been granted to us, but we had failed utterly in complying with its conditions. To make reparation for our wrong was impossible, for our moral power had become fatally prostrated. Nay, we had no desire to make any reparation, for we preferred sin to holiness, time to eternity, the indulgence of our passions to the love and service of God. A moral helplessness more complete cannot be imagined. Within the limits of created power we were utterly without hope. God could not pardon us unless his law was made honorable. We could not make it honorable; and we loved to violate it. No created power could help us. We must perish, or the justice of the Most High be trampled under foot. There remained for us nothing but a fearful looking for of judgment, and fiery indignation, which must devour the adversary.

Now, these are not mere theological dogmas, to be intellectually comprehended, they are the simple statement of the facts concerning our relations to God, revealed to us without the least ambiguity. As soon as a soul has been made aware of its condition by the illumination of the Spirit, they become the most vital truths of which the mind can conceive. The moment the eyes of the understanding are opened to see things as they are, the man perceives that all this is true *of himself.* It is he himself that is just such a sinner, and thus exposed, and justly exposed, to the wrath of God. No matter what the estimation is in which he has been held among men, or what may have been his views of his own desert, — no sooner does he compare himself with the holiness of God, than he discovers his helpless misery. Thus said Job, Though I wash myself with snow water, and make myself ever so clean, thou wilt plunge me in the ditch, and my own clothes shall abhor me. Thus Paul declares, I was alive without the law once, but when the commandment came, sin revived, and I died.

It was for our race, thus overwhelmed in helpless guilt, that our Father in heaven provided a way of restoration. His law must be honored, and he gave up his well-beloved Son to magnify and make it honorable. That divine Being, who was with God and was God, took upon him our nature, was made flesh, and dwelt among us. He honored the law by his perfect obedience in our stead, and took it out of the way, nailing it to his cross. He bore every thing that infinite holiness could require, so that we might be pardoned, and the purity of the Godhead be unspotted ; or, in the words of the apostle, that God might be just, and the justifier of him that believeth. God so loved the world, that he gave his only begotten Son, that whosoever believeth on him might not perish, but have everlasting life. The whole race of man, from being under hopeless condemnation, was henceforth placed in a salvable state. Every obstacle to our pardon arising from the holiness of God was removed; and from henceforth it became a faithful saying, and worthy of all acceptation, that Christ Jesus came into the world to save sinners. The conditions of the old probation had been violated, and it was taken out of the way. A new probation is set before us through the offering up of Jesus Christ once for us all. This is the one great stupendous truth which the Scriptures reveal. To it every ceremony points, and to illustrate it every prophet has spoken, for the testimony to Jesus is the spirit of prophecy.

The Scriptures teach us that the atonement of Jesus Christ was made for the sins of the whole race of man. The whole of our apostate family is considered as one, and for all that family is the salvation provided. The remedy was as extensive as the disease. All had broken and dishonored the law, and in behalf of all was the law magnified and made honorable. The effect of this sacrifice reached as far and as wide as the ruin that had been caused by sin. Its benefit extended from our first parents to all their posterity. God so loved the *world* that he gave his only begotten Son. As by the offence of one, judgment came upon all men to condemnation, so by the righteousness of one, the free gift came upon all men unto justification of life. And in harmony with this declaration is the universal offer of pardon through Christ. Go ye into all the world, and preach the good news to every creature. The Spirit and the bride say, Come ; and let him that heareth say, Come ; and whosoever will let him come, and take of the water of life freely. It matters not, then, where or when a child of Adam has sinned against God ; it matters not how vast the number, or how great the enormity of his sins ; Christ Jesus came into the world, said St. Paul, to save sinners, of whom I am chief. When writing to the Corinthians, after enumerating some of the most atrocious crimes which have ever disgraced and defiled humanity, he adds, And such were some of you ; but ye are washed, but ye are sanctified, but ye are justified, in the name of the Lord Jesus, and by the Spirit of our God. A fountain has been opened for sin and iniquity, and every individual of the race of man may wash and be clean.

Thus far we have contemplated two facts which enter into the plan of salvation. One is the guilt and moral helplessness of man, the other the abundant provision which has been made for his pardon. It becomes us, in the next place, to inquire what are the conditions on which man may avail himself of this provision. On this subject the Scriptures are full and explicit. The conditions are repentance towards God, and faith in our Lord Jesus Christ.

Repentance towards God. — The case here stands on this wise. Man has broken, times without number, the great moral law on which the happiness of the universe depends. He has preferred his lusts to God. He has loved and obeyed every one, and every thing rather than God. He has lived to himself rather than to humanity. He has set at nought the authority of God, and is engaged in rebellion against him; and this opposition goes to the deepest recesses of his nature, for the carnal mind is enmity against God.

But all this while God has been absolutely in the right, and man absolutely in the wrong. God has required of man nothing that was not holy, and just, and good. The man has causelessly injured and grieved his Father in heaven. It is right that he should come to God and confess his guilt, acknowledge that he deserves just what the law denounces as the punishment of transgression, even if the full penalty of the law be exacted of him. It is meet that he take all the blame upon himself, declaring from his heart that throughout this controversy God has been always in the right, and he always in the wrong. He has been engaged in rebellion against God; it is proper that he submit himself wholly, body, and soul, and spirit, to the will of his Maker; resolving, from his inmost spirit, that he will henceforth make the service of God the great business of his life. All this, I say, is the duty of man, irrespective of any hope of pardon. It is the temper of the returning prodigal, who could not have been received, had he come to his father in any other spirit. This is repentance towards God. This he requires of every one born of woman, before he can become a partaker of the blessings purchased by the sacrifice of Christ.

Faith in our Lord Jesus Christ. — The sacrifice of

Christ was made for the purpose of reconciling mercy with justice; so that the abhorence of God to sin might be manifest to the universe, at the same time that he pardoned the sinner, and received him to favor. The penitent sinner, as I have said, acknowledges his guilt, and confesses that if the penalty of the law were enforced, it would be just. How then can he be justified? As the case now stands, he is utterly without hope. But Christ has obeyed the law in his stead, and by his atonement taken away every obstacle to his pardon. God, through Christ, can now be just, and justify him. His only hope must rely, not on any thing that he can do, but on what Christ has done in his stead. If he ever is saved, he must receive salvation as a free gift, purchased by Him that died for our sins, and was raised again for our justification. He must come renouncing all merit, acknowledging his own ill desert, and casting himself as a perishing sinner on the mercy of God in Christ Jesus. This is faith in Christ — the other condition on which our pardon and salvation depend.

Now, to every penitent and believing sinner our Father in heaven holds out the offer of unconditional pardon. No matter how deep may have been the stain of his guilt, no matter how long-continued the life of rebellion, — a pardon is offered to all who thus come to God, trusting in the merit of his Son. The blood of Jesus Christ cleanseth from all sin. The promise is, Though your sins be as scarlet, they shall be as wool; though they be red like crimson, they shall be whiter than snow. There is henceforth no condemnation to those that are in Christ Jesus, and whosoever cometh unto him he will in no wise cast out. Such is the offer of eternal life made to every penitent sinner; an offer of free, unconditional pardon, and an inheritance among them that are sanctified.

Here, then, we have a sinner convinced of his guilt, and acknowledging the justness of his condemnation, an atonement for sin, through which a full and free pardon is offered, and the terms made known by which every one may avail himself of this offer of pardon; and these terms are the most reasonable, the most merciful, the most compassionate that could be conceived. What, then remains in order that a sinner may be saved?

One thing is now needful. It is that he come before the God against whom he has sinned, and acknowledge all this *to him.* It will not do that a man know it all, and feel it all, and keep it all within his own bosom. Religion is not a series of emotions, shut up within ourselves; it is a transaction between ourselves and God. The man has sinned against God, and he himself must, as an individual sinner, be reconciled to God. It is just as much a transaction between himself and God, as though he and his Maker were the only beings in existence. The prodigal son was first *convinced* of his wretchedness; but this did not help him. He *resolved* to arise and go to his father. This did not bring about his reconciliation. *He arose and went to his father.* This was the point on which his destiny was suspended. When he arose and went, and not till then, his father had compassion, and when he was yet a great way off, ran and fell on his neck and kissed him. Thus is it with us. We may know that we are sinners, guilty and justly condemned; this will not do. We may resolve that we will break off from sin; this will not do. We may know that we can have no peace of conscience until our wills are in subjection to the will of God; this will not do. We may believe that there is salvation in no other name but the name of Christ; this will not do. We must go, each one for himself, before God, and act out our beliefs at his feet. We must acknowledge our sins before him, and confess to him our guiltiness. We must surrender up our whole selves to him, desiring hereafter to do nothing but that which shall please him. We must renounce all hope of saving ourselves by any thing that we can do, and plead for a free and full pardon for the sake of Him that loved us and gave himself for us. This is submission to God. This is faith in Christ. The sinner acknowledges himself to be just what God has declared him to be, and in child-like obedience, comes to his

Father in heaven, bows before him in penitence, and looks for pardon to the blood of the everlasting covenant.

Now, to such a one the promise of God is in words like these : Him that cometh unto me I will in no wise cast out. Repent and be converted, that your sins may be blotted out. As Moses lifted up the serpent in the wilderness, even so is the Son of man lifted up, that whosoever believeth in him should not perish, but have everlasting life. And God fulfils this promise to the letter. Whenever a sinner thus penitently draws near to God, looking for salvation to the blood of the atonement, that moment God *does* pardon him. He places him at once beneath the shelter of the atonement, and gives him a title to all the blessings which that atonement has purchased. The law in his stead has been satisfied. It has no more claim upon him, that being dead by which he was held. To every one of its demands he can now plead the finished obedience of Christ, who for him magnified the law, and made it honorable. He has from his heart accepted the terms of the new probation, and is entitled to all its blessings. From being an enemy he has become a child of God. God can be more honored in pardoning than in condemning him. He is one with Christ, and his life is hid with Christ in God. He is received into the family of the redeemed, and there is joy in the presence of the angels of God over another sinner that has repented. Being justified by faith, he has peace with God through our Lord Jesus Christ, through whom he has received the atonement.

And now, concerning this act of our Father in heaven, I remark, it takes place at the moment when a sinner repents of his sin, and casts himself without reserve on the sacrifice of Christ. God has promised that if the sinner will repent and believe, he shall be saved ; the sinner repents and believes, and God saves him. There may be yet about him much imperfection and evil ; this will be cleansed away in the work of sanctification. Day by day he gains victory over the sin that dwelleth in him, as he is made more and more meet to be an inheritor with the saints in light. The progress may be gradual, but this has nothing to do with the fact that his relations with God are changed for eternity. He has already become an heir of God and a joint heir with Jesus Christ.

And again, it is a *full* justification. It covers all his sins. He is delivered forever from the curse of the law. He has cast himself on the righteousness of Christ; he has been received and placed under the shadow of the atonement, and for the sake of the Redeemer he is, in the sight of God, as though he had never sinned. And it is a *free* salvation. He has nothing wherewith to purchase it, and he offers nothing. He accepts it as the free gift of God to the most undeserving. His whole salvation, is thus the work of God in Christ, and hence his song will ever be "Unto Him that loved us, and washed us from our sins in his own blood, be glory, and honor, and power, forever and ever."

But an anxious inquirer may perhaps suggest, All this is very encouraging, and I delight to think of it; but how shall I ascertain that this is my portion. What you have told us is concerning an act of God. He does thus pardon sins and receive the returning penitent; but how can I know that he has pardoned and received *me*? I will endeavor to answer this question as distinctly as I am able.

In the first place, when a soul thus repents of sin and casts itself for salvation on Christ, this very act frequently is blended with a confident trust that God has done as he has said. The soul relies with full faith in the promises, and the consciousness that we have really submitted to God creates the assurance that He has received us into the number of his children, and thus the awful dread of the judgment to come is exchanged for the peace that passeth understanding.

But some one will say, This consciousness is a mere emotion; it is liable to pass away, and leave the man in a condition in no manner improved. At best it is but evanescent, and seems hardly a foundation on which to build for eternity. Is there no other evidence of pardon bestowed upon a penitent sinner? I answer, There is another and more infallible evidence; it is the change which a man perceives in his own moral affections. When God pardons a sinner, and receives him into the family of the holy, he puts his mark upon him, the image of Christ, engraved upon his inmost spirit. The Holy Spirit, by his almighty power, transforms the affections of the soul so that the man feels within himself that he is another creature; old things have passed away, and all things have become new. He was the slave of passion and appetite; now his love for the things that perish is subdued, and he is conscious that he is delivered from the bondage of sin. He was living for himself; now he lives only to please his Savior. The pleasures of the world have lost their attraction, for his affections are taken from things below, and fixed on things above. The objects that were once most distasteful are now the sources of his most refined enjoyment. He loves the word of God; he loves to pour out his soul in secret prayer and praise; he loves to bear hardness and endure suffering for Christ, and takes joyfully the loss of all things, for the sake of Him who died to redeem him. He has now no pleasure in the company of sinners; but his chosen companions are the men in whom he sees most evidently the image of Christ. And from such a change of moral affections there results, of necessity, a change in his manner of life. This is the law of Christ that we keep his commandments. The frivolous and unsatisfied child of fashion is transformed into the thoughtful, earnest, heavenly-minded saint. The faithless man becomes truthful, the vindictive forgiving, the passionate man becomes meek, the sensual temperate, the selfish man self-denying, and the habitually-profane would rather die than utter an oath. Such are some of the fruits of the Spirit — the outward evidences of that inward change wrought in the soul by the almighty power of God, when he pardons and accepts it for the sake of the Beloved. He who is conscious of such an inward change, and observes its transforming power upon his whole character, cannot but know that he is a new man. He is certain that such a change can have been wrought by nothing but the power of God, and he knows that God exerts this power only in those who are called to be saints. This change in his moral affections is the unmistakable evidence that he is a child of God. Thus he that believeth hath the witness in himself. This change of our spiritual affections, manifesting itself in our outward conduct, is the evidence, not only to ourselves, but to others, that we have passed from death unto life.

Such, then, as I suppose, are the essential elements entering into the change which we denominate conversion, change of heart, being born again, or regeneration; the change without which, our Savior declares, we cannot see the kingdom of God. I say these are, as I suppose, the essential elements. I do not say that they can always be recognized in this precise order, or that the several spiritual changes are manifested to our own consciousness always in the same manner. Sometimes light breaks in upon the soul suddenly; at other times it is revealed to us almost insensibly. Sometimes conversion is attended by great mental distress; at other times the goodness of God leads us to repentance. With one the change in moral affections seems at once universal, and suddenly transforming; with another it seems to display itself gradually, as from time to time the occurrences of daily life call it into exercise. In all these respects the Spirit of God acts with great diversity of operation. What is essential to conversion is, that we do really submit ourselves, without any reserve, to the whole will of God, that we renounce from the heart every thing sinful, that we acknowledge his justice in our condemnation, and as lost sinners look for pardon through Jesus Christ. If we do this, God does really pardon us; and the evidence that he has done it is found in the spirit which he has given us — a spirit of active, filial obedience, an honest, prevalent desire to bear hardness for Christ, and under all circumstances to prefer his favor to all that this world can offer, and in defiance of all that it can threaten. If we can recognize within us such elements as these, it matters not how they have arisen, or when they first appeared; they are the evidences, according to the Scriptures, that we are the children of God.

And now, let me inquire, is there not in these truths much ground for consolation to many a trembling believer? You may be doubting your acceptance with God, because your religious experiences are unlike those of many around you; or because the intensity of your emotions is less than theirs; or because you see such imperfection in the discharge of your religious duties, and gain so few victories over the world, which is ever alluring you. Let me then ask, Do you really repent of sin? Do you desire with your whole heart to be delivered from it? Do you, in practice as well as in theory, submit yourself to the whole will of God, and rely for pardon entirely on the great sacrifice of the gospel? And is it your sincere desire to please Christ, taking up your cross and following in his footsteps, and bearing hardness for his sake? If such be your character, then God has pardoned you, and received you into the number of his children. You are a redeemed soul, purchased by the blood of Christ, and you may humbly, and yet confidently, take to yourself all the blessing of the promises. Your salvation is not the work of your own hands, but the result of the righteousness of Christ. You may go to God as your reconciled Father in Christ. Your best obedience is imperfect; you frequently err, and grieve your Savior; but if you make no allowance for sin, and really strive to be holy, as he is holy, you have an Advocate with the Father, even Jesus Christ the righteous. Rely with child-like and affectionate confidence upon him. Be assured that he loves you, and is touched with the feeling of your infirmities. You may seem to yourself to be fighting this warfare alone, forgotten and neglected by your Savior; but it is not so. He is every moment watching over you, delighted to see in you every struggle against evil, and every victory over the sin that besets you. He never forgets a single cross you bear, or a single pain you suffer for him. Go to him with all your trials, and all your unbelief, and plead with him as one of the redeemed ones, for whom he has died, and to whom he has promised eternal life. Thus you will honor him by confidence in his promises, and the joy of the Lord will be your strength.

And the same remarks may be addressed to those who are convinced of their lost condition, and, so far as they know, have submitted themselves to God, but yet have no hope of pardon and salvation. They are expecting some miraculous manifestation, or some overwhelming emotion, or some overpowering consciousness of acceptance; and experiencing none of these, they are in painful doubt and sore perplexity. It may be that the view which we have here taken of conversion may shed some light upon the path of such a one.

Let us, however, in the first place, be honest with you Have you really renounced your sins, submitted your whole being to God, and asked for mercy through Christ, as a free gift from him? It is not enough that you know yourself to be a sinner, overwhelmed in helpless guilt. You must go to God, and acknowledge it *to him.* You must confess your ill desert *at his feet*, and while you tell him that he would be just if he never heard your prayer, plead with him for mercy for the sake of his well-beloved Son. You must *arise and go to your Father.* Nor is this a distinction without a difference. It is by no means uncommon to meet with persons who are thus fully aware of their guilt, but who have never bowed the knee to God in prayer. In such cases, frequently after a long season of most agonizing distress, the very first time the sinner has bowed himself before God, his burden has been removed, and he has felt that his deadly wound has been healed. Nor is it enough to do this theoretically; it must be a *real acting of the soul.* We sometimes meet with anxious inquirers, who have been long in darkness, who tell us that they have submitted their hearts to God, and yet have no hope of salvation. They, in feeling, submit themselves to God, but they are not doing his will. They mean to *obey* him when he shall reveal himself to them; but they suppose that until this has been done they are under no obligation to serve him. They are, in fact, making a compromise with God; they will serve him, *if* he will first pardon and save them. Hence there is much within them which is not yielded up to God, and they suppose it is not to be yielded up until they receive assurance of pardon. Now, all this is an error, and it may be fatal. We are not only to say that we submit our whole selves to God; we are actually and without reserve to do it. We are not only to be willing to renounce every thing at variance with his will; we are actually to renounce it. We are not only to be willing to serve him; we are, at once, to do whatever we believe will please him. We are not only to believe that Christ is a complete Savior; we are to come, renouncing every merit of our own, and cast ourselves on him alone for salvation. Now, I would say to such an inquirer, Hast thou sincerely and from thy heart not only thought about all this, but actually done it? If so, the promise of God standeth sure to thee — "Him that cometh unto me I will in no wise cast out." Christ has not cast thee out; he has pardoned and received thee. It is not a thing to be done at some future time; it has been done already. And thou wilt find the witness in thyself if thou wilt but look for it. Thou wilt discover, if thou wilt compare thy present with thy former character, that thy moral affections are even now transformed. Thy desires, thy aversions, thy pleasures, the object for which thou art living, have all been changed. The process may have seemed gradual. The time when it commenced may not have been evident to thy own consciousness, but it is apparent, if thou wilt only observe, that thou art not the same person thou wast a short time since. Old things have passed away, and all things have become new. This is the evidence which God has bestowed upon us, that he has received us. Accept it with thankfulness, do his will from the heart, and go on thy way rejoicing.

And now, lastly, let me ask, is there in all this, any thing mystical, mysterious, or incomprehensible? Does it not, on the contrary, approve itself to the common sense and common conscience of every thoughtful man? If we have done wrong, if we have abused confidence, if we have trampled on rightful authority, if we have grieved our best friend by the basest ingratitude, ought we not to be deeply sensible of it, and from our hearts regret it? If we have done all this to God, should we not *go to him* with our confession, and, each one for himself, cast ourselves at his feet, disavowing our conduct, and humbly asking that he will forgive us? If we can make no reparation for our conduct, but are helplessly guilty, and God has provided a way, at the cost of an infinite sacrifice, by which he can pardon us without sullying his holiness, ought we not thankfully to accept of his mercy, and cast ourselves for salvation upon the merits of his well-beloved Son? And he has promised that, if we will do this, he will accept us as if we had never sinned, and bestow upon us the gift of eternal life. Can any terms be imagined more full of compassion, or better adapted to our sad and helpless need? I call, then, upon every man at once to repent, and believe in Christ, and to do it now. There is no time to be lost. God will not always continue to offer to you salvation. If you despise and wonder, you will certainly perish. If you do nothing but delay, and day by day put off the work of conversion until to-morrow, you will just as certainly perish. This controversy with your Maker must come to a crisis at some time or other. You may be reconciled to him now, while it is an acceptable time. You may delay until death shall seize you at a time when you are not aware, and then it will be settled at the day of judgment, when the books are opened, and the sentence goes forth upon every impenitent sinner, "Depart, ye cursed, into everlasting fire, prepared for the devil and his angels." From such a doom may God, for Christ's sake, deliver us.

IMITATORS OF GOD.

"Be ye therefore followers of God."
Ephesians v. 1.

To beings like ourselves, heirs of immortality, shortly to be judged according to the deeds done in the body, the cultivation of our spiritual nature must be the great end of our probation. We can carry beyond the grave no distinction except that founded on moral character. At death the prince puts off his purple, and the beggar his rags; the judge lays aside his ermine, and the convict his chain; the rich man bids adieu to his banquet, and the pauper to his crust. The flashing diamond and the snow-white pearl no longer adorn the child of luxury as she sleeps her dreamless sleep, and the worm riots no more daintily on her than on the unknown peasant girl that slumbers at her side. The dust of both is scattered without distinction to the winds of heaven. The places that once knew them shall know them no more forever, and their record is quickly blotted out from the memory of man.

All this is of the earth, earthy. The dust returns to the earth as it was, and the spirit returns to God who gave it. The soul, distinguished only by its moral lineaments, appears without disguise at the bar of eternal justice. Every one of us must give account for himself before God. By the moral character which we have formed on earth will our destiny be determined forever. Every one of us will then stand confessed the friend or the enemy of God. Classes so intensely unlike must, by necessity, be separated from each other. "Then shall the King say, Come, ye blessed of my Father, inherit the kingdom prepared for you from the foundation of the world;" or, "Depart, ye cursed, into everlasting fire, prepared for the devil and his angels. These shall go away into everlasting punishment, but the righteous into life eternal."

That every one of us must thus die, be forgotten on earth, and be judged by God for the deeds done in the body, I presume you all believe. Did I not, then, say truly, that the cultivation of our spiritual nature is the great end of our present existence? All else that men seek after, — wealth, rank, political power, social position, nay, even learning, and intellectual improvement, — are, in comparison with the preparation of our souls for heaven, but as the small dust of the balance. "What shall it profit a man to gain the whole world, and lose his own soul?" Nay, "What shall a man give in exchange for his soul?"

But how shall our spiritual nature be cultivated? I answer, By doing our duty. We are not prepared for the awards of eternity by the accumulation of wealth, by the enjoyment of pleasure, by the attainment of position, or the exercise of power; but by keeping the commandments of God, and thus being transformed into his image. He is our Father, our Lawgiver, and our Judge. His favor is life, and his loving kindness is better than life. If our moral character is in harmony with his, if we love him with child-like affection, and serve him with filial obedience, every where, in this world or the next, throughout all duration, whether now or millions of ages hence, we must, from necessity, be happy; for we are always surrounded by the presence of a loving Father, and we are ever greeted by his approving smile.

Hence we learn the unspeakable importance of those teachings respecting our duty which he has scattered so profusely around us. The heavens above and the earth beneath speak to us of his boundless wisdom and irresistible power, and present before us innumerable indications of his will.

The dealings of his providence, both with individuals and with nations, teach us his love of righteousness and his hatred of wrong, and clearly intimate that though he hears the sigh of the penitent, he will in no wise clear the guilty. We may thus, from the things that are made, understand much of his eternal power and Godhead; so that, if we had no other teaching, we should be clearly without excuse. Had our Father in heaven, having bestowed upon us our various endowments, given us no other light than the light of nature, he would have dealt with us justly. With these means alone of knowing our duty and becoming imitators of him, we should have been under imperative and solemn obligations to love and serve him.

But such was not his will. Our condition was too momentous to be left to the least contingency. Hastening as we were to eternity, — an eternity depending for its happiness or misery wholly on our moral resemblance to him, — he condescended, by a written revelation, to make us acquainted with our duty. Age after age he spoke to us by prophet and by seer, and thus made known to us spiritual truth. For this purpose he appeared to Moses amidst the lightnings and thunderings of Mount Sinai. He touched the lips of Isaiah with fire from the altar, and revealed himself to Daniel, the man greatly beloved, and to other inspired men, in the visions of the old dispensation. Last of all, he spoke to us by his Son, who is the brightness of his glory and the express image of his person. Lest his will should be misunderstood, when made known to us by men weak and fallible like ourselves, God was made flesh and dwelt among us to reveal the pure light from heaven, unobscured by transmission through the medium of a sinful and finite intelligence. The will of our Father in heaven is thus made known to us so clearly that we cannot mistake it, unless we love darkness rather than light. And lest, even then, we should still remain thoughtless and unmoved, he has sent his Spirit to take these truths and present them before us, so that we cannot help knowing both our duty and our danger. Behold, then, the boundless compassion of our Father in heaven. He knew, as no finite intelligence can know, the infinite importance of the preparation of our souls for heaven, and he has left no conceivable means untried, to give us a perfect knowledge of his will, and teach us how, by being made like him, we may dwell in his presence forever. I put it to your consciences, my fellow-men — could our Father in heaven do more for us than he has done? He has taught us by men like ourselves, and has sent his beloved Son to be our instructor, and has enforced his instructions by the enlightening of his Holy Spirit. If, now, we will not learn our duty, our case must be desperate, and we must fail under the condemnation of those that knew their duty, but they did it not.

And here we cannot but observe what seems a peculiarity, if not an infirmity, of our nature. Precept alone rarely produces upon us the impression which might justly be expected. We may acknowledge the authority of the teacher, we may comprehend the reasonableness of the command; but not unfrequently our spirit rises in resistance simply because it is a command. "When the commandment came," said the apostle, "sin revived." We wait to see the precept exemplified by the obedience of others before we yield to it the practical control over our conduct. Hence the wonderful effect of example in swaying the affections and directing the opinions of mankind. Without any precept whatever, example frequently accomplishes what the naked commandment could never hope to effect. John Howard might have spent his life in discoursing upon criminal jurisprudence, and have died, without seeing the woe of a solitary prisoner alleviated. He, however, took the opposite course, and chose to act by example. He set himself at work to reform the prison in his own immediate neighborhood, and when this was done he proceeded to the regions beyond; nor did he cease from his labor until he had fathomed the depth of misery that existed in every prison house of Europe. It was in this manner that he inculcated the precept, "Remember those that are in bonds as bound with them," and so inculcated it as to work a change in the opinions of mankind. Robert Raikes wrote no works, that I ever heard of, on the religious education of the young, or the obligation of Christians to instruct the children of the poor in the knowledge of God. He established a Sabbath school, however, in the city of Gloucester, and the consequence has been that Protestant Christendom is, at this moment, covered with Sabbath schools. In this manner he inculcated the precept, "Train up a child in the way he should go, and when he is old he will not depart from it."

My brethren, do you not perceive the lesson that is to be learned from all this? Do you not see that a power for the accomplishment of good has been bestowed upon you which you never yet apprehended? When the duty is pressed upon you of doing good to your brethren, one of you replies, "I am not learned;" another, "I am not wealthy;" another, "I cannot write a book;" another, "I am not eloquent;" and another, "I have no influence." All very well; but what of it? You have hands, and feet, an understanding, and a conscience. Employ them, just as God has given them to you, in doing some good thing, no matter how small it may seem to human appearance. Put your own heart into it, and labor at it in deep humility, and with child-like faith. Do not ask others to help you until you have set an example of doing all you can yourself. Do not wait until an opportunity presents itself of doing some great thing a thousand miles off; but take the first thing that presents itself at your very door. Labor at it until God, by his providence, shall command you to cease, and see what will come of it. If it be a seed which the Lord has planted, it will assuredly spring up and bear fruit; and though the beginning be small, the latter end will greatly increase. And, even if nothing comes of it beyond the immediate good which you do with your own hands, be not discouraged; you will have received a rich blessing in your own soul. " Inasmuch as ye have done it to the least of these my brethren, ye have done it unto me."

Intimately allied to this is another peculiarity of our moral nature. The idea of law, as indicating restraint, is specially distasteful to the human mind, unless the legislator is himself subjected to the enactment which he enforces upon others. We require that he who makes the law shall himself present the first example of submission to it. When this is done, our repugnance generally vanishes. We look at it as a rule made for all of us in common, and feel assured that it was intended for the public good, inasmuch as the legislators themselves are the very first to bow to its authority.

Now, even for these peculiarities of our nature our Father in heaven has mercifully made provision. In infinite condescension, he has practically exemplified obedience to every precept which he has imposed upon us.

The laws under which he has placed us are substantially two. The first is the law of simple benevolence and universal love. We are commanded to love him with all our hearts, and our neighbor as ourselves. This commandment was imposed upon our first parents on the day of their creation. It binds us to child-like and supreme affection to God, and impartial love to universal man. It bids us look upon every human being as our brother, no matter how stolid may be his ignorance, how brutal his degradation, and how causeless the injury which he may have inflicted upon us. We are to treat all men, simply because they are men, the children of one common Parent, with fraternal good will, ever desiring to minister to the happiness and alleviate the sorrow of our brethren, so that each one of us may be a centre of social endearment to every circle by which we are surrounded. For this reason God has placed in our hands, in different proportions, the blessings of this life. He has made some rich and others poor, and long ago he announced to us that the poor should never cease out of the land. We are to consider every possession as a sacred trust, placed in our hands, not for our own benefit, but for the benefit of all. Such is the rule which our Father in heaven most mercifully has laid down for the government of our conduct.

And he who enacted this law has enforced it, first of all, by his own example. Creation, from its first conception to ts last result, is one unceasing act of love to man. This goodly heritage was prepared for us, by omniscient wisdom, before the morning stars sang together, or ever the sons of God shouted for joy. Man was not placed upon the earth until every arrangement had been made, not only for his reception, but for the sustentation and well-being of all the myriads that ever should inhabit it. Year after year, through the long lapse of ages, has he visited the earth with the inexhaustible loveliness of spring, the maturing heat of summer, the abundant gifts of autumn, and the solemn repose of winter, filling our hearts with food and gladness. But this universal provision did not satisfy the infinite benevolence of our heavenly Father. His eye rests with compassion on every single intelligent being. These countless millions through the ages have been individually dependent upon his bounty; day by day he has sent a portion to every household, and spread a table for every family. Nor does he limit his benefits to those that love and adore him. The bold blasphemer and the humble penitent share alike in his daily bounty, and at night are soothed to rest under the shadow of his protection. Even the tribes of irrational beings seek their meat from God. What he giveth them they gather; he openeth his hand and satisfieth the wants of every living thing. He hears the young ravens when they cry, and stoops down to scatter crumbs in the pathway of the sparrow.

And now, having given us such a precept, and set before us such an example, God calls upon us not only to obey, but to imitate him. "Be ye therefore followers [imitators] of God." Speaking to us by the lips of his well-beloved Son, he saith to every one of us, "Love your enemies, bless them that curse you, do good to them that hate you, and pray for them that despitefully use you and persecute you, that ye may be the children of your Father who is in heaven; for he maketh his sun to rise on the evil and on the good, and sendeth rain on the just and on the unjust. Be ye therefore merciful, as your Father in heaven is merciful."

But this world has been ruined by sin. Every child of Adam has corrupted himself, and in consequence of rebellion against God, is exposed to the condemnation of everlasting death. It was the purpose of God to redeem our race, and transform it again into his own image. To accomplish this, God made a most gracious provision for the pardon of our sins. The way of escape from the doom which we deserved was thrown wide open. God could be just, and justify him that believeth. Nay, more, he sent his Holy Spirit to show us the things which respect our salvation. And having done all this, he committed the work to the ministration of men themselves. He requires that every one of his children shall be a co-worker with him, and make it the business of his life to rescue men from everlasting death, and thus carry forward his purposes of mercy towards our lost and sin-smitten race. "Ye are," said the Savior, "the light of the world."

But it seems to be an established law in the government of God, that we are never permitted to confer great blessings upon our brethren except through the medium of suffering and self-sacrifice. The patriotism that has rescued nations from oppression, presents itself before us scarred and gory from the battle field and the scaffold, scorned by the few, neglected by the many, but opening a new career of liberty and honor to the very men who could not comprehend the greatness of its undertaking. And thus the religion of Christ has won its most signal victories in dungeons and at the stake, and its holy champions, who by faith subdued kingdoms, had trial of cruel mockings and scourgings, yea, moreover, of bonds and imprisonment; they were stoned, they were sawn asunder, were tempted, were slain with the sword, and wandered about in sheepskins and goatskins, being destitute, afflicted, and tormented, of whom the world was not worthy.

The great work of the disciple of Christ is to subdue the world to his Master; and this work he can hope to perform only by self-sacrifice. The faith of the gospel is then something more than trust in Christ, and grateful love for his pardoning mercy. It involves nobler, and higher, and sterner elements than these. It calls upon us to universal self-sacrifice for the salvation of men. It has nothing that it calls its own; all is laid on the altar, and all is consecrated to the service of the Master. Immortal souls for whom Christ died are at stake, and there is nothing that we must not cheerfully suffer, nothing that we must not relinquish, that we may be the means of conferring on them the boon of eternal life. Does the work of Christ require our property, we must give it. Is our personal service demanded, we must render it; nay, we must seek for occasions in which to employ it. Do the pleasures of sense, or of taste, or of literature, or of social distinction impede us in our labor we must surrender them. If a right eye causes us to offend, — and a right eye is very dear, — we must pluck it out. If a right hand interferes with our entire consecration to Christ, — and a right hand is very useful, — we must cut it off. The path of duty may lead through the valley of humiliation, — we must follow it fearlessly. We may be called to suffer reproach and have our names cast out as evil, — let us bear it exultingly, rejoicing that we are counted worthy to suffer reproach, for the name of Jesus. A service may be laid upon us which can only be performed at the peril of our lives, — we must willingly peril them to save the souls for whom Christ died. "He that saveth his life shall lose it, and he that loseth his life for my sake shall find it." Such are the precepts of Jesus.

But, as I have said, our Father in heaven imposes upon us no precept, obedience to which he has not himself first exemplified. In condescension such as finite mind can never comprehend, he loves us with the affection which he requires us to cherish towards him. He commands *us* to love *him* with our whole heart; and "God *so loved* the world that he gave *his only begotten* Son, that whosoever believeth on him should not perish, but have everlasting life." He forbids us to make any reserve, or to withhold from him the dearest objects of our affection. But *he* has done *this* for *us all.* When he gave up his well-beloved Son, he gave him up wholly, and shrunk back from nothing that was needful for our redemption. He yielded up the Son of his love to hunger and thirst, to cold and nakedness, to persecution, shame, and reproach, to the temptations of Satan such as no created being had ever undergone, nay, to the hiding of his face in the hour of his deepest agony, that such sinners as we are might be brought back to the family of the holy. Well might there be silence in heaven when this purpose of mercy was first revealed to the angelic hosts. They had for ages contemplated the unspeakable love of God; but when it was announced that he would make such a sacrifice for such a race, they were struck dumb in holy amazement. A new and transporting view of the condescension and love of God burst upon the sight of the seraphim. No finite mind could fathom its depth or explore its immensity. It was love to a race of rebels, guilty, odious, and despicable, who had trampled on his laws, and did not even like to retain him in their knowledge. And remember, redeemed sinner, this love reached even unto thee. God so loved thee that he gave his well-beloved Son; and if he so loved us, surely we ought to love one another. I put it to your own hearts, beloved — ought we not to be followers of God?

But there is another aspect of this subject, slightly differing from that which we have taken. We hear much in the New Testament about giving up our whole selves to the Savior, of being constrained by the love of Christ, and doing, not our own will, but the will of him that loved us. He requires us to give up ourselves, our affections, a living sacrifice to him for time and eternity. But remember he first set us the example by giving up himself wholly for us. And what a sacrifice was this! Here was self-sacrificing benevolence that must stand forever without a parallel in the history of the universe. He thought it not robbery to be equal with God. By him were all things created, visible or invisible, whether they be thrones, or dominions, or principalities, or powers, all things were created by him and for him. Yet, when the fulness of time was come, he emptied himself of his glory, and took upon him the form of a servant. When he had put his hand to the work of our redemption, there was no sacrifice which he did not make, there was no humiliation which he did not undergo, in order to accomplish it. He, whose arm upheld the universe, subjected himself to the law of humanity. The high possessor of heaven and earth had not where to lay his head. He, before whom the mightiest created intelligences bowed down in lowly adoration, condescended to be railed at as a madman. The Holy One of Israel was accused of collusion with the chief of the devils. His life was worn out in labors, and watchings, and fastings, while he was ever putting forth miraculous power to relieve the woes of others, though never to relieve his own. Follow him to the last supper, and see him, like the humblest menial, washing the begrimed feet of fishermen and publicans. Go with him to the garden of Gethsemane; remark the bloody sweat, the agony of that thrice-repeated prayer, "Father, if it be possible, let this cup pass from me;" observe the arrest by the mob, the flight of the disciples, the blows and mockery of the soldiery; hearken to the preference for Barabbas, while the air is rent with the cries, "Crucify him, crucify him;" see the crown of thorns, the nails driven home through those hands and feet that sin had never polluted; and listen to his cry, "My God, my God, why hast thou forsaken me?" Think of this, ye who have washed your robes and made them white in the blood of the Lamb, and if the Holy Spirit condescend to help you, you shall know something of the love of Christ which passeth knowledge. He withheld nothing from you, and can you withhold any thing from him? Does not your heart melt within you as you think of his love? and does not every power of your soul cry out and shout, "I will be an imitator of Jesus." "We love him because he first loved us."

And when you are thinking of all this, do not lose yourselves in vague generalities, but take each element of this transaction, and meditate upon it singly. Jesus Christ was no imaginary character, but, in his human nature, a man like any one of us, exposed to all the pains, and moved by all the impulses, of humanity, yet without sin. Endowed with an intellect of incomparable power, and capable of teaching the sages of this world as if they were children, he spent his life in imparting instruction to a few illiterate peasants. His taste was surpassingly exquisite, yet he so spoke that the common people heard him gladly. With eloquence such as to prompt the exclamation, "Never man spake like this man," his common audiences were rustic Galileans. His social sympathies were refined and delicate; yet his chosen companions were not the highly bred and illustrious, but those of every rank, who did the will of his Father in heaven. Borne down under the weight of his mighty undertaking, like any other man, he yearned for companionship; but there was not a being on earth who could comprehend his character, or understand his mission, or to whom he could unbosom his cares. He trod the wine press alone, and of the people, there was none with him. When, indeed, was there a single precept for the cultivation of Christian character which he did not exemplify in his own life? O, what shame does the life of Christ cast upon the pride, and vanity, and self-indulgence of multitudes of us who claim to be his disciples!

And here, my brethren, you observe the appropriateness of the exhortation, "Run with patience the race set before you, *looking unto Jesus*." Look to him as the interpreter of his own precepts. He has told us how to live, and he has exemplified every precept in his own life. You are frequently in doubt as to your duty. You may, perhaps, without difficulty, discover the precept, but you doubt as to the mode of its application. There is a worldly and a spiritual mode of understanding it, and you hesitate between them. In every such case look unto Jesus. See how he understood it, and how he put it in practice, and all your doubts will readily be dissipated. And even when you do not readily discover the rule of conduct, you never need be long in uncertainty. Look unto Jesus. Ask yourself in simplicity of heart, "What will best please my Savior?" and you will find small room for hesitation. The love of Christ furnishes the surest and simplest rule of duty. Giving our affection to him, we shall always do the things that are pleasing in his sight.

Let us look to Jesus for moral impulse. The path of duty, though a safe, is a rough one. Think of it as we may, when we come to the actual trial, to bear reproach, to be sneered at and neglected, to have men separate us from their company, in a word, to lose caste with our fellows, is by no means pleasant to flesh and blood. Specially is this the case in youth, when the social impulses are the strongest, and the power of resistance to public opinion the weakest. When, under the pressure of all these influences, the faith of the believer begins to falter, then is the time to look unto Jesus. Consider the example which he has set before us, and let us plant our feet in his footprints. Think how he triumphed over the world by scorning its delights, and meekly bearing all that it could inflict. Did the Son of God set thee such an example, and hast thou neither the courage nor love to follow it? Did he do all this for thee, and dost thou refuse to bear so light a cross for him? Keep thine eye fixed on Christ, and as thou gazest upon him thou shalt be strengthened by might, through his spirit, in thy inner man. As thou fillest thy soul with devout conceptions of the example of Jesus, the world will dwindle into insignificance, and, emancipated from its thraldom, thou shalt walk abroad in the noble liberty of the sons and daughters of the Lord Almighty.

And, my brethren, let us look to Jesus if we would estimate the reward of those that follow his example. As Messiah, the Mediator between God and man, the incomparable glory to which he is exalted is ever spoken of as the reward of his sufferings and humiliation. It was because he thus humbled himself that he was raised to the right hand of the Father. And the rule is the same for him and for all who imitate him. Every reproach endured for him, every self-denial suffered rather than grieve him, every labor distasteful to flesh and blood performed simply to please him, will render that crown the brighter which the Lord will give to them that love his appearing. When fainting under trial, and harassed by temptation, look unto Jesus, the author and finisher of your faith, who, for the joy that was set before him, endured the cross, despising the shame, and is now set down at the right hand of the throne of God. Let this mind, my brethren, be in you, which was also in Christ Jesus, who, being in the form of God, thought it no robbery to be equal with God; but made himself of no reputation, and took upon him the form of a servant, and was made in the likeness of man, and being found in fashion as a man, he humbled himself and became obedient unto death, even the death of the cross. *Wherefore* God hath highly exalted him, and given him a name that is above every name, that at the name of Jesus every knee should bow, of things in heaven, and things in earth, and things under the earth; and that every tongue should confess that Jesus Christ is Lord, to the glory of God the Father. Wherefore, beloved, comfort one another with these words.

GRIEVING THE SPIRIT.

"HE SHALL TAKE OF MINE AND SHALL SHOW IT UNTO YOU."
John xvi. 15.

THE Being referred to in these words is the Comforter, which is the Holy Ghost. The work which he accomplishes is also defined. All things, saith the Savior, that the Father hath are *mine*, therefore he shall take of *mine*, and shall show it unto you. That is to say, the Son possesses all the knowledge of the Father. As the Father knoweth me, so I know the Father. The Holy Spirit also possesses all the knowledge of the Godhead, for the Spirit searcheth all things, yea, the deep things of God. This knowledge in such measure as he pleases he reveals unto us. He communicates with the spirit of man, and teaches us truth which we could not otherwise know ; and enables us to comprehend, and receive, and apply to ourselves truth which, without his aid, would be sterile and unproductive. The power of truth over the mind of sinful man is thus ascribed to the agency of the blessed Comforter.

It is manifest that a fact of this nature must be a matter of revelation. Reason could never discover it. Natural religion could never discover it. Our senses could never perceive it. As it acts, except in the case of miraculous inspiration, in perfect harmony with all the faculties of the mind, our consciousness could not recognize it. All the knowledge we possess concerning it must come directly from God himself. We must therefore go to the Scriptures exclusively, if we would learn all that can be known on this subject. In such a case, to affirm what can be, and what cannot be, must evidently be to darken counsel by words without knowledge.

In considering at this time some of the aspects in which the work of the Spirit is made known to us, it is my intention to confine myself entirely to the teachings of the word of God. It is not my purpose to treat of the work of the Spirit in general, but only of that part of it which has respect specially to the soul of man in regeneration. If such an agency is exerted, and if it be the source of all spiritual illumination, it is important that every man should understand it, who is seriously asking the momentous question, What must I do to be saved?

I shall therefore take it for granted, that there is a divine Being, termed in the Scriptures the Holy Spirit, whose special office it is to reveal to the mind of man that truth which relates to our spiritual nature and eternal destiny. It was this Spirit which inspired the prophets of old. It was by the illumination of the same Spirit that the apostles and evangelists made known to us the will of God in the New Testament. Nay, the Messiah, on earth, spake not by himself; the Spirit was poured out upon him without measure, and thus he revealed to us truth pure and transparent, as it flowed through his lips from the bosom of the ever-blessed God. Nor is the influence of the Spirit confined to prophets, apostles, and holy men of old. The Scriptures represent the Comforter as dwelling in the hearts of all the children of God. We are told that the submission of our wills to the monitions of the Spirit is the evidence of our adoption into the family of the redeemed, for as many as are led by the Spirit of God, they are the sons of God. Ye are not in the flesh, but in the spirit, if so be that the Spirit of God dwell in you. If any man have not the Spirit of Christ, he is none of his.

Nor is the influence of the Spirit upon the soul of man confined exclusively to the children of God. The Scriptures represent bad men as resisting the Spirit, grieving the Spirit, and turning a deaf ear to all his monitions. Such was the case under the old dispensation. This truth is, however, made known to us more emphatically in the New Testament. Men are there addressed directly, and told that they are at this moment resisting the Holy Ghost. The sin against the Holy Ghost is also singled out, as the sin for which there is no forgiveness. A man may speak against the Son of man and be forgiven; but whosoever speaketh against the Holy Ghost, it shall not be forgiven him, neither in this world, nor in the world to come. It would seem, then, that the influences of the Holy Spirit are very generally bestowed upon man. Both good and bad men are, in some sense, taught by him. The one obey and the other disobey his instructions.

While, however, I thus speak of the universality of the Spirit's agency, I would remark that, under the old dispensation, this blessing seems to have been bestowed almost exclusively upon the Hebrews. It was given only in rare and exceptional cases to the Gentiles. With the Christian dispensation a new era commenced. The Gospel was to be preached to all nations; the promise was given that the Holy Ghost should attend upon the faithful preaching of the news of salvation. We are all living in the full enjoyment of this promised blessing. Christ is preached to us every Sabbath day, and every one of us has beheld the power, if he has not felt, in his own soul, the strivings of the Holy Spirit.

It is of importance here to remark that this gift is always spoken of, in the New Testament, as the crowning proof of the love of God to man, and his last effort to redeem us from the curse of sin. If this fail, the case of the sinner is hopeless. If the Spirit is grieved and withdraw from the soul, the man is lost beyond the possibility of redemption.

Nor is this without reason. We were justly condemned for our sins. Had God made no provision for our pardon, but left us to the consequences of our transgressions, his throne would have still shone spotless in holiness. The fallen angels were left, for their transgression, in chains under darkness, to the judgment of the great day. But for man God provided a way of escape, at the cost of an infinite sacrifice. He so loved the world that he gave his only begotten Son, that whosoever believeth in him should not perish, but have everlasting life. The atonement made for our sins was as extensive as the ruin by the fall. A pardon, free, full, and universal, was offered to all who would penitently and in faith come and accept of it. Jesus Christ came to seek and to save that which was lost; if any man, therefore, be lost, he may be assured that Christ came to seek and to save him. A pardon is provided for him, if he will, in a right temper of heart, come and ask for it. The door of heaven is thus thrown wide open, and whosoever will may come and take the water of life freely.

But men, with one consent, begin to make excuse. They prefer sin to holiness. They do not choose to have God to reign over them. The eyes of their understanding are blinded, so that they have no suitable appreciation of spiritual things. The coming, the invisible, the eternal is shut out from their thoughts by the present, the visible, the temporal. In this our hopeless exigency, our Father in heaven makes one more effort to save us. He sends the Holy Spirit to arouse us from our moral lethargy, and direct our attention to our relations to him, and the fearful danger of our present position. More than this, he has promised that this Spirit shall abide ever with those who sincerely desire it, to guide them into all truth, confirm them in all goodness, and lead them in safety to his kingdom in heaven. If we reject this last proof of the love of God, what can remain for us but to be left to the result of our own choices, and thus perish without remedy?

It is in view of this heavenly influence upon the minds of both saints and sinners, that our Lord declares, "It is expedient for you that I go away; for if I go not away, the Comforter will not come unto you; but if I depart, I will send him unto you." In these words our Lord teaches us, not only the infinite importance of the presence of the Com-

19*

forter, but intimates that this blessing is one of the results of his atoning sacrifice, and his ascension to the right hand of the Father.

We may thus learn something of the solemn responsibility which rests upon us who live under the new dispensation, and are partakers in this last and most astonishing proof of our heavenly Father's love. He has provided for us a way of salvation; he has freely offered to us eternal life; he has sent his Holy Spirit to persuade us to accept of the blessings purchased by the death of his Son. If, under such circumstances, we perish, who can tell the inexcusableness of our guilt? who can measure the solemnity of our doom?

But it may be important to inquire, What is the object of the agency of the Holy Spirit upon the minds of men?

I would answer, in the first place, the Holy Spirit is not given in order to furnish us with any new revelation. "Holy men of old spake as they were moved by the Holy Ghost." Under both dispensations they were inspired to reveal to us the will of God, and the authenticity of their message was attested by miraculous gifts. All that we receive as a revelation is the result of such inspiration. But with the teachings of those who were personally commissioned by Christ, we believe that the communications of God to us, concerning our salvation, have forever ceased. To the Scriptures which he has given to us no man may add, and from them no man may take away. God has here revealed to us all that he desires us to know of his dealings with man, and then closed the book forever. The Spirit of God speaks no more to us by way of inspiration. It is to the Bible alone that we must go, if we would learn his will concerning us. The voice of the Spirit is not heard in the floating, contradictory, and baseless fables of tradition. He speaks not to us in bulls of popes, the decrees of councils, or synods, or convocations, in the resolutions of conventions, or in the words of any man, or any association of men, claiming power over the conscience. To the law and the testimony: if they speak not according to this word, it is because there is no light in them. If we yield up the direction of our consciences to such guides, we do it at our peril, and it may be to our eternal undoing. What the Spirit has taught is to be found in the Scriptures of the Old and New Testaments; all else is the teaching of men. No man can claim for his utterances authority over the conscience, unless he authenticates his message by the manifestation of miraculous power.

Secondly. The Holy Spirit is not bestowed upon men in order to place them under any new obligation to love and obey God, and repent and believe the Gospel. These duties are forever binding upon us from the fact that Jehovah is our God, and such a God, and that we are his intelligent and accountable creatures. "He hath showed it [his eternal power and Godhead] unto them," saith the apostle Paul; "therefore they are without excuse." Every moral intelligence is bound by the strongest obligations to love God with the whole heart, and serve him with filial obedience. Every such intelligence who has sinned, is, in the same manner, bound to repent and humble himself before God. These obligations are fixed and unalterable as the throne of Jehovah. And this duty is not a thing of time or place — it presses upon us under all circumstances, and at every instant. There can be no moment in the existence of an intelligent creature, in which it can cease from loving God without being guilty of atrocious wickedness. There cannot be a moment in the existence of a sinner in which it is not his duty immediately to repent. God and himself are the only beings concerned in this controversy, and it is the first duty of his existence to draw near in humble acknowledgment, and ask for forgiveness of Him against whom he has sinned. Hence we see how greatly men err who suppose that they are under no obligation to repent, because they have never been visited by the influences of the Holy Spirit. Let them remember that if it was not their duty to repent until the Holy Spirit were sent to awaken them, it would never be their duty at all; for the Spirit of

God creates no new obligation. Let such a man, then, know that by this subterfuge he is deceiving his own soul; he is hardening his heart, and rendering his condition daily more hopeless. Instead of slumbering in this false security let him arise and call mightily upon God, lest, peradventure, he perish not. The Holy Spirit bestows no new faculties—it creates no new obligations. We must come to God just such sinners as we are, with just the powers we possess, or we can never come at all. Any reasoning, which teaches us that we may safely continue for a moment impenitent, and enemies to God, is from the father of lies, and if we believe it, we do it at the peril of our souls.

But you will ask, If such be the case, what is the need of any agency of the Spirit in our conversion and sanctification? I reply, There is no reason whatever for such an agency that is not found in our own hardness of heart, and our deep and sinful insensibility to spiritual truth. The facts which concern our relations to God do not affect us like any other well-known truth. Every act of sin, by a natural tendency, stupefies the conscience, and renders the soul less susceptible to spiritual impressions. We have been sinners from the beginning, and thus this insensibility has become fixed and immovable; and it furnishes one of the most significant evidences of our incorrigible depravity.

Let me illustrate my meaning by a few plain examples. You are humbled and ashamed if ever you have been guilty of ingratitude to man; but your unceasing ingratitude to God never has awakened in your bosom a single emotion of penitential sorrow. We fear for the result when we have justly deserved punishment at the hands of man; we know that we are exposed to the righteous judgment of God, and remain utterly unmoved. To escape the most trifling inconvenience, or secure the most momentary gratification, we deliberately defy our Maker, and knowingly incur his extreme displeasure. Self-sacrificing benevolence naturally fills us with admiration; but we can contemplate the sacrifice of

Christ, who, though he was rich, for our sakes became poor, without a single throb of grateful affection. In other cases, when we know that danger is impending, we leave no means unattempted by which we may avert it. Your dwellings and warehouses are liable to be consumed by fire, and your ships to founder at sea, and you take every precaution to have them fully insured. You know that your souls are exposed to everlasting woe, and that the irrevocable sentence may go forth against you at any moment, and you have never yet put forth one honest effort to escape the wrath to come. When an opportunity occurs of making an unusually favorable investment, we mortgage our property, we strain our credit to the utmost, that we may secure as large a share as possible of the benefit, and men praise our boldness and forethought. But when mansions in heaven, when seats at the right hand of Christ, when glory such as eye hath not seen nor the heart of man conceived, are offered to us as a free gift, we will not abandon a single lust, we will not endure a single self-denial, nay, we will not make a single effort, in order to appropriate these blessings to ourselves.

All this, beloved, you know to be the truth. In what we have thus said, we bring not against you any strange accusation. We only repeat what many of you have deliberately told us. When I have urged you to seek first of all the salvation of your souls, you reply, that the truths of religion, for some cause or other, do not affect you like other truth, and that, in this respect, you only resemble all other men. It must surely be very wicked for you to live thus, and to have hardened your conscience against the solemn reproofs and the merciful invitations of your Maker and Redeemer. But the infinite goodness of God has not been exhausted by your long-continued contumacy. It is because he cannot bear to see you perish, although you are just so unreasonable, obdurate, and ungrateful, that he has sent his Spirit to arouse you from the slumber of sin, and persuade you to lay hold on everlasting life. Our Father in heaven knows how the habit of doing wrong has stupefied our consciences, and enslaved us under the dominion of the senses, and therefore he has sent his Holy Spirit to convince us of sin, and of righteousness, and of the judgment to come. If we persist in our rejection of all these offers of mercy, what can save us from destruction? God does not interfere with the freedom of will with which at our creation he has endowed us. If, in spite of all that he has done to save us, we still choose to disobey him, we must be lost, and our ruin must rest upon our own heads.

But you will very naturally ask, What is the nature of that influence which the Holy Spirit exerts upon a human soul. With the metaphysical topics involved in this question, I have nothing to do. I confine myself to the facts concerning it which have been revealed in the Scriptures. These alone concern our moral nature, and these alone can affect our eternal destiny.

Our Lord, when speaking on this subject, gives us, I think, all the knowledge which we can ever obtain concerning it. "When the Comforter, which is the Holy Ghost, is come, he shall take of mine, and show it unto you." By *mine*, he means the truth common to him and the Father. The office of the Holy Ghost is, then, in some manner peculiar to himself, to *set before us the truth.* He withdraws the veil which our sinful habits have spread over spiritual facts, and we see them in their naked reality. I have said that whilst the truth which respects only the present world produces upon us its legitimate effect, the truths of the world to come lie in our minds powerless as though we knew them to be fables. Now, the Holy Spirit is given for the purpose of restoring to spiritual truth its natural and reasonable efficiency. It is as though we had our eyes fixed on a book in the deep gloom of twilight. We believe that the page reveals truth, we know the language in which it is written; but the light is so imperfect, that, though here and there we can distinguish a capital letter and now and then decipher a word, yet we are unable to make out distinctly a single sentence. But let light now fall upon the page, and every word and every letter is instantly revealed, the thought of the writer beams upon our understanding, and the channel of communication between his mind and ours is, for the time, fully established. Very similar to this is the case before us. We read and we hear about God, the Judge of all, and Christ, the Redeemer of men, about sin and repentance, heaven and hell, the wages of guilt and the reward of holiness, and we care so little about them that the words hardly awaken a thought, or leave a trace upon our recollection. But let now the Holy Spirit show these things of Christ unto us, and they are at once invested with the terrors or the joys of a most solemn reality. God, who, a little while since, seemed a mere powerless abstraction, now appears to us the living God, spotless in holiness, immutable in justice, a discerner of the thoughts and intents of the heart, before whom all things are naked and open. The sinner's life, which seemed to be sullied only here and there by a few venial transgressions, now appears nothing but one long act of unpardonable guilt, for which he can make no reparation. Eternity, which before was only a wonderful metaphysical conception, now spreads out before him as an overwhelming verity, which he cannot think of without a shudder; for it is not simply eternity, but an eternity of woe, that now appears before him in all its dread solemnity. The Holy Spirit thus sets the things of Christ, the truths of revelation, distinctly before the mind of the sinner, and, so long as this influence is exerted, he feels, intensely, the powers of the world to come.

On this subject I need make no reference to the experience of the disciples of Christ. They know full well, that for all their true knowledge of God, for all their convictions of sin, for every emotion of penitential sorrow, for every act of faith, for every glimpse of the glory that is to be revealed, they are indebted to the influence of the Holy Spirit. They have abundant occasion to know that the reading, or the hearing, of the word of life, is utterly powerless without the illumination of the Spirit of God. Hence the reason of their incessant prayer,

Open thou mine eyes, that I may behold wondrous things out of thy law. Hence their supplication for that heavenly teaching, which alone can make them wise unto salvation. Hence their frequently bitter cry, Cast me not away from thy presence, and take not thy Holy Spirit from me. Hence the earnestness with which they plead for an outpouring of the Spirit upon themselves, their children, their congregation, the whole Israel of God, and a world perishing in sin. Hence, also, the reason why our Lord so often inculcates upon us this duty, and teaches us that God is more willing to bestow upon us this last, best gift than any other. "If ye, being evil, know how to give good gifts unto your children, how much more shall your heavenly Father give the Holy Spirit to them that ask him!"

It is not, however, of Christ's people that I here desire to speak. I wish to address particularly those persons who have, for many years, listened to the preaching of the gospel; who, perhaps, habitually read the Scriptures; who, in the Sabbath school and the Bible class, have studied the meaning of the oracles of God. There are many who, while they are doing all this, remain unchanged in their love of the world, and have never yet taken the first step in the path of preparation for heaven. Some of you who now hear me, know this to be your own case, and may possibly be congratulating yourselves that you have none of this sin to answer for—that the Holy Spirit has never been sent to arouse your conscience or call you to repentance. You may possibly derive some satisfaction from the belief that though you have not yet obeyed the gospel, you have not incurred the still greater guilt of grieving the Holy Spirit.

Should it be as you say, thoughtless fellow-sinner, you have small cause for self-gratulation. I should be most unwilling to believe that it is as you suppose. Can it be that there is here a single soul that has been from the beginning forsaken of God, on whose moral darkness the Holy Spirit has never poured a single ray of light? Is there here a conscience so obdurate that no warning of the Spirit has ever awakened in it a single religious emotion? How sad beyond expression must be the condition of such a soul! What hope can remain of its salvation? Like a tree twice dead, plucked up by the roots, the sun may shine upon it with meridian warmth, the rain may descend with refreshing moisture, but they tend only to hasten its decay. Its vitality is extinguished; it is good for nothing but the burning.

But I will not, I do not, believe this of any one of you. I believe that the Holy Spirit is even now striving with you. Look back with me over some of the events of your past history, and determine for yourselves, whether you have not frequently been visited by the Holy Spirit, and whether you have not as often grieved him by your neglect.

I would have you remember that you have, from childhood known the Holy Scriptures, and have long been familiar with the conditions of the plan of salvation. For the most part, you think of these solemn truths without any emotion whatever. The favor of men moves you to action, rather than the fear of God; the present, the visible and tangible, seem to you the real, while the spiritual and the eternal are to you the shadowy, the uncertain, the valueless. This I think you will admit to be the common and ordinary condition of your soul.

But, if I do not greatly mistake, there have been occasions, brief parentheses, as it were, in your existence, when it has been otherwise. You can recall the time and the place when the truths which were as familiar to you as household words were clothed with a power before which you trembled in moral agony. It may have been while hearing the oft-repeated message of salvation, or when some friend has told you of a Savior's love, or in the solitude of your own thoughts, or even while the shout of boisterous hilarity was dying away upon your ear, that eternity, with all its realities, burst suddenly on your affrighted vision. The bottomless pit seemed to yawn before you, and the next step might plunge you into the abyss. Imagination placed you already in the presence of your Judge, and you heard beforehand the awful sentence, Depart, ye cursed, into everlasting fire, prepared for the devil and his angels. While you acknowledged the sentence to be just, you shrank back from your doom, shrieking in agony, How can I dwell with devouring fire? how can I lie down in everlasting burnings? The world, with its pleasures and cares, its hopes and its fears, seemed to you less than nothing and vanity, and an interest in Christ the only thing needful in all the wide universe.

What produced this transient difference in your moral sensibilities? The truths which at such a time so deeply affected you, were the same that you had known from childhood. You have listened to them Sabbath after Sabbath, until you have grown weary of hearing them. You have a hundred times been placed in precisely the same external circumstances, and no emotion has been awakened within you. Nay, you have frequently, since then, remembered these very moral feelings with a heart as hard as adamant. What was it that then clothed well-known truth with so overwhelming a power? Think, and judge for yourself. It was surely none of your own doing. You could not recall these feelings at will. The surrounding circumstances did not thus awaken you, for in them there was nothing peculiar. It was the Holy Spirit, taking the things of Christ and showing them to you. God, who caused the light to shine out of darkness, by his Spirit shone into your heart, and made known the gulf that was lying directly across your path. The view was too appalling. You closed your eyes upon it. When you opened them again, the light was withdrawn, and you were again groping in your former darkness.

Sometimes, however, the Holy Spirit awakens our attention with scarcely any appeal to our emotional nature. He makes use of our understanding to teach us our danger and our duty. The truths which we have ever acknowledged assume to us an unwonted practical character. The man, without any particular excitement, calmly compares time with eternity, and he at once perceives the littleness of the one and the vastness of the other. He looks upon all that he is now pursuing, and confesses to himself that, were it all attained, it would be but a miserable portion for an immortal spirit; nay, he not only confesses it, but he feels that it is true. To secure the salvation of the soul appears to him the most reasonable thing of which he can conceive, and he wonders that it should ever have seemed otherwise. At the same time, the world and the things of the world have lost their attraction, and the chains that bound him to the earth are relaxed, if they be not severed. There is not, and he sees that there is not any reason worthy of a moment's consideration, why he should not seek first of all the kingdom of heaven. It is as clear to him as a mathematical demonstration. It was not always so. This peculiar conviction, however, passed away, and it is not so now. What was it that, at that time, so strangely affected him? It was the Spirit taking the things of Christ and showing them unto him.

Such visits of the Spirit may recur several times and the man remain unchanged in moral condition. As a general rule, they become less frequent and less impressive, until at last they cease altogther. Sometimes, however, they assume a more definite character. The realities of eternity and the frivolities of time, the claims of God and the allurements of the senses, are placed before the soul in deliberate contrast, and the man feels that he must determine which he shall choose, and that he must do it *now*. The strait gate and the broad way stand visibly open before him, and he must enter either the one or the other, and the choice is for eternity. At such a time as this, there is no opportunity for procrastination. The Holy Ghost saith, to-day the decision must be formed. The man must now choose, and, in such a case, I believe he actually does choose. Most frequently he cannot resist the pleadings of the Spirit; he surrenders himself to God, and lays hold on the hope set before him. But it is not always so. Sometimes, under all this moral pressure, the love of sin gains the victory; the man succumbs to the power of his lusts, chooses the way of death, and deliberately bids the Spirit depart from him. He is taken at his word; the Spirit retires, and, alas! too often retires forever.

You see, then, beloved, the nature of the operation of the Spirit of God upon a human soul. It consists in showing to us, with distinctness, the things of Christ. It enables us to appreciate the truths of religion, just as we appreciate every other truth. Its visits are brief, and are easily interrupted. We may heed its monitions or reject them, as we choose. It reveals to us our danger, and suggests to us a way of escape. It is with us, free and independent creatures of God, to choose for ourselves eternal life or eternal death.

Have I, in these remarks, brought to recollection any facts in the history of any of you who now hear me? Has not the Spirit taken of the things of Christ and showed them to many of you here? You have, then, shared in these blessed influences the last gift of your Father in heaven. What has been the result? Have you yielded yourselves to the influences of his persuasive love? Have you turned your eyes to the light, or have you turned them away towards the darkness? For all this you must give an account. It is a solemn thing to turn away from the manifestation of a Savior's love, but it is still more solemn, besides all this, to grieve the Spirit of the living God.

Need I add that the soul which has thus far grieved the Spirit of God is at this moment in imminent peril? God hath said, "My Spirit shall not always strive with man." If you, by your neglect, or procrastination, or love of sin, grieve the Holy Comforter, he will leave you to the darkness which you have chosen. The decree will go forth, "Ephraim is joined to his idols; let him alone." Your doom will then be irrevocably sealed. No tear of penitence will ever moisten your eye. No emotion of godly sorrow will ever agitate your bosom. No view of a Savior's love will ever kindle in your soul the flame of adoring gratitude. Nay, the soul thus deserted of God can look even upon the reality of a lost eternity with stolid indifference. Henceforward there is no hope. "Hadst thou known, even thou, at least in this thy day, the things that belong to thy peace — but now they are hid from thine eyes."

In view of all this, may I not hope that some of you are already inquiring, How shall I escape this impending doom? To such an inquiry I would answer, briefly, as follows: —

First. It is against God that you have sinned, and it is to him that you must seek for reconciliation. You have broken *his* law, you have rejected *his* mercy, you have grieved *his* Spirit. No other being can pardon you, no other being can save you. You must settle this controversy with him, for you and he alone are the parties concerned in it. Retire to your solitary chamber, banish every distracting thought, and concentrate every power within you upon the concern of your soul's salvation. Fall prostrate before your Father in heaven, confess to him all your guilt, and beseech him once more to bestow upon you the gift of his oft-rejected Spirit. Beseech him to reveal to you your sins, and by his divine energy to quicken your torpid conscience. Ask him for strength to look up to that Redeemer who is exalted a Prince and a Savior, to grant repentance unto Israel and remission of sins. Look up to him in humble trust, and repent of your whole life of guilty disobedience and ingratitude. You are utterly lost unless he appear for your salvation. He would be just though he never should hear your prayer; acknowledge that it is so, but still, in trembling hope, plead his promise, "Him that cometh unto me I will in no wise cast out."

Secondly. You must obey the very first teachings of the Spirit, if you desire him to lead you to life everlasting. Whatever he makes known to you, do it, and do it immediately, and do it at any sacrifice. His command is, "Seek ye first the kingdom of God;" and do it *now*. Obey him implicitly. Give your undivided attention to the securing of your soul's salvation. Withdraw from all company, deny yourself every amusement, put aside every business that would interfere with this, the most important concern of your existence. Be not afraid of the sneer of your companions. You have not been ashamed for so many years to offend your Father in heaven and grieve his Holy Spirit; why should you be ashamed to acknowledge that you are seeking to be reconciled to him? And resolve in your inmost soul, that, God helping you, you will seek until you find, you will knock until it be opened unto you. Be thoroughly in earnest on this subject. Give up yourself wholly to it. Begin to obey the first intimations of the Spirit, and though the light that shines upon you be feeble, he will increase it; continue to do his will, and it will shine more and more unto the perfect day.

And, thirdly, do not waste your time and peril your soul in any attempt to make yourself better. Come to him acknowledging your guilt and ill-desert, and rely for pardon and eternal life solely on the mercy of God in Christ Jesus. You can never make any compromises with the Most High. You can never, by any thing that you may do, bring him under any obligation to pardon you. You are a sinner justly under condemnation, and the fact cannot be denied. As a sinner helplessly guilty, trusting in the sacrifice of Christ, with the returning prodigal say, I will arise and go to my Father. Do more than resolve, and as he did, arise and go to your Father. Even when you are a great way off, your Father will see you, and have compassion, bestow upon you a free and full pardon, receive you into his redeemed family, and clothe you in a Savior's righteousness.

All this is freely offered to every one of you. What will you do? The Holy Ghost saith, "To-day, if you will hear his voice, harden not your heart." If you do not hear it, your guilt will be rendered more inexcusable by this additional act of disobedience. There is no reason why you should not now, this very day, return to your Father in heaven, and be accepted of him. On your own souls does the responsibility of this decision rest. The gate of heaven is thrown wide open. The Spirit and the bride say, Come, and whosoever will, let him come, and take of the waters of life freely.

A DAY IN THE LIFE OF JESUS OF NAZARETH.

"And the apostles, when they were returned, told him all that they had done," etc.

Luke ix. 10–17.

It was the sagacious opinion of, I think, the late Professor Porson, that he would rather see a single copy of a daily newspaper of ancient Athens, than read all the commentaries upon the Grecian tragedies that have ever been written. The reason for this preference is obvious. A single sheet, similar to our daily newspapers, published in the time of Pericles, would admit us at once to a knowledge of the habits, manners, modes of opinion, political relations, social condition, and moral attainments of the people, such as we never could gain from the study of all the writers that have ever attempted to illustrate the nature of Grecian civilization.

The same remark is true in respect to our knowledge of the character of individuals who have lived in a former age. What would we not, at the present day, give for a few pages of the private diary of Julius Cæsar, or Cicero, or Brutus, or Augustus; or for the minute reminiscences of any one who had spent a few days in the company of either of these distinguished men? What a flood of light would the discovery of such a manuscript throw upon Roman life, but especially upon the private opinions, the motives, the aspirations, the moral estimates, of the men whose names have become household words throughout the world! A few such pages might, perchance, dissipate the authority of many a bulky folio on which we now rely with implicit confidence. Not only would the characters of these heroes of antiquity stand out in bolder relief than they have ever done before, but the individuals themselves would be brought within the range of our personal sympathy; and we should seem to commune with them as we do with an intimate acquaintance.

It is worthy of remark, that we are favored with a larger portion of this kind of information, respecting Jesus of Nazareth, than almost any other distinguished person that has ever lived. He left no writings himself; hence all that we know of him has been written by others. The narrators, however, were the personal attendants, and not the mere auditors or pupils of their Master. The apostles were members of the family of Jesus; they travelled with him, on foot, throughout the length and breadth of Palestine; they partook with him of his frugal meals, and bore with him the trial of hunger, weariness, and want of shelter; they followed him through the lonely wilderness and the crowded street; they saw his miracles in every variety of form, and listened to his discourses in public as well as to his explanations in private. Hence their whole narrative is instinct with life; a vivid picture of Jewish manners and customs, rendered more definite and characteristic by the moral light which then, for the first time, shone upon it. Hence it is that these few pages are replete with moral lessons that never weary us in the perusal, and which have been the source of unfailing illumination to all succeeding ages.

The verses which I have read, as the text of this discourse, may well be taken as an illustration of all that I have here said. They may, without impropriety, be styled a day of the life of Jesus of Nazareth. By observing the manner in which our blessed Lord spent a single day, we may form some conception of the kind of life which he ordinarily led; and we may, perchance, treasure up some lessons which it were well if we should exemplify in our daily practice.

The place at which these events occurred was near the

head of the Sea of Galilee, where it receives the waters of the upper Jordan. This was one of the Savior's favorite places of resort. Capernaum, Chorasin, and Bethsaida, all in this immediate vicinity, are always spoken of in the Gospels as towns which enjoyed the largest share of his ministerial labors, and were distinguished most frequently with the honor of his personal presence. The scenery of the neighborhood is wild and romantic. To the north and west, the eye rests on the lofty summits of Lebanon and Hermon. To the south, there opens upon the view the blue expanse of the lake, enclosed by frowning rocks, which here and there jut over far into the waters, and then again retire towards the land, leaving a level beach to invite the labors of the fisherman. The people, removed at a considerable distance from the metropolis of Judea, cultivated those rural habits with which the simple tastes of the Savior would most readily harmonize. Near this spot was also one of the most frequented fords of the Jordan, on the road from Damascus to Jerusalem; and thus, while residing here, he enjoyed unusual facilities for disseminating throughout this whole region a knowledge of those truths which he came on earth to promulgate.

Some weeks previously to the time in which the events spoken of in the text occurred, our Lord had sent his disciples to announce the approach of the kingdom of heaven, in all the cities and villages which he himself proposed to visit. He conferred on them the power to work miracles, in attestation of their authority, and of the divine character of him by whom they were sent. He imposed upon them strict rules of conduct, and directed them, to make known to every one who would hear them, the good news of the coming dispensation. As soon as he had sent them forth, he himself went immediately abroad to teach and to preach in their cities. As their Master and Lord, he might reasonably have claimed exemption from the personal toil and the rigid self-denials to which they were by necessity subjected. But he laid claim to no such exemption. He commenced without delay the performance of the very same duties which he had imposed upon them. He felt himself under obligation to set an example of obedience to his own rules. "The Son of man," said he, "came not to be ministered unto, but to minister, and to give his life a ransom for many." "Which," said he, "is greater, he that sitteth at meat, or he that serveth? but I am among you as he that serveth." Would it not be well, if, in this respect, we copied more minutely the example of our Lord, and held ourselves responsible for the performance of the very same duties which we so willingly impose upon our brethren? We best prove that we believe an act obligatory, when we commence the performance of it ourselves. Many zealous Christians employ themselves in no other labor than that of urging their brethren to effort. Our Savior acted otherwise. In this respect, his example is specially to be imitated by his ministers. When they urge upon others a moral duty, they must be the first to perform it. When they inculcate an act of self-denial, they themselves must make the noblest sacrifice. Can we conceive of any thing which would so much increase the moral power of the ministry, and rouse to a flame the dormant energy of the churches, as obedience to this teaching of Christ by the preachers of his gospel?

It seems that the Savior had selected a well-known spot, at the head of the lake, for the place of meeting for his apostles, after this their first missionary tour had been completed. "The apostles gathered themselves unto Jesus, and told him all things, both what they had done, and what they had taught." There is something delightful in this filial confidence which these simple-hearted men reposed in their Almighty Redeemer. They told him of their success and their failure, of their wisdom and their folly, of their reliance and their unbelief. We can almost imagine ourselves spectators of this meeting between Christ and them, after this their first separation from each other. The place appointed was most probably some well-known locality on the shore of the lake, under the shadow of its overhanging rocks, where the cool air from the bosom of the water refreshed each returning laborer, as he came back beaten out with the fatigues of travel, under the burning sun of Syria. You can imagine the joy with which each drew near to the Master, after this temporary absence; and the honest greetings with which every new comer was welcomed by those who had chanced to arrive before him. We can seem to perceive the Savior of men listening with affectionate earnestness to the recital of their various adventures; and interposing, from time to time, a word either of encouragement or of caution, as the character and circumstances of each narrator required it. The bosom of each was unveiled before the Searcher of hearts, and the consolation which each one needed was bestowed upon him abundantly. The toilsomeness of their journey was no longer remembered, as each one received from the Son of God the smile of his approbation. That was truly a joyful meeting. Of all that company there is not one who has forgotten that day; nor will he forget it ever. With unreserved frankness they told Jesus of all that they had done, and what they had taught; of all their acts, and all their conversations. Would it not be better for us, if we cultivated more assiduously this habit of intimate intercourse with the Savior? Were we every day to tell Jesus of all that we have done and said; did we spread before him our joys and our sorrows, our faults and our infirmities, our successes and our failures, we should be saved from many an error and many a sin. Setting "the Lord always before us, he would be on our right hand, and we should not be moved." "He that dwelleth in the secret place of the Most High shall abide under the shadow of the Almighty."

The Savior perceived that the apostles needed much instruction which could not be communicated in a place where both he and they were so well known. They had committed many errors, which he preferred to correct in private. By doing his will, they had learned to repose greater confidence in his wisdom, and were prepared to receive from him more important instruction. But these lessons could not be delivered in the hearing of a promiscuous audience. Nor was this all. He perceived that the apostles were worn out with their labors, and needed repose. Surrounded as they were by the multitude, which had already begun to collect about them, rest and retirement were equally impossible. "There were many coming and going, and they had no leisure, even so much as to eat." He therefore said to them, "Come ye yourselves apart into a desert place, and rest a while." For this purpose, he "took ship, and crossed over with his disciples alone, and went into a desert place belonging to Bethsaida."

The religion of Christ imposes upon us duties of retirement, as well as duties of publicity. The apostles had been for some time past before the eyes of all men, preaching and working miracles. Their souls needed retirement. "Solitude," said Cecil, "is my great ordinance." They would be greatly improved by private communion both with him and with each other. It was for the purpose of affording them such a season of moral recreation, that our Lord withdrew them from the public gaze into a desert place. Nor was this all. Their labor for some weeks past had been severe. They had travelled on foot under a tropical sun, reasoning with unbelievers, instructing the ignorant, and comforting the cast down. Called upon, at all hours, both of the day and night, to work cures on those that were oppressed with diseases, their bodies, no less than their spirits, needed rest. Our Lord saw this, and he made provision for it. He withdrew them from labor, that they might find, though it were but for a day, the repose which their exhausted natures demanded. The religion of Christ is ever merciful, and ever consistent in its benevolence. It is thoughtful of the benefactor as well as of the recipient. It requires of us all, labor and self-sacrifice, but to these it affixes a limit. It never commands us to ruin our health and enfeeble our minds by unnatural exhaustion. It teaches us to obey the laws of our physical organization, and to prepare ourselves for the labors of to-morrow by the judiciously conducted labors of to-day. It was on this principle that our Lord conducted in his intercourse with his disciples. "He knew their frame, and remembered that they were dust."

May we not from this incident derive a lesson of practical instruction? I well know that there are persons who are always sparing themselves, who, while it is difficult to tell what they do, are always complaining of the crushing weight of their labors, and who are rather exhausted with the dread of what they shall do, than with the experience of what they have actually done. It is not of these that we speak. Those who do not labor have no need of rest. It is to the honest, the painstaking, the laborious, that we address the example in the text. We sometimes meet with the industrious, self-denying servant of Christ, in feeble health, and with an exhausted nature, bemoaning his condition, and condemning himself because he can accomplish no more, while so much yet remains to be done. To such a one we may safely present the example of the blessed Savior. When his apostles had done to the utmost of their strength, although the harvest was great, and the laborers few, he did not urge upon them additional labor, nor tell them that because there was so much to be done they must never cease from doing. No; he tells them to turn aside and rest for a while. It is as though he had said, "Your strength is exhausted; you cannot be qualified for subsequent duty until you be refreshed. Economize, then, your power, that you may accomplish the more." The Savior addresses the same language to us now. When we are worn down in his service, as in any other, he would have us rest, not for the sake of self-indulgence, but that we may be the better prepared for future effort. We do nothing at variance with his will, when we, with a good conscience, use the liberty which he has thus conceded to us.

Jesus, with his disciples, crossed the water, and entered the desert; that is, the sparsely inhabited country of Bethsaida. Desert, or wilderness, in the New Testament, does not mean an arid waste, but pasture land, forest, or any district to which one could retire for seclusion. Here, in the cool and tranquil neighborhood of the lake, he began to instruct his disciples, and, without interruption, make known to them the mysteries of the kingdom. It was one of those seasons that the Savior himself rarely enjoyed. Every thing tended to repose: the rustling leaves, the rippling waves, the song of the birds, heard more distinctly in this rural solitude, all served to calm the spirit ruffled by the agitations of the world, and prepare it to listen to the truths which unveil to us eternity. Here our Lord could unbosom himself, without reserve, to his chosen few, and hold with them that communion which he was rarely permitted to enjoy during his ministry on earth.

Soon, however, the whole scene is changed. The multitude, whom he had so recently left, having observed the direction in which he had gone, have discovered the place of his retreat. An immense crowd approaches, and the little company is surrounded by a dense mass of human beings pressing upon them on every side. These are, however, only the pioneers. At last, five thousand men, besides women and children, are beheld thronging around them.

Some of these suitors present most importunate claims. They are in search of cure for diseases which have baffled the skill of the medical profession, and, as a last resort, they have come to the Messiah for aid. Here was a parent bringing a consumptive child. There were children bearing on a couch a paralytic parent. Here was a sister leading a brother blind from his birth, while her supplications were drowned by the shout of a frenzied lunatic who was standing by her side. Every one, believing his own claim to be the most urgent, pressed forward with selfish importunity. Each one, caring for no other than himself, was striving to attain the front rank, while those behind, disappointed, and fearing to lose this important opportunity, were eager to occupy the places of those more fortunate than themselves. The necessary tumult and disorder of such a scene you can better imagine than I can describe.

This was, doubtless, by no means a welcome interruption

The apostles needed the time for rest; for they were worn out in the public service. They wanted it for instruction; for such opportunities of intercourse with Christ were rare. But what did they do? Did our Lord inform the multitude that this day was set apart for their own refreshment and improvement, and that they could not be interrupted? As he beheld them approaching, did he quietly take to his boat, and leave them to go home disappointed? Did he plead his own convenience, or his need of repose, as any reason for not attending to the pressing necessities of his fellow-men?

No, my brethren, very far from it. The providence of God had brought these multitudes before him, and that same providence forbade him to send them away unblessed. He at once broke up the conference with his disciples, and addressed himself to the work before him. His instructions were of inestimable importance; but I doubt if even they were as important as the example of deep humility, exhaustless kindness, and affecting compassion which he here exhibited. When the Master places work before us which can be done at no other time, our convenience must yield to other men's necessities. "The Son of man came not to be ministered unto, but to minister." You can imagine to yourself the Savior rising from his seat, in the midst of his disciples, and presenting himself to the approaching multitudes. His calm dignity awes into silence this tumultuous gathering of the people. Those who came out to witness the tricks of an empiric, or listen to the ravings of a fanatic, find themselves, unexpectedly, in a presence that repels every emotion but that of profound veneration. The light-hearted and frivolous are awe-struck by the unearthly majesty that seems to clothe the Messiah as with a garment. And yet it was a majesty that shone forth conspicuously most of all, by the manifestation of unparalleled goodness. Every eye that met the eye of the Savior quailed before him; for it looked into a soul that had never sinned; and the spirit of the sinner felt, for the first time, the full power of immaculate virtue.

Thus the Savior passed among the crowd, and "healed all that had need of healing." The lame walked, the lepers were cleansed, the blind received their sight, the paralytic were restored to soundness, and the bloom of health revisited the cheeks of those that but just now were sick unto death.

The work to be done for the bodies of men was accomplished, and there yet remained some hours of the summer's day unconsumed. The power and goodness displayed in this miraculous healing, would naturally predispose the people to listen to the instructions of the Savior. This was too valuable an opportunity to be lost. Our Lord therefore proceeded to speak to them of the things concerning the kingdom of God. We can seem to perceive the Savior seeking an eminence from whence he could the more conveniently address this vast assembly. You hear him unfold the laws of God's moral government. He unmasks the hypocrisy of the Pharisees; he rebukes the infidelity of the Sadducees; he exposes the folly of the frivolous, as well as of the selfish worldling; he speaks peaceably to the humble penitent; he encourages the meek, and comforts those that be cast down. The intellect and the conscience of this vast assembly are swayed at his will. The soul of man bows down in reverence in the presence of its Creator. "He stilleth the noise of the seas, the noise of their waves, and the tumult of the people." As he closes his address, every eye is moistened with compunction for sin. Every soul cherishes the hope of amendment. Every one is conscious that a new moral light has dawned upon his soul, and that a new moral universe has been unveiled to his spiritual vision. As the closing words of the Savior fell upon their ears, the whole multitude stood for a while unmoved, as though transfixed to the earth by some mighty spell; until, at last, the murmur is heard from thousands of voices, "Never man spake like this man."

But the shades of evening are gathering around them. The multitude have nothing to eat. To send them away fasting would be inhuman, for divers of them came from far, and many were women and children, who could not perform their journey homeward without previous refreshment. To purchase food in the surrounding towns and villages would be difficult; but even were this possible, whence could the necessary funds be provided? A famishing multitude was thus unexpectedly cast upon the bounty of our Lord. He had not tempted God by leading them into the wilderness. They came to him of themselves, to hear his words and to be healed of their infirmities. He could not "send them away fasting, lest they should faint by the way." In this dilemma, what was to be done? He puts this question to his disciples, and they can suggest no means of relief. The little stock of provisions which they had brought with them was barely sufficient for themselves. They can perceive no means whatever by which the multitude can be fed, and they at once confess it.

The Savior, however, commands the twelve to give them to eat. They produce their slender store of provisions, amounting to five loaves and two small fishes. He commands the multitude to sit down by companies on the grass. As soon as silence is obtained, he lifts up his eyes to heaven, and supplicates the blessing of God upon their scanty meal. He begins to break the loaves and fishes, and distribute them to his disciples, and his disciples distribute them to the multitude. He continues to break and distribute. Basket after basket is filled and emptied, yet the supply is undiminished. Food is carried in abundance to the famishing thousands. Company after company is supplied with food, but the five loaves and the two fishes remain unexhausted. At last, the baskets are returned full, and it is announced that the wants of the multitude are supplied. The miracle then ceases, and the multiplication of food is at an end.

But even here the provident care of the Savior is manifested. Although this food has been so easily provided, it is not right that it be lightly suffered to perish. Christ wrought no miracles for the sake of teaching men wastefulness. That food, by what means soever provided, was a creature of God, and it were sin to allow it to decay without accomplishing the purposes for which it was created. "Gather up the fragments," said the Master of the feast, "that nothing be lost." "And they gathered up the fragments that remained, twelve baskets full."

Dissimilar as are our circumstances to those of our Lord, we may learn from this latter incident a lesson of instruction.

In the first place, as I have remarked, the Savior did not lead the multitude into the wilderness without making provision for their sustenance. This would have been presumption. They followed him without his command, and he found himself with them in this necessity. He had provided for his own wants, but they had not provided for theirs. The providence of God had, however, placed him in his present circumstances, and he might therefore properly look to Providence for deliverance. This event, then, furnishes the rule by which we are to be governed. When we plunge ourselves into difficulty, by a neglect of the means or by a misuse of the faculties which God has bestowed upon us, it is to be expected that he will leave us to our own devices. But when, in the honest discharge of our duties, we find ourselves in circumstances beyond the reach of human aid, we then may confidently look up to God for deliverance. He will always take care of us while we are in the spot where he has placed us. When he appoints for us trials, he also appoints for us the means of escape. The path of duty, though it may seem arduous, is ever the path of safety. We can more easily maintain ourselves in the most difficult position, God being our helper, than in apparent security relying on our own strength.

The Savior, in full reliance upon God, with only five loaves and two fishes, commenced the distribution of food amongst this vast multitude. Though his whole store was barely sufficient to supply the wants of his immediate family, he began to share it with the thousands who surrounded him.

Small as was his provision at the commencement, it remained unconsumed until the deed of mercy was done, and the wants of the famishing host were supplied. Nor were the disciples losers by this act of charity. After the multitude had eaten and were satisfied, twelve baskets full of fragments remained, a reward for their deed of benevolence.

From this portion of the narrative, we may, I think, learn that if we act in faith, and in the spirit of Christian love, we may frequently be justified in commencing the most important good work, even when in possession of apparently inadequate means. If the work be of God, he will furnish us with helpers as fast as they are needed. In all ages, God has rewarded abundantly simple trust in him, and has bestowed upon it the highest honor. We must, however, remember the conditions upon which alone we may expect his aid, lest we be led into fanaticism. The service which we undertake must be such as God has commanded, and his providence must either designate us for the work, or, at least, open the door by which we shall enter upon it. It must be God's work, and not our own; for the good of others, and not for the gratification of our own passions; and, in the doing of it, we must, first of all, make sacrifice of ourselves, and not of others. Under such circumstances, there is hardly a good design which we may not undertake with cheerful hopes of success, for God has promised us his assistance. "If God be for us, who can be against us?" The calculations of the men of this world are of small account in such a matter. It would have provoked the smile of an infidel to behold the Savior commencing the work of feeding five thousand men with a handful of provisions. But the supply increased as fast as it was needed, and it ceased not until all that he had prayed for was accomplished.

Perhaps, also, we may learn from this incident another lesson. If I mistake not, it suggests to us that in works of benevolence we are accustomed to rely too much on human, and too little on divine, aid. When we attempt to do good, we commence by forming large associations, and suppose that our success depends upon the number of men whom we can unite in the promotion of our undertaking. Every one is apt thus to forget his own personal duty, and rely upon the labor of others, and it is well if he does not put his organization in the place of God himself. Would it not be better if we made benevolence much more a matter between God and our own souls, each one doing with his own hands, in firm reliance on divine aid, the work which Providence has placed directly before him? Our Lord did not send to the villages round about to organize a general effort to relieve the famishing. In reliance upon God, he set about the work himself, with just such means as God had afforded him. All the miracles of benevolence have, if I mistake not, been wrought in the same manner. The little band of disciples in Jerusalem accomplished more for the conversion of the world than all the Christians of the present day united. And why? Because every individual Christian felt that the conversion of the world was a work for which he himself, and not an abstraction that he called the church, was responsible. Instead of relying on man for aid, every one looked up directly to God, and went forth to the work. God was thus exalted, the power was confessed to be his own, and, in a few years, the standard of the cross was carried to the remotest extremities of the then known world.

Such has, I think, been the case ever since. Every great moral reformation has proceeded upon principles analogous to these. It was Luther, standing up alone in simple reliance upon God, that smote the Papal hierarchy; and the effects of that blow are now agitating the nations of Europe. Roger Williams, amid persecution and banishment, held forth that doctrine of soul-liberty which, in its onward march, is disenthralling a world. Howard, alone, undertook the work of showing mercy to the prisoner, and his example is now enlisting the choicest minds in Christendom in this labor of benevolence. Clarkson, unaided, a young man, and without influence, consecrated himself to the work of abolishing the slave trade; and, before he rested from his labors, his country had repented of and forsaken this atrocious sin. Raikes saw the children of Gloucester profaning the Sabbath day; he set on foot a Sabbath school on his own account, and now millions of children are reaping the benefit of his labors, and his example has turned the attention of the whole world to the religious instruction of the young. With such facts before us, we surely should be encouraged to attempt individually the accomplishment of some good design, relying in humility and faith upon Him who is able to grant prosperity to the feeblest effort put forth in earnest reliance on his almightiness.

Such were the occupations that filled up a day in the life of Jesus of Nazareth. There was not an act done for himself; all was done for others. Every hour was employed in the labor which that hour set before him. Private kindness, the relief of distress, public teaching, and ministration to the wants of the famishing, filled up the entire day. Let his disciples rn to follow his example. Let us, like him, forget ourselves, our own wants, and our own weariness, that we may, as he did, scatter blessings on every side, as we move onward in the pathway of our daily life.

But no matter how onerous or incessant were the duties that pressed upon our Lord; he always found leisure for private devotion. "When he had sent them away, he departed into a mountain to pray." My brethren, does not our Lord's conduct on this occasion suggest to us an important monition? We frequently suppose that the earnest discharge of a Christian duty renders communion with God less necessary to our spiritual improvement. This supposition finds no support in the example of the Savior. Though mind and body were weary in the labor of doing good, yet every moment of the day had been spent in the company of the disciples, or in a crowd, and he needed to be alone with God. Wearied as he was, he might have been seen toiling up the steep mountain side, that he might spend the silent hours of the night in secret devotion. Let every Christian, and specially every minister, remember this. The holiness of our calling and our active labor in it, do not render private prayer at all the less needful to our souls. Irreligious labor in religious things exposes the soul to the most subtile power of temptation. Let every day's labor close with prayer, confession, and thanksgiving, if we would with renewed strength enter upon the labors of the morrow.

THE BENEVOLENCE OF THE GOSPEL.

"AND WHETHER ONE MEMBER SUFFER, ALL THE MEMBERS SUFFER WITH IT; OR ONE MEMBER IS HONORED, ALL THE MEMBERS REJOICE WITH IT."

1 *Corinthians* xii. 26.

IN this passage the apostle is enforcing the truth that God bestows upon us nothing merely on our own account. Every talent with which we are intrusted is committed to us rather for the good of others than ourselves. This doctrine, so essential to every true conception of Christianity, he illustrates by a reference to the uses of the several members of the human body. Neither the eye, nor the ear, nor the hand, is made for itself; all are made for each other and for the whole. If any one of them acted for itself, and not for the body, all would suffer injury, and the offending member would bear its full part of the mischief which it had brought upon the rest. On the contrary, the action of each part for the whole produces universal health, in which each member participates. In a word, the union of the several members is so intimate, the sympathy which pervades them is so intense and vigilant, that whatever affects one member, by the necessity of our constitution, affects all the others. If one member suffer, all the members suffer with it; if one member is honored, all the members rejoice with it.

The apostle is here speaking of a Christian church, and in this verse he teaches us an important lesson. We thus may learn the obligations which every Christian owes to every other

Christian brother. Every believer is a member of that body of which Christ is the head. One bond of affection unites every disciple to the whole brotherhood of saints, and unites the whole body to the same Redeemer, who has purchased us with his blood. We should all sympathize in the sorrows, and rejoice in the joys, of each other, as if they were our own. No matter how wide the distance which separates us from each other; no matter how great the difference in our external circumstances; no matter how much we may believe a brother to be in error; if he be a brother, we must love him with an earnest and unswerving Christian affection. We must rejoice in his prosperity, sympathize in his adversity, bearing each other's burdens, and so fulfilling the law of Christ. Each is a member of the same body; all are pervaded by the same spirit; all are beloved by the same Redeemer; and every one is bound to live, not for himself, but for his brethren for whom Christ died.

But is this principle of action peculiar to the church of Christ? or is it common to humanity? Manifestly the latter. The assertion is true, in some sense, whenever we associate ourselves with our fellow-men. It enters into the very idea of a society, that we confide some portion of our happiness to the keeping of others. We and they are reciprocally affected by whatever affects every member. It is just as true of humanity as of Christianity, that if one member suffer, all the members suffer with it; if one member is honored, all the members rejoice with it. It is the law under which we are created, that we cannot really benefit ourselves without also benefiting others; we cannot injure others without also, in some way, and at some time, inflicting injury upon ourselves. We are as truly social as we are individual beings. We find ourselves members of various societies as soon as we exist. To these we add voluntary associations of our own. Isolate ourselves as much as we please, we are still members of the brotherhood of man; we and our fellow-men reciprocally influence each other, and no being but God can tell what power the very weakest of us may exert over the destinies of humanity. We are bound together by ties which we cannot sever if we would, and we can neither suffer nor enjoy without awakening an emotion of pleasure or of pain in the bosom of others.

Take, for the sake of illustration, that domestic circle which we designate the family. In this society we find ourselves at the first dawning of consciousness, and we never leave it until we enter upon eternity. Let, now, one member of this body suffer, though it be the youngest and the least considerable, and what a shade of sadness is spread over the whole household! What nights of sleeplessness and what days of anguish are consumed in watching over the suffering infant! When, at last, every effort has proved fruitless, and Death has impressed his seal upon that face so lately radiant with innocent joy, how sadly earnest is the gaze of parents, and brothers, and sisters upon the placid loveliness of that beautiful corpse! Long afterwards shall that image remain deeply embedded in the memory, when these brothers and sisters have become men and women, gray-headed and care-worn; and this first bereavement will ever hold a conspicuous place in their calendar of sorrows, until they themselves have put on immortality.

Let, now, this family grow up to maturity, and each member enter upon the appropriate duties of his individual calling. It might, at first, seem as though the chain which once bound them so closely together had been severed, and that any one of them might suffer or enjoy, without affecting, either for good or for evil, the destiny of any of the others. They rarely meet, they but occasionally correspond, and the thought of each other rarely breaks in upon the pressing cares of each one's daily occupation. But let any of these brothers, by the display of unusual talent, or the manifestation of surpassing character, attain to high distinction, and what a lustre is at once reflected on all who bear his name! Their connection with him is enough to raise them from obscurity to renown, and their fellow-citizens confer upon them honors, not for what they have done themselves, but on account of their relationship to a public benefactor.

Or let it be otherwise. Be it that a member of a family has disgraced himself by crime, nay, by crime with which no relative whatever has had the remotest connection. Observe how mournfully the disgrace settles down upon parents, and brothers, and sisters, and kindred. No one accuses them of any participation in the wrong doing, and yet they all feel that, whether justly or unjustly, their hold upon society has been loosened, if not broken. They dread to meet the gaze of their fellow-citizens. The very pity which their condition awakens, only reminds them of the calamity which has fallen upon their lineage. They may flee to foreign climes, they may strive to hide their degradation under a change of name, but it is all in vain. Nothing can obliterate the fact that a brother is a felon. The barbed arrow rankles in the wound, and it cannot be extracted. It clings to them in their flight, and the poison drinks up their spirit. They have done nothing wrong; nay, they have labored to the utmost to correct those evil tempers from which the wrong doing has proceeded. All this is true, all this may be known, but yet it avails not. The law cannot be broken; if one member suffer, all the members suffer with it.

But we are members of a larger society, the community in which we live. Our happiness here is subject to the same law; and we can enjoy the gifts of God's providence in no way so well as by making others the sharers with us in his bounty. If our fellow-men around us suffer, we shall suffer also, unless we do all in our power to relieve them. We may be living luxuriously, surrounded by all that can render life desirable. We understand the laws of health, and we obey them. We do more than this; we deal out our bread to the hungry, but we go no farther; for we leave the poor around us to grow up unblessed by our personal care. There are intemperance, and ignorance, and filth in our vicinity; our brethren are herding together in squalid cabins, breathing air loaded with foul miasmata, unconscious of the laws of their being as the brutes that perish. The social chasm which divides them from ourselves is so wide and so deep that we seem to have escaped the operation of this universal law. But let now a deadly epidemic be borne on the wings of the wind, and we shall see it alight with inevitable certainty upon this forlorn and neglected neighborhood. It strikes down at first the bloated and gorged inebriate; then his poor but temperate and industrious neighbor sickens and dies. Soon the disease nestles in this unclean and repulsive hamlet, and breathes its unseen poison into the surrounding atmosphere. It is wafted by the passing breeze to the dwellings of the opulent, the virtuous, and the intelligent. The foremost man in the whole community is borne to his grave, followed by a neighborhood in tears. A strong rod is broken and withered, and every man feels that the state has suffered a loss which no survivor is able to supply. The plague spreads from house to house until the town falls prostrate under the pressure of a universal calamity. And all this sorrow sprang from a few neglected hovels, whose population seemed hardly of sufficient importance to sully the fair reputation of the smiling village in its vicinity. Neglected and forgotten as these paupers were, they were a part of our common humanity; and the pestilence which they first attracted, and then scattered abroad, utters in solemn accents the words of the text — if one member suffer, all the members suffer with it.

Or we may take an illustration from a more extensive field. How often has the form of social organization been constructed for the sole benefit of the few, rather than the whole! The titled, the wealthy, and the refined assume to be the favorites of Heaven, whose rights must be guaranteed and their happiness provided for, while the masses remain unprotected by law and unbefriended by benevolence. You will see the face of the land here and there beautified by the mansions of the proprietors, whose broad acres overspread the landscape, while the million, the children of ignorance and vice, herd together in cabins like brutes, and uncheered by any hope of improving their condition, and "hammered to the galling oar for life," know of no higher enjoyment than sensual gratification. All this goes on quietly, it may be, for many generations. At last, some general famine drives the multitude to despair, or some giant act of oppression maddens them to frenzy, or the infection of revolution is caught from some neighboring nation, and some plebeian, endowed by nature with power to command, sets before his brethren the history of their wrongs, and points out to them the means of redress. At once the underlying stratum is upheaved, and a social convulsion crumbles into dust the fabric of government which ages had cemented. Prince and peasant, wise and unwise, the rude and the refined, the innocent and the guilty, are overwhelmed in a common catastrophe; and, after ages of untold calamity, they may not yet have found a solid basis on which the foundations of the social edifice shall rest. And they will never find it, until they shall learn to reverence and love the humanity of the New Testament, and practically to obey the precept, "Thou shalt love thy neighbor as thyself." And if oppression always recoils with redoubled violence upon the head of the oppressor, our own country may, from such instances as these, learn a lesson of solemn instruction. It will be well if we learn it in season.

Or we may, if you please, observe the relations of a single individual to a whole nation. Suppose that a government lays its hand unrighteously upon the smallest portion of the property of a citizen,—it matters not whether he be rich or poor, high-born or lowly. It may be, for instance, the ship-money of Hampden, or the trifling tax on tea that inaugurated our revolution. The act of oppression is resisted, and the case is carried up from court to court until a decision is had from the highest authority in the land. The unjust claim is enforced by the whole power of the government. At once the shock is felt by the remotest citizen of the realm. One member has suffered, and all the members have suffered with it. Every man feels that his rights are prostrated by the blow which has struck down the rights of his neighbor. The property of every man is henceforth placed within the grasp of arbitrary power. By inflicting injustice on a single citizen, the government has outraged the moral sentiment of the nation. And it must retrace its steps, and acknowledge its own submission to social law; or else, unless the love of liberty be wholly extinguished, a revolution must ensue which will trample the throne and altar in the dust, and scatter the minions of despotism like the dust of the summer threshing floor.

And lastly, I will take an illustration from a still wider field. Were I to ask any one of you to-day, What concern have we, in this country, and at this time, with Warren Hastings and his conquests in British India? your reply would naturally be, None at all. We pity the sorrows of the nations and their rulers, and are shocked at the barbarity with which vast regions were devastated for the sake of gold; but in what respect we, or ours, are either the better or the worse for all that was then done and suffered, we cannot tell. But we are all more intimately connected with these events than we might at first suppose. It is said, and I believe truly, that the cholera, that scourge of our race, was generated in Bengal in that awful famine so eloquently described by Burke; and thus it is the direct result of the oppressions of which I have spoken. In Bengal it has established its permanent abode, and from time to time sets out from the banks of the Ganges on its mission of wrath, encircling the earth with the voice of mourning, lamentation, and woe. Thus we and those whom we love suffer at this day from deeds done on the other side of the globe, by a man whose name has long since passed into history. Thus we see that there is not a being on earth whose actions may not be a source of sorrow or of joy to us or to those that come after us.

We perceive, then, that if such be the law under which we

are created, the proper love of our own happiness would lead us, first of all, to seek the happiness of our brethren. If each one rejoices in the happiness of the whole, then the greater the happiness of the whole, the greater must be the happiness of each. If every member suffers in the suffering of all, every one will shield himself from suffering by alleviating the sufferings of humanity. The intelligent and opulent neighborhood would have saved itself from epidemic by transforming the filthy hovels of the hamlet into comfortable dwellings, and imbuing the minds of their inhabitants with the principles of temperance, piety, and self-respect. The hereditary nobility of France would have averted that most fearful of revolutions, had they, instead of living basely to themselves, lived to minister blessings to those who, in the social scale, occupied a position beneath them. If the monarch of England, eschewing the fallacy of kingly prerogative, had risen to the true conception of his office as the chief magistrate of a nation of freemen, and, in utter self-forgetfulness, sought only the highest good of the people committed to his charge, he might have prevented the catastrophe which brought him to the block, and transmitted his sceptre, wreathed with imperishable glory, to his remotest descendants. Had Warren Hastings treated the nations of Hindostan like brethren of the human race, and, instead of visiting them with exterminating warfare, scattered broadcast among them the benefits of knowledge and the blessings of religion, to say nothing of the late sepoy mutiny, mankind might have escaped that fearful pestilence which has so often swept the earth with the besom of destruction, and consigned millions after millions to an untimely grave.

We see, then, in a word, that happiness in a human bosom is a reflection from the happiness we have created in the bosom of another. We are made to be happy, not by selfishly seeking after personal gratification, but by laboring to promote the well-being of our brethren. That family is the happiest in which every member, in entire forgetfulness of self, is earnestly seeking the highest interests of the whole. That town, or state, or nation is the happiest in which the largest amount of talent, and capital, and influence is devoted to the benefit of the community. Acting upon this principle, every individual augments the happiness of all, and, in so doing, is attaining his own highest gratification. Acting on opposite principles, we care nothing for the happiness of our brethren, and suffer in our own persons the misery reflected from the manifestation of our mean and degrading selfishness. Such is evidently the law of our social constitution. God has made us for such a law, and his enactments can never be repealed.

But, if such be the fact, another truth, equally important, springs directly out of it. If God has made our happiness to depend upon the course of life here indicated, he has done so to teach us his will. Whenever he has indissolubly associated our own happiness with any manner of living, he thus teaches us that such a manner of living is prescribed for us by him, our Creator. Hence the ground of a moral obligation. We must live, not for ourselves, but for others; not only because it is expedient for us, but because it is right, because it is the command of our Father in heaven. A moral necessity is thus laid upon us. We cannot live to ourselves without doing violence to our conscience and incurring the consequences of disobedience to God. We bury our talent in the earth instead of improving it, and incur the doom of the unprofitable servant.

But, in a matter of so much importance, we are not obliged to ascertain our duty by the unassisted light of natural religion. The Bible teaches us this doctrine on every one of its pages. God is here represented to us as the God of love, pouring forth a flood of happiness over the whole universe, and rejoicing in the well-being of creatures, rational and irrational, that he has made. But the Bible informs us that God has gone much farther than this. When our race, insignificant as it is, had offended him by sin, and were at universal enmity against him, he gave up his well-beloved Son to redeem us from the doom which we had merited. When the fulness of time was come, we behold him who is the brightness of the Father's glory, by whom all things were created, whether they be visible or invisible, taking upon him the form of a servant, bearing our sins in his own body on the tree, becoming obedient to death, the death of the cross, that he might open for us the door of everlasting life. Every aspect of the plan of salvation presents to us our Creator and Redeemer, by every means which infinite love could devise, laboring at inconceivable sacrifice to save us from merited destruction, and confer upon us the blessing of a heavenly inheritance.

Our Father in heaven, as I have elsewhere said, imposes upon us no duty of which in his own person he has not set us the example. We are to imitate his boundless beneficence, by using the talents of every kind which he has committed to us for the good of others. We are to imitate his self-sacrificing love in the plan of redemption, by reclaiming the vicious, relieving the unfortunate, raising the fallen, and carrying the good news of salvation to the lost and abandoned in the highways and hedges, to those whose souls no man has cared for. Such was the Spirit of Christ, and we are told that unless we have the Spirit of Christ we are none of his. No one of us liveth unto himself, and no one dieth unto himself. In utter self-renunciation, we must, first of all, live unto God, and we cannot live unto him without following his example. At the last day, those only will be numbered with the blessed of the Father who have manifested their love to him by love to their brethren. Then shall the King say unto them at his right hand, "Come, ye blessed of my Father, inherit the kingdom prepared for you from the foundation of the world. For I was an hungered, and ye gave me meat; I was thirsty, and ye gave me drink; I was a stranger, and ye took me in; naked, and ye clothed me; I was sick, and ye visited me; I was in prison, and ye came unto me. Verily I say unto you, Inasmuch as ye have done it unto the least of these my brethren, ye have done it unto me."

Such, then, my brethren, is the teachmg of our blessed Lord on this subject. Such is the law under which we were originally created. Such is this law spiritualized by the revelation of our Lord and Savior Jesus Christ. By the law of our constitution we are taught, as we love our own happiness, to care for the well-being of our neighbor. By the law of Christianity we are commanded to do this, not for our own advantage, nor yet solely for the love of our neighbor, but from the love of God, who receives this as the most acceptable sacrifice that we can render unto him. Christianity elevates and expands the natural affections, until they embrace, not only the clique, the caste, the sect, the nation, but the whole family of man. It ennobles charity by elevating it to piety, and raises those graces which endear men to each other into the evidences of our union to Him who came from heaven to earth to seek and save that which was lost. God is love, and he that dwelleth in love dwelleth in God, and God in him. He that loveth not knoweth not God; for God is love.

You see, then, at a glance, the difference between a selfish and a religious life. In the one we live directly to gratify ourselves. We labor for wealth, for power, for pleasure, for social position, or political eminence. We ask, day by day, What shall we eat, what shall we drink, and wherewith shall we be clothed? From centre to circumference our sphere of action is bounded by selfishness, or if it extends beyond that narrow circle, it comprehends only those who are bound to us by the ties of personal relationship, or instinctive affection, or the little clique to whom we are affianced by the bond of mutual admiration. We live unto ourselves, and we die unto ourselves. We have made sacrifices for no one; we nave advanced no single interest of humanity. We have lived on earth, and have conferred on it no benefit. It is in no respect either happier or better for our having lived in it. It has no cause to remember us, and it consigns us to oblivion. We have consumed our probation in cultivating our appetites for the things that perish, until, hardened in selfishness and stupid insensibility, we have not a single desire for that which is not of the earth earthy, and a holy God has become an object too dreadful for contemplation. Death solidifies our characters into adamant, and separates us forever from the only objects in the universe which we have learned to love. Our hearts are fixed in enmity to God, and we must meet him at the bar of judgment, to receive the just desert of a life of sin. We have hidden our talent in the earth, and we must bear the doom of the unprofitable servant.

The Christian life proceeds upon wholly dissimilar principles. The very first act of such a life, as I have said, is the surrender of the whole man, body and soul and spirit, to the will of God. Henceforth the man's will, his desires, and his affections, become subject to the holy and all-wise will of his Father who is in heaven. From being his enemy he is henceforth his loving and obedient child. As a redeemed sinner he yields himself up joyfully to Him who has purchased him with his own blood, thus judging, that those that live shall not live unto themselves, but unto him who died for them and is risen again. The Spirit takes up his abode in the heart of the man who is now a new creature in Christ Jesus, and it is henceforth his delight to do the will of God. His desire is, to do, in his feeble and imperfect manner, as his Father in heaven is doing with all the wisdom and love of the Godhead. The world becomes to him an object of interest, not because it furnishes the means of selfish gratification, but because it presents a field for boundless usefulness, a sphere for the exercise of every benevolent affection. The whole brotherhood of man stands before him, suffering all the miseries entailed upon it by sin. Jesus Christ has appeared to put away sin by the sacrifice of himself, and open wide the door of heaven to every one that believeth. He has put forth his own hand to the work, and, by the sacrifice of himself, has insured its entire accomplishment. He has conceded to every disciple the privilege of being a co-worker with him in this his great labor of love. He has promised his almighty aid to every one who, in humility and faith, devotes himself to the performance of any good work. It is in this belief, and animated by these assurances, that the disciple of Christ goes forth to the labor of his life. In the name of the Lord God he lifts up his banner. Forgetful of his own gratification, he seeks, first of all, the happiness of others, and mainly that happiness which springs from the renewal of the soul in the image of Christ, the only preparation for the enjoyment of heaven. In every effort to promote the highest interests of man, he takes his place in the front rank of earnest, faithful, and self-sacrificing laborers. In him the young find a counsellor, the oppressed a defender, the poor a benefactor, the cast-down a comforter, and the children of infamy and vice a sympathizing brother, who will pity their sorrows, and lead them into the path of purity and eternal life. His course through life may be traced by the blessings that have been sown in his footsteps. The name of the wicked shall rot, but the righteous shall be held in everlasting remembrance. The blessing of him that is ready to perish shall come upon him and his children after him, for he delivered the poor when he cried, the fatherless and him that had no helper, and so an entrance shall be abundantly ministered to him into the everlasting kingdom of his God and Savior.

My hearers, we are spending our probation under the most solemn of all possible conditions. The choice between these two modes of life is presented to every one of us. Each one of us must individually decide whether he will live to himself or to God, for time or for eternity. Which of the two do you choose, nay, which have you already chosen? If you have made an unwise choice, your decision is not yet irrevocable. You may yet retrace your steps, surrender your heart to God, believe on his Son Jesus Christ, and receive into your soul the renewing influences of his blessed Spirit. What will you do? Will you live unto yourself, and lose your own soul, or will you live unto God, and enter into the rest that remaineth? Now is the time for decision. Decide,

I pray you, in view of time and eternity, of the love of God in Christ Jesus, and of the great day of account, when you shall stand before the throne of your Redeemer and your Judge.

You see, my brethren, that the religion which saves the soul is something more than a mere profession. It is not the performance of rites and ceremonial observances. It is not a belief in doctrines, however true or however solemn. It is not the mere indulgence of emotions, however pleasurable or however self-satisfying. It is a radical change in our moral nature, by which our selfishness is eradicated, and we are transformed, truly and in fact, into imitators of Christ. "If ye love me, keep my commandments. He that hath my commandments and keepeth them, he it is that loveth me; he that loveth me shall be loved of my Father, and I will love him, and will manifest myself unto him." Religious joy and and a religious life are thus inseparable. If we do the will of God, and follow the example of his Son, he will manifest his love to our own consciousness. Let us try ourselves by such tests as these, if we would assure our hearts before him. "Many will say unto me in that day, Lord, Lord, to whom I will testify, I never knew you."

THE FALL OF PETER.

"AND WHEN HE THOUGHT THEREON, HE WEPT."

Mark xiv. 72.

FEW narratives in the gospel history are more deeply imbued with practical instruction than that which relates the fall and the repentance of Peter, the apostle. The character of the man, his ardent zeal, and yet too fluctuating purpose, the circumstances of the case, its intimate connection with the sacred supper, the agony in the garden, the hall of Pilate, the betrayal and the crucifixion of the Redeemer, all conspire to bring this portion of the sacred writings frequently and vividly to our recollection. And yet, my brethren, I am not sure that we are disposed to view this subject in so practical a light as it manifestly deserves. We naturally consider an apostle, in many respects, as a peculiar man, and the circumstances in which this apostle was placed as peculiar circumstances; and thus we see in the whole case so much of peculiarity that each one escapes from that practical application of the history, which the Holy Spirit intended to carry home to the bosom of every disciple who reads it.

I freely grant that there is much of this sad story that may be considered peculiar. You are not the apostle Peter. Thi city is not Jerusalem. Your place of daily occupation is not the hall of a Roman magistrate. You are never in the personal presence of Jesus Christ. Here, however, if I mistake not, the peculiarity of the case ends. Though not an apostle, you are, it may be, by public profession, a disciple of Jesus

Christ. Though you are not Peter, yet your heart is probably as deceitful as his. Though this city be not Jerusalem, it is a province of that world which lieth in wickedness. Your placce of business is not the hall of Pilate; yet it may surround you with as insidious temptations as those which there encircled the apostle Peter. It is, perhaps, on this account that the Holy Spirit has marked the various circumstances attending this event with a particularity which allows us to apply every part of it to our own instruction. If, therefore, we look upon this history in its true light, I think we shall discover that, far from presenting us with an isolated and solitary case, which might possibly be of use to us only on rare and uncommon occasions, it presents us with precisely the reverse. It teaches many a lesson which we must practise every day; it utters notes of warning to which it becomes us continually to give heed, if we would escape the sorrows which fell upon the head of this falling and penitent apostle.

My object in the present discourse will be to place before you some of the lessons which may be derived from a contemplation of this portion of scriptural history. May the Holy Spirit carry home to each heart the instruction which it contains, so that our repentings may be enkindled within us, and that, looking backward over our past wanderings, we also may think thereon and weep.

With all the facts connected with the fall of Peter I suppose you to be already familiar. I need not, therefore, consume your time by recapitulating them, but may, at once, proceed to consider them in their order.

Commencing, then, with the narrative in the Gospels, I remark, in the first place, —

Peter was forewarned of his danger. He thought the warning needless, and slighted it. "All of you," said the Savior, "shall be offended because of me this night." Peter answered, "Though all men should be offended because of thee, yet will I never be offended." Jesus said unto him, "This night, before the cock shall crow twice, thou shalt deny me thrice." "But he spake the more vehemently, If I should die with thee, I will not deny thee in any wise."

We, like Peter, are commonly forewarned of the approach of moral danger. Conscience, especially when enlightened by the teachings of the Spirit of truth, admonishes us of the peril before it becomes imminent. It puts to us the solemn questions, Can this be right? Will this be well pleasing to God? Can I expose myself to this temptation unnecessarily and be innocent? If I am called by my convictions of duty to walk amidst temptation, have I armed myself by humility, faith, and prayer? Happy is the man whose conscience, habitually void of offence, is many times a day whispering in his ear such questions as these. But happier far is that man to whom they are never addressed in vain, who, without demur and without parley, instinctively, and with his whole soul, flees from the very appearance of evil.

Peter was self-confident, and deemed the warning needless. But, blind to futurity, who, under the same circumstances, would not have been self-confident? As the immediate family of Jesus, they had just partaken of the sacramental supper. They had just listened to the parting words of the Savior. They had been melted into tears at the announcement of his approaching and mysterious departure. At no moment of their discipleship had he seemed so peculiarly dear to them. If the question had then been *directly* put to Peter, whether he would deny Christ or die, I believe that he would instantly have chosen death. After rising from supper, they walked together to the garden of Gethsemane, that they might spend the remainder of the night in prayer. Jerusalem was wrapped in slumber. It was impossible to discern the remotest indication of danger. Only a day or two had elapsed since their Master had entered Jerusalem amidst the shouts of grateful and exulting multitudes. The moral danger of hypocritically professing attachment to Christ seemed far greater than that of denying him.

As they threaded their way through those quiet streets, and

clustered together to hear every syllable that fell from the lips of their Master, and marked the fixed melancholy, the exceeding sorrowfulness, even unto death, which, without any visible cause, settled upon his countenance, how strangely must have come over their souls the recollection of his recent warning, "Verily I say unto you, that all of you shall be offended because of me this night"! To which of us, under these circumstances, would not such an event have seemed incredible? Who could have foreseen the trials that were already impending? Who could have believed that the warm affection which now glowed in his bosom, could, by any possibility, be so suddenly chilled? Surrounded as they were by acquaintances, who of them could seem capable of such hardihood as to deny that he was a disciple of Christ?

Peter, as well as the rest of the apostles, could foresee no danger, and therefore felt himself in no special need of protection. He went forth that night in his own strength, and the result was such as might have been expected.

The enemy of souls did not, however, directly assail the virtue of Peter. He first stimulated his self-confidence until it exploded in folly, and exposed him to public disgrace. The moral power that is built upon natural self-reliance, crumbles into dust when self-reliance is smitten with confusion. It was on this principle that Peter was assaulted with the first temptation. It resulted in his second error.

The sad company, listening to the solemn instructions of our Lord, pursued their way to the garden of Gethsemane — a place to which they, together with their Master, often resorted for the purpose of quiet and secluded devotion. As soon as they had arrived there, Jesus desired them to sit down and pray, lest they should enter into temptation, while he went somewhat beyond them, and prayed also. Taking with him Peter, and James, and John, he retired into a more unfrequented part of the garden. Here he began to be sorrowful and very heavy, and said to these, his confidential friends, "Tarry ye here and watch with me while I go and pray yonder." All that he asked of them was, that they would protect him from interruption while he was preparing himself by prayer for the awful events that were approaching.

Soon the Lord was overwhelmed with his sore agony. Falling to the ground, his body bathed in blood, he cries, "Father, if it be possible, let this cup pass from me; nevertheless, not as I will, but as thou wilt." He rises and approaches these selected disciples, and they are already asleep. He arouses them, exhorts them to pray, and again retires to agonize in prayer. This was done thrice before the arrival of Judas. How sad a change has, within a few minutes, been wrought in this apostle! But just now, and he seemed to love Christ better than life. Already has the tide of affection ebbed so low that he cannot keep watch for the Savior even for one hour. Thus sadly does mere emotion wither away when exposed to the test of self-denying reality. Almost the last occasion in which it was possible for him to testify love to his Master, has passed away unimproved. The Savior, in this hour of his dire necessity, might as well have relied upon strangers, as upon his chosen disciples.

But the time for prayer and watching had now passed by. The time for action had arrived. The soldiery, with lanterns and torches, broke in upon the stillness of the scene. Jesus arouses the sleepers, and informs them of the approach of the betrayer. Starting suddenly from his guilty and unfeeling slumber, Peter desired to recover himself at once from his false position. Finding himself surrounded with armed men, the recollection of his Master's warning flashed upon his mind. He supposed that this was the trial to which Jesus had alluded, and that this was the occasion on which it had been predicted that he should deny his Lord. Strong in his own strength, he resolved boldly to meet the danger. He would show to Christ, and to his brethren, that he feared neither soldiers nor swords, neither wounds nor death. Anxious to give immediate proof of his courage, and to demonstrate that, though just now asleep, he was already quite prepared for any emergency, he draws his sword, smites a servant of the high priest, and cuts off his ear. In how few moments may an act be conceived, resolved upon, and committed, of which the consequences may affect our destiny forever! Before he had become aware of his danger, pride, vain-glory, nay, perhaps anger and revenge, had swept with unresisted force over his soul. This was his second error.

Observe, my brethren, the connection of these events. The self-confidence of Peter led him to spend this hour in sleep, which he should have spent in guarding his Master from interruption, and in earnest prayer for divine assistance during the unknown trial that was approaching. Had he been awake and in prayer, he would not have been so abruptly surprised by the appearance of Judas with the soldiery. Had he been at this moment humble, watchful, and devout, his ardent temper, calmed by solemn reflection, would not have precipitated him into an act which had so important a bearing upon all his future conduct. My brethren, we are never in greater danger than when our own passions become mingled with religious emotion. There are few states of mind on which God looks down with sterner displeasure.

The Savior rebuked the rash zeal of this disciple, healed the wounded man, and submitted himself to arrest. "Put up thy sword into its sheath," said the Lamb of God. "The cup which my Father hath given me, shall I not drink it?" These words were sufficient to discover to Peter his error, and fill him with regret and shame. He had displeased his Lord, he had prejudiced his cause, he had incensed the soldiery. He had made no friends, he had made many enemies, and his conscience testified to him that he had done wickedly. He had, by his sin, rendered the subsequent trial through which he must pass severer; while he had, at the same time, enfeebled the moral power with which he must meet it. Nothing awakens fear like the consciousness of guilt. His self-confidence fled, and with it all his boasted fortitude. This sudden explosion of impetuosity was instantly succeeded by trembling cowardice.

Seeing that Jesus offered no resistance, but suffered himself to be bound and led away like any other prisoner, he, with the rest, forsook him and fled. This man, who, but an hour before, had said, "I am ready to lay down my life for thy sake," and "though all men should be offended because of thee, yet will I never be offended," is already fleeing from the sight of the guard, and skulking in darkness amid the trees of the garden. This was his next error. Such, my brethren, is always the end of pride. A haughty spirit goeth before a fall. Such is the result of confidence in ourselves. Nothing will prepare us for the hour of trial like heartfelt humility. Nothing will sustain us amidst appalling dangers, but unshaken confidence in God.

The guards soon disappeared with their prisoner. The glare of lanterns and torches faded away in the distance. Gethsemane was again as still as when they entered it. Peter groped away from his hiding-place. He had escaped the present danger and eluded the grasp of the soldiery. His alarm began to subside, and he reflected upon his condition. His affection partially revived. His Master was on his way to the hall of the high priest. Not a single disciple was in his company. Was it right that the compassionate Jesus should thus be left in the midst of his enemies? Should no friend be near him to utter a word in his defence? Should no disciple stand forth to testify to his holy life, and bear witness to his deeds of mercy? The heart of Peter relented, for, though a rash and impetuous, he was also a kind and humane, man. Again he felt the throb of gratitude. He remembered his Master's love, his Master's warning, and his late and bitter agony. He cannot forsake his Savior altogether. He sees the glimmer of the torches on the road to Jerusalem. He turns his steps in that direction, and slowly follows the crowd that was bearing his Lord to the judgment seat. But what can he now do? Shall he go at once among the soldiers, and avow his inviolable attachment to Christ? This will expose him to more imminent danger than that which he has just escaped. The effects of his recent rashness spread themselves out before him in all their appalling reality. Yet he could not persuade himself wholly to abandon his Master. Distracted to the uttermost by contending emotions, he resolved to do as probably many of us, in the like circumstances, would have done. He pursued a neutral course — a course which would enable him to act according to circumstances. He followed Christ afar off. This was another and a fatal error. He had already begun to repent; but his repentance was baffling, undecided, and half-hearted. Had he even now resolved to surrender all for Christ, could he have brought himself manfully and publicly to confess his error, had he dared to take only one decided step, even now the ground which he had lost might have been retrieved. But he hesitated, he doubted, he trembled, until the time for action was past. He did not take that step, and the result proved that, in cases of moral trial, no man can come to a more fatal decision than that which fixes him upon neutral ground, and allows him to act for the future according to circumstances.

Whenever we hesitate about performing a clearly apprehended duty, trials multiply around us. Thus was it with Peter. Since the last setting sun, with a heart melted in love and gratitude, he had sat, with his brethren, around the sacramental supper, listening to the farewell address of our Lord. Within two or three hours, he had declared that he would die rather than deny him. How changed from all this is his present condition! He had disregarded the warning of his Master. He had been publicly reproved for his rash impetuosity. He had basely deserted the Savior at the first approach of danger. He was now, under cover of the darkness, following the Lord afar off, not daring to avow his discipleship, and prepared only to change his position when circumstances favored; that is, when nothing was to be risked by his fidelity. And in this hapless condition, with every moral principle quivering, and bowing before the whirlwind of contending emotions, he was approaching a trial under which the stoutest resolution might well nigh have quailed.

In this state of fearful indecision, he approaches the palace of the high priest. Well would it have been for him if he had never entered it. The apostle John, however, offered to gain him admittance; and he, like any other man in this condition, obedient to any impulse from without, accepts the invitation, and immediately finds himself in the common hall surrounded by servants and soldiers. He takes his seat among them like any unconcerned spectator, and, warming himself by the fire, waits at his leisure to see the end.

The trial of the Son of God had already commenced. The Holy One was accused of blasphemy, and appealed to those who had heard him in proof of his innocence. Peter said not a word. He was accused of threatening to destroy the temple. Peter well knew all the circumstances to which this accusation alluded, yet he offered no explanation. There was not a being present who was so minutely acquainted as Peter with the whole history of the Savior's life, and whose evidence could so fully have disproved every charge alleged against him; but yet he uttered not a word. His testimony, offered in boldness and sincerity, might have baffled the malice of the Savior's accusers, and would at least have shown that those who knew him best believed him wholly harmless, undefiled, and separate from sinners. All this Peter knew. But his lips were strangely sealed in silence. Terrified, doubting, and guilty, he suffered the opportunity for doing his duty to pass by forever.

The Savior was condemned, not for the doing of evil, but for revealing himself in his true character as the Son of God, the Savior of the world. He was mocked at and spit upon. He was surrendered up to the brutality of heathen soldiers. They blindfolded him, and, in ridicule of his claims to supernatural knowledge, cried out, "Prophesy unto us, thou Christ, who is he that smote thee?" Was there no one present who would offer his own body to shield the Lamb of God from insult, pain, and indignity? Yes; there sat one of his chosen apostles, who was tamely beholding the whole of this atrocious outrage. It was he who, a few hours before, had said, "I am ready to lay down my life for thy sake," but who now had resolved to act according to circumstances. The circumstances surely called loudly enough for the expression of his affection. But this resolution had been fatal. Every moral energy within him had vanished. He was trembling in every nerve, in a paroxysm of cowardice and guilt, incapable of making successful resistance to the slightest temptation.

While in this condition, a more decisive trial awaited him. As the light of the fire shone upon his pale and ghastly countenance, a little maid, coming up, said, without apparently much intention, "Thou also wast with Jesus of Nazareth." He felt at once the inconsistency and sin of his situation. Here he was, associated with the servants and soldiers, looking like an unconcerned spectator upon the injuries heaped upon his Lord. To confess himself a disciple of Christ under such circumstances would have been to plead guilty to inexcusable ingratitude, and would, moreover, have exposed him to personal danger. And yet he was not quite prepared to deny his Master in full. He adopted the usual expedient of a weak, irresolute, and double-minded man. He sought to escape detection by equivocation. "I know not," said he, "what thou sayest;" and immediately the cock crew. Equivocation is at best a poor refuge for guilt. Least of all will it avail in a disciple of Christ. He who resorts to it will speedily be put to shame. It would have been far better, even now, for Peter, had he at all hazards humbly confessed his sin, and boldly acknowledged the truth.

Fearing lest the same accusation should be pressed upon him again, he escapes from the hall, and retires to the porch. Here he hoped at least to elude detection. But where can a guilty conscience hide? Where shall a soul find rest that has been false to the Savior? His very change of place only gives rise to further inquiry. Another servant met him with the same tormenting message, "This fellow also was with Jesus of Nazareth." He was advanced too far for retreat.

To confess the truth would now convict him both of ingratitude and falsehood, for every one understood his former answer as a denial of Christ, and he well knew that he meant it to be so understood. He was now prepared to go still farther. A simple denial would now hardly suffice. He declares with an oath, "I know not the man." He escapes in haste from the porch, and, harrowed by an accusing conscience, he again enters the hall, and finds himself in the immediate presence of Christ. But even here his sin finds him out. Again the tormenting accusation is brought against him, not by a little maid, but by the whole company of the soldiers. One cries out, "Surely thou art a Galilean, for thy speech betrayeth thee." Another, steadfastly beholding him, asks, in the hearing of them all, "Did not I see thee in the garden with him?" Surrounded on all sides by the evidences of his guilt, agitated with shame and remorse, every unholy passion within him burst forth into ungovernable rage. "He began to curse and to swear, saying, I know not the man." This was the consummation of his crime. Immediately the cock crew.

The deed was done. But, as the storm of passion subsided, who can conceive of the agony that rent the bosom of that miserable, fallen, old man? He had heard his master falsely accused, and had not uttered a word in his defence. He had tamely looked on, while Jesus was smitten and spit upon, and neither came near to succor nor console him. Once, twice, thrice, he had denied him in the presence of a multitude who knew that he spoke falsely. He had dishonored his gray hairs by indecent passion and shameful profanity. In spite of his denials, he was well known to be a disciple of Jesus of Nazareth. Who would not condemn the teacher, if such were the effects of his doctrines? This chosen disciple, this intimate friend of the Savior, has inflicted an infinitely greater injury on the Lamb of God than the soldiers who bound him, the mob who reviled him, or even the High Priest who condemned him. Brethren, it is an evil and a bitter thing to sin against God. I suppose that, amid all the varieties of wretchedness which this world then witnessed, there was not a man under the face of the whole heaven whose agony would not have been light in comparison with that which pressed upon the soul of this much-loved and highly-favored apostle.

Where should he look for consolation? His denial had stupefied his brethren. His profanity had astonished the soldiery. Gazing around in horror, he turns towards the judgment seat, and his eye meets the eye of his Savior. The self-condemned disciple, with the oath yet quivering on his lips, bending under the weight of remorse, overwhelmed with astonishment at his own atrocity, looks upon the face of the immaculate Jesus. That face revealed even now nothing but unchanged benevolence. Those features were not darkened by a single cloud of reproach. They were as placid as when he stood in glory on the holy mount. There beamed forth from that countenance nothing but love; yet it was love saddened unto death, not by the buffeting, the shame, and the spitting, but by the ingratitude of his chosen disciple. That look of love subdued him. It recalled the whole history of the Savior's life. The solemn warning, the last supper, the farewell address, the intercessory prayer, the garden of Gethsemane, the bloody agony, — all came with one overwhelming gush to his recollection. That knitted brow is smoothed. That wrathful eye is quelled. That angry flush is followed by a deadly paleness. His knees smite one against another. The fountains of his grief are opened. He could not look again. He went out and wept bitterly.

Thus ends this sad narrative. Every portion of it is filled with practical instruction. To some of its lessons I have alluded in the progress of the discourse. Let us endeavor, before we close, to impress them yet more deeply upon our recollection.

1. The first error of the apostle was confidence in the strength of his own virtue, followed by its natural result, — the want of watchfulness. This was the commencement of his aberration, and the origin of all his subsequent sorrow. We have within ourselves no power to resist the assaults of tempta-

tion. Our only strength is in humble and earnest reliance upon the grace of Christ. St. Paul understood this when he said, "I can do all things through Christ, which strengtheneth me," "for when I am weak, then am I strong." It is rare, my brethren, that an humble and watchful soul is overcome by temptation. Never did a careless and proud man overcome it. And it would be well for us to remember that we are frequently in the greatest danger when we think ourselves most secure. Temptations are seldom nearer than when we suppose them most distant. On the evening of this sad night, Peter was sitting at the sacramental table, filled with devout and tender affection to Christ. Who could have foretold that such moral perils were closing around him, or that, by a series of indirect temptations, he could, before the morning light, be led into sins which then seemed to him far more terrible than death. Let this teach us the importance of constant watchfulness unto prayer. Let us enter upon no day without commending its duties, its trials, its cares, its conversations, to the all-seeing and all-sustaining grace of the Savior. If we commit our way unto the Lord, he will direct our steps. If, conscious of our own weakness, and earnestly desirous to be delivered from all sin, we look to the hills from which cometh our help, the God in whom we trust will never deliver us up to the will of our enemies. What misery would Peter have escaped had he thus acted! What miseries should we have escaped had this been the habit of our lives.

2. The first sinful act of Peter arose from vain-glory. He wished to make a display of his courage. The occasion which gave power to this temptation was, his inexcusable slumber at the solemn hour of the Savior's agony. Desirous in any manner whatever to escape the imputation of want of affection, the emotion of love to his Master was intimately commingled with the fiery impetuosity of his natural temper. Such is the natural action of an ill-disciplined heart. Let this teach us the necessity of frequently and prayerfully scrutinizing our motives. How much of our religious zeal, when weighed

in the balances of the sanctuary, would be found alloyed with pride, sectarianism, vanity, and evil temper! Thus are we, like Peter, constantly liable to injure the cause of our Master, at one time by sloth and indifference, and at another by rash impetuosity. Peter was really doing no more for Christ, when, in his anger, he smote off the servant's ear, than when, stretched at length in the garden, he slumbered while Jesus was at prayer.

One extreme is always liable to be succeeded by its opposite. Rashness is naturally followed by cowardice. He who smote off the servant's ear was seen, in a few minutes, hiding himself in the darkness among the trees of the garden. But two extremes of wrong, though ever so closely united, never lead to rectitude. If we have sinned against Christ in one way, this can form no excuse for sinning against him in precisely the opposite way. If we find that our efforts in the cause of Christ have been mingled with pride and vain-glory, does this make it right for us to fold our hands in indolence, and resolve that we will do nothing? Much less does it justify us in forsaking him entirely, and being found associated with his avowed enemies.

3. The vacillation of Peter produced its natural result — insufficient and undecided repentance. He could not forsake his Master entirely. He dared not openly confess his fault, and meet the consequences of doing right. He followed Christ afar off. Thus difficult is it to do right, after we have once commenced the doing of wrong. Yet, after all, the bold, manly, and immediate forsaking of sin is the only safe course that can be taken. A course only half way right, is as perilous a one as can be chosen. Hence, let us learn, then, never to allow sin unrepented of to remain upon the conscience. At the last, it will bite like a serpent and sting like an adder. It will wither our spiritual strength, and inevitably lead us to aggravated transgression. Nothing could have restored to Peter the moral courage of innocence, but going at once to Christ, confessing his sin, and avowing his attachment, no

matter what the avowal might have cost him. The rule is the same for every one of us. We may be surprised into sin. Our only safety consists in forsaking it immediately. If we hesitate, our conscience will become defiled and our resolution weakened. It is also of the utmost importance that our reformation be bold, manly, and universal. A mere formal return to our duty, lip-service, shame, regret, desire to repent, like Peter's, following Christ afar off, will only lead us into greater moral dangers.

4. Peter heard Jesus falsely accused, and he uttered not a word in his defence. The Son of man was buffeted and spit upon, yet Peter never rebuked the ruffians who were insulting him. This was a grievous and inexcusable sin. Yet, observe, it was not his doing, but his not doing, that was guilty. He was the friend and the witness of Christ. It was his duty to act, and to act promptly. By quietly looking on, when he ought to have acted, Peter prepared himself for all the guilt and misery that ensued. There can be no doubt that this friend and apostle of Christ, by standing there in silence, was doing a far greater wickedness than the very soldiers who were torturing him with every refinement of barbarian malignity.

Hence let us learn the danger of being found in any company in which the cause of Christ is liable to be treated with indignity. If we enter such company from choice, we are accessory to the breaking of Christ's commandments. If our lawful duties call us into society, where the name of Christ is not revered, we can never remain in it innocently, for a moment, unless we promptly act as disciples of Christ. Whenever our love to Jesus demands it, we must, without flinching or shamefacedness, boldly defend his cause. Whenever his name is reviled, we must meekly, yet boldly, rebuke the transgressor. Every where, and at all times, we are required to be ready to offer our testimony in favor of that Savior by whose blood we hope to be redeemed. To fail in the performance of this duty, is a grievous sin, and it always exposes us, in the end, to inextricable embarrassment and overwhelming temptation. Thoughtless and irreligious men themselves look upon such a disciple with contempt. They quickly apprehend the inconsistency of his conduct, and not unfrequently put to him the taunting question, "Did I not see thee in the garden with him?"

5. Peter attempted to escape from the embarrassments of his situation by equivocation. "I know not," said he, "nor understand what thou sayest." This only in the end rendered his embarrassment the more inextricable. It soon reduced him to a situation in which he had no alternative except confession of Christ, under still more disadvantageous circumstances, or the open and violent denial of him altogether. Let this part of the history teach us the importance of cultivating, on all occasions, the habit of bold and transparent veracity. Equivocation is always a sort of moral absurdity. It is an attempt to make a lie answer the purpose of the truth. He who does this when his attachment to Christ is called in question, has already fallen. He denies his Lord in the sight of his all-seeing Judge, though his cowardice will not permit him to do it openly. He cannot, however, long maintain this dubious position. His next step in sin will be open and avowed apostasy. The Lord, whom we serve, is a jealous God. He will not long suffer us to wear his livery when we are in heart united to his enemies. The man who has gone thus far will soon be brought into circumstances which will openly reveal his guilt.

6. Peter was rapidly led on to the commission of crimes in themselves most abhorrent to his nature, and crimes of which, at the commencement of his wrong-doing, neither he nor any one else would have believed him capable. He began by nothing more guilty than self-confidence and the want of watchfulness. He ended with shameless and repeated lying — the public denial of his Master, accompanied by the exhibition of frantic rage, and the uttering of oaths and blasphemy in the hearing of all Jerusalem. And how is this

sudden and awful transformation to be accounted for? My brethren, it may all be explained in the most simple manner possible. The first step in sin placed him in a position in which he must either humble himself in penitence, or, by a second step, plunge still deeper in guilt. He did not repent, but took that second step. Here, again, the same choice was offered to him, but with increased difficulty of repentance, and diminished moral power of resisting temptation. Thus, step after step, he plunged headlong into more and more atrocious guilt, until, without the power of resistance, he surrendered himself up to do the whole will of the adversary of souls.

From this, let us learn the danger of little sins, and especially of sinning against God in the temper of our hearts. If, in any case, we find ourselves cherishing wrong dispositions, let us learn immediately to repent of them. Still more imperative is this necessity, if we have gone so far astray as to sin against God by the actual commission of wrong. In such a case, we are always in imminent peril. Our only way of escape from impending moral danger, is immediate and sincere repentance. If this be neglected or delayed, we may be sure that more formidable temptation will soon surprise us, and that, while sin unrepented of palsies our conscience, we shall most surely be overcome. Nothing but penitence will either remove us beyond the reach of temptation, or with the temptation make a way also for our escape.

In closing this sermon, what need have we of application? If you have not already brought these truths home to your own consciences, all that I can say will be unavailing. Are there not some of us here present who are under those circumstances which the history of Peter illustrates? Is there no one here slumbering in false security, and saying to himself, "Though all men should be offended, yet will I never be offended"? Is there no one here who, by his boisterous and misplaced zeal, has brought dishonor on the cause of Christ? Is there no one here who, for some time past has been following Christ afar off, in darkness, hardly knowing whether he shall number himself among the friends or the enemies of his Redeemer? Is there no one here who, though cherishing a hope of acceptance with Christ, is found habitually in company with those who reject and revile him, and who yet never offers a word in favor of religion? Is there no one here who has, by word and action, once, twice, thrice, brought dishonor on the profession which he has made, who is fast sinking under the power of temptation, and denying the Lord that bought him? Professor of religion, thou art the man to whom this sermon is addressed.

CHARACTER OF BALAAM.

"FOLLOWING THE WAY OF BALAAM, THE SON OF BOSOR, WHO LOVED THE WAGES OF UNRIGHTEOUSNESS."

2 *Peter* ii. 15.

IN the history and character of Balaam every one of us must frequently have felt a peculiar interest. Among the prophets of the Gentile world, he holds a high, if not the very highest position. His conceptions of the character of God may challenge comparison with those of the most gifted writers of the Old Testament. The knowledge and the practice of duty were, however, in his life, strangely contrasted. While his intellect dwelt in the regions of inspiration, his heart revelled in all the abominations of paganism. The dealings of God with him in the great act of his life, the attempt to curse the children of Israel, were in many respects remarkable. God permitted him to go with the princes of Moab, and yet was displeased with him for going. He uttered his prophecy precisely according to the divine commandment, and yet he is spoken of as by way of eminence a sinner. These seemingly inconsistent facts are at first view irreconcilable with our moral conceptions. There is a mystery enveloping the whole transaction, which we do not satisfactorily penetrate. We are struck with the graphic power of the narrative; we are deeply moved by the sublimity of Balaam's apprehension of the character of God; we perceive that his life was a continual struggle between conscience and passion; we doubt not that there is much to be learned from his history; but we do not find the practical instruction as apparent as we might reasonably expect.

It may, perhaps, be profitable to examine this passage of Scripture history afresh. We may possibly discover the reason for the dealings of God with this Gentile prophet, and we may also learn from it some lessons that may tend to our own spiritual improvement. In fact, my brethren, the history of Balaam is more analogous to our own, than we might at first suppose. There must of course be much respecting events which occurred three or four thousand years since, which we of the present day cannot adequately explain. All that we know of this personage is contained in a few chapters of the book of Numbers, with brief references to them in other passages of the Old and New Testaments. Enough may, however, be learned from the narrative to furnish us with the materials for profitable reflection.

Balaam, a contemporary with Moses, was a native of Pethor, supposed to be a town of Mesopotamia, on the bank of the Euphrates. He had acquired a high reputation, which extended to the surrounding nations, as a diviner, or one endowed with the power of foreseeing the future. It was even supposed that the future was subject to his will, at least that prosperity was created by his blessing, while inevitable ruin waited on his curse. It is in this character that he is introduced to us in the history of the Israelites. The king of Moab, alarmed at the progress of the Hebrews, and convinced that they were led by supernatural power, inferred that they could not be resisted by merely human agency. In this trying emergency, he sought the aid of Balaam. He desired this powerful diviner to curse these hitherto invincible invaders, in the hope that thus he might possibly arrest their progress, and save his nation from inevitable destruction.

And here, at the commencement, there is, I confess, something apparently mysterious. Balaam seems to have been favored with intimate communion with the Most High, and to have received from him distinct and sublime revelations concerning the future; and yet he died a very wicked man. It may have been that his character changed, and that late in life he became an apostate. At the time of his first correspondence with Balak, his piety was, however, at best, but ambiguous, and he, before long, became an open enemy of God. Here, then, we behold miraculous gifts of the most extraordinary description, conferred on a man whose end was destruction.

There is, clearly, in such a bestowment of supernatural powers, something at first view inexplicable; and yet the Scriptures record many cases in no material respect unlike it. In the old time, God frequently chose men to be the deliverers of his people, and held with them special communication, who, so far as we can discover, exhibited at the best but dubious evidences of piety. We have no reason to doubt that the power of working miracles was bestowed as liberally on Judas as upon any of the apostles, though he was a thief and a traitor. Our Lord teaches us that miraculous gifts may be bestowed when no saving grace has been imparted. "Many will say unto me at that day, Lord, Lord, have we not prophesied in thy name, and in thy name cast out devils, and in thy name done many wonderful works? and then will I profess unto them, I never knew you; depart from me, ye that work iniquity." And, saith the apostle, "Though I have the gift of prophecy, and understand all mysteries, and all knowledge, and though I have all faith, so that I could remove mountains, and have not charity, I am nothing." If, then, God did endow with miraculous power this wicked man, there is nothing in the fact at variance with the analogy of Scripture. It is evident that no extent of religious knowledge, no possession of extraordinary gifts, no degree of usefulness in the church, can furnish adequate evidence that our hearts are right with God. Without charity — love — we are but sounding brass and a tinkling cymbal. How often has it occurred that ministers of the gospel, distinguished by eminent abilities, fascinating eloquence, and remarkable success in the conversion of sinners, have shown by their subsequent lives that they themselves have been fast held in the bonds of iniquity! "Let him that thinketh he standeth take heed lest he fall."

One fact, however, deserves to be specially remarked, because it does much to dissipate the mystery that seems to hang around this mode of God's dealing with men. Miracles are the universal credentials, by which the Most High authenticates a communication from himself to men. When he bestows this power upon an individual, he holds himself responsible for the truth of the message which, under such circumstances, shall be delivered in his name. If God permits the worker of miracles to utter nothing but the simple truth, then, how corrupt soever may be the heart of the prophet, men are in no danger of deception. So was it with Balaam. He had been endowed with supernatural power, and his utterances were to be received as the teachings of God. Hence the impressive and oft-repeated warning, Whatsoever I shall say unto thee, that shalt thou speak. But the care of God in this respect was not confined to admonitions. He held this wicked prophet fast in the grasp of his omnipotence, so that, much as he might desire it, he was actually unable to utter a single syllable either more or less than God put into his mouth. It is on this fact that the explanation of the subsequent narrative essentially depends.

The endowments of Balaam placed him in the rank of the foremost men of his time. His conceptions of the character of God are scarcely inferior in clearness and sublimity to those of the most gifted of the prophets. Nor did his knowledge of God pertain merely to his natural attributes. No one has spoken in more impressive language, or with more awful reverence, of the veracity, justice, and faithfulness of Jehovah. His mind dwelt naturally in the region of the loftiest contemplations, and he spoke in strains of matchless eloquence, such as became the man who had heard the words of God, and knew the knowledge of the Most High, and had seen the visions of the Almighty.

The conscience of this prophet was as remarkable as his intellect. His moral preceptions were distinct and discriminating, revealing to him clearly the moral sublimity of piety. His convictions of duty were almost irresistible, but they wrought within him nothing but anguish. He knew too well the character of God to dare directly to disobey him, but his obedience — if obedience it may be called — acknowledged no higher motive than the trembling fear of a slave. The clearest teachings of conscience awakened within his agitated bosom neither a sincere love of virtue, nor a single sentiment of holy obedience. He knew himself to be encircled by a power which it was absurd to resist, and wise to propitiate, and he crouched before it in hypocritical obeisance, while his heart was meditating falsehood and rebellion.

The whole course of the narrative teaches us that Balaam was a man of ungovernable passions. In his character were united towering ambition, insatiate love of power, a ravenous appetite for sensual pleasure, and a rapacious greediness of gain. His conscience and his passions grew up side by side, each in turn claiming the ascendency, but neither for a while gaining the undisputed mastery. Under ordinary circumstances, the balance was so well maintained that to outward seeming his conduct was correct, if not exemplary. If even for a time he was overcome by passion, the splendor of his abilities and the availableness of his talents easily pleaded his excuse among his admiring contemporaries. And then, again, conscience, in turn, asserted her supremacy, and he would be known as the preacher of righteousness, the eulogist of virtue, and the stern and eloquent rebuker of every form of evil doing. But with all this, there was no stable foundation on which a right moral character could be built. He had never, without reserve, submitted his whole heart to the teachings of conscience and the government of God. A being endowed with those mighty energies cannot long maintain a neutral position; he must act, and his action must tell powerfully on the destiny of coming generations. If these noble capacities are consecrated to the service of God and humanity, they will create a Luther, a Howard, or a Washington. If the voice of conscience is silenced, and these glorious endowments are made the venal slaves of selfishness and passion, the man is known as the scourge of nations, sacrificing the dearest interests of man to the gratification of his own ungovernable lust.

A being of so remarkable a character is always beset by temptations unknown to ordinary men. Such was the case with Balaam. The king of Moab sent to him the elders of his people, with the reward of divination in their hands, saying, " Come now, therefore, I pray thee, curse me this people, that we may smite them, and that I may drive them out of the land; for I wot that he whom thou blessest is blessed, and he whom thou cursest is cursed." At this time Balaam seems to have been ignorant of the character and destiny of the children of Israel. The ordinary rewards of divination were also as yet insufficient to arouse him to ungovernable cupidity. He, as was at this time his wont, retires to ask the Lord what he shall say to the messengers. Here he learns, probably for the first time, that the people are blessed of God, and he is peremptorily forbidden to curse them. He knew from the character of God that this decision was irreversible. " God," said he at another time, " is not a man, that he should lie, neither the son of man, that he should repent; hath he said, and shall he not do it? or hath he spoken, and shall he not make it good?" Impressed with these convictions, whatever may have been the secret wish of his heart, he obeyed the voice of God, and refused to go with the messengers.

Before long, however, the temptation is renewed with greatly additional allurement. Balak sent yet again princes more and more honorable than they. A splendid retinue, clothed in oriental magnificence, stood before the humble dwelling of the Gentile prophet, bearing an urgent message from a mighty monarch. " And they came to Balaam, and said unto him, Thus saith Balak, the son of Zippor, Let nothing, I pray thee, hinder thee from coming unto me; for I will promote thee to very great honor, and I will do unto thee whatsoever thou sayest unto me. Come, therefore, I pray thee, and curse me this people."

Balaam requests the messengers to tarry until he had inquired the will of the Lord. But what was there to ask of the Lord? The Lord had already pronounced an irrevocable decision, and he would not reverse it. Balaam knew that it was impossible to obtain the divine permission to curse Israel, and therefore, if he wished to obey God, there was no conceivable object for going. Notwithstanding all this, he still desired to go, that he might feast his eyes and stimulate his cupidity by gazing on the rewards, which could only be obtained by disobedience to God. He had, perhaps, an idea by no means uncommon, that the guilt of sin is modified by the presence of extraordinary temptation; he was, therefore, desirous to be tempted, so that, if he sinned, he might escape in some manner, at least the severity of punishment. Besides, he well knew the character of the ancient oracles, and probably supposed that by uttering some equivocal prophecy, he might satisfy the king of Moab, and obtain the promised rewards, without literally disobeying the command of God. If I do not mistake, these are forms of self-deception by no means uncommon. Men who would not resolve to disobey God, will frequently place themselves in circumstances where the temptation to disobedience is so great that they have no hope of resisting it, and think to escape the penalty, because they did not resolve to sin, but only to place themselves in the way of temptation. My brother, does memory recall no facts in thine own history which bear an analogy to this sin of Balaam? Hast thou never, of thine own deliberate choice, gone into the very thickest of temptation, silencing the voice of conscience with the suggestion that thou didst not intend to yield to it? And when, overcome by temptation, you have plunged deeply into iniquity, have you never comforted yourself with the hope that God would not deal with you severely, because the temptation was so great that it was impossible to resist it? The conduct of Balaam has in every age found many imitators; it is well if there be not many of them here in this congregation.

In answer to his urgent request, God gave him permission to go to the king of Moab, forbidding him, at the same time, to utter any thing but the simple verity. The words in the narrative do not, as I suppose, express a command; for no command was evidently necessary; they denote merely a concession to his earnest desire. God, in this respect, dealt with him just as he deals with us. He allows us to go in the way of temptation if such be our choice. He, by conscience and his written word, makes known to us his will, but at the same time, he gives us an opportunity to disobey him. Men must of necessity have the power to break the commands of God, for otherwise there could be no probation. Every act of sin is an exertion of this power, for without it sin could not exist. So, in this case, it is as though God had said to Balaam, You know my will; you are forbidden to curse them; there can be no virtuous reason for going, and by going you expose yourself to temptation, where you can ask for no aid from my protecting grace. Go if you choose, but the consequences must rest upon your own soul. Hearer, has the voice of God never uttered these monitory words in thine ear? Didst thou heed or disregard them? Hast thou to record, in this respect, none of the experiences of Balaam?

Such, then, was the moral condition of Balaam, when he set forth on his journey to meet the king of Moab. His lust of power and wealth was stimulated to the utmost. He desired to find some possible means by which he might secure the wages of sin, and revel in the delights that could only be enjoyed by transgression. He was going to expose himself to temptation, and place himself in a position in which he must, almost of necessity, be overcome, and utter a lie in the name of the God of truth.

Any one of us, if we could have looked into his heart,

would doubtless have said that, in such a moral state, to resist temptation was almost impossible. It was precisely for this reason that an angel was sent to meet him in the way. God, by granting to him miraculous power, had rendered himself responsible for all that he should utter. Though Balak was a wicked man, yet the Lord would not suffer him to be insnared by a prophet that spoke in his name. It was therefore necessary to arouse the conscience of Balaam by another and sterner monition. The permission to go is not recalled, but the warning is again most solemnly repeated, "Only that which I say unto thee, that shalt thou speak."

We see the condition to which he is now reduced. He dares not, from the fear of impending judgments, utter any thing which God has not commanded. He must not speak a syllable that is not true; while to do this must inevitably defeat the whole object of his journey. Under such circumstances, what possible object could a good man have for going at all? He must not disobey God, while without disobeying him, the attainment of promotion and wealth was absolutely hopeless. Reason and conscience must both have counselled him at once to return home. But the wages of unrighteousness were too tempting to be relinquished without an effort; and he resolved to go, in the hope, I presume, that something would occur, which, in some way or other, he might turn to his advantage.

The result was such as might have been expected. He who is allured by temptation at a distance will surely succumb when directly within its power. Balaam, with all his knowledge of God, was probably tinged with the oriental superstition, that by incantations and offerings it was possible to subject the Creator to the will of the creature. Nor let this surprise us. These intense moral contrasts are among the most common exhibitions of our fallen nature; and they are most frequently seen when a wicked heart and an enlightened conscience meet in the same individual. Balaam commences by offering sacrifices first at Kirjath Uzzoth. From thence he removes to the high places of Baal, as though he would enlist an idol god on his side, in this controversy with Jehovah. Here he builds seven altars, and offers a sacrifice upon each of them. But God commands him to bless Israel, and he dares not, however unwillingly, refuse to deliver the message put into his mouth. Next he removes to Pisgah, to the field of Zophim, and here again builds seven altars, and offers a bull and a ram upon every altar. Again the blessing of Israel is put into his mouth, and he is compelled to utter it. Not yet satisfied, he selects another more elevated position, and ascends to the top of Peor, as it looketh to Jeshimon; and here again he offers his accustomed sacrifice. This also proving unavailing, he went not, as at other times, to seek for enchantments, but set his face towards the wilderness. All these sacrifices, you see, were not offerings to God, but only the means used in unholy divination. Neither thus could he accomplish his purpose. He could by no means oblige God to permit him to curse the people, but was forced, in a most remarkable manner, to predict their future and unexampled prosperity.

Here let us pause for a moment, and reflect upon the moral condition of this man during these memorable transactions. He had been blessed with a knowledge of God such as had been granted to but few of his contemporaries. He knew that the Israelites were the people of God acting under his immediate supervision, while the Moabites were the enemies of God, idolaters of the basest type, cruel, sensual, and vindictive. Knowing all this, it was his earnest desire to destroy the children of God, and aid in the triumph of their enemies. By every device in his power, by sacrifices without number, and by every art of divination, he sought, with perseverance worthy of a better cause, to accomplish his object. And all this was done for the infamous purpose of rising to power and revelling in wealth. Gladly would he have deluded Balak by a lie, or destroyed the Israelites by a curse; but his lips were sealed to the utterance of every thing but the truth.

He obeyed the letter of the command simply because he could not help it; but his heart revolted from the words which he uttered. At the very moment when he was blessing the children of Israel, he longed to take part with their enemies, and wage war against the Almighty himself.

Thus, though in outward act Balaam formally obeyed the commandment, his heart was the seat of ungovernable ambition and inextinguishable love of gain. He would have sinned in act if he dared, but he durst not, and thus lost the poor rewards for which he was bartering his soul. His obedience was destitute of virtue, and hence he lost the peace of mind and self-sustaining energy of piety. This state of mind, in which external service is combined with determined love of sin, cannot long continue. The mind ere long yields itself to the dominion of its chief affection. Thus Balaam, finding even external obedience incompatible with the gratification of his passions, resolved to abandon it altogether. The character of a prophet failing to serve his purposes, he seems to have laid it aside, and the true disposition of his heart henceforth acted without control. He openly united with the Moabites in their attempt to destroy the people of God. Here his previous knowledge of religion gave him great advantage. He knew that it was impossible to compass the ruin of the Israelites, so long as they retained the favor of God. The only course that remained was, by alluring them into sin, to expose them to the judgments of Jehovah. If by their wickedness God should be made their enemy, they would be as easily overcome as any other people. By his advice, therefore, the Moabites cast off the appearance of hostility, and, under the guise of friendship, spread before the people the allurements of idolatry and the seductions of lust. This stratagem succeeded when hecatombs of offerings had failed. The Hebrews united in sacrifice to the gods of Moab, Israel joined himself to Baal Peor, and the encampment became a scene of universal and unblushing licentiousness. As Balaam had anticipated, the anger of the Lord was kindled against

Israel; a plague broke out in the camp, and twenty-four thousand of the people died. Thus, what could not be effected by open hostility, was accomplished by the blandishments of sin. The wicked prophet seemed to have triumphed, and the nation, for their sins, to have been deserted of God.

But God is not slack concerning his promises, as some men count slackness. He remembered his covenant with Abraham; and had he spoken, and should he not make it good? Though he punishes his people for their sins, his faithfulness endures to a thousand generations. By fearful judgments he recalled the Hebrews to their allegiance, and broke up their alliance with idolatry. War was again proclaimed between his friends and his enemies. There was now no ambiguity in the position of Balaam. His choice was irrevocably made. He joined the Moabites with his whole heart in their attack upon the Israelites, and, in the battle that ensued, was found among the slain. His name has been handed down to succeeding generations to designate a man of preëminent ability, destitute of principle, given over of God to work all manner of wickedness with greediness.

How different might have been the result, had Balaam consecrated his distinguished talents to the cause of truth, of conscience, and of God! Resisting the allurements of appetite, mortifying the lust of power, subduing the greed of wealth, and allying himself to the cause of God, he might have shone resplendent in that constellation of patriarchs and prophets of whom the world was not worthy. Had he chosen to suffer affliction with the people of God rather than enjoy the pleasures of sin for a season, he might with Moses have become a leader of the Israelites, with Joshua entered the promised land, and his name might have come down to us laden with the benedictions of ages. Indeed, of the distinguished men of antiquity, I know of none whose moral trials were so analogous, and whose end was so dissimilar, as those of Moses and Balaam. Both of them took rank among the most gifted of their race. Both were in a remarkable degree taught by the Spirit of God. To both were the allurements of the present world presented in the largest measure. Both were equally free to choose between virtue and vice, duty and pleasure, time and eternity. The one resigned without a murmur the luxuries of wealth and the companionship of princes, to unite himself with the enslaved people of God; and he received a hundred fold in this present life. God communed with him as a friend; he became the founder of the only people that has come down to us, through the wrecks of time, praising Jehovah in the identical words that were used by their fathers four thousand years ago; and his name is enrolled high on the list of those who have conferred blessings on humanity. The other meanly shrunk back from the trials of virtue; for a while he hesitated, then yielded to the seductions of passion, became the associate of those whom God had abandoned, and perished ignominiously, a scorn and a by-word to all coming time. "The name of the wicked shall rot, but the righteous shall be held in everlasting remembrance."

Of the many moral lessons which this narrative suggests, I will select only a few.

Some of you, in the vigor of youth, are naturally aspiring after eminence in the occupation which you have chosen. This is well; for why should we not wish to accomplish a noble destiny? He is a weak and a base man who wraps his talent in a napkin, and buries it in the earth. Let this discourse remind us that there are two paths by which men may seek for distinction. In the one, to the very best of our ability, in spite of every obstacle, we honestly DO OUR DUTY, leaving the result to God, and receiving thankfully whatever reward he shall graciously bestow. In the other, without any settled principle, we grasp at the prize, indifferent to the means by which our end may be attained. The latter was the choice of Balaam. It was not successful, and it never will be, for it ignores the fact that omniscience, omnipotence, and holiness govern the world. The end is rarely attained, and if attained, the soul is corrupted by the effort, and success becomes as the apples of Sodom and the grapes of Gomorrah. On the other hand, the faithful, disinterested doing of duty has ever been found the most direct road to eminence. In proof of this, I might summon the testimony of all history; but why should I do this, so long as on the annals of our country are inscribed the names of George Washington and Benedict Arnold?

Let us now apply this lesson more directly to our relations to God.

Among those who have been educated in a Christian land, and have enjoyed the teachings of the fireside and the sanctuary, there are many who are, at this moment, undergoing essentially the same trial as Balaam. There are, I doubt not, many in this assembly, who believe every truth revealed in the Bible, whose conscience is yet susceptible, who are perfectly aware of the consequences of a life of impenitence, in whom, nevertheless, the love of wealth, or pleasure, or social position, is uncontrollable. They cannot be persuaded to yield their affections to God, and yet they dare not openly and contumaciously disobey him. Whenever they refrain from doing what he has forbidden, they act only from fear. It is a service into which filial love never enters. They even listen gladly to any reasoning which teaches that the restraints of the law of God may be cast off with impunity. But this ambiguous moral condition cannot long continue. Its natural tendency is to hardness of heart and stupidity of conscience. If it does not terminate in sincere submission to God, the Holy Spirit will withdraw and leave us to our own choices. A man in this condition has not a moment to lose. What he does must be done quickly. If he delay until the power of the passions is increased, and the power of conscience is diminished, what hope can he have of salvation? If *now* the love of pleasure be strong enough to resist successfully all moral progress, when it increases to a flood, what shall prevent him from being carried down headlong?

Or, again, we frequently find men who have passed this dubious position, and whose power of resistance to evil is already beginning to yield. The man has begun to inquire how near he may approach to wrong without being guilty of wrong doing. He is ever pressing upon the extreme limit of right, that he may look over it, and gaze upon the temptations beyond. You will see him at questionable places of amusement, in the company of the wicked, if thus he can gratify a desire or subserve a purpose. In his intercourse with others, he will readily find some end that shall sanctify the means, until at last neither end nor means is capable of sanctification. The man is ever running after temptation, fooling himself with the belief that he is in no danger, and that there is no harm in taking fire into our bosom if our clothes are not burned. Now, what is all this but acting over again the scenes of the life of Balaam? What is it but going to Balak to feast our eyes upon the wealth, and gloat upon the delights which we may obtain by sinning against God? He who of his own choice places himself in the power of temptation, secretly wishes that he may be overcome. He who is allured towards forbidden pleasure at a distance, cannot surely hope to deny himself when it stands before him in all the power of a present and fascinating reality. If the unseen attraction of the whirlpool turns aside the mariner from his course, how shall he resist its power, when he is already ingulfed in its vortex?

And let this example teach us that we can never walk securely unless we walk uprightly. We can never escape the moral perils that beset us, except by yielding prompt obedience to the monitions of conscience. Formal service, from which the heart is excluded, will never confirm us in virtue. God is a Spirit, and they that worship him must worship him in spirit and in truth. No man ever obtained the rewards of piety without being really pious. The word of God is quick and powerful, sharper than any two-edged sword, piercing to the dividing asunder of soul and spirit, and of the joints and marrow, and is a discerner of the thoughts and intents of the heart. Neither is there any creature that is not manifest in his sight, but all things are naked and open unto the eyes of him *with whom we have to do.* Keep, therefore, thy heart with all diligence, for out of it are the issues of life.

VERACITY.

"FOR HE THAT WILL LOVE LIFE, AND SEE GOOD DAYS, LET HIM REFRAIN HIS TONGUE FROM EVIL, AND HIS LIPS THAT THEY SPEAK NO GUILE."

1 *Peter* iii. 10.

ONE of the attributes by which the Most High specially desires himself to be known by his intelligent universe, is, absolute and unchanging veracity. Whatever he reveals to us, he would have us receive as the pure and simple verity. Whatever he has promised, though heaven and earth should pass away, he will assuredly perform. Whatever he has threatened, he will execute to the very letter, and at the very moment which he has fixed upon for judgment. It is in language such as this that he has revealed himself to us: "He is the rock, his way is perfect; for all his ways are judgment." "A God of truth, and without iniquity, just and right is he." "The fear of the Lord is clean, enduring forever; the judgments of the Lord are true and righteous altogether." "The word of the Lord is right, and all his works are done in truth." "Forever, O Lord, thy word is settled in the heavens, thy faithfulness is unto all generations." "Justice and judgment are the habitation of his throne; mercy and truth go before his face." And one of the songs of the redeemed in the heavenly Jerusalem is, "Just and true are thy ways, thou King of saints."

It is in virtue of this attribute, to the existence of which the history of the universe, from the outgoings of eternity, has borne witness, that God claims of his creatures implicit and unquestioning belief. "Hath he said, and will he not do it? hath he spoken, and will he not make it good?" To give no credence to his declarations, or place no reliance upon his promises, he esteems one of the most insulting forms of human wickedness. An apostle has said, "He that believeth not God hath made him a liar;" and this is no poetic exaggeration — it is nothing but the simple verity. We cannot disbelieve what God has spoken, unless we suppose that he has promised what he did not intend to perform; that is, that he is capable of falsehood. And of this defiant iniquity the whole race of man has, ever since the fall, been preëminently guilty. Neither the promises nor the threatenings of God enter any more into the practical motives of the multitude of men, than the laws of Menu, or the sayings of Confucius. Is it wonderful, then, that the Most High has a controversy with our race? Must he not, at some time, vindicate his veracity, and teach an assembled universe, that though heaven and earth may pass away, not one jot or one tittle shall pass from the law until all be fulfilled?

In this attribute of inviolable truth, God commands us to be imitators of him. He wills us never to utter any thing but the exact verity. In the commandment given to our race by Moses it is written, "Thou shalt not bear false witness." In the text, as in other places, he has promised his special favor to those that speak no guile. He has taught us that "all liars shall have their portion in the lake which burneth with fire, which is the second death." Our Lord himself has declared that liars are the children of the devil; for he is a liar, and the father of lies.

It is manifest that these teachings have not been without effect, wherever the Bible has been openly and plainly spread before the people. Wherever the word of God is freely circulated, and generally read, a barefaced and habitual liar is rarely to be met with among men who lay any claim to the respect of their fellow-citizens. In this country, for instance, we do not often find a man who will deliberately and daily utter what he knows to be false, or make a promise, which he feels himself under no obligation to perform. He who thus disgraces himself is at once banished from the society of honorable men; he is branded as a knave; and we pay no regard to his word, unless it be accompanied by a bond which he must recognize at the bar of a judicial tribunal.

While, however, such cases are rare, I fear that indirect, and what are termed minor variations from strict veracity, are by no means uncommon. I cannot but believe that one of the causes of this moral dereliction is to be found in the fact that men do not adequately understand the requirements of the law under which they are created. They form the habit of looseness of statement and thoughtlessness of engagements, and thus, without consciousness of sin, violate the plain principles of the law of God. Men professing godliness are liable to a similar peril. To do wrong, with even imperfect knowledge, grieves the Spirit, paralyzes our piety, and perils our souls. It may therefore be proper to devote the time allotted to this service to a brief consideration of this subject. I speak to you all, my brethren, but especially to the young of this congregation. I would have you, my young friends, know the moral law under which you live, and by which you must be judged, that I may warn you of some of the dangers by which you are environed.

The law of absolute veracity would require that we should utter nothing but the perfect verity. We are, however, limited in comprehension, and imperfect in knowledge. We know but in part, and hence are liable to mislead when we have no intention to deceive. To this our imperfection the law of God has respect, and it requires of us no more than our nature can perform. It is supposed that we have a belief of what is the truth concerning an event. We are required, if we speak, to utter that belief precisely as it lies in our minds, without exaggeration, disguise, or subterfuge. We profess, when we speak, to convey to another the conception which exists within us; if we convey to him some other conception, we violate the law of veracity and disobey the command of God.

I have said it is supposed that we have a belief of what is the truth concerning any event. I here use the word *belief* in its strict acceptation, meaning by it a conviction founded on sufficient evidence. Hearsays, guesses, and suppositions are not such evidence. He who asserts any thing as a fact is responsible for the truth of his assertion, and is under obligation to take sufficient means to assure himself that the ground of his belief is legitimate. To assert as the truth what we do not know to be true, justly exposes us to the charge of falsehood.

But some one may ask, Are we obliged to tell every one whom we meet all that we know and all that we are thinking about? Do we violate the law of veracity because we do not make a confidant of every companion, or reveal all our thoughts, even to our most intimate friends? I reply, that what I have said has no reference whatever to any of these questions. I have not uttered a word concerning the law of *not saying;* I have only spoken about the law of *saying.* I have merely set before you the rule which should govern us when it is our duty to speak. I have not considered the question, *When* shall we speak, and *when* shall we be silent? This latter may be decided by the principles of duty or by the simple dictates of practical wisdom; but in neither case has it any thing to do with the law of veracity. We may ask ourselves, and it would be well if we asked ourselves much oftener, whether it is or is not our duty to speak. If we decide, either from moral or prudential reasons, that it is our duty to be silent, it is clear that the law of veracity has no command to utter. If we, on the other hand, decide that it is our duty to speak, then the law pronounces its decision, and forbids us to speak any thing but the truth.

But the inquiry may arise, Are we always obliged, when we speak, to speak the whole truth? Are we guilty of falsehood when we declare what is true as far as we go, but keep back a part which we might communicate if we chose? I reply, If we intend to convey the impression that what we say is the *whole* truth, when we know that it is only a *part*, we violate the law of veracity. If we have no such intention, but merely relate the fact as a fact, without any design to create any other impression, then we are innocent. If I mention to another that I walked half a mile, I violate no law of veracity by not telling him the name of every man whom I met, or the number of carriages that passed me on the road. If, however, I professed to give him a minute account of all that I saw, or if, in any manner, I intended to convey the impression that I saw no one, I spoke falsely. A man may thus speak what is strictly true, and yet be guilty of uttering an untruth. He tells what is true, but tells it with the intention of creating a false impression; that is, he wilfully deceives; and wilful deceit is falsehood.

The same law applies to promises. A promise is the expression of our intention to do something, with the design of creating in another the expectation that it will be done. Simply to express an intention is not to make a promise. If, in the course of ordinary conversation, I happen to mention my purpose to leave town to-morrow, this is not a promise, for I did not intend to create an expectation. If I not only say that I am going, but enter into an engagement with another to accompany him, this constitutes a promise. We are morally bound to fulfil the expectation which we have voluntarily created. I say which we have voluntarily created, for a man may expect what we never intended to promise. For his erroneous or injurious interpretations we are not held answerable. We are accountable, not for the expectation which he may have formed, but for that which we ourselves voluntarily created.

In such cases as these, it is evident that our intentions may easily be misunderstood, and we ourselves also tempted to sin. On the one hand, men are prone to mistake a conditional for an unconditional engagement, and thus hold us to the performance of what we never intended to promise; and, on the other hand, we are too often disposed to consider a slight change of circumstances a sufficient reason for the violation of an agreement. The moral question in such a case is, I suppose, simply this: when the engagement was made, would the present condition of things have been considered by both parties a valid reason for terminating it? If such be the fact, it terminates, of course. But, in deciding such a case, we are bound to act on the principles of high disinterestedness, and in the fear of God. If a moral obligation exists, it must be fulfilled. If a doubt remains, we must decide against ourselves, or leave the question to the decision of others. In no other manner can we retain our love of veracity unimpaired. By the habit of deciding doubtful cases in our own favor, selfishness gains the victory over our love of truth, and, before we are aware of it, we become reckless of our obligations and regardless of the sanctity of our word.

And here, again, it may be asked, — for questions on this subject seem to be almost innumerable, — Are we bound to fulfil to the letter every promise which we make, even when it is without any condition? I would not say even so much as this. The very object for which the promise was made may have become unattainable, and of course the whole engagement falls to the ground. I promise to walk with a friend at a certain hour for the sake of healthful exercise. In the mean time a storm has arisen, and to fulfil the promise would defeat the very object for which it was made. Here, of course, there can be no obligation. But, if I break such an engagement from idleness, or because I prefer at the moment to read some book which happens to interest me, I am guilty. It is of no avail to say my friend will excuse it: this may be, but it alters not the fact that I have trifled with my conscience, degraded my moral nature, and sinned against God.

All this should plainly teach us several quite important lessons. In the first place, a promise should always, if possible, be definite, and distinctly understood by both parties. Again, if there be from necessity a contingency, this contingency should be as accurately defined as the promise itself. And, lastly, when we are in doubt respecting the validity of any obligation, — that is, when there is a conflict in our minds between the claims of veracity and those of interest and convenience, — it is always safe to decide in favor of veracity. This may, it is true, cost us trouble, and sometimes apparently useless trouble, but it will confirm our virtue and teach us practical wisdom. We shall love truth the better for every sacrifice we make for it; our moral principles are strengthened by every act of submission to them; and the inconvenience arising from thoughtless engagements will render us more careful for the future. He who holds himself under moral obligation to do as he has said, will be careful of his words, and will excite no expectation which he is not able to satisfy.

And now, my brethren, if we should review these brief suggestions, we might sum up their substance in a very few words. We see that the law of veracity has no direction to give as to the question *when* we shall *speak*, and *when* we shall be *silent*. It simply teaches us our duty in the act of speaking, and then it requires that the thought which we embody in words shall be precisely the thought which lies in our own minds. If it be a fact, we must state it as a fact; if an opinion, as an opinion; and, in either case, we must do it without exaggeration or diminution. The same rule applies to promises. We must make known to another the intention as it actually exists, and the expectation which we thus voluntarily excite we are under moral obligation to satisfy, unless subsequent events shall render the performance impossible, or, in the judgment of disinterested men, would justly nullify the agreement. The law thus understood applies to all our conduct, at home or abroad, in the retirement of the family or in the publicity of the market place, in the workshop and behind the counter, in the gayety of the social circle and in the private dealing of every man with his neighbor. God knows what we think, and he hears what we say, and he observes the minutest discrepancy between the one and the other. It surely then becomes us ever to speak as seeing Him who is invisible.

Such, then, is the law of God, revealed to us in the Scriptures. But, let us ask, Is this law obeyed? Do men recognize the obligations of veracity, and do they speak as in the presence of the God of truth? Let us glance at a few of the occasions which give rise to the violation of the precept, and we shall see how easily men are seduced into disobedience to the law of God.

The inordinate love of wealth gives occasion to frequent violations of the plainest precepts of veracity. When large profits can be secured by falsehood, I am told that, in our large commercial centres, lying and even false swearing are matters of daily occurrence. A custom-house oath has, in fact, come to designate words which impose no manner of obligation. Men will swear to false invoices, knowing them to be false; nay, they will direct two different invoices to be made out, the one by which they sell, and the other to which they swear. If they fear to swear themselves, a clerk must do it for them, or they will employ some poor sinner, for a consideration, to do such swearing whenever it shall be found convenient. If I have stated this too strongly, I shall sincerely regret it; but I only affirm what, on competent authority, has frequently been stated to me. The common adulteration of articles of traffic comes under the same condemnation. Men take every means to give to a worthless compound the appearance of a genuine product, and then solemnly declare it to be what they know that it is not.

Or we may come to facts which transpire every day, in every city and village in our land. The seller represents his goods as of the very best quality, and offers them to the buyer at a price which he declares to be scarcely above cost; then he will sell them at cost; and, at last, will dispose of them to this particular friend at a ruinous sacrifice. The buyer, on the other hand, considers the quality inferior, the price unreasonable, and, at most, is willing to purchase only on a very long credit. The bargain is at length concluded, the goods are delivered, and the parties separate. All at once the language of these men is suddenly transformed. The seller is rejoicing that he has disposed of his merchandise at so handsome an advance, the buyer that he has received so good an article at so low a price. Now, it is apparent that the mere change of hands has neither affected the quality of the goods, nor the opinions of the parties concerning them. Neither of these men spoke as he thought, and the Searcher of hearts marked the violation of his law in every word that was uttered. The love of a little paltry gain overcame the love of truth, and was motive strong enough to set at nought the authority of God.

Idle curiosity gives occasion to a large amount of false speaking. Many persons have an insatiable desire to know all the affairs of their neighbors, their likes and dislikes, their domestic arrangements, their opinions on all matters and of all persons, and thus to worm themselves into the most secret recesses of their confidence. This is commonly done from no malicious design, — for such persons are commonly good natured, — but from mere childish inquisitiveness. To accomplish our purpose, however, not a little management is necessary, and we are obliged to pretend to know already much of which we are entirely ignorant. This is the first departure from truth. We obtained our knowledge under the injunction of secrecy. But a secret which does not belong to us is not easily kept, for this intense desire to know is always accompanied by an equally intense desire to tell. We must reveal it to our intimate friends; and here is departure from truth the second. Or, again, we may meet with another person as inquisitive as ourselves, in whom we dare not confide, and whose prying curiosity we can elude in no other way than by falsehood or prevarication; here is departure the third. Thus the habit grows upon us. Idle curiosity leads to the first falsehood, and the first falsehood creates the temptation to all that follow in its train. I will not here speak of the infinite mischief that is done by this prying inquisitiveness; I here only refer to its effect on our moral character. It affords a sad illustration of the fact that the most contemptible motive is frequently powerful enough successfully to tempt us to violate the commands of God.

Another frequent occasion for falsehood is found in the fear of speaking or acting at variance with received conventionalities. We express joy when we feel none. We counterfeit sadness when we suffer no sorrow. We use the expressions that are in vogue without any regard to the truthfulness of their application, but merely because we hear them used by others. The commonest things, the most unimportant events, are splendid, magnificent, glorious, or abominable, shocking, horrid, detestable. We do not mean what we say: there is no emotion within us corresponding to such exaggerated expressions. Why, then, should we use them? The same conventionality assures us that it is right and proper to escape a trifling inconvenience by telling a lie, or obliging others to tell it for us, and that to say what is false ceases to be a lie, if it be told very frequently, and by a great number of persons. It is said that every one understands us when we direct another person to say we are not at home when we are at home. If a servant or a child lies *to* us, we are indignant, and mourn over the mendacity which is every where so prevalent. But where, I pray you, is the moral difference between lying *for* us, and lying *to* us? Has God ever made any such distinction? It is in vain to say that here no temptation to lie is created, because every one understands it. Many a family has become habitual liars by the daily repetition of these conventional falsehoods. Children know that such language is false, and they must have more than usual virtue if they are not fatally corrupted. A friend of mine once called on a gentleman with whom he had a positive appointment, and was met at the door by his son, who told him that his father was not at home. My friend replied that there must be some mistake; for they had agreed to meet at this very hour. "No," replied the son, "he is not at home; he went out a few minutes since." He, of course, retired, but had scarcely left the house when the gentleman himself appeared at the door, inviting him in, and saying, "I had no idea that it was you." As he entered, the son, ashamed and confounded, turned to his father with these words: "Father, I will never tell another lie for you as long as I live." Had that son grown up to be a liar and a knave, at whose hands would the ruin of his soul have been justly required?

But I will pursue these illustrations no farther. I have said enough to draw your attention to the subject, and you yourselves can easily multiply instances for yourselves, and impress the truth upon your own hearts much more forcibly than another can do it for you.

But some one will say, To do as you advise, and avoid the errors against which you have cautioned us, would require great care and intense watchfulness in all our conversation. We should be obliged to think before we speak, abandon many of the ordinary topics of discourse, and be content to improve men rather than amuse them. Be it so. In this we shall only follow the examples of better and wiser men. It was the prayer of David, "Set a watch, O Lord, over my mouth; keep the door of my lips." He found the advantage of such a prayer when he said, "By the word of my lips have I kept myself from the paths of the destroyer. I said, I will take heed to my ways, that I sin not with my tongue. I have set the Lord always before me, that I sin not against him." "If a man," said the apostle James, "offend not in word, the same is a perfect man, and able also to bridle the whole body. Who is a wise man, and endowed with knowledge among you, let him show forth, out of a good conversation, his works with meekness and wisdom." You see, then, that it has been the earnest prayer of good men that they might be specially aided in this respect, for they were convinced that there could be no attainments in holiness while the tongue was a thoughtless and ungoverned instrument of duplicity or falsehood. Can we expect to please God, or do good to man, unless we are in the exercise of the same prayerful caution? But let us bring the subject to a practical test — let us review, for a moment, our past lives. With what a multitude of immortal souls has every one of us held conversation! Every one of these might have been made better by our words, and every one has been made either the better or the worse by our intercourse. What has been the result? To how many of this multitude can we point as the evidences that we really have consecrated our conversation to the Savior, and that our example has ever promoted the love of truth, and piety, and charity? Had we been more careful of our words, and ever spoken as seeing Him that is invisible, how rapid would have been our progress in piety, and what blessings should we have scattered along our pathway through life! Do you not wish, then, that you had in the past set a guard over your lips? and this you could never have done but by cultivating this very truthfulness which I here recommend. But it is evidently our duty to do in the future what we wish we had done in the past. Let us then begin this reformation at once.

But you will say, To obey these precepts with strictness, to speak nothing but the simple verity, and utter only what God will approve, would render us very peculiar. Our maxims of business must be greatly changed, and in our intercourse with the world we must bid adieu to many of the amenities and courtesies of society.

That the principles of religion carried into any of the departments of life would render us peculiar I will not deny. It belongs to the necessity of the case, for religion is designed to make men better; and if we would make them better, our manner of life must, of course, be in advance of theirs. The world lieth in wickedness, and how can a child of God live in it, and not be peculiar? Wicked men imitate the example of the father of lies; and can we be imitators of the God of truth without being peculiar? Was there ever a being on earth so peculiar as Jesus of Nazareth, the Author and Finisher of our faith? It was to his peculiarity in this very respect that he appealed as the evidence of the divinity of his mission. "Which of you," said he, "convinceth me of sin? [he referred to the sin of falsehood;] and if I speak the truth, why do ye not believe me?" Ought not the followers of such a Savior to be exemplary in all things, and, above all, in their conversation? Unless the teachings of Christ exert their effect on our intercourse with our fellow-men, what do we more than others? and how shall the world be the better or the wiser for our having lived in it?

But, you will say, this is a lesson most difficult to be learned. It requires that we should be always on our guard, watching over ourselves with a vigilance such as we had never imagined. We speak before we think; we become interested in conversation, and forget ourselves; we naturally follow the course of thought of those that are about us, and, before we are aware, commit sin with our tongue. How shall we gain the victory over ourselves? how shall we ever make our conversation a means of good to others, and so speak as ever to please a God of truth? To such an inquirer I would reply, The gospel of Christ has provided for us all needful assistance. The cure must be performed in thy inmost spirit, and the Spirit helpeth our infirmities. The blood of Jesus Christ *cleanseth* us from all sin — the sins of the inmost soul, the moral imperfections that have grown up within us, as though they were a part of our original nature. The word of God is quick and powerful, piercing to the dividing asunder of the soul and the spirit. If, then, you find yourself prone to thoughtlessness in speech; if in conversation and in promises you are liable, even in little things, to forget your obligations to God; if the fear of man or the love of gain ever seduce you to utter what the law of veracity condemns; and, especially, if any or all of this has grown into a habit from which your own power cannot deliver you, — come to that Fountain that cleanseth from all iniquity. Confess your sin before God, and look to him for pardon through the blood of the atonement. Resolve in his strength that you will never yield, but that you will contend against this sin that dwelleth in you, until you have trampled it under your feet. Implore of God the aid of his Spirit. Beseech him to make you thoughtful, self-possessed, vigilant, and endow you with presence of mind in the moment of the most subtile temptation. Ask of him all this with a simple and earnest heart, and he will do it all for you. There is balm in Gilead, there is a Physician there, and you shall certainly be healed. Day by day you will gain victory. Every failure will increase your sensibility to every deviation from right, and will also render it more odious in your eyes. Strengthened with might by his Spirit in the inner man, you will grow stronger and stronger, until by divine grace you have triumphed over this form of evil, and rejoice in the indwelling of his Holy Spirit. "Blessed are they that hunger and thirst after righteousness, for they shall be filled."

And while you are engaged in these moral conflicts with the sin that easily besets you, remember the innumerable cloud of witnesses who have, through grace, gained the victory over the very same enemies. Think of the Savior who has met and vanquished all your spiritual foes, and who looks upon you with approving love, as he sees you following in his footsteps. Think of that crown that shall be bestowed on every one that overcometh, and which shall be made brighter and brighter by victory over every sin. Think of this immortal soul, on which a new lineament of the image of Christ is engraved by every triumph over inbred corruption. Think of all this, and run with patience the race set before you, looking unto Jesus the Author and the Finisher of your faith. So run that ye may obtain.

THE CHURCH OF CHRIST.

"NEITHER PRAY I FOR THESE ALONE, BUT FOR THEM ALSO THAT SHALL BELIEVE ON ME THROUGH THEIR WORD; THAT THEY ALL MAY BE ONE, AS THOU, FATHER, ART IN ME AND I IN THEE, THAT THEY ALSO MAY BE ONE IN US, THAT THE WORLD MAY BELIEVE THAT THOU HAST SENT ME."

John xvii. 20, 21.

THESE words form a portion of that memorable prayer offered up by our Lord in the company of his disciples, on the night that preceded his crucifixion. They were uttered just before he proceeded to the garden of Gethsemane, whilst his mind was deeply impressed with the thought that before another sun should set, his work on earth would be finished, and the sacrifice for our sins offered up. The sentiments of the text, then, come to us clothed with all the authority of the last message from a dying Friend. They express to us the last wish of the Redeemer, and teach us the nature of those blessings which, at that solemn hour, he most earnestly craved in behalf of those for whom he was about to die. There must be in these words, then, something specially worthy of our prayerful attention. Let us endeavor to ascertain their meaning, and draw from it such lessons of instruction as are most appropriate to our present condition.

Let us inquire, in the first place, For whom was this prayer offered?

And here, at the commencement, we are met by the fact that this prayer of our Lord is remarkable for one striking peculiarity. Its object is definite and exclusive. The propitiatory work of Christ was wrought for the whole world, for the whole race of Adam. This prayer, on the contrary, was offered for only a part of that race. He himself declares, "I pray for them; I pray not for the world, but for them that thou hast given me out of the world." At first, the Redeemer seems to have prayed for the apostles who immediately surrounded him, or, at most, for those who had, up to that time, become his disciples. "Those whom thou hast given me I have kept, and none of them is lost but the son of perdition." As, however, he proceeds, his supplications become more general, until he includes within the scope of his intercession, not only the apostles, but all those who, through their word, should believe on him in all coming time.

We perceive, then, that while our Lord excludes the world from any interest in this particular prayer, he includes, within the number of those for whom he supplicates, certain persons taken out of the world. These two classes of mankind are placed in distinct opposition to each other. Those denominated the world, are not those for whom he prays. Those for whom he prays are not of the world. The peculiarity of character which designates this latter class of persons, and which distinguishes them from the world, is frequently alluded to in this last discourse of our Lord, in terms that cannot be misunderstood. They are those for whom a mansion is prepared in heaven; with whom the Comforter shall abide forever; with whom the peace of Christ dwells: they are the branches of that vine of which Christ is the stem; who keep his commandments and abide in his love; who are chosen out of the world, therefore the world hateth them; whom the Father loveth because they love Christ: they are those who have believed on him; whom the Father hath given him out of the world; they have kept his words, they are not of the world, even as Christ is not of the world; the glory which the Father gives to Christ, Christ gives to them; God loves them; the love wherewith the Father loves the Son is in them; Christ is in them, and he wills that they may be with him where he is, that they may behold his glory.

Such are the persons for whom Christ prays. Such are they for whom he supplicates that they may be one. Now, it is obvious that precisely equivalent terms to these are always used in the Scriptures with reference to the church of Christ. The church is always represented to be a portion of the human race possessing the very moral attributes which our Savior, in the passages which I have quoted, enumerates. Thus the apostle Paul addresses his various epistles either to the churches, or to the saints, or to the church of God; to them that are sanctified in Christ Jesus, called to be saints. The church in any place, and the saints in that place, mean, with him, precisely the same persons.

The church is repeatedly denominated by the apostle Paul the *body of Christ*, and every individual believer is a member of the body of which Christ is the head. Thus Eph. 1 : 22. "He hath given him to be head over all things to the church, which is his body." Eph. 4 : 15. "That ye may grow up into him in all things which is the head, even Christ, from whom the whole body, fitly joined together, maketh increase of the body." Col. 1: 18. "And he is the head of the body, the church." The illustration here used is precisely analogous to that derived from the relation of the vine and its branches. The idea in both cases is the same. That portion of matter which obeys my will, and is pervaded by my spirit, and partakes of my animal life, is a part of my body. So the members of the body of Christ are those who obey his will, are influenced by his spirit, and partake of his moral life. These, taken together, form the church, which is his body. All the rest are of the world. It is this spirit of Christ dwelling in them that distinguishes them from other men. "In Christ Jesus, neither circumcision nor uncircumcision availeth any thing, but faith, that worketh by love." "If any man be in Christ Jesus, he is a new creature." "Christ has purchased the church of God with his own blood." "He loved the church, and gave himself for it, that he might sanctify and cleanse it, that he might present it unto himself a glorious church, not having spot or wrinkle, or any such thing, but that it should be holy and without blemish." All the members of such a church, being holy persons, must, of course, be happy in heaven. "Ye are come to Mount Zion, and unto the city of the living God, the heavenly Jerusalem, and to the general assembly and church of the first-born which are written in heaven, and to God the Judge of all, and to the spirits of just men made perfect." From these, and a multitude of passages such as these, it is evident that the church of God is always spoken of in the New Testament, as the company of redeemed souls pervaded by the spirit of Christ, and that they are the persons of our race who possess exactly the same moral attributes as those for whom he prays that they may be one. They are the whole company of those who have come out from the world, who are united to Christ by a faith which worketh by love, who obey his commandments, and are laboring to be conformed to his likeness, that they may enter with him into his glory. Such are the children of men who form his spiritual body, and for whom he offered up his intercessory prayer.

In this statement we express no other truths than those which are fully revealed in other portions of the sacred Scriptures. The whole doctrine of conversion or regeneration is in perfect harmony with all that we have above recited. Thus we are taught that the whole race of man has apostatized from God, is at enmity against him by wicked works, and is under the condemnation of his righteous law; "for all have sinned and come short of the glory of God." Our Father in heaven, moved by sovereign and abounding grace, has provided for all men a way of pardon and reconciliation through the merits, obedience, and intercession of his well-beloved Son. "God so loved the world that he gave his only-begotten Son, that whosoever believeth on him should not perish, but have everlasting life. The offer of pardon and everlasting life is freely made to every individual of our race, on the condition that he truly repent of his sins, receive by faith the Lord Jesus Christ, and maintain a life of holy obedience. The commission which he gave to his disciples, when he ascended, was in these impressive words: "Go ye into all the world and preach the gospel to every creature. He that believeth, and is baptized, shall be saved; but he that believeth not shall be damned." Whenever an individual of our race accepts of these terms of salvation, and by faith yields up his whole nature in love and obedience to Christ, he becomes a new creature, the Holy Spirit takes up his abode in the renewed soul, working in it that which is well pleasing to God; God, for Christ's sake, pardons his sins, and receives the returning prodigal as a well-beloved son. The man becomes an heir of God and a joint heir with Christ; he is delivered from the slavery of sin, and "has his fruit unto holiness, and the end everlasting life." Henceforth, being influenced by the spirit of Christ, he is no more of the world, as Christ is not of the world. He was a sinner; he is now a saint. He was an enemy of God; he is now a child of God. He brought forth the fruits of the flesh; he now brings forth the fruits of the Spirit. He was under condemnation; now "there is a crown of righteousness laid up for him, and for all who love the appearing of the Lord Jesus Christ."

Such, then, is the character which the New Testament ascribes to the individual disciples of Christ. All, then, by partaking of his spirit, are united to him, and form a part of that spiritual body which is his church. Every one who possesses this moral character is a member of this body. The rest of mankind, by what name soever they may be known among men, are of the world, and are not of the church. The term *church*, you perceive, properly and originally designates a class of persons possessing a particular moral character, precisely as the term *world* designates a class possessing an opposite character; the one being precisely equivalent to the term *saints*, and the other to the term *sinners*. Thus all those, in the times of the apostles, who, in the sense that I have described, were disciples of Christ, were spoken of as members of the church. "Having put on the new man, which is renewed in knowledge after the image of him that created him, there was no more either Greek or Jew, circumcision or uncircumcision, barbarian, Scythian, bond, or free," that is, all human distinctions were abolished, and "Christ was all and in all." Thus, in the same manner, in every other age, all that portion of living men who have turned from sin to holiness, and are new creatures in Christ Jesus, are the church of God in the world, at that particular period. Thus, also, in a smaller society of men, in a nation, or city, or even a family, those who are the disciples of Christ are the church of God in that society. Thus all, in all ages, who have ever lived upon earth, and been received into glory, together with those who now by patient continuance in well-doing, are making their calling and election sure, the church militant below, with the church triumphant above, constitute "the general assembly and church of the first-born." And, when the mystery of redemption shall have been finished, and Christ shall have collected home all his ransomed ones into his house not made with hands, then the body of Christ shall be completed, and one church — the multitude which no man can number — shall surround the throne of God, singing, with one voice, the song of Moses and the Lamb, saying, "Thou hast redeemed us to God by thy blood, and made us kings and priests to our God;" "Salvation, and glory, and honor, and power, unto Him that sitteth upon the throne, and to the Lamb forever and ever."

Such, then, is the simple notion of the church of Christ, as it is presented to us in the New Testament. It is a term used to designate a class of persons possessing a peculiar moral character, right affections towards God and their fellow-men. Whoever possesses these moral affections belongs to this class, or is a member of this church, no matter by what other peculiarities he may be distinguished. Whoever is destitute of these moral attributes is not a member of this church, or does not belong to this class, no matter by what name he may be called, or what profession soever he may have assumed

But, it may be said, this truly is the conception of the church, as it exists in the mind of Him that searcheth the heart. The Lord knoweth them that are his. But there is not in us this knowledge. We can form no such church. What, then, is the scriptural idea of the church as it actually exists here upon earth? Let us proceed to answer this question.

In the first place, then, I think it must be obvious that if this be the pure and original idea of a church, it must lie at the foundation of every practical and visible manifestation of it which we are authorized to constitute among men. We are not omniscient, and therefore cannot organize a church which shall inevitably include every true disciple, and exclude every one who is not a disciple. We are, however, bound to use, for this purpose, all the means of discrimination which the Holy Spirit has given us, honestly endeavoring, to the utmost of our power, to render the church visible coëxtensive with the church invisible. The model is placed before us; and, though we are unable to attain to perfect conformity with it, we should labor to attain to as perfect a conformity as our limited knowledge will permit.

I remark, secondly, Christ has commanded all his true disciples to come out from the world, by making an open and avowed profession of their attachment to him. He has appointed a solemn rite, by the reception of which this profession is to be made. But, as there must be some authority under which this rite is administered, so that no other, if possible, than true disciples may be admitted to it, Christ has committed this authority to those who are already disciples. By these, every one who wishes to come out from the world, and profess his faith in Christ, is to be received into the number of visible disciples.

Again: Christ has appointed a solemn rite, in memory of his atoning death, which his disciples are commanded, from time to time, to celebrate. This second rite, like the other, is to be administered to those who are members of his body and partakers of his spirit. The meaning of it is, that they, in partaking of it, profess to be one with him, and one with each other. As none have a right to partake of this ordinance but true believers, Christ has authorized the disciples themselves to admit to it such persons as give evidence of faith in him, and to exclude from their fellowship all those in whom the evidences of piety are wanting.

And, besides all this, religion is intimately connected with the social principles of our nature. In our warfare against sin, and our endeavors after holiness, we are greatly assisted by the sympathy of our brethren. It is natural that those whose hopes and fears, whose joys and sorrows, are similar, should associate together, that they may strengthen their faith by fraternal communion with each other.

Again: it is made the duty of every disciple of Christ to extend the spiritual reign of his Master. He must hold forth the word of life, bear testimony against whatever is sinful, and devote himself to the work of saving men from the destruction which awaits the ungodly. Christ devoted himself to the labor of unceasing benevolence; and we are disciples of Christ in just so far as we follow his example. Much of this labor can be carried on only by associated effort. Men earnestly engaged in such an undertaking will naturally unite with each other for the purpose of more successfully accomplishing the object to which each one has consecrated himself.

For such reasons as these, our Lord has taught us that his disciples in any place should form themselves into fraternal societies. The object of such societies is purely spiritual. He only has a right to belong to them who is a member of the body of Christ; and the reason for which he unites himself with them is, that he may do the will of Christ more perfectly. A society thus formed is a church. It has nothing to do with any other association, nor has any other association any thing to do with it. Its laws and its authority are all derived from Christ, who is its head. It is composed of those who are "a chosen generation, a royal priesthood, a holy nation, a peculiar people — that they should show forth the praises of Him that hath called them out of darkness into his marvellous light."

From what we have said, it is evident that such a society as this is designed for action. There are things to be done by the members as a community. All are not, however, endowed with powers for doing the same things. Each one must labor according to his several ability. Hence the necessity for some form of organization, and for the creation of such a system of agencies as is commonly called a government, and for such laws as shall prescribe the duties, privileges, and responsibilities of each member. It, however, hardly need to be remarked that the organization of such a society should be exceedingly simple. The sole object of the association is to aid us in making other men, as well as ourselves, holy. This surely can demand no very complicated arrangements. Whatever we find in any ecclesiastical organization which is not directly productive of this object, whether it be innocent or noxious, can claim no sanction either from the precepts of Christ or his apostles.

The question, however, may be asked, What is the form of government which Christ has ordained for these various communities of Christians? I answer, I do not perceive in the New Testament any directions on this subject. I see there mention made of pastors, or religious teachers, who were to preach the word, and be examples to the flock; and deacons, whose office it was to distribute the charities of the disciples. But how these were to be appointed, or what was to be the form of the ruling authority, has not been authoritatively made known to us. I see nothing in the New Testament which would prevent any community of Christians from adopting any form of church government which they may esteem most for their edification. The forms which have been adopted, have, in fact, been very analogous to those which have obtained in civil society. All of these are allowable. Each one of them has various points of excellence. One may be better adapted to the habits and associations of one company of disciples, and another to another. But neither of them can, in my opinion, claim any divine authority. One of them is as acceptable to the Master as the other, if it be administered as much to his glory and the edification of those who have chosen to adopt it. Of one thing, however, we may be certain. The form of government is not the church of Christ, any more than a republican constitution is the people of the United States, or a monarchy the people of Great Britain. The people existed before the constitution, and the true church, the body of Christ, existed before the establishment of any ecclesiastical organization. The church is the body of sincere disciples; the form of government is the manner in which they have chosen to administer the laws of Christ in their intercourse with each other. The true disciples of Christ, who, in any place, hold forth the word of life, and are examples to the world, would, in the most important sense, be the church in that place, without any ecclesiastical organization whatever. Those who were destitute of his spirit, and were living to themselves, would not be his church, but the world; no matter how perfect, or how time-honored, may be the form of organization under which they may have been associated.

Now, if this be true, it is evident that the church of Christ must be something quite unlike any visible association existing on earth. The qualifications which unite a man to the real church are moral dispositions, of which man can but imperfectly take cognizance. Organizations, called by the name of Christ, have frequently been formed, from which every true disciple is deliberately excluded. Societies calling themselves churches have too often become synagogues of Satan, and haters of all that is good. But names cannot alter things, nor can the designations of men make him a member of the body of Christ, of whom Christ himself has said, "I never knew you: depart from me, all ye workers of iniquity." He is a member of the church who is a penitent and believing disciple of Christ. He is no member of the church who is not such a disciple, no matter by what name he may be called.

Thus Christendom is not the Church of Christ. By this term we generally designate those nations which acknowledge the Bible to be a revelation from God, and have forsaken the idolatry and paganism in which they had in former times been educated. Among these millions, a great number of the members of the church may be found; but these nations are not the church, for they contain multitudes who have no hope, and are without God in the world. For the same reason, the religion of Christ cannot recognize such a thing as a national church. Such a church, if consistent, admits to its communion every citizen of the nation. But the qualifications for admission to the church are entirely unlike those of citizenship. To be a member of the church, a man must be a member of the body of Christ, while the mere accident of birth within its territory entitles him to the privileges of citizenship. No being but Christ himself can alter the conditions of admission to his church. For man to assume such an authority, would be acknowledged as impious, if the frequent contemplation of the wrong had not blinded us to its real moral character. By what right, in the times of the apostles, could the emperor have enacted that every Roman citizen should be a member of the church of Christ? And it is obvious that a government possesses no higher authority over the church of Christ at the present day, than at any preceding period. Religion is, and ever has been, the intercourse which the spirit of man holds with the unseen and uncreated Spirit; and with it no created being has any conceivable right to interfere.

Nor, again, can any one of the sects into which the disciples of Christ are divided, claim for itself the exclusive title of the Christian church. What sect can claim that all of its members are the unfeigned disciples of Christ, and that all without its pale are reprobates? What sect of the Christian church is so distinguished by a holy life, by abounding self-denial, by victory over the world, and by universal charity, that, in the sight of God or man, it can dare to claim such a preëminence? The sect which approached most nearly to the spirit of the Master, would be the last to indulge in so arrogant an assumption. Let any man take the New Testament in his hand, and, selecting those passages which describe and define the character of a disciple of Christ, examine the fruits of the Spirit which are produced by the different denominations of Christians with which he is acquainted, and he must be sadly biased by prejudice, if he does not perceive in all of them, as communities, a lamentable deficiency of spiritual religion; while it will be strange if he do not discover, among them all, some of those who are honestly striving, according to their knowledge, to do the will of Christ from the heart. True piety, membership of the church universal, includes all of no sect; it excludes all of no sect; but in every sect, as in every nation, "he that feareth God is accepted of him." While, however, I say this, I by no means would assert that differences in religious opinion are matters of no importance; or that any one is forbidden, by the principles of charity, from proclaiming, in all faithfulness and love, whatever he believes to be true. All truth is good, for it comes from God; and all error is evil, for it is derived from the fountain of evil. But, while this is granted, we should still remember, that it has not been given to us to determine, in any particular case, what is the degree of ignorance or error which shall exclude a man from the kingdom of heaven. If he bear in his life the fruits of the Spirit, we know that the Spirit of God must dwell with him, and we know that, whatever be his errors, they are not, in his particular case, fatal. This does not render his error the less erroneous, nor does it prove that the same degree of error would be consistent with salvation in the case of another. The admission that his heart may be right, while his opinions are wrong, does not make true what is false; but it does furnish a reason why notwithstanding his errors, we should honor the spirit of Christ wherever we discover it, and by all Christian means strive to teach him the way of God more perfectly.

Hence, I think that we greatly err, if, in our efforts to extend the kingdom of Christ, we confine our interests to the sect to which we happen to belong; as though it were alone, or even by way of eminence, the company of true disciples. The kingdom of Christ is extended as the number of true believers is increased, and as new members are added to his spiritual body, and in no other manner. Hence we should rejoice unfeignedly in the progress of true piety in any sect, and by any sect; and we should, by such means as are in our power, strive to promote it. To oppose it, or to undervalue it, because it is not the work of the sect with which we are connected, is unchristian and selfish. If a man cast out devils in the name of Christ, we should imitate our Master's example, and forbid him not, because he followeth not with us. The Christian's watchword should ever be, Grace, mercy, and peace, be multiplied unto all them that love the Lord Jesus Christ. In this spirit should we labor, in this spirit should we pray, and in this spirit should we rejoice in every event which advances the cause of true godliness among men.

Again, as I have intimated before, the church of Christ is a totally different thing from any form of ecclesiastical organization. The various forms of church government are merely accidents; the church can exist in connection with any of them, as it existed anterior to any of them. Nor have the two ideas any essential or necessary connection. The external organization represents the union of men with each other; the church of Christ represents the spiritual union of men to Christ, who is the head. The two ideas may come practically into diametrical opposition. It is very possible to construct an organization by which men may be held together under a particular name, and which will pledge them to uphold particular doctrines, and unite in the performance of particular rites, even for a long succession of ages. This organization may continue after the last vestige of true piety, and every distinctive feature of spiritual Christianity has perished from among them. Such is the fact, at the present moment, among many of the nations denominated Christian. In many parts of what is called Christendom, the very words of Christ are kept from the people; the doctrines of the cross are a grievous offence, and the preaching of the gospel has been made the occasion of persecution of which the heathen would be ashamed; and this persecution has been excited by ecclesiastics themselves, bearing the name of Christ, and claiming to be the successors of the apostles. If, then, an organization may unite men under the name of Christianity, while it cultivates inveterate hostility to the very teachings of Christ, — if, while it claims to be the church of Christ, it persecutes unto the death the true members of his body, — this organization and the church of Christ, must be, as I have said, essentially different communities. Nor do these remarks apply exclusively to any particular form of ecclesiastical organization. The same facts have at different times occurred in the history of them all; and they will occur again, until men shall have learned that Christianity exists not in rites, but in the temper of heart to God; not in the letter, but in the spirit.

And I may add, that I do not perceive in what manner any peculiar form of organization can be of special advantage more than another to the cause of true religion. Some forms have, I grant, a greater power of association than others, and are better able to transmit names and creeds, and conformity to external rites, from one age to another. But has any one of them any power whatever to implant in the heart of fallen man the principle of holiness? to translate a soul from the kingdom of Satan into the kingdom of Christ, and make it, by the renewing of the Holy Spirit, a member of the body of Christ? If not, in what respect can any of them advance the real interests of the cause of Christ? Of what value is the power to retain the form, when there is no power to retain the substance? Of what use is it to bedeck the corpse with the habiliments of life, when the spirit has departed? I grant that a sect possessing no general and central organization must fall to pieces as soon as the animating spirit of piety has left it. And is it not better that it should fall to pieces? If the body be dead, let it be buried; it will otherwise become a source of corruption. A company of men, calling themselves Christians, destitute of the spirit of Christ, are not of Christ, but of the world. They belong not to Christ; why should they wear his livery, and, by being false witnesses for him, lead immortal souls to destruction? The cause of Christ and the welfare of man demand that they be disbanded. Let them be divided in Jacob and scattered in Israel." Let the displeasure of God be seen to rest upon them. But let them not hold the form of godliness while they deny its power; and, while they profess to be witnesses for Christ, by their conduct declare that they are living without God in the world. And I cheerfully accept this alternative with respect to the sect with which I am connected. If it be not a pious sect, earnestly engaged in the work of promoting the cause of true godliness, as a distinct organization, it must perish. It is better that it should. "If the salt have lost its savor, it is meet that it be cast out, and trodden under foot of men." The sole object for which a visible church is organized, is to advance the cause of Christ by rendering men more holy; if it accomplish not this object, it is an offence which ought to be removed, a moral nuisance which ought to be abated. The principle which I thus apply to my own sect, I may, as I hope, without offence, apply to every other sect of the Christian church.

In making these remarks, I shall not, I presume, be misunderstood. I speak here as the advocate of no sect, but as, I believe, in the true spirit of universal Christianity. In addressing you, young gentlemen, I am of no sect. Never, since I have been an instructor, — nay, I might, with truth, go farther, — have I uttered a word with the conscious intention of proselyting you to the denomination of which I am a member. I have no right to use what little influence I may possess, as an instructor, for such a purpose. You have all your own religious preferences, as you are connected with the different persuasions of Protestant Christianity. We would have you enjoy these preferences to the uttermost; and in this institution you have, from the beginning, enjoyed them to the uttermost, not as a favor, but as an inalienable right. We would say to you all, Search the Scriptures, each one for himself; and, by the exercise of your own understandings, ascertain what is the truth which Jesus Christ has revealed to us. Having done this, unite yourselves, if you have not yet done it, to that sect whose belief and practice seem most in harmony with the teachings of the holy oracle. Understand what you profess, and be always ready, as intelligent men, to give to others a reason of your faith. But guard yourselves against the notion that your sect is, in any exclusive sense, the church of Christ, or that, in any special sense, it imbodies the heirs of heaven or the favorites of God. Reverence, and love, and imitate real piety, wherever you may find it. Your great distinction is not that you are a member of this or of that sect, but that you are a child of God, and an humble, self-denying disciple of the blessed Savior. Study, by all the means in your power, to advance the cause of truth and holiness among men; and rejoice as much and as truly to witness the prosperity of religion among other sects as in your own. This, if I understand it, is the spirit of real, universal Christianity. This is the spirit exemplified by Him who came to seek and to save them that were lost; who died to create in us a new life; and who accepts the worship of all who worship him in sincerity and truth.

And, finally, let this discussion teach us that our connection with a particular sect is no evidence whatever that we are members of the church of Christ. Sects are of human origin, the work of man, and by the will of man are we admitted to them. The disciple of Christ is born, not of the will of man, but of God. The church of Christ is composed exclusively of those that are new creatures in Christ Jesus, who are crucified to the world, and are living by faith in Jesus Christ. Let us not then deceive ourselves by living contented with any mere profession of Christianity. Against this fatal and most common error, our Lord has specially forewarned us. "Not every one that saith unto me, Lord, Lord, shall enter into the kingdom of heaven; but he that doeth the will of my Father who is in heaven." "Many will say unto me in that day, Lord, Lord, have we not prophesied in thy name, and in thy name cast out devils, and in thy name done many wonderful works? And then will I profess unto them, I never knew you; depart from me, ye that work iniquity." Let us, then, look far beyond our profession, and try ourselves by the temper of our hearts. "We must judge ourselves if we would not be condemned." It is moral character alone which unites us to Christ. It is the indwelling of the Spirit which creates us the children of God. And if that Spirit dwell not in us, whatever be our profession, at the great day we shall be cast out as reprobates.

THE UNITY OF THE CHURCH.

"NEITHER PRAY I FOR THESE ALONE, BUT FOR THEM ALSO THAT SHALL BELIEVE ON ME THROUGH THEIR WORD; THAT THEY ALL MAY BE ONE, AS THOU, FATHER, ART IN ME AND I IN THEE, THAT THEY ALSO MAY BE ONE IN US; THAT THE WORLD MAY BELIEVE THAT THOU HAST SENT ME."

John xvii. 20, 21.

HAVING, in the previous discourse, attempted to define the character of the church of Christ, I proceed to inquire into the nature of that unity for which the Redeemer, in the text, makes supplication.

Does this unity consist in identity of knowledge? Plainly not. The disciples of Christ differ in this respect as much as other men. In the school of Christ are to be found the child, whose intellect has but just begun to unfold itself, and the sage, to whose teachings nations listen with reverence; the savage, who has not yet heard even the name of science, and the philosopher, whose discoveries have filled the world with his renown. Nor is this true alone of human knowledge. There are to be found in the church of Christ believers, the eyes of whose understandings have been but lately opened upon the wonderful truths of redeeming love, as well as those who, by the habitual contemplation of the doctrines of the cross, have arrived at the stature of perfect men in Christ Jesus. It is obvious that inasmuch as piety is a temper of heart, it may exist amid every variety and with every degree of spiritual knowledge. It cannot, therefore, be in identity of knowledge that the unity spoken of in the text consists.

Does this unity consist in identity of opinion on all the

truths even of religion? I answer again, Plainly not. Diversity of knowledge, and of intellectual and spiritual culture, must, by necessity, produce differences of opinion. The light of the sun, always pure, always the same, is reflected in different colors, as it falls upon the differently organized surfaces of the objects which surround us. So, the same truth will be differently apprehended by men of unequal endowments, of dissimilar attainments, and of diversified opportunities for spiritual cultivation. The apostle Paul, who had profited in the Jews' religion above many who were his equals, and had moreover drunk deeply at the wells of classical learning, formed conceptions of divine truth very dissimilar to those of a Jew who had devoted his whole life to the traditions of the fathers, and whose intellectual thirst had been slaked only at the streams which trickled, in muddy obscurity, from the cisterns of rabbinical logomachy; although both of them might have truly submitted themselves to the teachings of Jesus. Every thing, as the schoolmen have said, is received according to the nature of the recipient. Seed, under the proper conditions of warmth and moisture, will spring up and bear fruit any where; but the vegetation will be more vigorous, and the fruit richer and more abundant, in the well-tilled field than on the stony and neglected heath.

But this is not all. The truths which are essential to salvation are revealed to us in the Bible with indubitable clearness. But, beyond these, there is much knowledge at which we would gladly arrive, which has not been revealed, and concerning which, we may form opinions, and nothing more than opinions. On such subjects as these, it is not remarkable that different opinions should be formed by men of dissimilar degrees of knowledge and great variety of intellectual culture. And, still more, the Bible generally reveals to us facts; while the theory of these facts is commonly unrevealed. When men form theories for the purpose of explaining truth, they will form them in harmony with their previous habits of thought. Of these various theories, in explanation of a particular fact, but one, at best, can be true, and most likely all of them will be false, since it is very difficult for man to discover what God has seen fit to conceal. To illustrate my meaning by a single case: The Bible reveals to us the fact of man's universal sinfulness, and of a connection between this sinfulness and the sin of our first parents. This is all that it behoves us to know. This is sufficient to show the necessity of a way of salvation by grace. This granted, all the doctrines that flow from it assume their position by the necessity of reason, no less than by the teaching of revelation. But the precise manner in which man at first becomes a sinner, and the manner in which our moral constitution has been affected by the sin of Adam, have not, that I know of, been any where revealed; and yet, on these questions, how many volumes have been written, how many controversies waged, and how much animosity excited! All men who receive the Bible as a revelation from heaven must agree as to the revealed fact; but they may all differ among themselves in respect to the unrevealed theory. And yet it is in respect to this unrevealed theory that they have so fiercely insisted upon uniformity of opinion. The same remarks apply with equal force to the controversies which have been waged respecting the doctrines of the sovereignty of God and the free agency of man. It is evident, then, that the unity of the church of God does not consist in identity of belief in matters of opinion.

Does the unity of the Christian church consist in uniformity of practice, even in matters strictly religious? I answer again, Clearly not. This uniformity of practice did not exist even in apostolic times, and under the preaching of inspired teachers themselves. There was seen in the church at Rome considerable diversity of practice. "One believed that he might eat all things, another would eat only herbs." "One man esteemed one day above another, another esteemed every day alike." So, in the church at Corinth, there were some who, knowing that the whole system of mythology was a childish absurdity, could, without offence, eat the flesh of an animal that had been killed in sacrifice to an idol, others, whose minds were not freed from early associations, refused to do it. In other churches, again, there were those who believed that the rite of circumcision should be observed for the sake of expediency; others wholly rejected it. The apostle Paul by no means condemned these differences of opinion or of practice. He merely taught that every one should be fully persuaded in his own mind, and that, whatever might be his practice, he should observe it, because he believed that, in so doing, he would be most acceptable to God. He held forth the principle by which every disciple of Christ must be governed,—"No man liveth to himself, and no man dieth to himself;" and allowed every man to apply it to his own case, in matters of this kind, as his own understanding and conscience should direct. I do not perceive any other manner in which an intelligent moral agent, accountable to God, can be guided in the path of his duty.

In the Scriptures, the principles which should govern us in our relations to God, and in our essential relations to man, are clearly made known. It is required of us, that honestly, and in the fear of God, we govern our lives in conformity to them. But among the varieties of human character and education, and amid the exigencies of human condition, it is not possible that all men should apply these principles in the same manner and to the same things. The revealed will of God may seem to one man to render obligatory a course of action, as in the case of the Romans alluded to, which to another seems indifferent. Hence, if each one obeys what he believes to be the will of God, there must arise diversity of practice. The moral law teaches that, in these cases, where nothing is definitely prescribed, each one do, from the heart, what he believes to be commanded, or, in the words of the apostle, that every one be fully persuaded in his own mind. And the same apostle teaches us that, on account of these differences of practice, "no one should judge his brother, and no one should set at nought his brother, since we must all appear before the judgment seat of Christ, and it is to the Master alone that every one of us standeth or falleth.

Hence it will appear, that since the unity of the Christian church allows of all these differences both in opinion and practice, it presupposes the full enjoyment of the right of private judgment. It imposes upon us no obligation to believe according to the decisions of councils or synods, or ministers or prelates, or the sect, or party, to which we belong. What God requires us to believe, he has clearly made known to the understanding of each one of us, and what is left to our own inferences is not a matter for the dictation of our fellow-men. In the concerns of religion, no created beings can interpose between the soul and God; nor can any combinaion of men, without daring impiety, either add to or take from aught that God has commanded. With these views, the disciple of Christ unites himself with that community of Christians whose views harmonize most nearly with his own. He unites with them, in preference to others, because his belief and practice are in conformity with theirs; but he neither believes a doctrine nor performs a duty because he has united with them. Neither his sect nor his church can impose upon him any duty which the Master has not imposed. The point of union with each other is not obedience to ecclesiastical authority, but a similar understanding of the commands of the Master who is head over all.

The unity of the church of Christ cannot proceed from without; it must proceed from within. We cannot, with a good conscience towards God, either believe or act as our fellow-men shall direct; but we must believe what our intellect teaches us to be true, and do what our conscience, enlightened by the revelation from God, declares to be right. Nor, if we should choose to disobey this elementary instinct of our moral nature, could we by this suicidal sacrifice attain to unity. Suppose we choose to surrender our intellect and conscience into the hands of ecclesiastical teachers, — what teachers shall we select? Those who claim the right to exercise dominion over our faith, differ among themselves as widely as we should differ by the exercise of private judgment. We should gain nothing by the change; while, in submitting our conscience to man, we have bowed down to the creature instead of the Creator. Nay, more: if our Christian brethren, whether they be clergy or laity, assume authority over our conscience, and demand that we shall believe or act, in matters of religion, because they have so enacted, and not because Christ has commanded it, they are guilty of lording it over God's heritage, and their conduct merits nothing but contempt and detestation.

We inquire, then, In what does the unity of the church, spoken of in the text, really consist? I answer, It consists in identity of moral affections, in a right temper of heart towards God and towards our fellow-men. After what I have said in the preceding discourse, a few remarks will suffice to illustrate this part of our subject.

I have said that every member of the true church of Christ is a member of the body of Christ, and is pervaded by the spirit of Christ. The Spirit of God dwells in his heart, influencing him to do those things, and to exercise those affections, that are well pleasing to God. "If a man have not the spirit of Christ, he is none of his." "And as many as are led by the Spirit of God, they are the sons of God." There is, then, one infinite, all-wise, and all-holy Spirit to lead them all; there is in every one of them a disposition to be led by that Spirit. They must, then, all be taught alike; they must cherish the same moral affections, and be conformed to the same image — the image of Christ, who is the head. Identity of moral character, then, flows by necessity from renewal of heart and sanctification of the spirit; without which no man can be a disciple of Jesus Christ.

Those who are taught by the Spirit of God have the same moral affections to God. They look up to him as a reconciled Father in Christ Jesus; to him they joyfully surrender up their affections and their will; they desire that not their will, but his, should be done; they mourn over their past sins and their present misdoings; and, looking for pardon through his well-beloved Son, earnestly, and above all things, desire to be delivered from the power of evil, and to be made perfect in holiness. "They have not received the spirit of bondage again to fear, but the spirit of adoption, whereby they cry, Abba, Father."

Those who are taught of the Spirit have the same affections towards men. There is implanted in their bosoms the spirit of universal love. All men are their brethren — brethren for whom Christ died; and "if he laid down his life for us," his spirit teaches us that "we ought to lay down our lives for the brethren." The pen of inspiration has delineated the features of that temper towards man which dwells in the heart of every disciple of Christ, without which, whatever be our profession, we are as sounding brass or a tinkling cymbal. "Charity suffereth long and is kind, charity envieth not, charity vaunteth not itself, is not puffed up, doth not behave itself unseemly, seeketh not her own, is not easily provoked, thinketh no evil, rejoiceth not in iniquity, but rejoiceth in the truth; beareth all things, believeth all things, hopeth all things, endureth all things." Such is the temper towards man which the Holy Spirit creates in the heart of every disciple of Christ.

Again: the spirit of Christ proposes the same object of living for every true member of his body. The believer has been redeemed, not with corruptible things, but with the precious blood of Christ. All were dead, and "Christ died for all, that we, which live, should not live unto ourselves, but unto him which died for us and rose again." By the principle of gratitude, then, as a redeemed sinner, no less than of original duty as a creature of God, he is under obligation to consecrate all that he possesses, and all that he is, to the cause of Christ. His object of life is not to secure to himself the honors, or pleasures, or riches, or power of the present life; but to contend against all sin, and advance the whole race, as well as himself, in all goodness, so that the will of God may be done on earth as it is in heaven.

Such, then, is the manifestation of the Spirit in every renewed soul. Such is the peculiar type of character which the religion of the Bible creates and cultivates in the heart of every one who is a member of the body of Christ. In all ages, these elements of character may be discovered, wherever a man has been born of the Spirit. It is in this respect that the church is one. These moral dispositions unite together the saints of all ages, and nations, and of every variety of mental culture; and also unite the church on earth to the "general assembly and church of the first-born who are written in heaven." That this type of character ever exists in perfection amid the ignorance and blindness of earth, of course, I do not assert. It was only realized without spot or blemish, in the Lamb of God who took away the sins of the world, and, by his perfect obedience and death, wrought out our redemption. His disciples make nearer and nearer approaches to it as they make greater and greater attainments in holiness. But no one is a disciple of Christ who does not set the holy example of his Master before him, and honestly, earnestly, and above all things else, strive, in the temper of his heart and the practice of his life, to be transformed into the same image.

But, it may reasonably be asked, Does not such a temper of heart presuppose some identity of belief, and is not therefore a peculiar belief necessary to salvation? I reply, It is evident that our affections must be the result of our knowledge. No man can come to God, unless he believe that there is a God. No man can love God as a Father, unless he have some suitable conceptions of the character of God. No man can believe in Christ, unless he know what Christ has done for him. It is, therefore, evident that, unless there be a belief of the truth, there can never exist the affections which are its natural result. Fatal error begins where a man's belief on matters of religion is inconsistent with those tempers of heart which unite the soul to Christ. This point may not be the same in all persons, and under various circumstances of education and knowledge. God knows where it is for each one of us, but I do not know that he has revealed it to us. If we honestly, earnestly, and humbly seek for the truth, we shall never fall into fatal error. Hence, for a good and pious man to be lost, because he does not believe a particular doctrine, is impossible. No man is lost simply because of his belief; but because that belief is of such a nature that it is inconsistent with goodness and piety; and because he has sinfully clung to his error, turning away from all the light which a compassionate God has thrown around him.

But it may be well for us to examine this question by the light of history, and inquire whether it be the fact, that this identity of moral character has, in all ages, been manifested in the lives of those whom the Bible designates as the children of God. Have those who have subjected themselves to the teachings of revelation, exhibited the same moral affections to God, the same love to man, and the same unity of object?

All these questions may, I think, be easily answered in the affirmative. A peculiar and unique form of character is clearly to be observed in all those who are called the children of God, from the beginning of the inspired record to the present moment. It is totally unlike any form of character elsewhere to be observed; it is derived from moral views which this world does not present; it is not indigenous to our nature in its present lapsed condition; it is every where similar to itself, and unlike the world around it; and every where it reveals itself as the meet preparation for the society of that "city which hath foundations, whose builder and maker is God."

Take, if you will, the example of Abraham. Observe the filial confidence in God, the profound and unhesitating submission to his will, which shone forth in the whole life of this venerable patriarch; add to this, his meek and self-sacrificing love of peace, — though he was a man of Oriental loftiness of spirit, — and his interceding earnestness in behalf of the doomed cities of the plain; and you instantly recognize the elements of that character, which, under both the Old Testament and the New, designate a man as the friend of God, and an inheritor of the glory that shall be revealed. Make the allowance which belongs to difference of condition and culture, and you observe the same moral affections governing the life of Moses, "who chose rather to suffer affliction with the people of God than to enjoy the pleasures of sin for a season;" who, for forty years, bore with meekness the contradiction of his brethren in the wilderness, and refused the offer of being himself made a great nation, lest his people should be destroyed, and the name of God dishonored. You perceive the same, or similar elements, in the character of Samuel, the patriot seer; of David, the warrior minstrel; of Isaiah, the seraphic prophet, and of the other messengers of Heaven, who recalled their countrymen from the worship of idols, and revealed to them the holiness and the compassion of the God of Abraham.

And, besides this, the form of moral character which these men exemplified has been the study of the godly through all subsequent time. Their trains of thought on other subjects have, for ages, been forgotten; and could they be recalled, there would be scarcely any thing on earth with which they would now be in analogy. But the saint, walking in darkness, when every thing else has failed him but the promise of God, still strengthens his faith by meditating upon the example of Abraham. The confessor, who has surrendered all for Christ, remembers the example of Moses, and is comforted. The penitent sorrowing for sin, and the believer rejoicing in God, can find no language in which he can so adequately pour forth the deep emotions of his soul, as in that of David and of Asaph. Thus the pious, in all ages, have acknowledged themselves the children of those, who, under the comparative darkness of a distant dispensation, trusted in God; and, in the consciousness of moral feeling identical with theirs, joyfully accepted the evidence that they were the followers of those "who, through faith and patience, inherited the promises."

Or take, for instance, the ages which intervened between the early period of the church and the Protestant reformation, and, amidst the darkness which so long brooded over our race, under the despotism of an ignorant, profligate, and apostate priesthood, you will find that God, even then, did not leave himself without a witness. Scattered here and there, amidst the millions of Christian idolaters, you might find the true successors of the apostles — men who, following in the footsteps of Christ, were renouncing the world, living for heaven, shedding around them the lustre of a holy example, and cherishing in their hearts the true love of man. Such men as Bernard, Thomas a Kempis, Huss, Wickliffe, and the Waldenses of Piedmont, taking the word of God for the rule of their lives, and the consolations of the gospel for the ground of their hope, handed down, through successive ages, the light of everlasting truth to those for whom was reserved the dawn of a brighter and more illustrious day.

Since the reformation, the disciples of Christ have constituted for themselves different sects, as was natural, and without offence. On the various points upon which they have differed, there have arisen controversy, disputation, and frequently collision; although this latter has almost always originated in the unchristian and oppressive union of the church with the state. But, notwithstanding all this, the essential union of which I have spoken has been preserved among the true, not nominal, disciples of Christ. Where is the Protestant whose spirit has not been purified while listening to the persuasive piety and meek wisdom of Fenelon, or whose knowledge of his own heart has not been extended, while its deep recesses have been explored by the searching eloquence of Massillon? What member of the whole church of Christ has not trodden in the steps of the "Pilgrim" of Bunyan? Whose aspirations after holiness have not been quickened by reading the "Saints' Rest" of Baxter? Where is the man, of any sect, who has not derived spiritual advantage from the "Rise and Progress" of Doddridge? Who of us has not examined his title to heaven more carefully by the aid derived from the "Treatise on the Religious Affections" of Edwards? Whose devotions have not been animated by the prayers and meditations of Bishops Andrews, Wilson, and Hall? In bringing our spirits under the influence of these works, and such as these, we forget that there ever have been sects in the Christian church; we feel that the words of these holy men express the inmost sentiments of our souls; we are conscious that we and they are one with Christ and one with each other; and we long for the time when, having put aside these bodies of flesh, our union with them shall be perfected before the throne of God and the Lamb.

The authors whose names I have mentioned were, some of them at least, among the most voluminous among the writers even of theological controversy. Their treatises and disputations on topics incidental to piety would of themselves form, in amount, no contemptible theological library; and the bare enumeration of them would exhaust the time that remains to us of this discourse. But these works are now almost forgotten, and they have been transferred from the hands of the student to those of the antiquarian. The works by which these truly great men are now known, and through means of which they are now loved and revered, are precisely those which tend to cultivate in the heart of man true love to God and universal charity to man. When they treated on these topics, they touched a chord which awakened a corresponding vibration in every heart that had been attuned by the Spirit of God. These are the works which the sons of God would not willingly let die, while all the rest they have consented to surrender to oblivion. Thus it is that the piety of a soul in any age awakens a moral sympathy in the pious souls of every succeeding age. Though centuries may intervene between their sojourning on earth, each one acknowledges the other as a brother, and, forgetting the matters of opinion on which they may have differed, encircles him in the embrace of Christian fellowship, and humbly endeavors to tread in the footsteps of those "who, through faith and patience, have inherited the promises."

Now, in all this, I cannot but believe that there is something which could not have existed were not the religion taught by the Bible a revelation from Heaven. Here is a type of character peculiar and by itself, and, in many respects, decidedly at variance with the ordinary principles of human nature. It exists the same under every modification of revealed truth; it passes onward, through the current of controversy, without becoming commingled with it; every where it is recognized by every one who possesses it, and it unites them all in the brotherhood of the Spirit. It is designated by the exercise of the same affections, by the cherishing of the same hopes, and the dread of the same dangers; its sentiments in the most distant ages, and amidst every variety of social condition, are expressed by the same identical language; it tends ever to the same result; and all who possess it rejoice in the prospect of meeting the same Savior, with all his redeemed ones, in the same mansions of everlasting rest. If this be so, then, surely, in so far as this, the prayer of the Savior has been answered; those that believe on him are one, and this unity is an abiding evidence that the Father has sent him.

And, lastly, it is clearly the will of Christ that this unity of his disciples should be manifested to the world. He prays "that they may be one, that the world may believe that the Father has sent him." But the world cannot be convinced by the fact, unless, by our conduct, the fact be made obvious. He requires that those who are members of his body should confess their union with him before men. For the same reason, he requires that those who are members of each other should witness by their brotherly love the same confession. He himself gave the first illustration of this love by declaring it paramount to every other form of affection. "He stretched forth his hand towards his disciples, and said, Behold my mother and my brethren; for whosoever shall do the will of my Father, who is in heaven, the same is my brother, and sister, and mother." And, in the times of the apostles, and afterwards, this more than fraternal love of the disciples of Christ was fully and nobly exemplified. It was the universal badge of discipleship. "We know that we have passed from death unto life, because we love the brethren." "Every one that loveth is born of God, and knoweth God." And, in the early ages of the church, the manifestation of this love amid persecution unto death, became one of the most convincing proofs of the reality of religion. The heathen every where confessed that they knew of no principles which were capable of producing such effects, and were obliged to admit that love such as this was of God.

And, if this be true, it is also true that the manifestation of this love is an end to be desired for itself. It is an incomparable blessing, a source of pure, elevated, and ennobling joy, and it is one of the means which Christ himself has appointed for the conversion of the world. Were it exemplified as Christ and his apostles exemplified it, it would furnish a stronger and more convincing argument for the authenticity of the mission of Christ, than all the works of controversy that have ever been written.

If, then, the visible manifestation of this unity be in itself so desirable, it is an object for which we are bound to make sacrifices. We should sacrifice to it our love of sectarian aggrandizement, our desire to control the opinions of our brethren, our strife for ecclesiastical power, and even, if it be necessary, the good opinion of the members of our own sect. Christ, and the members of his spiritual body, should be dearer to us than any human organization. If it be not so, where is our love of Christ? And if it be asked, How far shall this sacrifice be carried? I answer, Up to the point of the sacrifice of principle. We cannot, for the sake of unity, do wrong, or be the parties to wrong-doing; we cannot declare that to be true which we believe to be false; or perform, as an ordinance of Christ, what we do not believe that Christ has commanded. When this limit meets us, we can go no farther. To go farther than this, would be to surrender up a conscience void of offence, and to value union with men more than union with Christ. But so far as this it is our duty to go. We should testify our love to our real brethren in Christ, by uniting with them in every thing, so far as we can do it without the surrender of truth and a good conscience. When this limit has been reached, we must separate; but we should separate, not in unkindness, but in mutual love; coöperating in all things, where we can do it honestly; regretting that we cannot coöperate in all, and always "keeping the unity of the spirit in the bond of peace." He who is not willing to do this, has much yet to learn of the spirit of Christ. He who is willing to render wider the apparent breaches which already exist between the various persuasions of Christians, and, by magnifying their points of difference, withdraw them farther and farther from each other, is wounding Christ in the house of his friends, and holding up the church of Christ to the merited reproach of a thoughtless and gainsaying world.

And if it be demanded, in what way may we cultivate in our own hearts, and make manifest to others, this spirit of universal love to the whole body of Christ, the answer, from what has been already said, is obvious. We cannot do it by striving to convert all men to our individual opinions. To do this, is manifestly impossible, when men enjoy freedom of discussion and investigation. Why should we wish to do it until we ourselves become omniscient and infallible? Nor should we strive to bring all men to imitate our particular practice. Differences in action must follow from the necessary differences of opinion. Why should we judge another man's servant? "To his own master he standeth or falleth." After faithfully and kindly setting forth the reasons of our belief and practice, we should rest. But we must go farther. Having done this, we must still strive for unity. We must do this by cultivating in our own hearts a more fervent love to Christ; and just in proportion to our love to him will be our love to his image, as it is displayed in the members of his spiritual body. Overlooking the narrow limits of sect and party, we should cultivate a spirit of universal love to the whole assembly of the redeemed of every age, of every sect, and of every variety of social condition. Wherever the spirit of Christ manifests itself, there it should be sure of our sympathy. Whenever our brethren are in adversity, we should proffer them our aid; whenever they are in prosperity, we should rejoice in their success. Wherever they are laboring to advance the interests of truth and righteousness, we should remember them, without ceasing, at the throne of grace, and unite our efforts with theirs, as we may have opportunity. It is thus that we shall bring the spirit of Heaven down upon earth, and it shall be seen that God is in the midst of us of a truth. Though separated in matters of opinion, as must be the case with honest, independent men, the disciples of Christ will still be one, and the world will believe that he is the Messiah sent by the Father.

THE DUTY OF OBEDIENCE TO THE CIVIL MAGISTRATE.

PART I.

"RENDER THEREFORE UNTO CÆSAR THE THINGS THAT ARE CÆSAR'S, AND UNTO GOD THE THINGS THAT ARE GOD'S."

Matthew xxii. 21.

THIS sentence was spoken by our Lord in reply to a question of casuistry presented for his decision by the Pharisees and Herodians of Jerusalem. It teaches us, that a disciple of Christ is under a moral obligation to obey the civil authority, but that there are limitations within which that obligation is restricted. I propose to ascertain the meaning of the passage, and then to derive from it such instructions as may be appropriate to the condition of a Christian citizen at the present day.

At the time when the conversation was held, of which the text forms a part, Judea was a Roman province. Its king was an Idumean, who held his authority under the Emperor Tiberius. Every important city through the Holy Land was garrisoned by Roman soldiery. The common currency of the nation was Roman coin. The law which transcended every other law, and to which every citizen had the right to appeal, was Roman law. The God of Abraham, Isaac, and Jacob, was worshipped only by sufferance. Every thing bore testimony to the fact, that the independence of the kingdom of David had passed away, and that Judea lay prostrate at the feet of the mistress of the world.

It was under these circumstances that the Pharisees and Herodians, waiving for the present their differences of opinion, agreed upon a question to be submitted to our Lord, for the sake of entangling him in his talk. They were unable to conceive how he could possibly answer it, without embroiling himself either with the people or the government. "Master," said they, "we know that thou art true, and teachest the way of God in truth, neither carest thou for any man, for thou regardest not the person of men. Tell us, therefore, what thinkest thou? Is it lawful to give tribute unto Cæsar, or not?"

The question thus artfully proposed, was intended, I presume, to suggest some such considerations as the following: This land was given to Abraham, and to us his posterity, for an everlasting possession. The family of David was selected by the Most High to be our hereditary rulers. We are the worshippers of the true God, while all other nations are senseless idolaters. The payment of tribute is an acknowledgment of submission to an authority which we believe to be usurped. By doing it we profess to receive as magistrate, and reverence as sovereign, a man who has never been appointed by God to govern us; nay, more, we acknowledge the right of unclean idolaters to bear rule over the chosen worshippers of Jehovah. Coming to Jesus,—as a teacher sent from God, a personage incapable of being swayed by the fear of man, who in a matter of right would look unawed upon the whole power of the Roman empire,—they ask him what, under these circumstances, they shall do. Can persons of as tender consciences as we, say they, pay this tribute without sin? or must we refuse, and bring upon ourselves all the consequences of resistance to the civil authority?

This was not the first, nor has it been the last time in which the rights of conscience have been pleaded as an excuse for deliberate wickedness. All this our Lord knew perfectly well. The question, however, in itself, was one of grave importance. Our Lord proceeded to answer it just as though the motive which prompted it had been ever so innocent. He, in very few words, announces the rule by which his disciples in all ages should be directed in their relations to the civil government. Let us proceed to examine this rule.

"Show me a penny," said he. "Whose image and superscription hath it?" That is, whom doth this piece of money testify to be the actual sovereign of this country? "They say unto him, Cæsar's." They thus acknowledge that their actual sovereign is Cæsar. "Render, therefore," said he, "unto Cæsar the things that are Cæsar's, and unto God the things that are God's." Cæsar, you perceive, is here put for the chief magistrate of the nation, the organ of civil government, the agent of civil society. The precept of our Lord then is, render to the civil government whatever is due to the civil government, and to God whatever is due to God. And you will observe that, in this connection, the precept to render unto God the things that are God's, is not absolute, but relative. It is not the simple command to worship, revere, and love our Father who is in heaven. It has special reference to the case in which there may seem to arise a collision between these two duties. Whenever such a case occurs, we, as beings responsible for all our acts to God, are bound deliberately to consider it. We are to determine precisely what belongs to the civil government, and then, as citizens and as Christians, we are under moral obligation to render it. But, then, in this, as in every other case, we are bound to consider also what belongs unto God. Nothing must either tempt or affright us from obedience to him. His claim over us transcends that of the civil magistrate. We ought to obey God, rather than man. And we may be confident, that, in obeying him, we shall never violate any duty which we owe to the magistracy, for if the magistracy command us to disobey God, it has transcended its proper powers, its commands are of no authority, and a Christian must not obey them.

There can be no doubt, however, that our Lord intended to direct them to pay the tribute money. He knew that they would be called upon for it, and he offers no reason why they should not pay it. But he goes farther. "Show me," said he, "the *tribute money*. Whose image and superscription *hath it?* They say unto him, Cæsar's." Holding it up before them, or pointing to it, as I presume he did, he replies, "Render unto Cæsar Cæsar's things." That is to say, this tribute money, on which his image is engraved and his name is written, belongs to Cæsar, and to him let it be paid. Now, this decision, if I mistake not, throws some light upon another question, which, in this connection, is very likely to be raised. It teaches us that Christianity has nothing to do with the *forms* of human government. The people were at this time living under an absolute monarchy. The reigning sovereign was a tyrant of atrocious wickedness. And yet our Lord directs that the government be respected and the tribute paid. He neither inquires into the title of Tiberius to the throne of the empire, nor the right of the empire to rule over Judea. He simply asks, "Whose is this image and superscription?" that is, what is the government actually established? and he commands them to render to that government its due. I do not say that Christianity forbids us to entertain preferences in regard to the forms of government. I do not say that Christianity does not create a tendency to free institutions. I firmly believe that it does. Teaching universal equality of right, it could not do otherwise. All the true freedom on earth springs essentially from the gospel. It is intended, however, to improve the condition of civil society, not by revolution and bloodshed, but by instilling into our bosoms a spirit of piety towards God, and of justice and mercy towards men. While Christianity is doing this, it is rendering good government necessary, and bad government impracticable. In the mean time, it treats every existing government in obedience to the precept given in the text. The civil authority is established; the image is stamped, and the superscription is engraved. The evidence of the actual existence of this authority is in the hands of every man. Its precept then is, Render to society, as represented by the magistracy of its choice, whatever society can rightfully claim. Such I understand to be the teaching of Jesus Christ.

This is, however, only a part of our Savior's precept. The remainder is at least equally important. "Render unto God the things that are God's." That is, Cæsar may claim things which belong to God, and these must never be rendered to Cæsar. While the Lord expressly teaches the duty of obedience to the civil magistrate, he forewarns his disciples that cases may arise in which such obedience would be treason against God. "Thus," saith he, "they will deliver you up to the councils, and will scourge you in the synagogues, and you shall be brought before governors and kings for my sake, for a *testimony against them* and the Gentiles. What I tell you in darkness, that speak ye in the light, and what ye hear in the ear, that preach ye upon the house-tops. And fear not them that kill the body, but are not able to kill the soul; but rather fear Him that is able to destroy both soul and body in hell." And the manner in which the apostles understood this commandment of our Lord, we may learn very clearly from their conduct immediately after his resurrection. When Peter and John were forbidden by the Sanhedrim to speak at all or to teach in the name of Jesus, they answered, "Whether it be right in the sight of God to hearken unto you more than unto God, judge ye; for we cannot but speak the things which we have seen and heard." And when they were discharged from arrest, the burden of their prayer was, "And now, Lord, behold their threatenings, and grant unto thy servants that with all boldness they may speak thy word." A few days afterwards, they were again arrested, and the high priest asked them, saying, "Did we not strictly command you, that ye should not teach in this name? and behold, ye have filled Jerusalem with your doctrine, and intend to bring this man's blood upon us." * To this accusation, the noble reply of the

* They had arraigned the civil magistrate before the bar of Eternal Justice. "Him ye have taken, and with wicked hands have crucified and slain."

apostle was merely this: "We ought to obey God rather than men;" and he forthwith began to preach to the high priest himself the same gospel which he had been forbidden to preach among the people.

Here, then, the disciple of Christ seems to be furnished with two apparently opposite rules of conduct. By the first he is commanded to obey the civil magistrate, without asking many of the questions which men are commonly disposed to ask on this subject. By the second, he is commanded to pay no respect to the civil magistrate whatever, but to act just as he would if such a magistracy did not exist. How, then, are we to harmonize these two apparently conflicting precepts? When are we to obey, and when are we to disobey?

This seeming contradiction can only be explained by supposing that the authority of society, and of government, which is its agent, is a limited authority. This is intimated in the words of the text, "Render unto Cæsar the things *which are Cæsar's;*" that is, there are certain things which are not Cæsar's, and to which he can claim no right. The authority of the magistracy is conferred for definite and specified objects, and it must accomplish these objects by innocent means. So long as it confines itself to its appropriate objects, and seeks to accomplish them by innocent means, Jesus Christ commands us to yield to it implicit obedience. When, on the other hand, it undertakes to accomplish objects for which no authority has been conferred upon it, or attempts to accomplish them by means which Christ has forbidden, the gospel imposes upon us no obligation to obey it; nay, it may command us to disobey it.

This distinction renders it necessary for us to inquire, What are the legitimate objects for the accomplishment of which civil government is established? To this question let us briefly direct our attention.

The great object for which civil government is established among men, I suppose to be, to protect every man in the enjoyment of those rights which have been conferred upon him by his Creator.

Every man is conscious that he is an independent moral agent, responsible to God for the use of the powers with which he is endowed, and at liberty, so far as man is concerned, to use them as he will, provided he do not interfere with the correspondent rights of his neighbor. The muscles, the sinews, the senses, the whole body of a man, are his own; and, provided he use them without injury to another, he may use them as he will. He has a perfect right to the natural results arising from the labor of his body, in what manner soever that labor may have been employed. His mind is his own. He may acquire with it such knowledge as he chooses, and, under the limitation above suggested, may disseminate that knowledge as he pleases among his fellow-men. He has a right to obey with perfect freedom the dictates of his conscience, that is, to worship God in such manner as he pleases, or not to worship him at all. The worshipping or the not worshipping cannot come under the cognizance of the civil magistrate, so long as the man refrains from infringement upon the rights of his neighbor.

But it is found that men are not naturally disposed to obey these obvious dictates of justice. Every man is more or less disposed to appropriate to himself the property or labor of another, to restrict him in the use of his mind, or to control the exercise of his conscience. As the indulgence of these dispositions would lead to universal war, society is ordained by God to prevent it. Its object is to oblige every man to use the means of happiness which God has conferred upon him, in such a manner that he shall not interfere with any of the correspondent means of happiness which God has conferred upon his neighbor. Though every man might be willing to encroach upon the rights of his brother, no man is willing himself to suffer encroachment, nor is he willing to tolerate encroachment in another. Hence men instinctively unite in societies for the purpose of mutual restraint. They naturally place themselves under the protection of society, that thus the rights of the individual may be guarantied to him by the combined power of the whole. Every man turns to society as the umpire whenever he believes that his rights have been invaded by his neighbor. Society, on the other hand, assumes the office, pronounces the award, and pledges its whole power to carry it into execution.

It is for the accomplishment of these purposes that the various forms of the civil magistracy are ordained. The legislature enacts the laws; that is, it declares what are the rights of the individual, and what shall be the penalty if they be violated. The judiciary ascertains whether or not a law has been violated, and pronounces the sentence which the law has affixed to the transgression. The executive carries into effect the decision of the judiciary. Here the great function of civil society ends. This is, I think, the view of the subject entertained by the authors of the Declaration of Independence. "We hold these truths to be self-evident; that all men are created equal; that they are endowed by their Creator with certain inalienable rights; that among these are life, liberty, and the pursuit of happiness; that to *secure these rights governments are instituted among men.*" Such, then, is the paramount object for which the magistracy is appointed of God.

I have said that civil society assumes the responsibility of protecting the rights of the individual. Having assumed this duty, it is under obligation to discharge it. If it cannot be discharged without the use of force, it is authorized to use force to the extent which the obligation that it has assumed renders necessary. In order to prevent wrong, it has a right to summon to its aid the assistance of every citizen, and he is bound to render it. Every individual is a member of that society which has promised to secure to his brother the enjoyment of those rights bestowed upon him by his Creator; and that promise every man is under moral obligation to redeem.

In all this, I think I have but enforced the doctrine of the apostle Paul, in the thirteenth chapter of the Epistle to the Romans: "Let every soul be subject to the higher powers; for there is no power but of God. The powers that be are ordained of God. Whosoever therefore resisteth the power, resisteth the ordinance of God; and they that resist shall receive to themselves damnation. For rulers are not a terror to good works, but to the evil. Wilt thou, then, not be afraid of the power? Do that which is good, and thou shalt have praise of the same. For he is a minister of God to thee for good. But if thou do that which is evil, be afraid; for he beareth not the sword in vain; for he is the minister of God, a revenger to execute wrath upon him that doeth evil."

But we may carry this principle a single step farther. I have shown that it is the duty of the society to protect the individual against injury from another member of the same society. But suppose that he is exposed to injury from a member of another society,—is he not entitled to the same protection? It seems to me that he is; and that the society to which he belongs is bound to protect him, whether he be assailed by one or by many. It is the duty of the society to which he belongs to restrain *him* from inflicting injury upon all *other men*, and to prevent *all other men* from inflicting injury *upon him.* Here, however, it is to be remarked, that the use of force can only be justified when employed for the prevention of injury, when directed towards the injurious person alone, and when employed to no greater extent than the accomplishment of the purpose renders necessary.

But besides this, the great object for which civil government is established, there are various other objects, which, for the sake of convenience, are, by common consent, committed to its care. Thus, for instance, it is found that common education can be much more successfully conducted by public than by private effort. The care of highways, of harbors, and many of the most important aids to civilization, are most properly left to the same agency. Every man receives the benefit of such arrangements, and hence every man may properly be obliged to bear his portion of the burden.

The cost of conducting all these departments of government

must be defrayed by taxes, or some other form of imposition Our share of this cost belongs properly to Cæsar, and a Christian is bound, by the principles not only of common honesty, but also of his religion, to render it even to the uttermost farthing. The blessings of a good government are absolutely incalculable. Shall any man ask to be a partaker in these blessings, and be unwilling to pay his portion of that expense by which they are procured? Can that man be honest, who would send his children to a public school, and refuse to pay his proportion of the tax for the support of education? Can he be a disciple of Christ who shrinks from bearing his part of the cost of repairing a road which he uses in common with his neighbors, or of lighting a public lamp of which he enjoys with them an equal and common benefit?

The apostolic precept on this subject is clear and explicit. "For this cause," (that is, for conscience' sake,) "pay ye tribute also, for they are God's ministers, attending continually upon this very thing. Render, therefore, to all their dues; tribute to whom tribute is due, custom to whom custom, fear to whom fear, honor to whom honor."

The precept of our Lord, however, goes farther than this, and teaches us that a Christian is not to limit his public service to the strict line of equity, but is to go farther, and set an example of enlarged public spirit. It encourages us to do more than can rightfully be demanded of us, so that we may by example cultivate a spirit of disinterested zeal for the general good. The precept of Jesus Christ is this: "If a man compel thee to go with him one mile, go with him two." The words here spoken allude to compulsory public service. In the time of our Lord, the public despatches were carried by officers of government, who had the power to compel any citizen to leave his occupation and forward them on their journey. The teaching of our Lord would then be something like the following: The public service can be done only by the assistance of every citizen in his turn. In all such cases, do your own part willingly. But be not content with this. Be ready and willing at all times to do more than can in strictness be required of you. You thus set an example of voluntarily doing good to the public. To cultivate this spirit is to lay deeply and securely the foundation of all public improvement. You will thus render it evident that you act, not for yourselves, but for others; and men, seeing your good works, will glorify your Father who is in heaven.

You all see how widely extended is the application, and how ennobling is the practice, of this precept. Let me suggest a few cases by way of exemplification. I frequently hear Christians, as well as other men, excusing themselves from serving as jurors, on account of the irksomeness of the duty, or the pressure of their private avocations. This is a violation of the precept of the text. The duty belongs unto Cæsar, and to Cæsar must it be rendered. We must bear our portion of this service, or we disobey Christ. If we refuse to perform it, we are guilty of injustice to our fellow-men. If our property or character is at stake, we expect them to do their part in protecting us from wrong. They have a right to claim that we shall perform the same service for them. It is an act of very stupid selfishness, to leave the most important judicial duty in the hands of men whose time is utterly valueless.

For the same reason I think that every Christian citizen is under obligation to vote in every case where a public officer is to be chosen. The happiness and virtue of the community, no less than the security of property, depend greatly on the character of the magistracy. If I am injured in person or property by a wicked public officer, I have a right to complain of my fellow-citizens who gave him authority over me, or who, when it was in their power, did not prevent his election. A Christian, in this country, above all others, has a duty to perform in this matter, and he disobeys the commandment in the text if he does not perform it.

The same principles teach us, that there can be nothing more diametrically at variance with the precepts of the gospel than any attempt to defraud the revenue. He who does this knowingly and wickedly, disobeys the precept, "Render unto Cæsar the things that are Cæsar's." He withholds from the public what belongs to the public. He receives the full benefit of protection, and refuses to pay his share of what that protection costs. Nay, he is guilty of a double injustice. He realizes to himself an exorbitant profit, the wages of unrighteousness, while he is able to undersell, and, it may be, ruin his honest neighbor, who, in an upright public spirit, is obeying the law of Christ. I need scarcely add, that overcharging the public, the waste of public property, and all the modes by which the post-office is defrauded of its due, come under the same condemnation.

I have thus endeavored to show what are the legitimate objects of civil government, and what are the duties which the ordaining of this government imposes upon a disciple of Christ. It is proper, however, that I remark, before closing this part of the subject, that a government, in carrying forward these objects, is ever amenable, like an individual, to the law of right. The goodness of the end will never justify wickedness in the means. Societies, as much as individuals, are bound to yield obedience to the commands of God. It is only when the objects of a government are right, and the means by which they are accomplished are innocent, that it can demand, on the principles of the gospel, the aid and coöperation of the disciple of Christ. Acting in obedience to these principles, the magistracy may claim the obedience of the Christian citizen, not from fear, but for conscience' sake, and from the love which he bears to the Savior, who loved him and gave himself for him.

THE DUTY OF OBEDIENCE TO THE CIVIL MAGISTRATE.

PART II.

"RENDER THEREFORE UNTO CÆSAR THE THINGS THAT ARE CÆSAR'S, AND UNTO GOD THE THINGS THAT ARE GOD'S."

Matthew xxii. 21.

IN the preceding discourse, I have endeavored to show that every disciple of Christ is under imperative obligations to obey the civil magistrate, so long as the civil magistrate obeys the social and moral laws by virtue of which his office has been created. While the magistracy employs itself in the administration of justice, in the protection of innocence, and the punishment of crime, and in the discharge of those duties, which, for the sake of convenience, the public has voluntarily confided to it, Christ commands us not merely to yield it our obedience, but to proffer to it our cheerful and disinterested support. We may not too closely scrutinize the extent of our obligation for the selfish purpose of ascertaining how little we may do and yet escape censure. We are to look upon civil society as one of our greatest sublunary blessings, and we must cherish, and succor, and sustain it, not from wrath, (the fear of wrath,) but for conscience' sake; not because physical force would, if necessary, compel us, but because we thus most effectually subserve the interests of good order and happiness, of virtue and religion.

So much as this, then, the gospel commands, in respect to

our obedience to civil government. Beyond this I know not that it utters any command whatever. The acts, therefore, the laws, the requirements of civil society, like the acts, the laws, the requirements of the church, or of any other society, are amenable to the tribunal of reason, and conscience, and the word of God. The Christian is at liberty to inquire whether any act of the government transgresses the limit within which its action is, by reason and revelation, restricted; and yet more, to determine, concerning every one of its actions, whether it be right or wrong. At liberty, did I say? He is more than at liberty, — he is obliged thus to inquire and to determine. He is a party to every act of the society of which he is a member. He is an intelligent moral agent, responsible to God for his actions, whether they be personal or associated, and therefore he must think about civil government, and act about it, according to the light which God has given him, all things else to the contrary notwithstanding.

I therefore, as a Christian citizen, look upon the civil government and the civil magistracy with as unblenching an eye as I look upon any thing else. In simplicity and godly sincerity, not in the spirit of strife or partisanship, I may pronounce my opinion upon its enactments and measures, just as I would express my opinions in any other case. I see in presidents, cabinets, senators, representatives, and all the array of the civil magistracy, nothing but men, fallible men, of like passions with myself. Every page of the history of the past has shown that men placed in such situations have been exceedingly prone to err and to do wickedly. I cannot, therefore, worship men in power. In so far as they are virtuous men, I love them. In so far as they are able men, I respect them. In so far as, with an honest and true heart, they labor to discharge the solemn duties to which they have been appointed, I honor and I venerate them. I will pay all due deference to the offices which they hold, and will bow with seemly respect to the men who hold them. These men are to me the representatives on earth of eternal justice and unsullied truth; and may my arm fall palsied from my shoulder-blade when I refuse to raise it in token of respect to him who is called of God to minister under so solemn a responsibility.

But all this veneration is due, not to the man, but to the magistrate; and it is due to him, therefore, only so long as he confines himself to the duties of his office, and discharges them with pure and patriotic intentions. I have a right to inquire whether his actions in his office conform to the principles of justice. He must claim for himself no immunity from scrutiny on account of the dignity of his station. If he use the power committed to him for any other purpose than that for which it was committed; if he prostitute his official influence to pander to the wishes of a political party; if he sacrifice the gravest interests of his country for the sake of securing to himself the emoluments of office; if he trample the national honor in the dust in order to minister to the grasping selfishness of a contemptible clique,—that moment every vestige of his sacredness is gone forever. He stands before me like Samson from the lap of Delilah. Shake himself as he may, it matters not to me,—his strength is departed from him. But this is not all: not only is his official sacredness departed,—he has become to me the most odious of despicable men. He has sacrificed his country to his lusts. He has bartered away the well-being of millions for food to nourish his vices. Whether in office or out of it, whether powerful or powerless, I can look upon him henceforth with no other feelings than those of pity and disgust.

But this may become a yet more practical matter. The magistrate may not only do wrong himself, but he may command me to do wrong. How shall I regard this command? I will regard it as I do any other command to do wrong,—I will not obey it. I will look the magistracy calmly and respectfully in the face, and declare to it that in this matter I owe it no allegiance. I will have nothing to do with its wrong-doing. I will separate myself, as far as possible, from the act and its consequences, whether they be prosperous or adverse. It is wickedness; it has the curse of God inwrought into it, and I will have nothing to do with it. From the beginning to the end, I will eschew it, and the rewards that it offers. The magistracy may punish me; I cannot help that. I will not resist, but I will not do wrong, nor will I be a party to wrong, let the magistracy or aught else command me.

In saying this, I hope that I arrogate to myself nothing in the least peculiar. I am only in the plainest and simplest manner stating the rights and obligations of an intelligent moral being, accountable to God for his actions, and bound to reverence his Creator above all else in the universe. Created under such a responsibility, can I transfer the allegiance which I owe to God, to legislative assemblies, to political caucuses, to mass meetings, to packed or unpacked conventions representing or pretending to represent the assumed omnipotence of public opinion? My whole moral nature with loathing forbids it. I could not do it without feeling that I had become a despicable slave. I could not do it without knowing that I had exchanged the glorious and incorruptible God for an image made like to corruptible man, and to birds and four-footed beasts and creeping things, and worshipped the creature more than the Creator, who is blessed forever. My fellow-citizens must not ask this of me; I will surrender, for my country, my possessions, my labor, my life, but I will not sacrifice my integrity; and that is unworthy of being the country of a good man which shall ask it.

But here it seems proper that I illustrate more clearly the nature of that limit, beyond which the Christian obligation of obedience to the magistrate ceases. I proceed to offer a few suggestions on this part of our subject.

I have said that the great end for which civil society is established, and the magistracy appointed, is, to secure to man the enjoyment of those rights with which he was endowed by his Creator. If society or the magistracy interfere with those rights, it is tyranny. If its acts transcend the limits of the authority committed to it, it is guilty of usurpation. In neither of these cases does the gospel of Jesus Christ command us to render to it obedience.

The civil magistrate has frequently persecuted men even unto death for believing the gospel of Jesus Christ. Here he not only does not secure the enjoyment of an inalienable right, — he goes farther and actually prohibits it. He demands of the conscience that it bow down to him rather than to its Maker. I need not repeat here the precepts of Christ which I have already quoted in reference to this subject. You all know that we are commanded under such circumstances, on the peril of our souls, to pay no respect to the precepts of the magistracy. "Fear not," saith our Lord, "those that kill the body, but are not able to kill the soul, but rather fear Him that is able to destroy both soul and body in hell." Here, then, is a plain case, in which the magistrate, by inhibiting instead of securing the rights conferred on man by his Creator, has forfeited his claim to obedience; I do not say to *all* obedience, but to obedience *in just so far* as his commands interfere with the rights of man or the commandments of God.

The magistrate may also forfeit his claim to obedience by usurpation, that is, by employing his official power for other purposes than those for which it was committed to him. One of the most common instances of this form of wrong is found in the case of war. To this case let us direct our attention.

I have already remarked that the supreme power is conferred on the magistracy for the purpose of securing to every individual the rights conferred on him by the Creator. I have also said that in the exercise of this power the magistracy may defend the individual against wrong, whether it be offered by its own citizens or by strangers. It may, consistently with this principle, use force in order to extend its protection to innocence, if it can accomplish this purpose by no other means. But, while all this is admitted, we are carefully to observe the limitations with which this admission is guarded.

The object for which this power is conferred is, to secure to the citizen the enjoyment of his rights. Hence, *for no other object* can the resort to force, on Christian principles, be justified. The only persons whom this object regards are the *evil-doers themselves;* hence, against no others can force be directed. The object being the protection of rights, as *soon as this object is accomplished, the reason for the employment of force ceases.* Such are, I think, the limits within which the employment of force by a government is, by the Christian religion and the principles of civil society, manifestly restricted.

Thus, suppose that a company of men should land upon our shores, for the purpose of destroying our property, or pillaging our houses, or murdering our brethren. We and our fellow-citizens have mutually promised to protect each other in the enjoyment of our rights. We are, therefore, bound to protect them. We may rightfully unite together, and, if it be necessary, repel the wrong-doers by force of arms. But, in this case, our object recognizes no other persons than the wrong-doers themselves. Their wives, their children, their innocent fellow-citizens, have done us no harm, and we have no authority to inflict injury upon them. If it be said that in perpetrating wrong they only obey the commands of their government, I reply, they are moral and accountable men, and have no right to obey a wicked command. All that is necessary in order to protect our rights is, to repel the invader; and hence our object allows us to employ force to no greater extent than is demanded for the accomplishment of this object.

Again: as soon as our object is accomplished, and our rights are no longer endangered, all reason for contention ceases. We wish the wrong-doer no harm. We have no desire of vengeance to gratify. Our object is not to harm him, but only to protect ourselves. He is still our brother, though he has intended evil against us. This danger being now averted, we will again treat him as a brother, and overcome evil by good. We will turn his enmity to friendship, and thus all strife between us must by necessity forever cease.

Again: it is, I think, evident that our rights are of very different degrees of importance, and therefore justify very dissimilar efforts to enforce them. The right to life and liberty is very unlike our right to property. The invasion of the one would authorize us to use means of redress, which could not be authorized by the invasion of the other. I may have the right to repel a murderer at the risk of his life, but this by no means would justify me in slaying a man, because he owed me a dollar, or entering his house by force of arms and seizing upon his property at the risk of the destruction of his family. We are reasonable, accountable, and sinful men. It becomes us, who owe a thousand talents, not to press too eagerly the payment of a hundred pence. There is, in our circumstances, much that persuades to forbearance and charity, both as individuals and as members of a community. It is surely better to suffer loss than to reclaim our property at the sacrifice of that which is of infinitely higher value. This principle of conduct must certainly approve itself to every virtuous man.

Were this principle universally adopted, wars would very soon cease altogether. National force would never be employed except for the sake of protecting the citizen from injury. In no greater degree than was necessary for the accomplishment of this object would force be employed. No one but the wrong-doer would suffer, and as soon as his wrong-doing terminated, the employment of force would cease. These principles of action restrict the infliction of pain within the smallest possible limits, and thus they are in harmony with the attributes of a just and all-merciful God.

But, in granting this, do we admit the innocence of war, as it is at present carried on between nations? The two conceptions scarcely resemble each other in any single respect, except that in both cases physical force is employed. The sheriff who arrests a criminal, and the highwayman who robs a traveller, both employ physical force to accomplish their object; yet we should hardly designate their acts by the same term. The one is a righteous and the other an unrighteous employment of force, and to concede the necessity of one, is by no means to admit the rectitude of the other. A declaration of war not only authorizes us to repel an *invader*, but it abolishes all the relations of peace between *two whole nations*, and substitutes in their place the relations of enmity unto death. It henceforth becomes the duty of our national force to destroy the lives and the property of our brethren whom we declare to be our enemies, to any extent that the prosecution of the war may render expedient. The more universal the slaughter, and the more terrific the destruction of property, the greater is the glory which we ascribe to the transaction. Innocent and guilty, combatants and non-combatants, men, women and children, are mingled in one common calamity, and our most gratifying success is that, in which, with the smallest loss to ourselves, we inflict the greatest misery upon our brethren. Can the right of self-protection, any more than the precepts of the gospel of Jesus Christ, ever justify atrocities such as these?

But this is only a part. The very declaration of war exposes us to all the calamities which we would inflict upon others. For this result we ourselves must be prepared. Every individual becomes in effect a soldier, liable at any moment to be led into battle. Military law supersedes all other law, whenever they come into collision. We, in fact, become parties in a war, and we must suffer the evils of the condition which we have chosen. We desire to inflict misery to the greatest extent upon our enemy, and we must prepare ourselves to receive at his hands whatever misery he can inflict upon us. Can any one believe the gospel of Jesus Christ, and not perceive that all this must be atrocious wickedness?

To illustrate this subject, let us suppose a case, which is not by any means without a parallel. A few months since, and we were at peace with all the world. We wished evil to none of our brethren of the human race, and none of them wished evil to us. Our property, wherever it might wander for the purposes of commerce, was every where protected by the arm of peaceful and universal law. On the other hand, the property and the lives of all our brethren of the human race were as safe under the guardianship of our constitution as under that of their own. Every good citizen felt it to be a point of honor to respect the rights of his neighbor, though he were separated from us by the diameter of the globe.

Suppose, now, that war were declared by this nation against Great Britain, and all these conditions would be, by a single word, reversed. The property of both parties ceases to be under the protection of international law. Each nation sweeps the ocean with its fleets, and each confiscates, and destroys by hundreds of millions, the property of the other. We exult in the misery which we inflict upon our correspondents, our friends, our relatives, and derive pleasure from the perpetration of indiscriminate slaughter. We send fleets and armies to devastate their coasts. We subject Liverpool to bombardment, and destroy its unoffending inhabitants by thousands; we advance to Manchester, and put to the sword every citizen who defends his home from our ravages, and prosecute the work of destruction until resistance ceases, or we ourselves are overpowered. The greater our skill in the work of desolation, and the greater the number of human beings whom we can slaughter, the greater is our glory; and at every report of wholesale murder, there arises from a hundred cities the peal of national exultation. But the work of death is not confined to one of the parties. The forces of Great Britain are landed at Boston. That beautiful city is reduced to a heap of ruins. Young and old, innocent and guilty, parents and children, are involved in one common desolation. An army, flushed with conquest and maddened by resistance, pursues its course to New York, and there, on a larger scale, a similar scene is enacted. Shells and shot do the work of death, until resistance ceases, and the city is surrendered up to the lusts of a brutal soldiery. And as the army moves in its gigantic force over our country, sweeping before it our flying and terrified people, destroying in its course whatever could be used for the purposes of defence, and consigning to instant death every man who defends himself or his property from aggression, each successive slaughter is chronicled by Englishmen as a victory; the leaders in this desolation are crowned with honors, and the cities in Great Britain blaze with illumination as they hear that tens of thousands of us their brethren are slain, that our hearths are steeped in blood, that our wives are widows, and our children fatherless.

Were the calamities which nations inflict upon each other in war to result from the agency of Divine Providence, what would be the feelings with which we should contemplate them? Suppose that an earthquake should work the destruction which we accomplish by a bombardment; that a tempest should sink our merchant ships, instead of a hostile fleet; that a hurricane, instead of an army, should sweep over the land, scattering desolation in its path, and covering field after field with the thousands of the slain; what would be the moral sentiments with which we should contemplate such a succession of disasters? The whole land would stand aghast at this strange work of the Almighty. The infidel would construct from it an argument to prove that a just Being could never have involved the innocent and the guilty in so frightful a common calamity; and the ministers of religion would be called upon, Sabbath after Sabbath, to silence the rebellion of the human heart, "to assert eternal providence and justify the ways of God to man." And can any thing be more atrocious than for us to work out a destruction so universal and so indiscriminate that natural conscience is staggered while she allows that the Eternal has the authority to inflict it? Can the right of self-defence ever justify atrocity such as this? Did we ever concede to government the right to perpetrate so measureless a crime? It is in vain to say that, in giving to the magistracy the power to protect our citizens, all this power is also surrendered. That power was granted for a *given purpose*, and *for no other*, and it was limited within correspondent restrictions. The magistrate is clothed with the power of life and death, so that he may defend us against injury from each other; but this by no means confers upon him the right to cut us off at his pleasure by indiscriminate slaughter. He is authorized to use the national force, in order to defend us from external injury; but this confers upon him no authority to use that force for the purpose of conquest. The guilt of such an abuse of power is enormous, when war is provoked by the infliction of aggravated injury; but how greatly is this guilt increased when it is waged for insufficient cause, and yet more in the perpetration of atrocious wrong!

War has nevertheless been frequently carried on for the purpose of extending religious sentiments or political institutions. Wars for the sake of what is called religion, have in former times been frequent. Of late, millions of men have been slain in the contest between monarchy and republicanism. Such was the character of the wars of the French revolution. Still later, it has been urged that a war may be waged by one nation upon another in order to enlarge the area of freedom, and it has also been pleaded that freedom may most successfully be extended by enlarging the domain of slavery.

It is obvious that every one of these reasons carries the mark of reprobation deeply branded upon its front. We have no right to interfere either by force or by intrigue with the religious sentiments or political institutions of another nation. If we possess this right, every other nation possesses, and may exercise it as freely as ourselves. The result of such an admission would be to declare the innocence of universal war, and to assert the right of murdering any man who does not think as we do. I ask, Is not this something very different from the right of self-defence?

Again: wars are sometimes waged for the sake of conquest. The soil of a neighboring nation is rich, or her harbors are commodious, and our power may be increased by adding them to our possessions. If we are the stronger party, we can generally find pretexts to cover our all-grasping covetousness; and if all other reasons fail, we may always plead our irresistible destiny, and thus cast the blame of our wickedness upon the perfections of the Most High. But can such a transaction, though it could be perfected without bloodshed, be designated by any other name than robbery? and is there any more predestination about robbery than about any other crime? Does our *desire* for our neighbor's possessions give us any *right* to our neighbor's possessions? If desire confer right, it confers it upon all nations, and to admit this would be to admit the right of universal destruction. What shall we say, then, when this iniquitous passion for territory is gratified at the expense of indiscriminate slaughter? Can we conceive of a more diabolical wickedness, than a war waged in the cause of national robbery?

But I go farther: I ask, Was the power of waging such a war, and for such purposes, ever intended to be conferred upon a government? *Can* it ever be conferred? Can man, under any circumstances, authorize his brother to do wickedness? Can any man offer the authority of his fellow-man in justification of wrong-doing? But I ask again, *Was* such authority ever given? I know that people have frequently conferred upon governments the power to declare and to carry on war. But did a people ever confer on a government the authority to carry on a war for the purpose of extending religious belief, or of establishing political institutions, or of increasing territorial dominion? Have we ever conferred this power upon our government? If, when our constitution was framed, this power had been asked for, would it ever have been granted? To these questions I apprehend but one answer can be returned by any thoughtful man.

I think, then, it must be evident that the right of self-defence in no manner involves the right to wage war as it is commonly waged between nations. The objects pursued in the two cases are entirely unlike, and the means of attaining them are widely dissimilar. For the accomplishment of one object, authority may be granted, but it cannot rightfully be granted for the accomplishment of the other. The well-being of society may require that in the one case this power be conferred upon the magistrate, while to concede it in the other would be to consign the race of man to universal and interminable war. The principles of the gospel may permi us to defend our fellow-citizens from injury, but we cannot inflict injury upon others without bringing down upon ourselves the judgments of a God who judges righteously.

In the previous discourse I endeavored to illustrate the object for which civil government was established, and to enforce the duty of cheerful obedience to it so long as its action was limited to the accomplishment of its legitimate object. In the present discourse I have attempted to show that a government may use unlawfully the power with which it is intrusted; that it may assume a power which neither social principles nor the written constitution ever conceded to it, and that it may, in doing this, also commit an act of atrocious wickedness. The question then arises, What is the course of conduct which the precepts of Jesus Christ prescribe for the citizen? To this part of the subject I propose to direct your attention in the following discourse.

THE DUTY OF OBEDIENCE TO THE CIVIL MAGISTRATE.

PART III.

"RENDER THEREFORE UNTO CÆSAR THE THINGS THAT ARE CÆSAR'S, AND UNTO GOD THE THINGS THAT ARE GOD'S."

Matthew xxii. 21.

THE question to be considered in this discourse is this: What is the duty of a Christian citizen, when he believes that the government of his country is engaged in the perpetration of wickedness?

I suppose that I need not here refer to the fact that a disciple of Christ acknowledges the law of God to be of infinitely higher authority than the command of man. And when I say man, I use the term generically. I do not mean a single man, but man under what forms of combination soever he may be associated. Ecclesiastical societies, civil societies, political parties, combinations for the purpose of amassing wealth or consolidating power, utter nothing but the voice of man, weak, selfish, depraved, and erring man; and man weaker, more selfish, more depraved, and more liable to err, in consequence of the combination which blends the individuals too frequently into one soulless and unprincipled mass. It has been said, with too much practical truth, that corporate bodies have no conscience. Judge ye, then, how debasing must be the idolatry which obeys the commands of such an association, in defiance of the commands of God our Father Almighty!

In order to present this subject in a form as intelligible as possible, I will commence our discussion by stating a few propositions which I suppose must lie at the foundation of a correct decision in regard to it.

1. It cannot, I think, be doubted that societies of all kinds are as liable to do wrong as the individuals of which they are composed. Merchants in partnership are as much exposed to the temptations of dishonesty as individual merchants. Incorporated companies, banks, joint stock companies, men associated for the promotion of any object whatever, have never, that I know of, been considered immaculate. The same is true of nations. We, at least, have always believed that Great Britain was guilty of grievous wrong in her treatment of us when we were her colonies. She must have been thus guilty unless our Declaration of Independence is a falsity. It is, I suppose, universally conceded, that France exhibited a scene of atrocious wickedness during the period of her revolution, and throughout all the wars which commenced with and which succeeded it. I think that no one, acquainted with the facts in the case, can deny that our government has been guilty of grievous wrong in its treatment of many of the tribes of Indians on our western frontier, and especially in the removal by force of the Cherokee nation from their ancient homes and the burial-places of their fathers.

2. I think it must be admitted that every member of a society is morally responsible for the wrongs committed by that society, unless he has used all the innocent means in his power to prevent them. Unless he have done this, he is a partaker in the wrong. It will constitute no valid excuse for him to plead that he was not the actual doer of the wrong, and that it was done by his agent. He who appoints an agent is, by every principle of law and of equity, responsible for his acts. Nor can we even plead in extenuation, that we, as members of the society, took no active part in the appointment and direction of the agent. The wrong is done, and the wrong might have been prevented by the exercise of

precisely such power as has been placed in our hands. Unless we have exerted that power for the prevention of wrong, which others have exerted in causing it to be committed, we are, on every principle of right reason, responsible for the act, and are partakers of the guilt.

This is the only rule, so far as I know, by which we estimate moral responsibility in all cases of association. If several men are united in a copartnership, we hold every one of them responsible for the acts of the firm, not only legally, but, under the conditions which I have specified, morally also. If one partner commit no act of dishonesty with his own hands, yet if he be cognizant of the dishonest acts of his associates, if he allow them to use his capital and then share with them the gains of wickedness, he is manifestly as guilty as they. Although he never told his clerk to defraud, yet if he see his clerk defraud at the command of his partners, and never put a stop to the villany, is he not as thorough a sharper as any one of his companions?

Such are the judgments which we invariably form in respect to the acts of a private association. Precisely the same principles guide our judgments respecting the obligations of a political society. A people is always held responsible for the acts of its government, be the form of that government what it may. No nation has ever maintained this doctrine more strenuously than ourselves. We have demanded restitution for wrongs inflicted under the government of a usurper, or even under the temporary subjection of a nation to a foreign power. But if this be the law of national responsibility, it is manifest that it applies to us with greater stringency than to any other people on earth. We exercise, in its widest extent, the right to elect our own rulers. We elect them for short periods. We demand a full knowledge of all their public acts, and of the reasons which have led to all their decisions. We remove them whenever their acts displease us. We thus employ them as our agents. We claim to be principals, and we must by consequence assume all the responsibility of principals. We thus forever shut ourselves out from the plea that we are not answerable for the acts of our rulers. No American citizen can ever offer this plea unless he has employed his constitutional power to its full extent for the prevention of national wrong-doing.

Let us suppose, for instance, that the legislature of a state borrows money for the purpose of constructing works of internal improvement. The question of effecting this loan was publicly discussed. It was believed to be a measure of great public utility. No citizen objected to it. The funds are received and appropriated, and the faith of the state is pledged for their redemption. The undertaking proves disastrous, or the loan is squandered by unfaithful agents. The enterprise becomes unpopular. The legislature refuses to pay it, and the people sustain their refusal by declaring that they will not be taxed to redeem their bonds. Can there be a doubt that the citizen who suffers this wrong to be done, without uttering his solemn remonstrance, is a partaker in the guilt of the dishonesty? Can any man, under such circumstances, be innocent, unless he not only is willing to pay his portion of the debt, but also exert all the influence which he possesses to persuade his fellow-citizens to be of the same opinion? Nay, even this is not enough. He cannot free himself from the stain of dishonesty until he has used all the constitutional means in his power to secure the election of those rulers who will redeem the solemn pledges of the state, and reassure the world that the national honor is inviolate.

3. It will, I presume, be admitted that the precepts of the gospel in no case whatever allow the disciple of Christ to be voluntarily a partaker, directly or indirectly, in the commission of wrong. This principle is of universal application. It governs us under all circumstances in which we can possibly be placed. It matters not whether the wrong be intended by an individual or by a society, whether we are to gain or to lose by the transaction. Our decision can be swayed neither by the terrors of power, nor by the allurements of affection; neither

by the frown of a tyrant, nor the frenzy of a mob. The disciple of Christ can bow down before nothing but right. We must hate father and mother, houses and lands, yea, and our own life also, for the sake of Christ. And Christ forewarns us that if we love him, we must keep his commandments in preference to those of man, whether individual or social, and irrespective of the consequences which may follow from our obedience. "Fear not them," saith he, "that kill the body, and after that have nothing that they can do; but fear Him who is able to destroy both soul and body in hell. Yea, I say unto you, fear him."

But even this is, in fact, the operation of nothing more than a generally admitted moral principle. If there be any distinction between virtue and vice, if guilt and innocence be not the mere figments of the nursery; if man be endowed with a conscience by which he is allied to God, and by the possession of which he is rendered accountable to him; if this life be a state of probation, and if every one of our actions here will continue to unfold its consequences after ages upon ages have rolled away; if the favor of God be infinitely the greatest blessing, and his displeasure infinitely the direst curse, of which the mind of creatures can conceive,—then, surely, our moral obligations must take precedence of every other impulse, and we must do what we believe to be right, not only in the face of danger, but, if need be, in deliberate defiance of the power of the unanimous world.

From these remarks it must, I think, appear evident, that every member of a society is guilty of the wrong-doing of that society, unless he has employed all the innocent means in his power to prevent it; that the essential principles of the Christian religion forbid us to participate, directly or indirectly, in wrong-doing; that they oblige us to put forth all the innocent means in our power to prevent it or to arrest its progress; and if this last be impossible, they command us to withdraw from all participation in what we believe to be displeasing to God.

Of the truth of these principles I think there can be no doubt. If I mistake not, they commend themselves to the reason and conscience of every man as soon as they are presented. The only question that remains to be considered is this: In what manner do these principles limit our obedience to the civil magistrate? or, in other words, how may we render unto Cæsar the things that are Cæsar's, and yet shun participation in the guilt of Cæsar?

I inquire, first, Do the principles of the gospel permit us to resist by force the wrong-doing of our government? This question may, I think, be easily answered by referring to the exposition previously given respecting the object of civil society. Civil society is instituted for the purpose of securing to man the enjoyment of those rights with which he has been endowed by his Creator. So long as it discharges this its office, making all due allowance for human imperfection, and so long as this is its honest intention, we have no authority to resist it. When, on the contrary, it not only ceases to perform this its only office, but also employs its power in depriving us of those rights conferred upon us by our Creator, then, in the view of reason and religion, it ceases to be a government.

Destitute of moral principle, it is nothing but *power without authority;* and we are justified in setting it aside, and constructing *a government* in its place. For no other reason, so far as I perceive, are we justified in resisting by force that which performs the functions of government. The magistracy may err; it may do wrong; it may, in many respects, treat me unjustly; it may treat foreign nations unjustly; but none of this, nor all of it together, justifies me in resisting it by force, so long as it accomplishes, or honestly intends to accomplish, the purpose for which it was established. The government of Rome, in the times of Christ and his apostles, was exceedingly corrupt and oppressive; and yet we find not a syllable in the New Testament which would authorize a citizen to rebel against it, but very much that inculcates obedience to it in all things not forbidden by the commandments of God.

If, then, we are forbidden to resist the civil magistracy by force, in what manner may a Christian citizen innocently deliver himself from the guilt of wrong perpetrated by the government of his country? To this question let us endeavor to return an intelligible answer.

First. I presume it will be admitted that every man is bound to understand the nature of every question on which he gives an opinion; especially when that opinion must lead to a practical result. This is as true of questions of public as of those of private concernment. If it be true in general, it is much more definitely true in those cases where we utter our constitutional opinion in the act of suffrage. If this be true of other governments, how much more emphatically is it true of our own! We have chosen a form of government in which all power emanates from the individual citizen. We declare, in the most unambiguous manner, that the officers of government are our agents, in all respects responsible to us their principals. If we claim the enjoyment of this right, we must not shrink from the responsibility which it imposes upon us. Can any thing be more obvious than this, that he who claims the right of directing the concerns of a community, is under a moral obligation to qualify himself for the discharge of the duty which he has voluntarily assumed?

When men unite in the establishment of a government, they mutually promise, in all their relations with each other, to yield obedience to certain fundamental principles. The object of these principles is, *to define and limit the power of the magistracy, and to prescribe the manner in which this power shall be exerted.* The enunciation of these principles forms what is called a constitution. This being once established, it binds all and it protects all. It is a solemn and mutual contract between every individual on the one part, and the whole community on the other part. Upon the faithful fulfilment of this contract depend the freedom of every individual and the security of his rights, whether civil or religious. We can neither assume powers not conferred upon us by this instrument, nor refuse to carry its provisions into practice, either ourselves or by our agents, without a violation of our solemn obligations. It matters not how overpowering the majority by whom the outrage is committed, nor how small the minority whose rights are infringed, nor how elevated the position of the functionary by whom the act is performed; it is a crime of the deepest dye, and merits, and should meet, the sternest reprobation of every virtuous man. If, then, such be the responsibility assumed by every citizen of a free government, it surely becomes him to understand the provisions of that instrument by which this responsibility is created.

The same remarks apply essentially to those parts of the social compact by which our intercourse with foreign nations is regulated. We appoint public officers to conduct all our affairs with other countries. We prescribe the limits within which their power in this respect shall be exerted. We assert the right of directing our agents according to our own will, and hence we are responsible for their acts. This right we must *exercise*, unless we consent to become slaves rather than freemen. Should we allow our rulers to violate the rights of other nations, to involve us in wars according to their own will, not only should we be principals in the guilt of bloodshed, but, while we boast of the freedom of our institutions, we should in fact become the minions of a despot.

Secondly. Supposing a Christian citizen to have made himself acquainted with the principles of the constitution under which he lives, he is bound to apply these principles to the decision of every public measure on which he forms an opinion. The first question for him to ask in respect to every public act is this: Can this act be done without violation of the compact by which I and my fellow-citizens have promised to bind ourselves in our relations with each other? If the answer to this question be in the negative, no matter what may be the advantage to be secured, no matter how urgent may be the demands of a political party struggling for place, a Christian and an honest man must shrink back from the act with indignation. Or again: suppose that we find the power to have been committed to the magistrate, — it by no means follows that his manner of using it is in accordance with the compact. It may have been committed to him for one purpose, and he may use it for another. This is a violation of the contract, and against it we are bound to protect ourselves and our fellow-citizens. Take, as an illustration, the case of a declaration and prosecution of war. The authority to declare war is granted by us to our legislators. But for what purpose was this authority conferred? Plainly for the purpose of defending us from aggression, and protecting us from injury. Was authority ever given by this people to their rulers to prosecute a war for conquest, or for glory, or to extend slavery, or to restrict it? In the formation of our constitution, as I have said before, if such a power had been demanded, would it ever have been conceded? Would not the concession of such a power have branded us at once as a nation of free-booters? In such ways as these, I suppose, we are to apply the principles of the constitution to the decision of every public act.

But this is not all. Suppose that the act be not in violation of the principles of the constitution, — we may yet inquire whether it be in violation of the principles of the gospel. Suppose a nation has given us cause of offence; a disciple of Christ must ask himself, Can I be a party to measures which seek for the redress of grievance by means of the slaughter of tens of thousands of innocent persons, and the destruction of hundreds of millions of treasure — treasure earned by the bone and sinew of my fellow-men, whether friends or enemies? Could I, in a matter of private grief, pursue my revenge in a similar manner? Every Christian, in the solitude of the closet, in the presence of his God, is bound to ask all these questions, and to answer them for himself. He must put far away from him the prejudice of sectional interests; he must close his ears to the mandates of a political party, and calmly and resolutely form his opinions in the sight of the omniscient God, and in the full conviction that the result to which he shall arrive will meet him again in the day when the secrets of men's hearts shall be revealed.

And now, supposing that, after such a review, a Christian shall be convinced that the acts of his government are in violation of the compact from which all authority emanates, or at variance with the moral law which Christ has revealed to our race, — what then shall he do? I answer, as a Christian, a citizen, and a freeman, he cannot be guiltless unless he put forth all his social and constitutional influence to prevent or to arrest it.

If it be asked by what means can this be done, the answer is at hand. Having formed his opinions in obedience to moral principle, let him freely and fearlessly *express them.* It is thus alone that a virtuous and independent public opinion can be formed. We are bound to do this in obedience to the dictates of humanity. He who possesses knowledge which he believes to be valuable to the community, is under obligation to divulge it. The command of our Lord has made this our duty, under the most imperative sanction. " What I have told you in darkness, that speak ye in the light; and what ye hear in the ear, that preach ye on the house-tops; and fear not those that kill the body." And, indeed, unless this be done, by what means shall truth and righteousness make progress in the world? The wicked labor without ceasing to extinguish moral light; and if we, to whom its custody has been committed, hide it under a bushel, instead of placing it upon a candlestick, we betray the cause of truth, and by our silence declare our willingness that it be banished from the earth.

And here I may add, that, in a free government like our own, this manly avowal of our adherence to right, and our opposition to evil, would commonly render a resort to other measures comparatively needless. The good men among us — and under this term I mean to include all men of virtuous sentiments, whether they profess themselves the disciples of Christ or not — have it perfectly in their power, by the calm and decided expression of their moral convictions, to direct the destinies of this nation. There never has existed, and there never can exist, either an administration or a political party, that would dare to trifle with the *uttered* sentiments of the men of principle in the United States. Were such an act done but once, there would be small temptation to repeat the insult. If you ask me why it is, then, that public wrongs are so frequently done, and the doers of them held scathless, I answer, it is because those sentiments *are not uttered.* There exists among us a fear of avowing our *moral* sentiments upon political questions, which seems to me as servile as it is unaccountable. It envelops society like a poisoned atmosphere. It is invisible and intangible, but every virtuous sentiment that breathes it grows torpid, loses consciousness, gasps feebly, and dies. To this result every man contributes who withholds the expression of his honest indignation on every occasion of public wrong-doing.

2. But the mere expression of our moral sentiments by no means discharges us from the responsibility which rests upon us as Christian citizens. Our sentiments are worthless, not to say savoring of hypocrisy, unless they lead us to correspondent action. When we believe an act to be wrong, we have no more right to appoint a man to office, who, as we believe, will perform it, than we have to perform it ourselves. For such a man we cannot, with a good conscience, vote. By refusing to vote for such a man, we in part deliver ourselves from the guilt of wrong-doing. But we must go farther. We must not merely have no part in wrong-doing, — we must see to it that wrong be not done. We must use all innocent, constitutional means to secure the doing of right. We must choose men to represent us whom we believe to be governed by moral principle, who will act in the fear of God, and who will love right, and justice, and mercy, better than personal aggrandizement or political power. By this, I do not mean that we should limit our selection to any religious sect, or to the professors of any form of belief. Far from it. All that

I claim is, that we shall choose men who will represent the *moral*, as well as the *political*, sentiments of this nation. A virtuous man has certainly a right to demand that his moral feelings be not outraged by the public agent whom he appoints. If we sternly enforce this demand, we ourselves shall be innocent, and the republic will be safe.

But suppose that our honest efforts thus put forth are ineffectual, and a course of public wrong-doing has been actually commenced, — what is then our duty?

I reply, the fact that our country has commenced a course of wrong-doing, in no manner whatever alters the moral character of the action. The greater the number of persons combined to perpetrate injury, the greater is the wickedness and the more interminable the mischief. A nation seems a vast and magnificent conception to us, the children of yesterday; but it is otherwise with "Him who sitteth on the circle of the earth, and the inhabitants thereof are like grasshoppers; who taketh up the isles as a very little thing, and before whom all nations are counted as less than nothing and vanity." What, then, is the will of a nation in comparison with the command of Almighty God? and what can be the measure of that impiety which exclaims, "Our country, whether right or wrong"? that is, our country in defiance of the Eternal One himself.

Every virtuous man must shrink back with trembling from so glaring an impiety, and look with abhorrence upon a cause which requires such sentiments to sustain it. If his country has done or is doing wrong, he must boldly and fearlessly express his opinion of the transaction. He must, as I have before remarked, use all the constitutional power which he possesses, in order to bring the public wickedness to a close. Were the good men of this nation thus to unite, national wickedness among us would be of very limited duration.

But this is not all. While the wrong-doing is in progress, we are bound to have no further participation in it than our social condition renders indispensable. The punishment which God inflicts upon the nation for its crime, we must bear in common with our fellow-citizens. This we cannot avoid, and we must bear it manfully and uncomplainingly. But we can go no farther. We may have no share in the gains of iniquity. A good man can arm no privateers against his brethren of another nation because his government has styled them his enemies. He can loan no money to government, no matter how advantageous the terms of investment, in order to carry on an iniquitous war. He can undertake no contracts by which he may become rich out of the wages of unrighteousness. He may not say, If I do not reap these gains, other men will reap them. They are the gains of wickedness, and let the wicked have them. If a good man believe that moral principle is better than gold, this is precisely the occasion on which he is called upon to show his faith by his works. The only question for a conscientious man to ask is this : Is the public act wrong in the sight of God ? If it be wrong, he must have nothing to do with it, and he can no more innocently aid it with his capital than with his personal service.

But it may be said, that a course of conduct like this would destroy all political organizations, and render nugatory the designations in which we have for so very long prided ourselves. If this be all the mischief that is done, the republic, I think, may very patiently endure it. The voice of history has surely spoken in vain, if it has not taught us that political parties have ever been combinations for the purposes of personal aggrandizement, advocating or denouncing whatever political principles would best subserve the selfish objects which alone gave efficiency to their organization.* And

---

* "The history of English party is as certainly that of a few great men and powerful families, on the one hand, contending for place and power, with a few others on the opposite quarter, as it is the history of the Plantagenets, the Tudors, and the Stuarts. There is nothing more untrue than to represent *principle* at the bottom of it ; *interest is at the bottom*, and the opposition of principle is subservient to the

besides this, if a disciple of Christ has learned to value his political party more highly than he does truth, and justice, and mercy, it is surely time that his connection with it were broken off. Let him learn to surrender party for moral principle, and stand forth, though he stand alone, the friend of righteousness. Let all good men do this, and they will form a party by themselves — a party acting in the fear of God, and sustained by the arm of omnipotence. Then would our nation present the glorious spectacle of a people governed by the laws of God; obeying, above all things, the rule of eternal rectitude. Then God would be our refuge and strength; a very present help in trouble. God would be in the midst of us, and we should not be moved. God would help us, and that right early.

To all this I know it will be answered, there are never more than two political parties; and though with neither can a good man harmonize, yet he must unite with either the one or the other, lest his influence be altogether thrown away. He must, therefore, become a party to much that is wrong, that thus he may accomplish a probable good. To this objection our reply must be brief. It declares it to be our duty to do wrong for the sake of attaining a purpose; or, in the

---

opposition of interest. Accordingly, the result has been, that unless perhaps when a dynasty was changed, as in 1688, and for some time afterwards, and excepting in questions connected with this change, *the very same conduct was held, and the same principles professed, by both parties when in office, and by both in opposition.* The Whig, when not in office, was for retrenchment and for peace; transplant him into office, and he cared little for either. Bills of coercion, suspensions of the constitution, were his abhorrence when propounded by Tories; in place, he propounded them himself. Acts of indemnity and of attainder were the favorites of the Tory in power; the Tory in opposition was the enemy of both. The gravest charge ever brought by a Whig against his adversary was the personal proscription of an exalted individual to please a king; the worst charge that the Tory can level against the Whig is the support of a proscription still less justifiable, to please a viceroy." — *Lord Brougham on the Effects of Party.*

words of the apostle, "to do evil that good may come." This is its simple and obvious meaning, and we leave it to the condemnation of the apostle. But, besides all this, when we urge such a plea, we seem to forget that there is a power in truth and rectitude, which wise men would be wiser did they duly appreciate. Let the moral principle of this country only find an utterance, and party organizations would quail before its rebuke. How often have we seen a combination, insignificant in point of numbers, breaking loose from the trammels of party, and uniting in the support of a *single* principle, hold the balance of power between contending parties, and wield the destinies of either at its will! Let virtuous men, then, unite on the ground of *universal moral principle*, and the tyranny of party will be crushed. Were the virtuous men of this country to carry their moral sentiments into practice, and act alone rather than participate in the doing of wrong, all parties would, from necessity, submit to their authority, and the acts of the nation would become a true exponent of the moral character of our people.

And unless we do this, it is both folly and injustice to complain of the magistracy which we have set over us. We have no reason to expect in a legislator a higher degree of virtue than we possess ourselves. It is ungenerous to blame him for being a selfish partisan, when we ourselves have set him the example. It is unreasonable to expect him to sacrifice office, emolument, and influence, for principle, while we dare not act from principle when we have none of these to lose. It is shameful to ask him to forsake his party for right, when we ourselves, if he obeyed our wishes, would be the first to abandon him. If we expect moral independence in our representatives, we must show them that we possess it ourselves. If we ask them to peril their political influence for right, we must at least show them that the moral principle of their constituents will sustain them in well-doing.

We see, then, that this whole discussion tends to one very simple practical conclusion. A virtuous man is bound to carry his principles into practice in all the relations of life. He can no more do wrong in company than alone, and be guiltless. If he be a true man, he must love right, and justice, and mercy, better than political party or personal popularity. If he fear God, he must obey God rather than man, and this fear must govern his conduct universally. In this matter, every man must begin not with his neighbor, but with himself; and, if he wish our country to be reformed, let him begin the work immediately. Let us all, then, lay these things solemnly to heart, and may God grant us grace to carry them into practice.

VALUABLE WORKS

PUBLISHED BY

GOULD AND LINCOLN,

59 WASHINGTON STREET, BOSTON.

SACRED RHETORIC: Or, Composition and Delivery of Sermons. By HENRY J. RIPLEY, Prof. in Newton Theological Institution. Including Ware's Hints on Extemporaneous Preaching. Second thousand. 12mo, 75 cts.

An admirable work, clear and succint in its positions and recommendations, soundly based on good authority, and well supported by a variety of reading and illustrations. — *N. Y. Literary World.*

We have looked over this work with a lively interest. The arrangement is easy and natural, and the selection of thoughts under each topic very happy. The work is one that will command readers. It is a comprehensive manual of great practical utility. — *Phil. Ch. Chronicle.*

The author contemplates a man *preparing to compose a discourse* to promote the great ends of preaching, and unfolds to him the process through which his mind ought to pass. We commend the work to ministers, and to those preparing for the sacred office, as a book that will efficiently aid them in studying thoroughly the subject it brings before them. — *Phil. Ch. Observer.*

It presents a rich variety of rules for the practical use of the clergyman, and evinces the good sense, the large experience, and the excellent spirit of Dr. Ripley; and the whole volume is well fitted to instruct and stimulate the writer of sermons. — *Bibliotheca Sacra.*

An excellent work is here offered to theological students and clergymen. It is not a compilation, but is an original treatise, fresh, practical, and comprehensive, and adapted to the pulpit offices of the present day. It is full of valuable suggestions, and abounds with clear illustrations. — *Zion's Herald.*

It cannot be too frequently perused by those whose duty it is to *persuade* men. — *Congregationalist.*

Prof. Ripley possesses the highest qualifications for a work of this kind. His position has given him great experience in the peculiar wants of theological students. — *Providence Journal.*

His canons on selecting texts, stating the proposition, collecting and arranging materials, style, delivery, etc., are just and well stated. Every theological student to whom this volume is *accessible* will be likely to procure it. — *Christian Mirror, Portland.*

It is manifestly the fruit of mature thought and large observation; it is pervaded by a manly tone, and abounds in judicious counsels; it is compactly written and admirably arranged, both for study and reference. It will become a text book for theological students, we have no doubt: that it deserves to be read by all ministers is to us as clear. — *N. Y. Recorder.*

THE CHRISTIAN WORLD UNMASKED. By JOHN BERRIDGE, A. M., Vicar of Everton, Bedfordshire, Chaplain to the Right Hon. The Earl of Buchan, etc. *New Edition.* With Life of the Author, by the REV. THOMAS GUTHRIE, D. D., Minister of Free St. John's, Edinburgh. 16mo, cloth, 50 cts.

"The book," says DR. GUTHRIE, in his Introduction, "which we introduce anew to the public has survived the test of years, and still stands towering above things of inferior growth like a cedar of Lebanon. Its subject is all important; in doctrine it is sound to the core; it glows with fervent piety; it exhibits a most skilful and unsparing dissection of the dead professor; while its style is so remarkable, that he who could *preach* as Berridge has *written*, would hold any congregation by the ears."

THE SIGNET RING, AND ITS HEAVENLY MOTTO. Translated from the German. Illustrated. 16mo, cloth, 31 cents.

☞ This little work is a polished gem of sparkling brilliancy. Seldom within so small a compass has such weighty teaching been presented with such exquisite and charming skill.

Clergymen, and all who make "essays to do good," are particularly invited to examine it. Benevolent persons, who, like Amos Lawrence, make it their pleasure to give away useful books by the quantity, will find this, from its small size, small price, intrinsic value, and attractive style, specially adapted to their purpose. (1.a)

DR. WILLIAMS'S WORKS.

RELIGIOUS PROGRESS; Discourses on the Development of the Christian Character. By WILLIAM R. WILLIAMS, D. D. Third ed. 12mo, cl., 85c.

This work is from the pen of one of the brightest lights of the American pulpit. We scarcely know of any living writer who has a finer command of powerful thought and glowing, impressive language than he. The volume will advance, if possible, the author's reputation. — DR. SPRAGUE, *Alb. Atlas.*

This book is a rare phenomena in these days. It is a rich exposition of Scripture, with a fund of practical religious wisdom, conveyed in a style so strong and massive as to remind one of the English writers of two centuries ago; and yet it abounds in fresh illustrations drawn from every (even the latest opened) field of science and of literature. — *Methodist Quarterly.*

His power of apt and forcible illustration is without a parallel among modern writers. The mute pages spring into life beneath the magic of his radiant imagination. But this is never at the expense of solidity of thought or strength of argument. It is seldom, indeed, that a mind of so much poetical invention yields such a willing homage to the logical element. — *Harper's Monthly Miscellany.*

With warm and glowing language, Dr. Williams exhibits and enforces the truth; every page radiant with "thoughts that burn," leave their indelible impression upon the mind. — *N. Y. Com. Adv.*

The strength and compactness of argumentation, the correctness and beauty of style, and the importance of the animating idea of the discourses, are worthy of the high reputation of Dr. Williams, and place them among the most finished homiletic productions of the day. — *N. Y. Evangelist.*

Dr. Williams has no superior among American divines in profound and exact learning, and brilliancy of style. He seems familiar with the literature of the world, and lays his vast resources under contribution to illustrate and adorn every theme which he investigates. We wish the volume could be placed in every religious family in the country. — *Phil. Ch. Chronicle.*

LECTURES ON THE LORD'S PRAYER. Third ed. 32mo, cl., 85c.

We observe the writer's characteristic fulness and richness of language, felicity and beauty of illustration, justness of discrimination and thought. — *Watchman and Reflector.*

Dr. Williams is one of the most interesting and accomplished writers in this country. We welcome this volume as a valuable contribution to our religious literature — *Ch. Witness.*

In reading, we resolved to mark the passages which we most admired, but soon found that we should be obliged to mark nearly all of them. — *Ch. Secretary.*

It bears in every page the mark of an elegant writer and an accomplished scholar, an acute reasoner and a cogent moralist. Some passages are so decidedly eloquent that we instinctively find ourselves looking round as if upon an audience, and ready to join them with audible applause — *Ch. Inquirer.*

We are constantly reminded, in reading his eloquent pages, of the old English writers, whose vigorous thought, and gorgeous imagery, and varied learning, have made their writings an inexhaustible mine for the scholars of the present day. — *Ch. Observer.*

Their breadth of view, strength of logic, and stirring eloquence place them among the very best homiletical efforts of the age. Every page is full of suggestion as well as eloquence. — *Ch. Parlor Mag.*

MISCELLANIES. New, improved edition. *(Price reduced.)* 12mo, 1,25.

☞ This work, which has been heretofore published in octavo form at 1,75 per copy, is published by the present proprietors in one handsome 12mo volume, at the low price of 1,25.

A volume which is absolutely necessary to the completeness of a library. — *N. Y. Weekly Review.*

Dr. Williams is a profound scholar and a brilliant writer. — *N. Y. Evangelist.*

He often rises to the sphere of a glowing and impressive eloquence, because no other form of language can do justice to his thoughts and emotions. So, too, the exuberance of literary illustration, with which he clothes the driest speculative discussions, is not brought in for the sake of effect, but as the natural expression of a mind teeming with the "spoils of time" and the treasures of study in almost every department of learning. — *N. Y. Tribune.*

From the pen of one of the most able and accomplished authors of the age. — *Bap. Memorial.*

We are glad to see this volume. We wish such men abounded in every sect. — *Ch. Register.*

One of the richest volumes that has been given to the public for many years. — *N. Y. Bap. Reg.*

The author's mind is cast in no common mould. A delightful volume. — *Meth. Prot.* **Bb**

UNIVERSITY SERMONS.

SERMONS Delivered in the Chapel of Brown University. By the REV. FRANCIS WAYLAND, D. D. Third thousand. 12mo, cloth, 1,00.

☞ DR. WAYLAND has here discussed most of the prominent doctrines of the Bible in his usual clear and masterly style, viz.: Theoretical Atheism; Practical Atheism; Moral Character of Man; Love to God; Fall of Man; Justification by Works impossible; Preparation for the Advent of the Messiah; Work of the Messiah; Justification by Faith; The Fall of Peter; The Church of Christ; The Unity of the Church; The Duty of Obedience to the Civil Magistrate; also, the Recent Revolutions in Europe.

The discourses contained in this handsome volume are characterized by all that richness of thought and elegance of language for which their talented author is celebrated. The volume is worthy of the pen of the distinguished divine from whom it emanates. — DR. BAIRD'S *Christian Union*.

Few sermons contain so much carefully arranged thought as these. The thorough logician is apparent throughout the volume, and there is a classic purity in the diction, unsurpassed by any writer, and equalled by few. — *N. Y. Commercial.*

The author has long been before the public as one of our most popular writers in various departments of science and morals. His style is easy and fluent, and rich in illustration. — *Evan. Review.*

No thinking man can open to any portion of it without finding his attention strongly arrested, and feeling inclined to yield his assent to those self-evincing statements which appear on every page. As a writer, Dr. Wayland is distinguished by simplicity, strength, and comprehensiveness. He addresses himself directly to the intellect more than to the imagination, to the conscience more than to the passions. — *Watchman and Reflector.*

Just issued, a noble volume of noble sermons, from the distinguished President of Brown University. These discourses are fine specimens of his discriminating power of thought, and purity and vigor of style. — *Zion's Herald.*

DR. WAYLAND'S name and fame will cause any thing from his pen to be eagerly sought for; and those who take up this volume with the high expectations induced by his previous works, will not be disappointed. The discourses are rich in evangelical truth, profound thought, and beautiful diction; worthy at once of the theologian, the philosopher, and the rhetorician. — *Albany Argus.*

This volume adds to Dr. Wayland's fame as a writer. This is commendation enough to bestow upon any book. — *Puritan Recorder.*

DR. WAYLAND is one of the prominent Christian philosophers and literary men of our country. His style is elegant and polished, and his views evangelical. — *Watchman, Cincinnati.*

His style is peculiarly adapted to arrest the attention, and his familiar illustrations serve to make plain the most abstruse principles, as well as to enstamp them upon one's memory. It is, in fact, scarcely possible to forget a discourse which we read from Wayland, and we have ever found his works to be highly suggestive. We think no minister's library complete without it. — *Dover Star.*

We must call the attention of our readers again to this attractive volume of sermons. They come from one who has attained a national reputation, and embody the views matured by the careful study of many years upon the most important topics in theology. — *Phil. Ch. Chronicle.*

It would be spending time to little purpose to attempt a eulogy on a work emanating from such a source. — *N. Y. Baptist Register.*

THE PERSON AND WORK OF CHRIST. By ERNEST SARTORIUS, D. D., General Superintendent and Consistorial Director at Konigsberg, Prussia. Translated from the German, by the REV. OAKMAN S. STEARNS, A. M. 18mo, cloth, 42 cts.

A work of much ability, and presenting the argument in a style that will be new to most American readers. It will deservedly attract attention. — *N. Y. Observer.*

DR. SARTORIUS is one of the most eminent and evangelical theologians in Germany. The work will be found, both from the important subjects discussed and the earnestness, beauty, and vivacity of its style, to possess the qualities which recommend it to the Christian public. — *Mich. Ch. Herald.*

A little volume on a great subject, and evidently the production of a great mind. The style and train of thought prove this. — *Southern Literary Gazette.*

Whether we consider the importance of the subjects discussed, or the perspicuous exhibition of truth in the volume before us, the chaste and elegant style used, or the devout spirit of the author, we cannot but desire that the work may meet with an extensive circulation. — *Christian Index.*

RECENT PUBLICATIONS.

THE EVIDENCES OF CHRISTIANITY, as exhibited in the writings of its apologists, down to Augustine, by W. J. Bolton, of Gonville and Caius College, Cambridge. 12mo, cloth. 80 cents.

The essay contained in this volume received the Hulsean prize (about $500) in England. The author is a professor in Gonville and Caius College, Cambridge, and evidently a very learned student of the patristic writings and the whole circle of ecclesiastical history. He has presented to the world in this essay an admirable compendium of the arguments for the truth of Christianity advanced in the works of the Apologetic Fathers during the third, fourth, and fifth centuries of the Christian era. These arguments are classified as being deduced from antecedent probability, from antiquity, from prophecy, from miracles, from the reasonableness of doctrine, from superior morality, and from the success of the Gospel. — *N. Y. Commercial.*

This is a work of deep research, and of great value to the theological student. — *Transcript.*

We had occasion, some time since, to notice this work, when we expressed a high estimate of its merits. We can only say that, in looking through it a second time, our appreciation of both the learning and the ingenuity which it discovers is heightened rather than diminished We thankfully accept such an effort as this of a profound and highly-cultivated mind. — *Puritan Recorder.*

The work bears the marks of great research, and must command the attention and confidence of the Christian world. — *Mercantile Journal.*

THE BETTER LAND ; or, Thoughts on Heaven. By A. C. Thompson, Pastor of the Eliot Church, Roxbury. 12mo, cloth. $1.00. *Just published.*

THE MISSION OF THE COMFORTER ; with copious Notes. By Julius Charles Hare. Notes translated for the American edition. 12mo, cl. $1.25.

We hardly remember any treatise which is so well calculated to be useful in general circulation among ministers, and the more educated laity, than this, which is rich in spirituality, strong and sound in theology, comprehensive in thought, vigorous and beautiful in imagination, and affluent in learning. — *Congregationalist.*

We have seldom read a book with greater interest. — *N. Y. Evangelist.*

The volume is one of rare value, and will be welcomed as an eloquent and Scriptural exposition of some of the fundamental doctrines of our faith. — *New York Recorder.*

THE VICTORY OF FAITH. By Julius Charles Hare, author of "The Mission of the Comforter," etc. 12mo, cloth. *In press.*

FIRST LINES OF CHRISTIAN THEOLOGY. In the form of a Syllabus, prepared for the use of Students, with subsequent Additions and Elucidations. By Rev. John Pye Smith. Edited from the author's manuscripts, with Additional Notes and References, etc. 1 vol. Royal octavo. $5.00

☞ A most important work for ministers and theological students.

THE RELIGIONS OF THE WORLD, and their relations to Christianity. By Frederick Denison Maurice, A. M., Professor of Divinity in King's College, London. 16mo, cloth. 60 cents.

The effort we deem masterly, and, in any event, must prove highly interesting by the comparisons which it institutes with the false and the true. His investigations into the Hindoo and Budhist mythologies will itself repay the reader's trouble. — *Methodist Quarterly.*

GUIDO AND JULIUS. The Doctrine of Sin and the Propitiator ; or, the True Consecration of the Doubter. Exhibited in the Correspondence of two Friends. By Frederis Augustut O. Tholuch, D. D. Translated from the German, by Jonathan Edwards Ryland. With an Introduction by John Pye Smith, D. D. 16mo, cloth. 60 cents.

☞ It might naturally be expected that a work by authors so distinguished in the literary and religious world would prove one of great interest and value. This expectation will not be disappointed. It is pre-eminently a book for the times — full of interest, and of great power.

H

IMPORTANT NEW WORKS.

THE TESTIMONY OF THE ROCKS: or, Geology in its Bearings on the two Theologies, Natural and Revealed. By HUGH MILLER. "Thou shalt be in league with the stones of the field." — *Job.* With numerous elegant illustrations. 12mo, cloth, $1.25.

The completion of this important work employed the last hours of the lamented author, and may be considered his greatest and in fact his life work.

MACAULAY ON SCOTLAND. A Critique. By HUGH MILLER, Author of "Footprints of the Creator," &c. 16mo, flexible cloth, 25c.

When we read Macaulay's last volumes, we said that they wanted nothing but the fiction to make an epic poem; and now it seems that they are not wanting even in that. — PURITAN RECORDER.

He meets the historian at the fountain head, tracks him through the old pamphlets and newspapers on which he relied, and demonstrates that his own authorities are against him. — BOSTON TRANSCRIPT.

THE GREYSON LETTERS. Selections from the Correspondence of R. E. H. GREYSON, Esq. Edited by HENRY ROGERS, Author of "The Eclipse of Faith." 12mo, cloth, $1.25.

"Mr. Greyson and Mr. Rogers are one and the same person. The whole work is from his pen; and every letter is radiant with the genius of the author of the 'Eclipse of Faith.'" It discusses a wide range of subjects in the most attractive manner. It abounds in the keenest wit and humor, satire and logic. It fairly entitles Mr. Rogers to rank with Sydney Smith and Charles Lamb as a wit and humorist, and with Bishop Butler as a reasoner.

If Mr. Rogers lives to accomplish our expectations, we feel little doubt that his name will share, with those of Butler and Pascal, in the gratitude and veneration of posterity. — LONDON QUARTERLY.

Full of acute observation, of subtle analysis, of accurate logic, fine description, apt quotation, pithy remark, and amusing anecdote. . . . A book, not for one hour, but for all hours; not for one mood, but for every mood, to think over, to dream over, to laugh over. — BOSTON JOURNAL.

A truly good book, containing wise, true and original reflections, and written in an attractive style. — Hon. GEO. S. HILLARD, LL. D., in *Boston Courier*.

Mr. Rogers has few equals as a critic, moral philosopher, and defender of truth. . . . This volume is full of entertainment, and full of food for thought, to feed on. — PHILADELPHIA PRESBYTERIAN.

The Letters are intellectual gems, radiant with beauty and the lights of genius, happily intermingling the grave and the gay. — CHRISTIAN OBSERVER.

ESSAYS IN BIOGRAPHY AND CRITICISM. By PETER BAYNE, M. A., Author of "The Christian Life, Social and Individual." Arranged in TWO SERIES, OR PARTS. 12mo, cloth, each, $1.25.

This work is prepared by the author exclusively for his American publishers. It includes eighteen articles, viz:

FIRST SERIES: — Thomas De Quincy. — Tennyson and his Teachers. — Mrs. Barrett Browning. — Recent Aspects of British Art. — John Ruskin. — Hugh Miller. — The Modern Novel; Dickens, &c. — Ellis, Acton, and Currer Bell. — Charles Kingsley.

SECOND SERIES: — S. T. Coleridge. — T. B. Macaulay. — Alison. — Wellington. — Napoleon. — Plato. — Characteristics of Christian Civilization. — Education in the Nineteenth Century. — The Pulpit and the Press.

LIFE AND CHARACTER OF JAMES MONTGOMERY. Abridged from the recent London, seven volume edition. By MRS. H. C. KNIGHT, Author of "Lady Huntington and her Friends," &c. With a fine likeness and an elegant illustrated title page on steel. 12mo, cloth, $1.25.

This is an original biography prepared from the abundant, but ill-digested materials contained in the seven octavo volumes of the London edition. The great bulk of that work, together with the heavy style of its literary execution, must necessarily prevent its republication in this country. At the same time, the Christian public in America will expect some memoir of a poet whose hymns and sacred melodies have been the delight of every household. This work, it is confidently hoped, will fully satisfy the [illegible]. It is prepared by one who has already won distinguished laurels in this department of [illegible]

NEW WORKS

THE TEACHER'S LAST LESSON. A MEMOIR OF MARTHA WHITING, late of the Charlestown Female Seminary, consisting chiefly of Extracts from her Journal, interspersed with Reminisences and Suggestive Reflections. By CATHARINE N. BADGER, an Associate Teacher. With a Portrait, and an Engraving of the Seminary. 12mo. Cloth. $1.00. Second Edition.

THE subject of this Memoir was, for a quarter of a century, at the head of one of the most celebrated Female Seminaries in the country. During that period she educated more than *three thousand* young ladies. She was a kindred spirit to Mary Lyon, the celebrated founder of Mount Holyoke Seminary, with whom, for strength of character, eminent piety, devotion to her calling, and extraordinary success therein, she well deserves to be ranked.

MY MOTHER: or Recollections of Maternal Influence. By a NEW ENGLAND CLERGYMAN. 12mo. Cloth. 75 Cents.

THIS is a new and enlarged edition of a work that was first published in 1849. It passed rapidly through three editions, when the sale was arrested by the embarrassment of the publisher. The author has now revised it, and added another chapter, so that it comes before the public with the essential claims of a new work. . . . It is the picture of a quiet New England family, so drawn and colored as to subserve the ends of *domestic education*. The central figure is the author's mother, around whom are grouped the various members of the family. Biographical sketches and lessons of practical wisdom are so intermingled, that while the former relieve the latter, these in turn give force and significance to the sketches. . . . . . . The author has already distinguished himself in various walks of literature, but from motives of delicacy towards the still surviving characters of the book, he chooses for the present to conceal his name. . . . . . A writer of wide celebrity says of the book, in a note to the publisher — "It is one of those rare pictures, painted from life, with the exquisite skill of one of the *old masters*, which so seldom present themselves to the amateur."

THE IMITATION OF CHRIST. By THOMAS A'KEMPIS. With an Introductory Essay, by Dr. CHALMERS. Edited by HOWARD MALCOLM, D. D. A NEW EDITION, with a LIFE OF THOMAS A'KEMPIS. By Dr. C. ULLMAN, author of "Reformers before the Reformation." 12mo, cloth. 85 cents.

⁎ This work has, for three hundred years, been esteemed one of the best practical books in existence, and has gone through a vast number of editions, not only in the original Latin, but in every language of Europe.

This may safely be pronounced the best Protestant edition extant. It is reprinted from Payne's edition, collated with an ancient Latin copy. The peculiar feature of this *new edition* is the improved page, the elegant, large, clear type, and the NEW LIFE of A'KEMPIS, by Ullmann. Born nearly five hundred years ago, Thomas A'Kempis is almost unknown. While the Memoir prefixed to former American editions, and purporting to give all the facts, is contained in a few paragraphs, this life extends to more than fifty pages.

Dr. Payson, in conversing with a young minister, once said, "If you have not seen '*Thomas A'Kempis*,' I beg you to procure it. For spirituality and weanedness from the world, *I know of nothing equal to it*."

EXCLUSIVENESS OF THE BAPTISTS. A Review of the Rev. ALBERT BARNES' Pamphlet on "Exclusivism." By HENRY J. RIPLEY, Newton Theological Institution. 12mo, printed cover, 13 cents.

A thorough, candid, yet searching Review of Dr. Barnes' unfounded charges against the Baptists. It contains much important information on controverted subjects between Baptists and Pedo-Baptists, especially that usually termed "Close Communion." No better work can be placed in the hands of any one desiring light on this subject. The manner of treatment, the size, and the price, all render it admirably adapted to general circulation.

www.ingramcontent.com/pod-product-compliance
Lightning Source LLC
LaVergne TN
LVHW020106110826
845151LV00001B/73